Amazed by His Glory

*Faith-building true accounts of God's grace,
drawn from our missionaries' experiences*

Compiled by Mary Amesbury

Edited by Nancy Freund & Elizabeth Mayner

Baptist Mid-Missions

Baptist Mid-Missions, Cleveland, Ohio 44130-8011 • www.bmm.org
© 2010 Baptist Mid-Missions

Scripture quotations are taken from the King James Version
of the Bible.

Additional proofreading by Martha Baldwin and Becki Beam
Cover photo: iStock.com

ISBN 0-941645-08-8

Printed in the United States of America
15 14 13 12 11 10   1 2 3 4 5

Contents

Introduction

Every story in this collection is true, taken from the experiences of missionaries who have served under Baptist Mid-Missions, an independent, fundamental Baptist mission organization founded in 1920. Baptist Mid-Missions' missionaries serve Christ around the globe in more than 55 countries. Most of these stories were written by the actual participants—ordinary men and women serving an extraordinary God. Like Moses of old, these servants of Christ have realized that their two greatest needs are the presence of God and a glimpse of His glory.

When Moses was confronted with the difficult task of leading a rebellious and stiff-necked people into the Promised Land, he begged God:

> Now therefore, I pray thee, if I have found grace in thy sight, shew me now thy way, that I may know thee, that I may find grace in thy sight: and consider that this nation is thy people. And he said, My presence shall go with thee, and I will give thee rest. And he said unto him, If thy presence go not with me, carry us not up hence. For wherein shall it be known here that I and thy people have found grace in thy sight? is it not in that thou goest with us? so shall we be separated, I and thy people, from all the people that are upon the face of the earth. And the LORD said unto Moses, I will do this thing also that thou hast spoken: for thou hast found grace in my sight, and I know thee by name.

> And he said, I beseech thee, shew me thy glory. And he said, I will make all my goodness pass before thee, and I will proclaim the name of the LORD before thee; and will be gracious to whom I will be gracious, and will shew mercy on whom I will shew mercy. And he said, Thou canst not see my face: for there shall no man see me, and live. And the LORD said, Behold, there is a place by me, and thou shalt stand upon a rock: And it shall come to pass, while my glory passeth by, that I will put thee in a clift of the rock, and will cover thee

with my hand while I pass by: And I will take away mine hand, and thou shalt see my back parts: but my face shall not be seen (taken from Exodus 33:13-23).

This book is a glimpse of God from the cleft of the rock. God delights in revealing Himself to His sons and daughters. In His love and mercy, God has given mankind a record of His acts among men and a declaration of His character. That record is the Bible. Within its pages we can begin to see what God is like. We see that God is a Person with a name—Yahweh. He acts in history and reveals Himself to humans and transforms their lives.

God never changes. He is the same, yesterday, today and forever. The attributes of God displayed in the Bible—omniscience, omnipotence, holiness, love, grace, mercy, faithfulness, and sovereignty—are the very same attributes that are demonstrated in this volume of true stories from our own time. Those who know the character of God trust Him completely because they have discovered that the Most High God is infinitely worthy of that trust.

It is my hope that these accounts will challenge the reader to take God at His Word and trust Him more. It is my prayer that the reader will get a glimpse of the righteous and holy Lord God Almighty as He intervenes in the lives of these His disciples.

—Mary Amesbury

God's Omniscience

The name a person carries often reveals something of his or her character. That is particularly true of God. In Genesis 16:13, God is referred to as El Roi—"The Strong One who sees." This term magnifies both the omniscience and omnipotence of God. The powerful God who created the universe thousands of years ago knew at that moment everything that would transpire on planet Earth to every one of its billions of inhabitants. He knew when they would be born and when they would die. Incredible as it is, He knows every thought of every person who has ever lived. It is staggering to consider.

God not only knows what will happen in the future, He has the power to make those events come to pass. In the Old Testament, a prophet of the Lord told King Jeroboam that his heathen altar would be desecrated by a man of the house of David whose name was Josiah. That event came to pass exactly as the prophet had proclaimed it—three hundred years later! (1 Kings 13:1-2; 2 Kings 23:15-17). Two hundred years before it happened, the prophet Isaiah proclaimed that the Persian king Cyrus would be used by God to return the Israelites to their land after the captivity (Isaiah 44:28; 2 Chronicles 36:22-23).

Psalm 147:4 declares, "He [the LORD] telleth the number of the stars; he calleth them all by their names." Astronomers can only estimate the number of stars in the universe. Their best guess is that there are approximately 1,000,000,000,000,000,000,000 stars. Not only does God have a precise number, He also has a name for each individual star. Wow!

The fact that the Lord has a name for every star attests to the personal nature of His knowledge. He even gives stars a name and remembers their names so that He can call them. Just as He knows each of the stars He has created, God precisely knows each one of the billions of people on the earth. "Then the word of the LORD came unto me, saying, Before I formed thee in the belly I knew thee; and before thou camest forth out of the womb I sanctified thee, and I ordained thee a prophet unto the nations …" (Jeremiah 1:4-5).

O lord, thou hast searched me, and known me.
Thou knowest my downsitting and mine uprising, thou
understandest my thought afar off. Thou compassest my

path and my lying down, and art acquainted with all my ways.

For there is not a word in my tongue, but, lo, O LORD, thou knowest it altogether. Thou hast beset me behind and before, and laid thine hand upon me. Such knowledge is too wonderful for me; it is high, I cannot attain unto it.

Whither shall I go from thy spirit? or whither shall I flee from thy presence? If I ascend up into heaven, thou art there: if I make my bed in hell, behold, thou art there. If I take the wings of the morning, and dwell in the uttermost parts of the sea; Even there shall thy hand lead me, and thy right hand shall hold me.

If I say, Surely the darkness shall cover me; even the night shall be light about me. Yea, the darkness hideth not from thee; but the night shineth as the day: the darkness and the light are both alike to thee.

For thou hast possessed my reins: thou hast covered me in my mother's womb. I will praise thee; for I am fearfully and wonderfully made: marvellous are thy works; and that my soul knoweth right well. My substance was not hid from thee, when I was made in secret, and curiously wrought in the lowest parts of the earth.

Thine eyes did see my substance, yet being unperfect; and in thy book all my members were written, which in continuance were fashioned, when as yet there was none of them. How precious also are thy thoughts unto me, O God! how great is the sum of them! If I should count them, they are more in number than the sand: when I awake, I am still with thee (Psalm 139:1-18).

A man actually counted the number of grains of sand in 1/8 of a teaspoon, and then by doing the math figured that there were around 12.5 million grains in just one cup of sand. If a cup of sand represented the number of thoughts that God has to each one of us for 10 years of our lives, He'd be thinking about us as individuals more than twice a minute. But the Scripture doesn't say that His thoughts toward us are more than a cup of sand, it says more than *the sand*. How many cups of sand are in the Sahara desert or along the ocean shores?

God's thoughts toward us are constant—they are infinite. Because God knows the needs of His children in advance and sees all things at once, He can supernaturally burden someone to pray a believer through a crisis. "Chased By An Elephant" and "The Peace That Passes All Understanding" are testimony to the powerful effect of long-distance prayer prompted by an omniscient Father.

The Bible attests that God knows our thoughts (1 Corinthians 3:20) and what we will say before a word is on our tongues (Psalm 139:4). He also has the ability to put words in our mouths that will be fulfilled many years in the future. "Prophetic Prayer" is the story of the prayer of a stranger that was fulfilled 28 years after it was uttered. In "Pray For Thousands" the omniscient Lord invites His servants to pray beyond their wildest dreams because He has already determined to fulfill those prayers. Because God knows all the circumstances involved in a decision, we can trust Him to guide correctly. In "Lord, Guide Me" the omniscient Lord knows that finding the right hairdresser will result in victories for eternity.

The omniscient God is willing to share His wisdom with His children. James 1:5 declares, "If any of you lack wisdom, let him ask of God, that giveth to all men liberally, and upbraideth not; and it shall be given him."

God does put a very important condition on the asking for wisdom. Verses 6-8 of James chapter 1 warn: "But let him ask in faith, nothing wavering. For he that wavereth is like a wave of the sea driven with the wind and tossed. For let not that man think that he shall receive any thing of the Lord. A double minded man is unstable in all his ways."

God's wisdom is infinitely superior to that of even the wisest man. When an African woman had a fishbone hopelessly lodged in her throat, missionary Loie Knight called out to God for wisdom and He provided the answer. The omniscient Lord knew that Maisie Anspaugh's heart was a time bomb ready to go off. But Maisie was unaware that anything was wrong until "God's Intervention." Isaiah 65:24 declares, "And it shall come to pass, that before they call, I will answer; and while they are yet speaking, I will hear." As children of God, we can take great comfort that God knows all about us. We are never out of His sight or beyond His ability to help.

A Pastor Who Speaks Portuguese
Joel and Beverly Shoaf

Joel and Beverly joined Baptist Mid-Missions in 1988. The Shoafs first served in Mt. Maunganui, New Zealand, in 1992 and began church planting in the city of Napier in 1994.

At a time when our church and ministry here in Napier, New Zealand, needed a boost, such an amazing event took place that no one could deny it was a work of God.

One Sunday morning as our service was about to begin, one of the ladies in our church told Beverly that there was a young couple out at their car looking uncertain as to whether they should come in. As Beverly went out and warmly greeted them, she learned the source of their dilemma—they had recently moved from Brazil and spoke very little English.

They at first expressed shock and then huge smiles as Beverly told them that her husband Joel was the pastor and that, having been an MK in Brazil, he spoke Portuguese. Later that day we learned that Alex and Ci were Christians from a Baptist church in Santa Catarina in southern Brazil. How amazingly and precisely God had guided them!

It is safe to assume that Joel is likely the only pastor in New Zealand who speaks Portuguese. Alex said that they had been very uncertain about which city they should come to and had decided on Napier. There are two other Baptist churches in Napier that are not sound, and of course the pastors speak no Portuguese. God had directed them to our church through our church advertisement that Alex had clipped from the paper.

Over the months that followed, Alex and Ci attended services and added much-needed excitement and passion to the congregation. Unfortunately for us, they could not obtain an extended visa, and they had to return to Brazil. But God is now using them incredibly in their Baptist church there in Brazil.

While Alex and Ci were with us, they began to bring Robson and Priscila, another Brazilian couple who were unsaved. Robson and Priscila were eventually saved and are now the strongest leaders in our church. We are currently having the joy of training them for ministry.

It was not until several years after Alex and Ci's first amazing visit that we learned, from Robson and Priscila, the most amazing detail of the whole story. On the morning of their initial visit, Alex and Ci had said to Robson and Priscila, "We are going to church this morning." Knowing that they spoke little English, Robson had said to them, "What? Do you think you'll find a pastor who speaks Portuguese?"

Later that day, it was Robson and Priscila's turn to be shocked when Alex and Ci told them the story of the mighty way in which God had worked personally for them!

Though Robson and Priscila have permanent residency here in New Zealand, we realize that God may also lead them one day to return to Brazil and minister there. Whatever takes place, our faith will each time be renewed as we remember the day that God worked in a way in which, clearly, only He could.

The Peace That Passes All Understanding
Mary Baker

With her vivacious personality, Mary used her gifts to serve the Lord in missions. She joined Baptist Mid-Missions in 1945 and served in Chad, Africa, mainly working with children. In 1981 she began serving in North American youth ministries, where she was well-loved by the children she worked with. Mary retired in 1990 and went to be with her Lord in 2007. Her story is told in her book, The Calling.

After I went to France in April of 1948, I received a telegram stating that my favorite brother, Howard, had died. My mother's telegram said, "Howard died very suddenly. Letter will follow." Of course I couldn't come back for the funeral because I was in language school. But even after receiving such terrible news, I had the most wonderful peace that I could not explain.

I just had the most wonderful peace; I had it and couldn't understand it. The missionaries in the hotel with me—they couldn't understand the peace, and they asked my roommate, "Boy, she's sure putting on a good front, isn't she?" My roommate, who doesn't usually get angry, got angry with those missionaries and said, "I'm in the same room with her. She has a peace that I can't explain. When I got word that her brother had died, I fell on the bed and sobbed and she came to comfort me."

A short time later, I received a letter from a lady named Doris Jean Clair. I thought, "I don't know any Doris Jean Clair. I wonder who it is that is writing me."

So I opened the letter and read:

> You'll remember me when I tell you this: You were standing at the door in Williamsport, Pennsylvania, and I came out and I said to you, "I'm not going to say that I will pray for you everyday. And I'm not going to tell you that I'm going to write to you, because many people say that to missionaries and never do it. So what I'm going to do is tell you that I'll never write to you and I'm going to pray for you only when God's Spirit reminds me of something that you said."
>
> But I was awakened in the night after a dream almost like a vision. Before me were rows and rows of missionaries that I had promised to pray for through the years. They were all standing there and I could see their faces. Then all their faces went dim and you stepped out in the middle. There you stood and I saw you clearly. And so I crawled out of bed and knelt and prayed for you until I had assurance that God had heard my prayer. I'm curious. Tell me, what was your need? This is the last letter you'll probably ever get from me.

The letter included the date and time of the woman's dream. She was praying the night before the morning when I got the telegram informing me that my favorite brother had died. So it was the peace that passes all understanding delivered by one prayer in Williamsport, Pennsylvania, and arriving in Paris, France.

Pray for Thousands
Mark and Nancy Sheppard

After joining Baptist Mid-Missions in 1982, Mark and Nancy served in Liberia for one term. When Liberia's bloody civil war erupted and they could not stay, the Sheppards moved to the neighboring country of Ivory Coast, where they ministered to those who had fled the conflict. After 11 years, the Sheppards were able to return to Liberia, where they currently work.

"Pray for thousands," the Lord said.

What? The Lord had been leading me for several months in a new adventure in prayer and faith, but this was impossible! I had just prayed aloud in our missionary prayer meeting for hundreds of people to come to Christ, when distinctly I heard God tell me to pray for thousands.

Here, Lord? "Challenging" would be the polite way to describe our ministry in the Ivory Coast, West Africa. The existing church was so cold it was embarrassing to be associated with it. Within the church, prejudice existed between the Ivorian French-speaking people and the English-speaking Liberian refugees. Although they shared a common dialect, rather than seeing themselves as brothers and sisters in Christ, an intense rivalry had developed. As missionaries coming into this situation, we felt our hands were tied; we could not tell an independent church to shape up. We prayed for God's wisdom and direction.

After eight months of this frustration, my husband Mark and our coworker Jeff Abernethy felt God leading us to start a separate English work. From its beginning in March 1996, God blessed with the peacefulness and unity we had longed for so desperately. Immediately we saw growth in the believers—a new willingness to forsake sin and look to Christ. We also sensed God was demanding a new level of purity in our lives as missionaries, as well as in the lives of a core group among whom we ministered.

Then, less than a year after the church's birth, God asked me to pray for thousands in our area to find Christ as personal Savior. I tentatively told the others on our team, wondering how they would respond to such a humanly impossible request. To my delight, everyone simply accepted it as from God. But how would this prayer be answered? We knew no human effort could produce this fruit. We waited with anticipation.

In the spring of 1997, Jeff Abernethy preached a sermon about Andrew and how, after seeing Christ, he ran to get his brother Peter to bring him to the Messiah. Jeff encouraged those who were interested in bringing others to Christ to stay after the service. Many stayed behind. In the month that followed, Jeff and his wife Kim worked with part of this group, and we with the other. During this training period, these volunteers learned the basics of presenting an individual with his or her need for Christ as Savior. The response of the class members was very exciting. Even while still taking the course, several led friends and neighbors to Jesus Christ.

And so "Operation Andrew" was born. Each Saturday, small groups went out to share the gospel. We asked God to lead us to people who were ready and eager to listen to the message of salvation. God answered, and many came to the Lord. The veil of Satan's confusion was lifted, and in its place came a willingness to believe God's truths. It was as though they were just waiting for someone to tell them about Christ.

With God working so visibly, our church felt electric. We were not just learning about God; we were seeing His hand moving powerfully in and through us! New believers eagerly drank in the truths of God's Word. At prayer meeting, excited Christians shared how God had allowed them the privilege of leading friends, neighbors, and relatives to Christ.

God also revealed Himself powerfully in evangelistic meetings. For example, in May 1997 the men scheduled a Saturday night open-air campaign in the nearby village of Diboke. A soldier from the village had received Christ after hearing the gospel at our clinic. Wilson, the worker who led him to Christ, started going to the village each weekend to preach. We prayed this meeting would give the fledgling fellowship a boost. With four vehicles carrying 45 people from the French and English churches in the city of Blolequin, the team descended on the village with great enthusiasm: setting up the meeting place, distributing tracts, and inviting people to the meeting.

An estimated 500 people showed up, many out of simple curiosity. They watched the evangelistic video with rapt attention. Videos are a real treat in an African village! As Jeff Abernethy preached with one of our African Christians interpreting, the Holy Spirit reached into the hearts of the hearers and applied God's Word.

Knowing all spiritual battles are won through prayer, not through well-executed plans, Kim Abernethy had opened her home for a prayer meeting. Twenty-five Christians met to pray over nine specific requests as the village meeting was taking place. Around 11:00 p.m. we found every one of those nine prayer requests wonderfully answered, including the prayer for souls. That night, 122 people made professions of faith! When the team returned with their report, the prayer group spontaneously broke into singing, "Praise God, Hallelujah, Praise God, Amen!" Wilson reported 98 in church the next day. A month later, he still had 75 or 80 of those coming faithfully. A new church had been born.

As God blessed, the devil fought tooth and nail. There were many trials and tests of our faith and of the faith of these new believers. Yet it is with awe and thanksgiving to God we report that thousands have indeed come to know the Lord in the area of Blolequin, Ivory Coast. By November 1998, a year and a half after beginning to pray that thousands would be saved, over 2,400 people had made professions of faith through the ministries of the English church, the French church, the village outreaches, and the mission clinic. The specific command to pray for thousands was from God, and the answer was also from Him.

Thank God He allowed us to be a part of this bountiful harvest of souls.

God's Intervention
Maisie Anspaugh

Maisie and her husband Fred began ministry with Baptist Mid-Missions in 1960 after serving with the Garden of Prayer Mission. Their first works were in Mexico, but they later transferred to North America and planted churches in Kentucky and New Jersey. The Anspaughs retired in 1982. Fred went to be with the Lord in 2005 and Maisie in 2010.

I woke up in the middle of the night with an overwhelming sense that something was not right. I got up and went to the bathroom and then returned to the bedroom. But still I could not rest. I didn't know what was wrong. So I lay in bed and prayed through the rest of the night.

The next morning, we were supposed to go on a trip, but at

breakfast time I told my husband Fred that we shouldn't go because something was not right. I didn't feel any pain nor did I have any symptoms. The Holy Spirit just impressed on me that something was very wrong with my health.

My husband called for an ambulance, and they came out to Missionary Acres, Baptist Mid-Missions' retirement village in Missouri, where we live. They took my blood pressure and other vital signs and determined that they needed to transport me to the hospital in Poplar Bluff. I was there in the hospital from Saturday until Thursday, when they transferred me to Barnes Hospital in St. Louis. They didn't tell me until I got to Barnes that my heart was bad and that I needed a valve replacement. I had major heart surgery on Friday. During surgery, they almost lost me three times.

I just praise the Lord for getting me to the hospital when He did. Without the Holy Spirit's intervention, I quite possibly would have had a major heart attack or a stroke. But the Lord spared my life.

The other aspect of this story is that the Lord used this incident to touch the heart of our daughter. After many years of rebellion, she again desired to be totally involved in our lives. I praise and thank the Lord for His goodness to me. All praise to Him.

Kept from Harm
Joy Spieth

Joy is a second-generation missionary serving in Brazil. Her parents, Albert and Naomi Spieth, began their service with Baptist Mid-Missions in 1941, and Joy joined in 1967. As did her parents, Joy serves in the Amazon region.

My missionary coworkers Ray and Jan Reiner had come to Manaus from Northeast Brazil to live for a while. When it came time for them to return to the Northeast, they had not sold their home. They asked me if I would deal with the buyers for them. Little did I know when I agreed to do it that one of the potential buyers would turn out to be a racketeer and a murderer.

This man called and arranged to come to my house. He wanted me to go with him to see the Reiners' house, which was located about 50 miles out of town. I always make it a practice as a single woman not to go in a car alone with a man, so I asked the girl that lives with me to come with us. As we drove out to the house, he told us about his work and said that he was a used car dealer. Then he talked about his family and his children and how wonderful they were. He portrayed himself as a real family man.

Well, when we got to the little town and saw the house, he decided that he wanted to buy it. On the way back we stopped and had lunch. It was all very pleasant.

This man had said that he wanted the house, but he took a long time to bring me a check for the purchase price. Once he gave me the check, however, he was very insistent that I sign the documents right away. But something made me hesitate. I made up my mind that I wouldn't sign any documents until Ray Reiner had received the actual cash, since the check had to go to a different state.

Sure enough, a couple of days later I got a call from Ray. "Joy, don't sign anything. The check bounced."

"It's OK, Ray. I haven't signed anything," I assured him.

The fellow came back and insisted that I sign the documents, but I wouldn't sign. A few days later, I got a telephone call from the lady I knew who had told this fellow about the house. She said, "Joy, did you see yesterday's newspaper?"

"No, I usually don't take time to read it," I replied. I decided to go to the neighbors and ask them if they had a newspaper. The paper had a story about my prospective buyer. He was part of a gang of car thieves. The gang's operation consisted of one member purchasing an imported pickup truck and then another member of the gang attacking the seller a few blocks down the street and taking back the money that had just been paid for the truck. But this last time, the man who had sold the truck happened to recognize the fellow I had been dealing with. So the gang decided to kill him and bury him at this fellow's ranch 84 miles out of town.

Chills went up my spine. That could have been me! But the Lord had His angels watching out for me, and I was protected.

Lord, What Do I Do?

Loie Knight

*Loie joined Baptist Mid-Missions in May 1953 after several years in prepa-
ration for a medical ministry in Central African Republic. Ted and Lila
Wimer and Linda Seymour were veteran missionaries who inspired and
encouraged her. Loie's story recounts her cry for help in one rare case at the
Kaga Bandoro Mission Dispensary—and God's all-knowing answer.*

One morning, I was working in the dental clinic at our Kaga
Bandoro station in the Central African Republic. I am a registered nurse,
but much of my time I spent in the dental clinic working alongside missionary Knute Orton. There I had learned to use a new anesthetic spray
that he had. I got a call to go across the yard to the dispensary because a
lady needed to see me. When I got there, this young lady had a fishbone
caught in her throat and couldn't talk.

She had been down to the government hospital. They had prod-
ded and poked around until her throat was roughed up pretty badly, and
they still hadn't been able to get that fishbone out. I didn't know what
more I could do, but I thought that I would at least start with the spray. I
was praying like crazy, "Lord what do I do? What do I do?"

I didn't have any of the instruments that I thought a person
would use. And so I was praying a little bit madly. Then as I sprayed her
throat, it just seemed like the Lord said to me, "Put some gauze on your
finger." So I cut a little piece of gauze and I put it on my finger, and then I
thought, "Loie, you'll lose that down her throat!"

So I discarded that piece and cut a bigger one and wrapped that
around my finger. Then I carefully put my finger down her throat. The
spray had done its job and her throat was anesthetized so she didn't gag at
me. I pulled my finger back and that little fishbone hooked right into that
gauze and came right out! I was amazed and so was everyone else. Thank
you, Lord.

God's Diagnosis

Mary Amesbury

Mary joined Baptist Mid-Missions in 1992 and served first in the Far East of Russia. Since 2000, she has been serving with Campus Bible Fellowship International in Cleveland, Ohio.

For seven years, from the spring of 1993 to 2000, I suffered from a mysterious disease that would come and go. Doctors could not determine what was causing my overwhelming fatigue, headaches, intermittent muscle pain, poor lung function, and a host of other random symptoms. Sometimes I would go for months without too much trouble, and other times it seemed my whole body was falling apart. The lab tests always came back inconclusive. Doctors would address one symptom or another but would never look at the entire list.

Eventually my fatigue, pain, and breathing problems became so pronounced that I could no longer live in Russia as a missionary. I came back to the States in January of 2000, not knowing what was wrong with me or whether I would recover or not. My health was so compromised that I wasn't sure I could continue as a missionary.

In the next couple of months, the Lord made it clear that He still had ministry for me to do. He was directing me to Cleveland, Ohio, to serve with Campus Bible Fellowship. And yet I was still sick, my chest hurt, and my breathing seemed impeded. Trips to the doctor and the physical therapist did little good.

One day while receiving a heat treatment at the physical therapists' office, I prayed in frustration, "Lord, You have called me to Campus Bible Fellowship, and it's not a rocking chair ministry. I need to know what is wrong with me and how to fix it." At that moment there was an overwhelming sense that He had heard and that He would answer. I have not often had such assurance, but this time I did.

1 John 5:14-15 says, "And this is the confidence that we have in him, that, if we ask any thing according to his will, he heareth us: And if we know that he hear us, whatsoever we ask, we know that we have the petitions that we desired of him."   -

About an hour later, I was done with my therapy, and I decided that I would go to the library and find a book about muscles so that I could understand why mine were not responding to treatment.

I went to the card catalog and looked up the number and then went to the proper shelf, but the book that I was looking for was not there. On the shelf was a book about fibromyalgia. I had never heard of fibromyalgia. I had no idea what the word meant. But for some unexplainable reason, I pulled this book off the shelf, flipped it open, and read a list of symptoms.

The page could have been written from the list of symptoms I had given my doctor! Nearly all of the items on the list described what I had been experiencing over the last eight years. In that same book was the treatment to reverse the disease.

None of the other books about fibromyalgia offered anything more than coping techniques to deal with this incurable disease. Only this book answered both components of my prayer—the diagnosis and the hope for fixing it. Interestingly, the book *What Your Doctor May Not Tell You About Fibromyalgia* had been in print for only six months. Most doctors had never heard of the protocol. Had I been diagnosed earlier, doctors probably would have given me little hope for recovery, and I might have resigned myself to giving in to the disease and stepping out of missionary service.

But because of God's diagnosis, that day I started on the road to recovery. Ten years later, I'm still doing well and have an energetic ministry among college students.

Divine Appointment
Janet Stinedurf

Janet and her husband Jim previously worked with another agency in Puerto Rico before joining Baptist Mid-Missions in 1972. They continued their service in that country and have been involved in church planting and theological education.

Giving your life to serve God as a missionary doesn't always mean you automatically give Him every hour and moment of the day. Complete consecration has been a hard lesson to learn, but it makes me all the more aware of God's faithfulness.

Being sensitive to God's direction is a daily goal for me, so I'm glad to share a simple account of His leading. I was all alone in a doctor's office waiting for my husband Jim when a lady and her husband walked in. She gave me an extra warm smile, and as I sat there I felt God wanted me to befriend her. I wasn't sure, but I felt Him remind me again.

So, following His lead, I went and sat down beside her, saying that I felt it would be nice not to be sitting all alone. Right away, she struck up a conversation and told me her name was Felicita. Before long, she was telling me of her problem with depression. When I asked her why she had this problem, she said that she and her husband were older, and that she did not know what would happen to them.

I reminded her that God does not forsake us. I then asked her if she had ever received Christ as her Savior. She told me that she was a Catholic, and that she did trust Christ, but that her church did not meet her spiritual needs.

I was then able to tell her about the church Jim had started just around the corner that now had a national pastor. I told her that the church was small, but that they would be able to help her. I also offered to help her personally. Shortly after that, she was called in to see the doctor and Jim came out. She left, asking me to pray for her. I encouraged her to call me.

I left the doctor's office, pleased that I had allowed God to lead me. I am newly aware that He wants us to be pliable tools in His hands as He continues to meet the needs of hurting people. God's great faithfulness to direct our lives to accomplish His purposes is awesome.

Praise God for Answering My Prayer
Alisha Colson

Alisha is the daughter of Jody and Terry Colson, who became part of the Baptist Mid-Missions Family in 1988. The Colsons served in Hawaii and there met a family from Micronesia in the South Pacific. This led to a Macedonian call, and the Colsons began serving in Micronesia's Chuuk Islands. Alongside her family, Alicia serves the Lord there also.

One Saturday morning, I prayed that Jesus would use me, a missionary kid, to reach someone for Him that day. My family and I were going to the Chuuk State Hospital to witness for Christ. The hospital is just down the street from our house. When we went to the hospital, there were many people waiting outside, because eight men had died that week, and the morgue was full.

When we reached the women's ward, I saw an old woman sitting on her bed, looking out the window. I went over to her and asked her in Chuukese what was the matter.

"My brother died this morning," she said, "and when I started to wail for him, my doctor told me to stop or I might have another heart attack."

After talking with her for a while, I asked her if she knew if she would go to heaven when she died.

"I don't know," she said. "All my life I've gone to church and I've listened to the preachers talk about Jesus. But they didn't tell me how to know Him or how to get to heaven."

I opened my Chuukese New Testament and read Romans 3:23 to her. She told me she knew she was a sinner. "No matter what I do, I can't get rid of an awful feeling of guilt wrapped around my heart," she told me.

After she understood the gospel, I led her in prayer as she asked Jesus into her heart. Then she took my hand in hers and said, "Thank you. Praise God for answering my prayer. This morning I couldn't stand that feeling of guilt any longer, so I prayed that God would send someone to help me, and He sent you! You are the answer to my prayer. I finally feel … free! All praise and thanks to Jesus. I know Him now."

We talked for a little while, and then it was time for me to go. We shook hands again, and I left. When I got home, I prayed and thanked the Lord for answering my prayer.

Maple Syrup
Carl Barton

In 1966, Carl and his wife Selma joined Baptist Mid-Missions to serve in Liberia. After a brief period, the Lord directed them to Australia. In 1983,

Carl accepted the position of Mission Advancement Representative, where he counseled with prospective missionaries and represented Baptist Mid-Missions in churches. The Bartons retired in 2007.

In 1996 my wife and I attempted to get permission from the Zimbabwean government to work as missionaries in Zimbabwe, Africa. During that period, we made three trips to try to work with government officials to obtain missionary visas, but to no avail. On the third trip, friends of ours—Gene and Doris Stockton, who were then working with Campus Bible Fellowship in Charleston, West Virginia—said they wanted to drive down and see us off at the airport in Atlanta, Georgia.

The day before our flight, British Airways went on strike, so we were rerouted to a different airline. There was no way to let Gene and Doris know about the change, though, because they were already on the road somewhere. So we did not expect to see them at the Atlanta airport. But minutes before we were to board the plane, Gene and Doris showed up! Somehow they had found us. As a parting gift, they gave us a tin of maple syrup and some other things.

We got on the plane with this tin of maple syrup from Cracker Barrel. We said to ourselves, "It is so nice of Gene and Doris to give us this gift, but what in the world will we do with maple syrup in Africa?" We kept that tin of maple syrup for four months in our suitcase. We never used it; we didn't know what to do with it; we just moved it around.

Then … the last week before we were to come home, an unsaved family who owned a plantation in the heart of Zimbabwe invited us to visit and spend the weekend with them on their farm. So we went, and they treated us very well. The last night we were there, the owner of the plantation started reminiscing and said, "You know what I miss, what I dream about? When I was 12 years old, I was down in South Africa, and a family gave me some ice cream with maple syrup on it. It was the most wonderful tasting thing that I have ever had. I've never had it since. Here it is 54 years later, and I still dream of maple syrup. I would love to have some maple syrup on my ice cream."

Selma and I looked at each other in amazement, because we had a tin of maple syrup in our suitcase, and we were able to give it to him. Finally we understood why God had worked it all out so that Gene and Doris had found us at the airport and had given us that tin of maple syrup to take to the middle of Africa. It just worked out great. After we left Zimbabwe, we went on to Australia and filled in for some missionaries there for nine months. Then we came back to the United States.

The week we returned from Australia, a pastor telephoned and offered to pay my way if I would go on a bus tour—a Baptist Historical Tour of New England—with 56 other pastors. I agreed to go, and for five days we toured in several New England states. Our 28-year-old driver was a man by the name of Seth. His parents make their living by making maple syrup. Seth takes the maple syrup with him on the bus and sells it to the passengers. All the pastors, of course, tried to tell Seth about Jesus Christ, but he said he believed in reincarnation and that he wanted to come back in the next life as a maple tree. So, of course, on the last day of the tour I just had to tell the account of the maple syrup in Africa.

Seth was amazed at the story. His last words to me were that he just couldn't get over the story of the maple syrup. He said he couldn't wait to get home to tell his parents about how a tin of maple syrup traveled all that distance to get to a man who had been longing for it. I don't know what God is going to do with all these interconnected events, but I am confident that He was the arranger of it all. It's just too incredible to think otherwise.

Lord, Guide Me
Evelyn Einfeldt

Evelyn Regier joined Baptist Mid-Missions as a single missionary in 1953. After many decades in Japan, she transferred to ministry in Hawaii. In 1987, she married Lynn Einfeldt and retired the following year. Lynn went to be with the Lord in 2006 and Evelyn in 2010.

In 1983, I moved to Hawaii after serving many years as a missionary in Japan. So it was necessary for me to find a new hairdresser, but I didn't know anyone in Hawaii. I didn't know where any of the shops were. I really did not even know the streets yet, so looking in the telephone book was not too helpful. So I prayed, "Lord, guide me to the right place." I got in my car, drove down the street, and looked for a hairdresser. All of a sudden I saw a sign that said, "Toyoko Beauty Salon." I knew she must be a Japanese lady. So I stopped there and asked if she accepted walk-in clients without an appointment. She said, "Yes."

That day began a friendship with Toyoko. For ten years I witnessed to her. She was a Buddhist and would not allow me to talk to her about Christ or the Bible or anything like that in front of other patrons. Finally, one day I took a video copy of the *JESUS* film with me, and I said, "Do you have a VCR? Would you like to see this?" She took it home. She watched the two-hour video once, then twice. She watched it three times. Finally, she accepted the Lord Jesus Christ as her Savior.

In 1995 I received a letter from Toyoko that said, "Rejoice with me. My daughter Faith has also received the Lord Jesus." When Toyoko was first saved, she said, "Pray for my husband John. I want him to be saved. He is a difficult man." But now she says, "Faith and I pray together. We go to church together. And we can pray that the rest of our family will be saved."

It takes a long time for some people to accept Jesus Christ, but God is always working even when we can't see immediate results.

Chased by an Elephant
Mary Amesbury

Mary joined Baptist Mid-Missions in 1992 and served first in the Far East of Russia. Since 2000, she has been serving with Campus Bible Fellowship International in Cleveland, Ohio. Here, she tells the story of Fred and Dorothy Waldock, veteran missionaries who are now with the Lord.

Fred Waldock and his wife Dorothy were in their first term of service in Assam, India, during the early 1950s. They were living on a tea plantation that had been purchased by the missionaries and converted into a leprosy colony. The Makunda Leprosy Colony was on the edge of a huge, dense jungle. Conditions on the mission station were primitive at the time, but God was a constant source of strength for the young couple.

One day, Fred and an Indian guide were deep in the jungle when they heard a rogue elephant crashing through the trees behind them. The Indian man ran up a hill, but Fred in his heavy boots could not run as fast and was tiring quickly. He ran until he thought he would collapse. The Indian man motioned to Fred that he should run in a zigzag fashion through the bamboo. The elephant would have to slow down to try to catch the scent and Fred would have a chance to get away. So Fred ran, zigzagging through the bamboo until he was exhausted. He finally evaded the pursuing elephant.

Years later, he was on furlough and related the story to his mother in Alberta, Canada. "Fred, what day was it exactly? Do you remember?"

"Why is the date important, Mother?" asked Fred after he told her the approximate date and time.

"One night I was unable to sleep. I was so very burdened for you. I could not rest until I prayed for you and received assurance from the Lord that He had heard my prayer," she answered. "The time difference between Alberta and India is 12^1/2 hours. I believe the Lord burdened me to pray for you at just the time you were fleeing that elephant."

Belem Earthquake
Isabelle Schopf

Isabelle (Gates) Schopf, known to most as "Izzy," entered the Baptist Mid-Missions Family in 1951. In 1955, she married John Jacob "Jake" Schopf, and he joined Baptist Mid-Missions the following year. The Lord gave them many fruitful decades in Brazil. In 1992 Jake became a Mission Advancement Representative and served in this position for 10 years. Jake has been with the Lord since 2005.

My husband Jake had a book in his library whose title always impressed me—*Another Hand on Mine!* We have often felt that "Hand" on our lives in so many ways. The following story was one of those times.

We had returned to Brazil from furlough in 1968 or 1969 to continue the work at Igreja Batista Luz Brilhante (Bright Light Baptist Church) in Belem do Para. We became burdened for a particular section of town. The people from that part of town would come to a nearby open air market for shopping but considered the distance "too far" to come for church. So Jake, with the men of the church, decided to rent a house and open a "congregation" with weekly meetings there.

Properties in the Belem area were mostly long and narrow, and this one was no exception. Stan Best, our fellow missionary in Belem, came to help Jake prepare the house for meetings. While Jake was downtown getting materials, Stan in his eagerness knocked out all the walls between the rooms. When Jake returned the roof was sagging. So first off, they had to shore that up. When the house was painted and ready and Jake had made folding pews, we set the date for a Tuesday night to begin the work.

Sunday afternoon, the people of the Bright Light Baptist Church met to canvass the area and pass out tracts and invitations to the meetings. Since we had not been back from furlough long enough to send away for tracts, we used the only two we had leftover from the previous term. One was *Os Sinais do Fin,* (Signs of the End Times), and the other was *Salvo Por Um Terramoto* (Saved by an Earthquake). Neither seemed especially appropriate, but they had a good salvation message, so we passed them out all over that section of town. We passed out several hundred of these tracts.

We then returned to our church, had a good evening service, and then went back to our house behind the church. We fed our four sons and settled them down for the night and then went to bed ourselves.

Sometime around two or three a.m., we were awakened by a terrible noise. Jake said it sounded like a train rushing through our house. We jumped out of bed and realized the house was shaking. An earthquake!

When Jake went out in the morning to open the gate, there was a long line of people waiting. Because of fear, most of the people wanted to get right with the Lord. At least one couple received Christ as Savior that morning!

What is most amazing is that Belem is not in an earthquake zone. There had not been a recorded earthquake in Belem for over 100 years. Most had never heard of an earthquake.

Tuesday night, when we opened the congregation for our first meeting, the place was packed! People were hanging in the windows and pushing in at the door. When Jake finished preaching and gave the invitation, 19 people came forward for salvation. What a thrill!

We knew God's hand was on ours. Who led us to pass out that tract about an earthquake? Who made us order them in the first place? Who sent the earthquake at such a time? God did. God did it all and proved to us in such a vivid way the truth of Proverbs 3:6, "… and HE shall direct thy paths."

Seeds in Swindon
Eleanor Brittain

*In 1950, as a single missionary en route to Liberia for the first time, Elea-
nor met Stan Brittain, then an officer on the ship Eleanor sailed on. They
married three years later, and Stan joined Eleanor in the work in Liberia. In
the 1970s, they served in New Zealand, Hawaii, and finally Great Britain
(Stan's home country), from which they retired in 1992. Stan went to be
with the Lord in 2003.*

Sometimes in our service for the Lord, we start out intending to
do one thing and then later discover that God had something entirely
different—but equally special—in mind. This was the case when our missionary team had the goal to plant a church on the east side of Swindon,
England. Our team consisted of my husband Stan and me and two single
ladies, Marcia and Reta.

God answered prayer and we finally obtained the use of a community hall in which to hold Sunday services. It bordered Park North
and Park South housing estates on the east side of Swindon. Marcia and
Reta bought a house in Park North. We put invitations and tracts in hundreds of doors and talked to every person who would listen.

It was an exciting Sunday morning in late 1986 as we waited for
the people to arrive. We were very pleased when about a dozen children
and a couple with their two little girls came. It was a start!

The next Sunday, we met Rachel for the first time. She came pulling a wagon with her little brother and the family laundry in it. Her two
younger sisters walked behind the wagon. There was a launderette in the
Community Square. We soon learned that Rachel, just 13 years old, was
the caregiver in her home in Park North. Rachel came to all the meetings
as faithfully as she could, including afterschool Bible Club and Saturday
Youth Night. She came to Marcia and Reta's house for Thursday Bible
study also. Rachel soon accepted Christ as her Savior and was growing
spiritually.

Then it happened! Social Services decided that the four children
were no longer safe in their own home and put them in foster care. God
had a plan and a purpose for Rachel. Jeremiah 29:11 says: "For I know
the thoughts that I think toward you, saith the LORD, thoughts of peace,

and not of evil, to give you an expected end." The four children were placed in the home of Sylvia, who lived in Purton. This was farther west of Swindon than we lived. Sylvia agreed that the children could continue coming to our church as long as we picked them up and brought them back. Of course, we agreed to do this.

Eventually, the two younger children were placed with another family. Rachel and Debbie continued to attend faithfully, and Rachel especially was a testimony to Sylvia, a widow, and her 20-year-old son, Stuart. One Sunday evening as we dropped off the girls, Rachel said, "You won't have to pick us up on Thursday evening. Sylvia asked if it's all right for her to bring us, and she will attend as well." How thrilling! Stan was teaching from the book of the Revelation. After two weeks, Sylvia was coming to Sunday services and soon accepted Christ as her own Savior.

The next thing we knew, Sylvia wanted us to have Bible studies in her home so she could invite her local friends. We were praising the Lord for the things He was doing. Stuart didn't attend but couldn't help hearing some things from upstairs once in awhile. He would leave the house most times but would always greet us.

One evening he had a tennis racket under his arm. He stopped to chat a bit, and Stan told him he had been keen on tennis since his younger days, and maybe they could have a game sometime. What could the poor lad say? Stuart said he would arrange a doubles match with a couple of his buddies. He figured if he partnered with Stan, it wouldn't be so embarrassing for the "old man." Months later, Stuart was still delighted to tell the story: "Stan played better than any of us young blokes, and we whopped 'em!" That started a friendship that never ended. Who can predict what the Lord will use to help bring someone to Himself?

A 10-member musical group from Cedarville College in Ohio came to minister to the various Baptist Mid-Missions churches in England that summer. We usually took such groups on at least one sightseeing tour. We chose the Roman city of Bath. The Cedarville group had ministered in the Evangelical Church in Swindon, and some of their young people were going along, so we needed two vans. Stan was driving the hired one, and we hoodwinked Stuart into driving our Ford Transit 12-passenger van so I wouldn't have to. Among the youth from the Evangelical church was the pastor's daughter, Anna, and she and Stuart met for the first time.

God had a plan and purpose for Stuart and Anna. Stuart, with our blessing, began attending the Evangelical church. He soon realized he was a sinner and accepted Christ as his own personal Savior. He started taking classes in our Baptist Bible College and rode with Stan to Bracknell. Stan taught every Monday evening and also en route on the 45-mile drive. On the way to and from Bracknell, Stan poured the truth and his own heart into Stuart. As a result, we began calling Stuart "Stan's Timothy."

Stan had the privilege of participating in the wedding of Stuart and Anna just before we left England in September 1992. When it was determined that Stan had terminal cancer in December 2002, Stuart phoned from London to ask if he could come. He was with us for a week before Stan was promoted to Glory January 10, 2003, the day after our 50th wedding anniversary.

Stuart has been assistant pastor of Trinity Chapel in South London since the mid-1990s and is also active in beach ministries. He and Anna are the proud parents of five lovely children.

What about Rachel? Sylvia found it necessary to give up being a foster parent, but decided to adopt Rachel. Debbie was placed with another good family, and the four siblings still keep in touch. Eventually Rachel married Simon, the son of a deacon from the Evangelical church. As of January 2005, they had three children and were serving the Lord alongside an ABWE missionary couple in a North Swindon church plant.

The "seeds" planted in Swindon never grew into a formal church, but God worked in the hearts of many individuals. His Word continues to bring forth fruit for His honor and glory, and His plan and purpose continue to unfold.

Saved by a Penny and a Prayer
Russel Mapes

Russel and his wife Mary began their service with Baptist Mid-Missions in 1955, starting in Ghana, Africa. The Mapes family also ministered in North America before retiring in 2002. Their son Dan and his wife Karis now serve with BMM in Ghana. This story comes from Russel and Mary's book, Why Not Leave Them Alone … They Have Their Own Religions.

One day when I was in town, a madman approached my vehicle and started spitting into the car. I got out and stood there. The man then raised his hand to strike me.

Just then, Mr. Continua, one of our Ghanaian believers, came by and saw what was going on. He quickly said to the man, "Come with me and I will give you a penny." The man lowered his fist, and walked away to collect his penny. I suppose he forgot all about his desire to attack me.

I wrote home about the incident and later received a reply from Pastor Lloyd Smith. I quote a portion of his letter:

> You mentioned in your letter a few weeks ago that a madman almost attacked you. My wife told me when she was reading your letter and came to this part where you told about the madman, she felt cold chills run all over her. Just a few weeks before that, one day while she was sweeping the floor, she suddenly felt strongly impressed to stop and pray for you. She knew when she read your letter that the Holy Spirit had warned her of your danger. God is a great God and watches over and cares for His children wherever they may be.

God protected me from harm that day through a penny and a prayer.

Prophetic Prayer
Joyce Oshiro

Joyce's parents, Roy and her late mother, Kimiko, and stepmother, Kiyo, served the Lord as missionaries in Okinawa, beginning in 1950. Joyce joined Baptist Mid-Missions in 1982 and continues to serve in Japan.

My dad was born in Brandon, Manitoba, in 1921. While my grandparents were at the hospital after the delivery, a missionary on furlough from Japan visited that same hospital and stopped by their room.

My grandparents were naturally delighted to talk with someone who knew their Japanese language and had been to their homeland.

Before this missionary left, he asked to pray for the baby. My grandparents did not know the Lord then, but they consented to his request. The missionary put his hand on the baby's forehead and prayed that when this baby grew up, the Lord would save him and send him to Japan as a missionary.

My dad grew up, but it wasn't until he was a 28-year-old schoolteacher that he heard the gospel and accepted the Lord. He immediately had a burden for the people in Okinawa. He went to Japan as a missionary in 1955 and met my mom, who was already a missionary there. My two sisters and I were all born and raised on Okinawa as missionary kids.

It wasn't until my dad was 50 years old that my grandparents came to visit us in Okinawa, and Grandpa told us for the first time how that missionary had prayed for my dad as a baby. We listened to his story in amazement, realizing that God had in fact answered that prayer! After 25 years on Okinawa, the Lord enabled my dad to establish Gushikawa Baptist Church in the very area where my grandparents were born and raised. Dad completed 51 years of ministry in Okinawa in 2006 before retiring at the age of 85.

We don't know who that missionary was that prayed for my dad, but I'm looking forward to meeting him in heaven someday and thanking him for his prayer.

God's Omnipotence

Word quickly spread across Galilee and Judea and even beyond the borders of Israel to the seacoast of Tyre and Sidon. The prophet from Nazareth had the ability to heal people and to cast out demons. For those who had suffered for years with different infirmities, it was news almost too good to be true. Was it possible that the blind could be made to see, that the mute could speak again, that the lame could walk and run? That the maimed could have their hands and feet restored? That those tormented by unclean spirits could be set free from demon possession and be normal again? That the dead could come back to life?

The accounts were too incredible to be believed and yet ... God had done miracles in the times of their fathers. He created the world in six days, and when His creation rebelled, He judged it. The fountains of the deep were broken up and the windows of heaven were opened and a great flood covered the whole earth. The tallest mountains were buried to a depth of 20 feet! Only those on the ark were saved.

With 10 plagues, God released the Hebrews from the mightiest nation on earth. God split the Red Sea and the Jordan River. He made the sun stand still for a whole day so that Joshua could have vengeance on his enemies. God defeated the powerful Midian army of 135,000 with Gideon's band of 300 men.

In Elijah's time, fire came down from heaven and consumed the sacrifice, the altar, and the 12 barrels of water in the trench, proving that Elijah's God was the one true God. Elisha brought the son of the Shunammite woman back from the dead and healed Naaman, the leper.

Now there were stories circulating that Jesus could do all these things and more. Great multitudes of people came to hear Him and to be healed of their diseases and to be freed from unclean spirits. And everyone was healed.

The whole multitude sought to touch Him, for power went out from Him and healed them all! Pandemonium broke out as person after person was made whole. The lame began to leap and shout. The blind marveled at being able to see their loved ones' faces. Those who had been mute began to shout and sing. People laughed and cried for joy and hugged their neighbors and friends. El Shaddai—the Lord God Almighty was also Emmanuel, God with us.

In the New Testament Greek, one of the words for God's power is *dunamis*, which means force and, specifically, "miraculous power." It is where we get our English word "dynamite." The other word is *exousia*, which carries the meaning of the authority to do something.

"And they were all amazed, and spake among themselves, saying, What a word is this! for with authority [exousia] and power [dunamis] he commandeth the unclean spirits, and they come out" (Luke 4:36). God's omnipotence includes both His might and His authority. He has the power to do anything, and He has the authority and the right to do anything.

God's power is evidenced in Christ's death and resurrection. Right after the fall, God warned Satan that the Seed of the woman (Jesus Christ) would inflict a wound to Satan's head. "And I will put enmity between thee and the woman, and between thy seed and her seed; it shall bruise thy head, and thou shalt bruise his heel" (Genesis 3:15).

Satan would not have ultimate authority over mankind but would be destroyed that many would be made free. "... through death he might destroy him that had the power of death, that is, the devil; And deliver them who through fear of death were all their lifetime subject to bondage" (Hebrews 2:14-15).

We think of death as defeat. Christ saw it as the means of victory. Death could not have dominion over Christ. In fact, God's power was so intense at the death of Christ that multiple supernatural events occurred.

> Jesus, when he had cried again with a loud voice, yielded up the ghost. And, behold, the veil of the temple was rent in twain from the top to the bottom; and the earth did quake, and the rocks rent; and the graves were opened; and many bodies of the saints which slept arose, and came out of the graves after his resurrection, and went into the holy city, and appeared unto many. Now when the centurion, and they that were with him, watching Jesus, saw the earthquake, and those things that were done, they feared greatly, saying, Truly this was the Son of God" (Matthew 27:50-54).

At the cross, Jesus defeated the most powerful created being who, nonetheless, does not come close to having God's power. Our world is not a struggle between equal forces of good and evil. Good has already won by the power of God.

> That the God of our Lord Jesus Christ, the Father
> of glory, may give unto you the spirit of wisdom and
> revelation in the knowledge of him: The eyes of your
> understanding being enlightened; that ye may know what
> is the hope of his calling, and what the riches of the glory
> of his inheritance in the saints, and what is the exceeding
> greatness of his power to us-ward who believe, according
> to the working of his mighty power, which he wrought in
> Christ, when he raised him from the dead, and set him
> at his own right hand in the heavenly places, far above all
> principality, and power, and might, and dominion, and
> every name that is named, not only in this world, but also
> in that which is to come (Ephesians 1:17-21).

Man's strength, in comparison, is downright pathetic. An Egyptian Pharaoh thought he was mighty. He said, "And Pharaoh said, Who is the LORD, that I should obey his voice to let Israel go? I know not the LORD, neither will I let Israel go" (Exodus 5:2). Yet just months later, the land of Egypt was decimated and Pharaoh's army was washed up on the shore of the Red Sea. Egypt and all the surrounding nations knew then that the God of Israel was more powerful than anything they had ever seen before.

Oh, that modern man would acknowledge the power of God as King David did. He wrote, "Thine, O LORD is the greatness, and the power, and the glory, and the victory, and the majesty: for all that is in the heaven and in the earth is thine; thine is the kingdom, O LORD, and thou art exalted as head above all" (1 Chronicles 29:11).

God has power over all that He has created. He can overrule the laws of nature because they are His laws. What He wills to do is accomplished. In the accounts "The Church That Would Not Burn" and "Through the Fire," Psalm 29:7 was literally fulfilled as God directed the flames like a conductor directs his orchestra. The testimony of a firefighter who saw the aftermath was, "Only God could have done this."

God is glorious in power. The compelling stories in this section are evidence of God's mighty hand. Each is testimony that God can do whatever He pleases when man is helpless to do anything at all. Each of the participants in these stories can echo the words of Jesus, "But Jesus beheld them, and said unto them, With men this is impossible; but with God all things are possible" (Matthew 19:26).

Snail Manna

Nancy Sheppard with Pastor Emmanuel Kollie

After joining Baptist Mid-Missions in 1982, Nancy and her husband Mark served in Liberia for one term. When Liberia's bloody civil war erupted and they could not stay, the Sheppards moved to the neighboring country of Ivory Coast, where they ministered to those who had fled the conflict. After 11 years, the Sheppards were able to return to Liberia, where they currently work.

Like the Israelites, one Liberian family experienced the thrill of seeing God provide in a most unusual way. After three months of being forced to harvest all 10 acres of his rice field under the guns of soldiers, Pastor Emmanuel Kollie understood the soldiers' intentions clearly. They would leave nothing for his family. Nothing—not even one kernel of rice.

The Liberian Civil War in West Africa was leaving its mark on yet another innocent family. What would happen to them? Weren't the beatings and the looting enough? Nine children to feed and not a kernel of rice for the year. How could they live without rice—the staple of their diet? The palm cabbage (inner edible part of the palm tree) would not last forever.

Desperate, Pastor Kollie made plans to close down the Bible school he directed and to leave the area. After all, they had to eat. However, after calling the students together to break the news to them, he just couldn't do it. He felt God would have him stay and trust Him to provide sustenance. And so he, his family, and the students prayed for God's supply.

And then the snails came—big ones, sometimes with shells four or five inches across. Of course, there had always been some snails, but never in such profusion. There were snails everywhere. The mission property was literally crawling with them. The family went out to gather, and each step would yield a snail. All they had to do was reach out and pick it up.

The French call snails escargot and consider them a delicacy. Pastor Kollie and his family likened the snails to manna from heaven. And what did they do with all those snails? Well, the same thing the

Israelites did with their manna. They thought of every possible way to prepare it. Snail with cassava leaf. Boiled snails. Snail with whatever else was available. There was such an abundance of snails that there was sufficient to sell or trade for other things. Things like rice. Things like clothes. And so they carried bags of snails on their heads to market and came home with provisions.

When the Israelites entered the Promised Land, the manna stopped just as suddenly as it had started 40 years earlier. The need was no longer there. So it was with Pastor Kollie and his family. When the next year's rice harvest was safely stored, the snails were gone. And now when he sees a lone snail crawling across the mission, Pastor Kollie is reminded of God's provision in their year of great need.

(First printed in Harvest *magazine, Winter-Spring 1999–2000.* Harvest *was BMM's main publication and is now called* Advance.*)*

The Church That Would Not Burn
Doug and Linda Ferrett

Doug and Linda have been serving with Baptist Mid-Missions since 1990. They still work among the people of Big Lake, Alaska, where their story takes place.

Doug

It had been an unusually hot, dry spring and summer in Big Lake, Alaska. Since January, we had planned for a work crew to come up from a church in Remus, Michigan, to help paint our house and church and to hold Vacation Bible School during the first two weeks of June. The crew arrived in Big Lake as planned. But they ended up ministering to us in ways that none of us had anticipated. On June 2, 1996, my wife Linda and I had taken two couples out to dinner. When we left the restaurant, we saw a huge plume of smoke coming from the direction of Big Lake.

Two weeks before, as a volunteer firefighter I had helped fight what I thought was a big forest fire—600 acres. I figured that fire had rekindled. Linda dropped me off at the fire station at about seven o'clock

Monday night. I discovered that this was a new forest fire burning between Big Lake and Houston and heading our way. I immediately got into an engine, and we firefighters raced off to where we thought the blaze would be going.

The fire was huge and incredibly fast. Flames leaped to 200 feet in the air and were rushing from 30 to 60 miles per hour through the tops of the trees. The fire was so intense by this time that it was creating its own weather patterns. From seven o'clock Monday night to eight o'clock Tuesday morning, the fire had changed direction 11 times. One of the phrases that the firemen repeated was, "This fire is hotter than hell."

"No," I said, "it doesn't even compare. If you think this is hot you have no idea what hell is like."

Linda

After dropping Doug off at the fire department, I took the two couples back to their hotel and then headed for home. When I got home I listened to Doug's pager, the radio, and the television all at the same time, trying to get information about the fire. Over the pager I could hear the fear in the firemen's voices as they talked about how big the fire was and how out of control it was getting.

At about ten o'clock Monday night, I started getting telephone calls from church members who lived on the side of the lake where the fire was. They could see the flames advancing towards them. The state troopers had told them that they needed to evacuate. Because our house was not yet in danger of the fire, they asked to come here. Within an hour or so, three families had evacuated to our house. Around eleven o'clock, one of the men staying with us came to me and said, "Linda, you have to come look at this." We went to the front door and looked across the lake. The other side was completely orange. It was totally consumed by fire. The smell of smoke filled the air. It was then that the families started panicking and said, "We've got to get out of here."

"Yes, I guess it's time to go," I agreed. The next half-hour or so was spent packing, and then our five cars made a convoy on the back road out of Big Lake towards Wasilla. There was no way that I could contact Doug at this point. He was somewhere in the thick of the battle against this inferno. The only place we could think of to go was the Wasilla High School, which had been turned into an evacuation center. We ended up staying there seven days.

Doug

While Linda and our three boys—Adam, Joel, and Luke—were evacuating to the high school, I was down at the lake pumping water and filling tanker trucks all night. Around midnight, one of the firefighters driving the trucks told me that our church building had gone up in flames. Then about an hour or so later another firefighter came up and said, "Man, there's fire everywhere around your church! But it's still there."

Between midnight and eight o'clock Tuesday morning, I was told three different times that the church building had burned up. Finally I just prayed, "Lord, if it's there when I get there, I'm going to praise You. And if it's gone, I'm still going to praise You because You've got another plan."

About eight o'clock Tuesday morning, I was down at the lake pumping water. One of our church families that lived on the other side of the lake had to evacuate by boat. The Lord brought them right to where I was working. The man came up and said, "Pastor, all my cars are back there. Can I borrow one of yours?"

"Sure," I said. "Go up and see Linda and she'll give you one of ours."

He came back about an hour later in my Toyota pickup and said, "I didn't see Linda. Nobody's around." Then I knew Linda had evacuated, but I didn't have a clue as to where.

I worked nonstop from seven o'clock Monday night to four-thirty in the afternoon on Tuesday. Then a medic told me that I needed to take a break. So I went back to the house and tried to find out where Linda and the boys were. I was there for two hours when the state troopers came and told me that I had to leave. So I went back to work.

Later I saw a Red Cross lady that I knew, and I asked her to see if she could find Linda. The morning of the next day—more than 36 hours since I had last heard from my wife—the Red Cross volunteer told me that Linda and the boys were fine and that they were at the Wasilla High School. At ten o'clock Wednesday night, I had two hours off again and I went to see them. But before I left Big Lake, I drove around to all my people's houses to check on them. Five of our church families and two families whose children came to our church had lost their homes. Their houses were dust. I just cried as I drove to Wasilla to find Linda.

I spotted her in the hallway of the school, looking at the message board. I ran to her and we hugged and cried. It was a very joyful reunion. It had been three intense days since we had seen each other. Then I had the sad task of finding the families in our church and telling them that their houses were gone. It was very emotional.

I worked the fire all the rest of the week. It was Saturday before I saw Linda again.

Linda

While we stayed at the evacuation center, we witnessed the most incredible outpouring from the community. People came to the evacuation center and dropped off armloads of clothing and food. Pepsi semi-trucks backed up to the school doors and started unloading case after case of pop. It was incredible how people came together to help. The work team that had come from Michigan had arrived in Alaska on the second day of the fire. They stayed at a Christian school and helped out wherever they could—unloading food trucks, counseling those who had lost their homes, helping the Red Cross.

Doug

On Saturday the troopers allowed us to go back in and see what we had lost. By that time the fire had come within a half-mile of our house and then the wind changed and blew it in another direction.

God saved our church building. Our church property had two acres. The acre of woods next to the building was completely gone. Everything behind the church except a little cabin was consumed. All the woods on the other side of us were completely burned. Across the street from the church was burned too. Even the grass on our property was burned right up to the edge of the building. But the building itself was spared. It wasn't even singed. We had a little shed out back on blocks with a plywood floor. The fire burned the grass under the shed but not the wood floor!

When some of the other firemen saw our church building they said, "Only God could have done this."

"That's right," I said. "Only God did this." In the week that the fire raged out of control, 430 structures and 42,000 acres were burned in the Big Lake area.

After the fire was out, the church was able to minister to a lot of people. A year before the fire, we had installed a shower and a kitchen in our church building. So those families who had lost their homes were able to come to the church to eat and wash up. The Lord enabled me to borrow a dump truck and a backhoe so that I was able to help our families clear away the rubble on their properties. Before they left, the Michigan work crew helped one of our church families frame in a new house.

Churches from across the United States sent approximately $10,000 to help out the families who had been burnt out. Baptist Mid-Missions' World Relief Fund also sent money to help the families rebuild their lives.

We were able to minister to people outside the church family as well. It was a real struggle emotionally for the people in our church, but the Lord continues to work. Our church went through a fiery trial, but by God's grace we survived and continue to serve Him today.

Bible Classes in the Public School
Hubert Broeckert

Hubert and his wife Mary have served in a variety of locations since joining Baptist Mid-Missions in 1985. Their first ministry was in Central African Republic. Hubert, a Vietnam veteran, jumped at the chance to serve in Vietnam when the opportunity arose in 1995. That door later closed, and the Broeckerts then took the challenge of learning yet another language when they transferred to Cambodia in 2001. The Broeckerts are church planters, and as a physician, Mary has done extensive medical ministry. Their daughter Cherith and her husband Jonathan currently serve with BMM in France.

I was working with youth at Ippy in the Central African Republic. I wanted to teach Bible to the students in the public school, so I first went to a friend of mine who was a teacher. He said, "Well, we'll have to talk to the director." We went to the director's office, and my friend said, "This missionary here—he wants to evangelize in the schools. Is that all right?"

The principal said, "Well, I guess so."

I had full opportunity to preach the gospel to the youth in the public school for three years. Then a new director came in with some different administrators and teachers. I went back in September asking for permission to again teach in the school. I told the new director what

I had been doing for the past three years, and he said, "Yes, there is no problem. You can continue to teach Bible."

But there was a teacher who controlled the scheduling of classes. He claimed to be a Christian but belonged to a new evangelical group where there was known immorality and other matters that prevented us from cooperating with the group. He said to me, "The only way you are going to teach here is if I can teach with you." I told him that wasn't possible. So he said, "Then there's no way you can teach here."

I went back home really discouraged. My wife Mary and I put the matter before the Lord in prayer and asked that He would open up a way for us to continue to teach the Bible in the school. I knew that God had the keys to open up that school to me once again. So I went back to the principal and said, "You know, I really would like to teach."

And he said, "Well, I already told you that you could."

"There seems to be a problem with the teacher who has the schedule," I replied.

So the principal called this fellow into the room and said, "What seems to be the problem?"

And the teacher said, "We don't have any time."

The principal said, "What do you mean we don't have any time? Let me see the schedule."

So he showed him the schedule and declared, "See, every hour of every day is all filled up. There is no time for him to teach the Bible."

So the principal looked at me and asked, "When would you like to teach?"

"Well, I'd prefer Fridays at about three o'clock," I replied.

Looking at the other teacher, the principal said commandingly, "Put him down for Fridays at three o'clock."

"But there is someone else scheduled," argued my adversary.

"Take him out," the principal demanded, impatiently. "Fridays at three o'clock. In fact, all classes will be canceled on Fridays at three o'clock, and only Bible will be allowed." And that's how the Lord opened up the way for us to teach Bible in the public schools again.

Radio Luce on the Air
Fred Whitman

Through the Lord's blessing and their tenacious effort since 1973, Fred and his wife Rachel have seen a church established in Italy, a country sometimes called the graveyard of missionaries because of the difficulty of establishing a Protestant church. The Whitmans have a telecast, La Bibbia Oggi, *seen daily since 1979 as well as* Radio Luce, *broadcasting in FM 24/7 in central Italy since 1981. In 2008 the Whitmans celebrated the milestone of purchasing their own church building—a first for a Baptist group in their area. The Whitmans' grown children now serve alongside them in the ministry.*

In 1982 we had just ordered a new FM radio transmitter for about $25,000 and had it installed on the mountain above our city of Perugia, giving us the possibility to cover almost half of our province with the gospel. Our transmitter shared a tower with a TV station and a commercial radio station. But we had not even paid for the transmitter yet when a terrible electrical storm swept through our area.

At the time I had already been on television for about three years with my daily 10-minute telecast, *La Bibbia Oggi* (The Bible Today). Our transmitter for *Radio Luce* was actually hosted on that TV station's broadcasting tower. One of the men who taped my television program was also their technician. So when their power went out on the mountain, he went up to see what the problem was.

He found that their transmitter, worth about $35,000, had been burned to a crisp by the lightning. The large transmitter of the other commercial radio station was also destroyed in the same instant. When he went over to look at our transmitter, he found that it was broadcasting as if nothing had happened. He exclaimed, "Only to Pastor Whitman could something like this have happened!" Praise the Lord for protecting us in those humble beginnings.

When we moved our transmitter up on the mountain, we gained a stronger signal, but soon we started receiving menacing telegrams from a station that claimed we were broadcasting on their frequency. We were sure that our frequency had been formerly unregistered by any other station, so we continued to broadcast. We found ourselves taken to court by this station, which ended up being the official radio station of the Communist Party, which was the ruling party of our province.

The Sunday before the first menacing telegram arrived, a casually dressed young couple visited our church. When they introduced themselves after the service, however, we found out that he was a law professor at the University of Perugia and his wife was also a lawyer. As they introduced themselves, they mentioned that if we ever needed any legal advice to feel free to call on them. That very next day, as soon as I had received that telegram, I was on the phone!

The law professor took me to meet one of his former students, who happened to work in one of the most prestigious (and most expensive) law firms in the city. He agreed to represent us—for free! The case was prepared, and the day for the first hearing arrived.

As I stood in the hall waiting to be called to testify before the judge in an attempt to defend our radio station against the most powerful political force in our province, I cried out to God and found peace in His promises. When I was called before the judge, he lifted his eyes from our document that he was reading and exclaimed, "Pastor Whitman, what a privilege to meet you! I have watched you many times on television and find your program most inspiring!" I lifted a silent "Praise the Lord!" to Heaven.

The court proceedings dragged on for several years with decisions in our favor and then their appeals, but at the end the Lord gave us the victory. It was shown that the station had broadcasted on that frequency without permission, and in a time of turmoil and confusion in the party, they had not paid the electric bill. After several months, the electric company shut off their power, and their transmitter had stood silent for several months. In that time period, we had begun broadcasting on that "open" frequency. The court decision in our favor ended up in the official national legal journal, and the legal precedence of that court case gave us legal recognition as a station even before needing to officially apply for a frequency after the law on private broadcasting was passed in 1990.

To this day we thank God daily for His miraculous protection as well as His miraculous provision for this ministry, which last year cost us about 25 cents per minute to broadcast 24/7 to a possible audience of 600,000 people in our region of central Italy on FM 96.9 and FM 105.6 as well as to countless cities around the world on www.radioluce.com. Praise the Lord!

The Lord's Conduit
"Barnabas"

During my first term on the foreign field, I received funds from the BMM Home Office on an as-needed basis. So over the years, quite a surplus was building up in my account. I was really puzzled as to why God kept providing funds in excess of what I needed for my ministry.

Many individuals and churches gave above and beyond, without any request or hint on my part that I needed the money. In fact, several times I explained the situation to my churches and asked them to stop giving above my regular support. It didn't work; they kept giving.

I was embarrassed that I was so well-supported and was perplexed to know what to do with it. All my personal needs and all the needs of my work on the field were amply supplied, and yet there were still more surpluses. I had no clue as to what the Lord wanted me to do with that money.

Then in March of 1997, Dr. Gary Anderson, president of Baptist Mid-Missions, wrote a letter to our Mission Family to let us know about a capital campaign that was being implemented to meet some very pressing needs at the Home Office. The two primary projects driving the campaign were a new roof and a new computer system for the Home Office. The 24-year-old roof had to be replaced. Emergency repairs had kept the Home Office from significant loss of equipment and materials when they had leaks, but patching was no longer effective in keeping the water out. The weary old Wang computer system was obsolete. Breakdowns were occurring with greater frequency, impacting the entire Mission Family. At the end of that letter, he asked the Mission Family to pray.

In the June 1997 *Family Letter* sent out to BMM missionaries, he challenged us missionaries to ask the Lord to direct us about what part we could play in meeting the needs of another part of the Mission Family. The Lord began to lay it upon my heart to contribute in a big way to the capital campaign.

At the end of August, I needed to fly to the United States to renew my visa. I planned a trip to the Home Office while I was there. At this point, it was evident that I could give $5,000 to the capital campaign and hardly miss it at all. However, the thought of giving away that big a chunk of cash really got my palms sweating—I was afraid people would think I was daft.

So it was with fear and trepidation that I approached Dr. Anderson to offer him the gift. He seemed a little taken aback when I said, "I'd like to give the capital campaign $5,000."

"Are you sure?" he asked.

"Yes, I have extra and I don't need it. You do," I said. "Members of the family need to help each other out."

I didn't realize what a thrill it would be to be obedient to the Lord in the area of giving. It was really fun to give away $5,000!

At that point, I figured that was the extent of what the Lord was going to do through me. But I was wrong. When I got back to the field, the Lord also began to burden me for the needs of poor people in my adopted country, which at the time, was just about everybody. Proverbs 28:27 was a particular challenge. "He that giveth unto the poor shall not lack: but he that hideth his eyes shall have many a curse." I determined to put the Lord's promise to the test. I began to routinely help three families with food. I have no idea how my funds on the field stretched, but they did. I had no lack. It was spiritually exhilarating to take Him at His word and to watch Him work. Even though I was feeding nine more people without any increase in resources, I was not in want. God was faithful to His promise!

At the end of October, the Lord began to burden me a second time to give $5,000 to the capital campaign. Because of a lack of security on our field, we were not getting our monthly statements mailed to us. We didn't want the wrong people to know our net worth. So I had no idea how much was in my account. But I was convinced that the Lord wanted me to redirect more of His funds into the capital campaign. So who was I to argue?

I sent a cryptic e-mail to the Home Office asking that a "second helping of potatoes, just the same size as the first, be placed on the Home Office's plate." The good folks in Cleveland understood the message. However, because of instability on my field, they were reluctant to bring my balance down to zero in case I had to fly home unexpectedly. So the transfer was not made until the end of December.

I appreciated their concern for me but was mildly irritated that it was taking so long for me to fulfill what the Lord had told me to do. This was especially true because the Lord had been prompting me since December 3 to pray towards giving a third "helping of potatoes."

The third $5,000 took longer for the Lord to bring in, but by October of 1998, it was complete. Between August of 1997 and October of 1998, I was used as the Lord's conduit to convey $15,000 into the capital campaign. Whenever I think of what God was able to accomplish, I get little chills running down my spine.

When I got back to the United States, I sat down with my monthly statements and a calculator and began to discover how God was able to provide $15,000 to give away through a missionary whose committed support was only about $18,000 a year. It was amazing! Most of that money was from donors who were not a regular part of my support team. It was money, over and above, that God had prompted them to send in over the course of five years. Few of those gifts were large—most of them were $10 here and $50 there, and yet those special gifts totaled about $12,000! Interestingly enough, when the special need was no longer there, the extra gifts stopped coming. All these years later, it's sort of a surreal feeling. Sometimes I wonder if it really happened, even though I know our faithful Lord really did accomplish it.

Power Transfer at 100 Feet
Bill Kettlewell

Bill and his wife Dorothy joined Baptist Mid-Missions in 1970 to serve in Brazil. Since arriving in December 1972, they have concentrated their ministry in church planting evangelism. Today they minister in multiple local churches, establishing Bible Training centers for training pastors and leaders.

"The eternal God is thy refuge, and underneath are the everlasting arms" (Deuteronomy 33:27a). We have always known this truth and lived it, but on January 11, 1986, our entire family experienced this promise of God in a dramatic way. On take-off from Juazeiro do Norte, Brazil, our small mission plane, with all the Kettlewells aboard, lost power.

The story begins back on January 6. We got up early to prepare for our trip to Martins in the state of Rio Grande do Norte. For some time, we had been planning our annual Field Council meeting in this cool mountain city where Pete and Louise Brooks lived and ministered. The gas tanks were full to provide fuel for our return flight. We were off by 10 a.m. for an hour and 40-minute trip. It was a beautiful day, with scattered clouds at 3,500 feet.

Upon arrival, we had dinner with Pete and Louise. We talked over final details for the conference. We sought God's wisdom and direction for the week of fellowship in His Word and work. There would be many items of business to deal with and new officers to elect. Others began to arrive in mid-afternoon by plane, car, and bus. In all, there were 83 of us.

The conference went well as we started out that evening around the Word. Pastor Milton Frazier from Hartsville, South Carolina, challenged us from the Word, and he and his wife also ministered to us in music. He spoke to us from Romans. We heard from the Romans 8:28-29 passage on Thursday. What precious truths!

Thursday was also picture-taking day. In the morning, there was a group photo taken with all of us. In the afternoon, all the pilots and all five Mission planes were lined up for pictures. The picture taking was followed by a fly-by for the city. This was quite an event for the people of Martins as well as for the missionaries.

Early Saturday morning, the missionaries began departing for their stations in the far reaches of Northeast Brazil. Things went smoothly that morning. All ground transportation was off by 8:30 a.m. We were the last to leave for the airport. Up until that time, our plans had been to fly directly to Campos Sales, 190 miles away. Upon arrival at the airport, we changed our plans and decided to fly with the other planes to Juazeiro to buy fuel and have lunch together. The change of plans seemed common and insignificant.

The flight to Juazeiro went well, and the time passed quickly as we stayed in radio communication with the other planes. We were comparing flight data and plane performance. It was one last little bit of fellowship before returning to our ministry in Campos Sales, far removed from our fellow missionaries.

After lunch, missionary Wayne Barber took us back out to the Juazeiro airport around 3:00 p.m. There we found Harold Reiner, our senior pilot, storing his plane. After some small talk, goodbyes, and preflight, we taxied toward our eventful takeoff for Campos Sales, 35 minutes away.

The Juazeiro airport is much different than any other in the Northeast, having over a mile and a half of runway. The preflight check ran smoothly. We were close to maximum weight with mild winds on a hot day. As we started our takeoff run, some of the family commented about the time it was taking to get airborne. I was quick to explain the effects of high temperature and little wind at gross weight.

All was normal with smooth air. Our wheels lifted off the runway, and we started to climb ... 50 ... 60 ... 70 feet—the kids could now see Harold and his plane on the ground.

Then the smooth purr of our Lycoming 180 turned into a turbulent series of loud backfires. All of us felt the sudden loss of power. All eyes turned to me and my concentrated expression of shock. Pilots train and try to anticipate what to do in such events, but they never really get experience dealing with it until that time of trial. Then when it happens you say to yourself—is this it? Thousands of thoughts flash by in split seconds.

Engine power cut, full flaps, nose down. There was still runway. "Lord, we're in your hands," I prayed. Seconds passed—they seemed like hours. Finally, we were on the ground with a smooth touchdown. We stopped just 20 feet from the end of the runway.

On the ground Harold heard the plane lose power and told Wayne Barber, "They're going in; let's go." When they arrived, we were all out of the plane, trembling and praising God. Surely the eternal God was our refuge and underneath were the everlasting arms, holding us up and then safely setting us back on the ground.

Hurricane Mitch
Paul Howell

When Paul and his wife Lois joined Baptist Mid-Missions in 1993, they embarked on ministry in the Howell family homeland of Honduras. Paul's grandfather, Edward Howell, was an islander and circuit preacher for many years. Several of Edward's children also became preachers, including Robert, Paul's father, who joined BMM in 1954. Paul's brother Marty and his wife Cheryl served in Honduras until Marty went to be with the Lord in 2010. Paul and Lois continue to serve in the city of San Pedro Sula.

In late October and early November 1998, Hurricane Mitch sat off the Honduran coast for nearly a week. This storm brought utter devastation to Honduras. Reports tell of 11,000 people dead and thousands more known to be missing. The statistics tell us that more than one million people became homeless and in need of food and shelter. The newspapers in Honduras said that in four days it rained more than six feet of rain—about the same amount that the country normally receives in a year. The rivers and creeks were swollen to incredible proportions, overflowing their banks, and making lakes out of the low-lying areas of Sula Valley where my brother Marty and my father, Robert, serve the Lord under Baptist Mid-Missions.

This valley is where most of the country's vegetables, bananas, and pineapples are grown and where cattle are raised. Many of the cattle died, and nearly 100 percent of the fruit was lost because of the floodwaters and mud. Many small towns were completely swept off the map by a single mudslide that covered entire groups of houses and huts, leaving no one alive. Many people were stranded on top of roofs or left clinging to trees to keep from being swept downstream and drowned in the surging waters.

For several months before Hurricane Mitch visited Honduras, we had been wondering why God hadn't brought in the last of our passage money. We had 100 percent of our support, but Baptist Mid-Missions wouldn't give us clearance until we had enough for our passage. We couldn't understand why He who owns the cattle on a thousand hills did not send us the few thousand dollars we needed to finish our deputation and get to the field of Honduras. Then Hurricane Mitch came and we understood why. God, in His infinite wisdom, knew the situation that would arise and knew we would be more useful here in the United States.

As soon as we heard the news, I began contacting every Christian and local organization I could think of to help with the relief effort for the people of San Pedro Sula. Within a few weeks, a 48-foot container of relief supplies, clothing, Bibles, and tracts was on its way to Honduras.

Baptist Mid-Missions' World Relief Fund quickly responded to the crisis and advanced $21,000 to its missionaries to assist in the mammoth task of providing relief. My brother and father began meeting the needs of the people immediately. Both churches were filled with refugees who had nothing but the clothes on their backs. As my brother and father passed out food and water and other supplies to the homeless, they told the people of the love of Christ and gave them a tract. Within days of the hurricane, 21 people had made professions of faith in Christ.

I had the opportunity to visit Honduras December 2–17. I saw firsthand some of the damage brought by the storm. I went with the men of the church to purchase large quantities of rice, red beans, cornmeal, lard, salt, powdered milk, coffee, sugar, and hand soap. Then the church met one evening and divided the purchase into smaller quantities, one for each homeless family. A committee had already done a survey to determine which families would qualify to receive the bags of food. The following day, the church folk loaded the church bus and drove to one of the areas that had been badly hit by the flooding. This day it was the village of La Democracia—where we desired to plant a church.

The bus pulled into the neighborhood that we had chosen and a crowd gathered. One of the Bible students began singing a hymn and the church members joined in. After several songs, another Bible student opened his Bible and began preaching to the crowd in Spanish. At the end of his message, he explained that many groups from America had organized distribution of hurricane relief goods, but that ours was different. He explained further that we had two things to give away for free. We offered salvation from their sin through faith in Jesus Christ, and we offered humanitarian aid from churches and individuals in the States. He explained that if they received Christ, they would receive the donated goods. If they refused to receive Christ as Savior, they would still receive the goods. We were different because we were introducing them to Christ who could solve all their problems—not just their physical ones. An invitation was given, and many received Christ.

The missionaries met with the mayor of San Pedro Sula and presented a plan to build 100 simple homes for the city's homeless. The mayor offered free land for the construction of homes and a church building! The same thing happened in the village of La Democracia. Building teams from America descended on Honduras and started construction with money provided by individuals and churches that contributed to Baptist Mid-Missions' World Relief Fund. More than $180,000 was allocated for the construction of homes.

We arrived in Honduras in April 1999 and plunged right into the work of bringing spiritual hope to Hondurans. We were glad to finally be part of all that God was doing to bring new life and new hope to this country.

In the summer of 1999, we had a dedication service for three of the homes, with a devotional and challenge to the new occupants. By fall of 1999 our new church building was under construction.

More than 450 people have trusted Christ as their Savior since Hurricane Mitch made its grand entry. Maybe more accepted Christ; only God knows the complete number. Hurricane Mitch took many thousands of lives, but it brought new life for those who have been touched by the gospel.

Watching God Work on My Behalf
Jacqueline Eaton

Jackie and her late husband Jerry began service with Baptist Mid-Missions in 1964. The Eatons spent more than 40 years as church planters, with their last church being in Elkhart, Indiana. After Jerry's homegoing, Jackie transferred to BMM's Bible translation division, Bibles International, where she now serves.

God took my husband Jerry to heaven in March of 2005 after a brief illness with a malignant brain tumor. After a period of grieving, I finally decided that I should start to clear out our fairly large home and throw out items that I no longer needed. So one day in July 2005, I decided to start in the basement.

Under some boards I saw a black metal sign that said "Home for Sale by Owner" and the phone number. We had used the sign some 11 years prior when we sold our last home. I literally laughed out loud as I dragged the heavy metal sign up the stairs. I said to myself, "I won't be needing this. I will hire a Realtor because I can't sell a home by myself." I put the sign out by the trash can to be set out with the garbage in a couple of days. Little did I know that God had other plans for that sign.

This happened on a Tuesday, and that very night around nine p.m. I heard a knock at the front door. Since I lived on a cul-de-sac out in the country, I was a little leery of answering the door at that time of night, since I now lived by myself. I peeked out and saw it was a neighbor who lived two doors down from my home.

So I answered the door, and John said, "Jackie, I know your husband died and you probably will be selling your home. I would like to show it to my friends; I think they will be interested."

Earlier, in May, four different Realtors had looked at my house, and each gave me an idea of how much I could sell it for if I ever decided to sell. But I explained to John that the house was not ready to sell yet. He was undeterred and asked me if he could show it to his friends on Friday night. I agreed to let him bring his friends, even though the house was not ready to show. My husband's office was just the way he left it, and several areas needed a little cosmetic paint here and there.

"But I can't bring them if you don't have a sign out front, because they will think your home is not really for sale," he said. "Will you please put a sign out front?"

My mind raced back to the "Home For Sale" sign that I had lugged up the basement stairs earlier in the day. I almost said out loud, "God, are you going to sell my home?"

I agreed to put the sign up. The next day, Wednesday, my brother came to help me, and I told him about it. He helped me change the phone number on the sign and then pounded it down in the front yard.

Friday night came, and my neighbor and 10 of his friends took a tour of my home. After viewing my home, John said that he was going back to India for two weeks, and that when he got back he would let me know what they had decided.

From Wednesday to Friday a lot of other folks had stopped to view the sign. I started receiving call after call. The next week one gentleman called and made an appointment to see it. He liked it so much that after two more walks through the house, he made an offer and I counter-offered, and he accepted.

God had sold my home, and the only advertising I did was to put that sign in the front yard! I knew of a local Christian lawyer who was a deacon in one of our Baptist churches. He drew up the papers and kindly helped me with all the details for a small fee.

By this time, I had decided to move from Indiana to Michigan to work for Bibles International. I thought that a condo would best suit my new situation. However, now I had a deadline of September 9 to find something. Since my son and his family live in the same town that I was moving to, they began to search. Nothing seemed to be what I wanted.

After coming to a dead end looking for places, my daughter-in-law went back once again to the first place we had looked at. She discovered that a couple had decided to buy an adjacent condo and had released the contract on just the one I felt would suit me. When I had looked earlier, that model was not available, and the builder was not currently building any more of that type. Because the lower level was not finished, I could afford it.

God once again took care of the closing on my home. My home in Indiana closed one day at four p.m., and I closed on my condo in Michigan the next day at nine a.m.

One week before I closed on my home, my daughter and her husband closed on a brand new home. They needed lawn equipment and some furnishings since they had always lived in apartments. They came to my house and loaded a U-Haul and took all they needed. The next week, God sent a retired missionary in the area to take the rest of the things that he could use and that we had not sold or given to others.

I was on the sidelines watching God work on my behalf. God had everything in place at just the time it was needed. I was just a spectator. No, I couldn't sell a home by myself, but God already knew that and had His plan in place. God only needed my help to put the sign out in the front yard, and He did the rest. How I thank Him for caring for me as I changed fields and now as I've been serving Him in Bibles International since January 2006.

An Eleventh-Hour Surprise
Kent Albright

Kent and his wife Belén serve in Spain, her homeland. Appointed with Baptist Mid-Missions in 1989, the Albrights served their early years in the Madrid area, teaching in the Bible institute and giving support to existing church plants. In 1996, the Albrights began a church in Salamanca, in western Spain. Kent is also now the director of the Spanish field's seminary program.

One of the moments in our missionary career that most caused us to see the hand of God arranging circumstances was when we were trying to purchase a storefront building for our budding church here in Salamanca.

We had arrived in Salamanca in 1996 with a clear sense of God's leading us to begin a new work in this monumental, medieval, scholastic city in western Spain. To this point, there had been no Baptist church in the province nor had there been any independent Baptist church in this entire region of Castilla y León. We knew we were in enemy territory but had no idea how much opposition we would face.

However, we began finding a handful of people willing to begin a new church. We met in our little apartment in the bedroom town of Santa Marta de Tormes, just across the river Tormes from the main city.

Salamanca, certainly the center of our radar, has a population of about 200,000. Santa Marta hosts a basically blue-collar population of about 15,000. For over 200 years, there had never been a Protestant church of any kind there. We were definitely the new kids on the block.

The Lord confirmed His guidance to the area when we saw our first convert receive Christ. She was an older Spanish lady, born and reared in the city. She had been a nun for several years but had never read the Bible. Her salvation and growth (she read the whole Bible in four months) showed us that God could transform the lives of even the staunchest of the religious lost.

After a couple of years, more than 15 people were attending services in our living room. The local city government allowed us to meet in the cultural center for the next year and a half while we began looking for rental space. When we found the corner restaurant dining hall, our hearts flipped. It was in an ideal location with a rock bottom price, "only" $137,000 for over 5,000 square feet of developed property!

It made no difference that we had only about $1,000. We had discovered the place God had reserved for us! At least, we thought so at the time. We began earnestly praying that the Lord would provide the funding and financing we needed. We were very aware, however, of the long shot we were facing.

After several months, the Lord had wonderfully used several churches and people to provide about $40,000, but we still needed local financing. I had been to several banks with the same typical response from each one—no deal. It didn't surprise us, since we were Baptists in a very Catholic society; but we were still disappointed. I felt the need to call the seller to ask for a little more time and to assure him of our interest and intent to buy.

My heart sank when he told us, quite matter-of-factly, not to worry—the building was sold. I was stunned. As he was about to hang up, I grasped at a straw. I asked the man to mention to the new owner to contact us if he would be willing to resell part of the building. Although it sounded ridiculous at the time, this request would prove to be providential.

Missing this opportunity was a tremendous letdown to Belén and me. Psalm 126:5 says that those who sow in tears shall reap in joy. The meaning of the verse is that we must keep sowing, even though the tears fall and the hardships arise. So we focused our attention back onto our ministry to the new Christians and the discipleship courses we were giving. We knew that God would someday open the doors in His own way.

About three months later, the phone rang—it was the new owner of the building! He was a well-known businessman in the city, Mr. Alfonso De Arco. He had been looking for an investment opportunity when he bought the building. He was more than willing to sell us half the building, but for a new price, of course. Now it would cost $96,000 for 2,300 square feet—still a bargain. We asked for time and hit the banks again. After six rejections, I sulked back to Mr. De Arco and confessed that we just could not get the financing we needed.

Amazingly, he invited us to come and talk to his own banker friend. The three of us sat down, and Mr. De Arco introduced me as the leader of the "Buddhist" church in Santa Marta. I whispered, "Baptist." At the time it just seemed like a silly slip of the tongue, but later I was impressed that this man was willing to help a group who were not just part of the despised Protestants but rather an Asian religion! That was indeed a wild stretch!

The banker reluctantly listened to our story. Mr. De Arco finally said, "Manolo, I want you to give these folks a loan, and besides, I'll be willing to cosign for it."

What a shock! Who ever heard of a businessman cosigning for a loan—to an unknown religious buyer?! While we were signing the contracts, he said that this was only the second time he'd ever cosigned for a loan. The other time was for a family member, which turned out so skewed that he had vowed to never cosign again. What made him do it for us, only God knows!

So the door squeaked open and we were elated. But our bubble would soon deflate when the banker called to let us know that his superiors would approve only $40,000 instead of the $45,000 we needed, and only for 10 years instead of the 15 we'd asked for. It seemed we'd reached another impasse.

We challenged our church friends to pray, but we had only a couple of days to decide. There was no time for fund-raising for the $5,000 we lacked. We'd reached the end of the line. I'd have to call the banker soon with our answer.

The morning arrived when I told Belén that I was calling the bank. But a last-minute impulse caused her to suggest we check e-mail one more time. Truthfully, I was skeptical. That was back in the day of slow dial-up Internet access. To save money, I checked our e-mail only once a night. I'd gotten all our messages the night before. Unenthusiastically, I acquiesced and sat down at the computer.

Our eyes nearly became unglued when we saw a short little message from a little church on the west slope of the Rockies. The message was in all capital letters: "OUR CHURCH VOTED LAST NIGHT TO SEND YOU $10,000 FOR THE PURCHASE OF YOUR BUILDING. LOVE PASTOR DUNDSON."

It was truly an eleventh-hour miracle for us. We could hardly contain our amazement. How close we were to the precipice of another disappointment; but how secure we really were in God's wise and loving superintendence of our circumstances. Astonishment, awe, admiration, and wonder flooded our hearts. We bowed to give thanks to our almighty and awe-inspiring God for the enormous and sacrificial gift of this missions-loving church.

Then I called the banker. He stuttered with confusion when I told him we'd accept the loan, but on different terms. I told him we needed only $30,000, and only for seven years, instead of ten. Two weeks later we were signing the title deed.

In 2006 we finished paying off that loan and now own the property free and clear. However, in the meantime the two cities have built a bridge over the river practically to the front door of the church. The entire area has become what they call "The Golden Mile" of commercial development.

Due to circumstances we could have never foreseen, the property is now worth well over half a million dollars. It seems to us more than an adage that the night is darkest just before dawn. Our experience has shown us on more than this occasion that no matter how dark the night, "The LORD is my light and my salvation; whom shall I fear? the LORD is the strength of my life; of whom shall I be afraid?" (Psalm 27:1). God is still God in spite of the lack of answers, even at the very last minute before midnight.

The Lord Cleared the Way
Linda Throop

*Linda and her husband Craig spent many years in Papua New Guinea serv-
ing in Bible translation with another agency. In 2004, the Throops joined
Baptist Mid-Missions and are now continuing their work on the island
nation through Bibles International, BMM's Bible society. In addition to
translation work, the Throops are helping to establish a church in the West
New Britain province.*

The first major mud hole loomed ahead. "Lord, please help us to
get through the mud okay and not get stuck or slide off into some dangerous place. Help it to have dried a bit this week," I whispered under my
breath.

Suddenly an angry-looking man motioned us to stop. I recognized him as Henry, the chief Catholic catechist for the Kaulong area in
Papua New Guinea. As we slowed, a crowd of men began to gather behind Henry, many of them carrying long bush-knives and some of them
looking as angry as Henry himself.

Henry had been chewing betel nut (a mild stimulant) and he spat
out a stream of red juice as Craig rolled down the window. Eyes bulging,
Henry yelled, "You cannot drive by here. You are stealing my people. You
are only a white man. You're not one of us, and you're not doing anything
for us, so just GO HOME!"

As he spoke, specks of betel nut spattered our window and a
couple specks even landed on my arm as I sat praying in the passenger
seat. I glanced back at our 10-year-old special needs son, Daniel, in the
back seat. Did he understand what was going on? Was he frightened?
With relief, I saw that he hadn't caught on yet to the tension in the air.

As my eyes searched the group of men behind Henry, noting the
knives and some angry faces, I prayed for protection. A couple of other
men spoke up, supporting Henry's angry words. Some of them appeared
to be working themselves up into a rage. I prayed that the Lord would
send angels to keep this crowd from harming us and that Daniel would
not become too frightened to return happily to our little church in the
bush with us in the future. I especially prayed that the Lord would give

Craig courage, patience, calmness, and real wisdom as he tried to calm the men.

I watched in awe as the Lord kept Craig calm and apparently saying just the right things.

"You steal my sheep and you don't do anything special for us! Have you started a hospital for us?" Henry challenged. "No! Have you started any schools for us? No! You don't belong here. Go back to America!"

"True. We haven't started any hospitals," admitted Craig. "We are not doctors or nurses, and we could not do that. There are only my wife and myself. We are hoping to begin literacy classes soon, but with just two of us we cannot open a big school. But we have tried to teach many people what God says in His Word, the Bible."

"But you baptize people whom we already baptized!" raged Henry. "You are stealing my people! Go back! We don't want you here!"

"Now, don't get so angry so quickly. Let's talk about this," Craig said soothingly.

Back and forth the dialogue went. I watched and listened as Craig answered lucidly and apparently calmly, though I did wonder about the way his right leg jiggled up and down so strangely.

Meanwhile, the electricity in the air began to weaken. Women standing to the side of the car came to peek in on Daniel, who was busy smiling at everyone, especially babies and small children. One man began calling Daniel's name and trying to talk to him through the window.

"Thank you, Lord," I whispered, "for keeping Daniel from becoming frightened and for allowing him to do his little 'P.R.' thing."

Gradually, Henry began to calm ever so slightly. Finally Craig offered, "Henry, I would love to take some time to talk about these issues with you and look in the Bible together to see what God has to say about them. Why don't you come to our house tomorrow, and we'll sit down and talk about them?"

Henry stuttered a little as he replied, "W-w-well, I'm too busy this week. No, I can't come this week," and then, picking up confidence, "but maybe I'll come a little later. Look, you go ahead and go on to your Bible study this time. I'll come see you a little later."

Motioning to us the best way to get around the large mud puddle, Henry directed us to go on. With thankful hearts, we continued on our way (and, incidentally, made it around the mud puddle with less trouble than usual!).

After we told them the story, our small gathering of believers prayed earnestly for the Lord's intervention.

Henry never did come by, but neither did he try to stop us from driving to our church each Sunday morning. A couple of weeks later, one of our group of believers, formerly treasurer of the Catholic church in his village, told this story: "Craig, did you know that Henry came to visit me last week? We talked for a while, and then I thought I should show him Sunday's Bible study notes. He read it over for a while. Then he looked up at me and asked, 'Oh, is this what Craig is teaching you? I don't see anything wrong with this! Well, it's okay, I guess!'"

And so the Lord cleared the way for us once again! It is His work, after all. God be praised!

Hough Riots
Norma Nulph

"Miss Norma," as she is affectionately known by the people in her inner-city neighborhood, joined Baptist Mid-Missions in 1960. Norma established Faith Baptist Community Center as a lighthouse for the Lord in an under-privileged area of Cleveland, Ohio. The center now has its own church and medical ministry and is overseen by Norma and her missionary colleagues.

The Hough neighborhood in Cleveland was one of the toughest neighborhoods in the city during the 1960s. Housing was poor and rat-infested. Absentee landlords didn't make repairs. Unemployment was high and education was inferior. One out of every four families in Hough had their children enrolled in the Aid to Dependent Children program, which provided federal funds to families whose head of the household could not provide an income.

Racial tensions were also high in the neighborhood. The area had formerly been a middle-class Jewish community. But the whites had long since moved out and had been replaced predominately by poor blacks. However, many of the small shops, bars, and markets were still owned by whites. These white businessmen charged high prices for inferior prod-

ucts. Residents of the area were frustrated and edgy. The crime rate in
the Hough neighborhood had tripled since the 1950s. Family instability
was more prevalent there than anywhere else in the city.

It was to the children in Hough that the Lord called me—a single,
white 30-year-old woman. I could identify with the children in the
Hough area. I had grown up in a very small town in rural, western Pennsylvania. I was the third of six children. My family was poor because my
father was a clay miner. When I was young, I never heard or felt expressions of love from my family … something that led to a great hatred in
my life. As a result, I became tough … I fought in school, associated with
a negative group of friends, and began to smoke. Then the Lord Jesus
saved me and delivered me from hatred and a fear of dying.

I wanted to reach the children in the Hough area for Jesus Christ
and show them how Jesus could turn their lives around just like he had
done for me. I was able to rent a storefront building next to a pool hall. It
had big glass windows in the front.

I didn't have much money, but the Lord always provided. A lady
invited me to live in her home, and so I could afford to rent the building
in the Hough neighborhood. The Lord provided the money to turn on
the gas and the electricity. Every month the Lord provided for the rent
and utilities.

I started having children's classes. There would be 30-40 kids per
class. I would take the kids on picnics and to camp. I was there about
three years working with the children before that fateful day in the summer of 1966.

That summer, it seemed everyone in Hough was angry with
everyone else. The young men especially seemed frustrated. Most did
not have jobs and had no hope for anything better. The trouble began at
the Seventy-Niners Café that stood at the corner of East 79th Street and
Hough Avenue, the geographical center of the neighborhood. The owners had not had a good relationship with the people of the area. When
a black customer requested a pitcher of ice water and a glass, one of the
owners refused to serve him. The outraged customer shouted to his
friends that he had been denied a drink of water. A crowd quickly gathered. The white bar owners called the police.

The simmering tensions boiled over. The crowd began to throw
rocks and bricks at police. A riot broke out. Stores were looted and
torched. Two blocks between E. 84th and E. 86th Streets suffered the
heaviest damage. Snipers began to shoot from apartment buildings. Fire-

fighters could not reach the riot zone because of the crowds. When they did get in, they were assaulted with bottles and rocks. Fire hoses were cut.

The mayhem that first night continued until about 4 a.m. One young woman was shot and killed as she tried to get permission to leave a building to get home to her children.

The next day the National Guard was called in, but they didn't arrive until about 11 p.m. Tuesday. The National Guard with their big trucks blocked the whole area. I tried to get into the neighborhood to protect my building, but the National Guard wouldn't let me in. They said, "No, you're a white lady. You can't go in there." I couldn't get into the area for a whole week. I knew the Lord was taking care of it. All I could do was watch it on TV.

The rioting continued each night for five days. Four people lost their lives, many others were injured, and the damage to the neighborhood was impossible to calculate.

On Monday, a week after the riots had broken out, I went down to the neighborhood. I got out of my car, and there were five men from the pool hall guarding my storefront meeting place.

The men ran up to me and said, "Miss Norma, we saved your building. You take care of our kids. You teach our kids about Jesus, so we didn't let anyone mess with your building." In gratitude for the message of Christ that I had been giving to their children, these unsaved men had courageously guarded the building day and night for an entire week while violence raged through the neighborhood. Our faithful Lord had preserved my building and the ministry that went on inside it, including that huge plate glass window. The mighty love of God had gloriously triumphed over hate and anger.

The Gates of Hades Shall Not Prevail
Dr. Matt

"Dr. Matt" is a pseudonym for the missionary described in this story. Because of his work in a Creative Access Nation, his identity is not given.

In 1990, Dr. Matt, his wife, and three children said goodbye to their home country of Japan. God's call led them to an Asian country where Muslims are in the majority and where Dr. Matt's skills as a physician were greatly needed.

But the difficulties were immediate: they struggled with the language, their children refused to eat the local food, and there was no schooling for them. To his dismay, Dr. Matt found that he needed much broader medical skills than what his training included. Nevertheless, people were won to Christ and the hospital work grew. A Baptist church was organized in 1993. Two days before organizing the church, nine Christians were baptized.

Some of these Christians were persecuted after their baptism. Muslims tried to hinder the hospital. Yet, God continued to overrule the opposition. Land was able to be purchased for a church building, and the Christians dedicated the land to the Lord in 1996. Within a month they started construction of a boundary wall.

A mob of Muslims accosted the workmen constructing the wall. Young Muslim men demanded money from the church. They threatened the church deacons, boasting that they would break down the church building, kill Christians, and set fire to Christians. The believers were intimidated, and construction on the wall stopped.

A few days later, the house of one of the deacons was set on fire and a part of the house burned. The police refused to investigate, saying it was an accident.

The next day, about 50 Muslims threatened two other deacons, demanding that they return to the Muslim faith. One man's younger brother twice attempted to kill him with an axe. The Lord protected him both times, and he was not hurt. That Christian made the decision that he would never deny Christ.

Dr. Matt and his wife were in a dangerous situation. They made the decision to stay in the country. In trust, they committed everything to the Lord. Second Corinthians 1:9 declares, "But we had the sentence of death in ourselves, that we should not trust in ourselves, but in God which raiseth the dead." They felt that they could not go away and leave the Christians to face persecution alone.

Fear gripped the church and new Christians were afraid to come. Attendance plummeted from 111 people to just 49. Some Christians who were the most persecuted, in fear, denied Christianity.

But God remained faithful. Some who had lost courage came back. He softened the attitude of some Muslims who had opposed the church building. Dr. Matt stated, "Even in a difficult place, if it is His will, God's church is built." Dr. Matt worked tirelessly treating patients, demonstrating and telling about God's love through Jesus Christ.

In early 1998, the church deacons made the decision to resume building the wall around the property and to start the church building. Nineteen months had passed from the start of the heightened persecution. Just like the wall-building project of Nehemiah's day, the Lord protected the construction from enemies.

On Easter Sunday of 1998, the new church building, with seating for 200 people, was dedicated. Persecution resurged. In the months of April and May, tormentors threw stones at the church building during meetings. They threatened the church security guard. He quit the job. The newly hired Christian security guard was also threatened during the night. Four young men wearing masks came over the boundary wall. They threatened the night guard with a long knife. He was told that if he continued to work for the church, they would kill him. That night they punched him and got away. This guard, too, decided to quit the job.

The church deacons were also threatened. Enemies tried to stop the church work. But Exodus 14:14 says, "The LORD shall fight for you, and ye shall hold your peace." The Lord did indeed fight for them, and within two months the persecution of the church stopped. People from the hospital began coming to church almost every week.

In October of 1998, they celebrated the fifth anniversary of the church. Brothers and sisters in Christ were bold and invited many people to come to church. Although it rained heavily on the anniversary day, 138 people attended the meeting and several made decisions to accept the Savior.

During that same year, a Bible college and ministries in two villages were also started. Often, new initiatives were accompanied by persecution, but the believers persevered.

Individual believers who submitted to baptism were often targets. One lady who had converted from Islam could not come to the morning service on the day she was to be baptized, because people blocked the road. But in the afternoon, just before the baptismal service, she appeared at the church. She came through the rice field. Her mother-in-law, who is a Muslim, helped her to come to church. The church praised the living Lord for preparing the way. Both she and her son were baptized. She was so happy, even though she knew that she would not be able to go home.

"Since Jesus started to build this church, Satan cannot destroy it," declares Dr. Matt. "By throwing stones at the church, it will not be destroyed. The church will be strong by persecution."

Today the church is well established. Its ministries include a Christian school and a book house where hospital patients can watch the *JESUS* film and receive Bibles and tracts. The church has done mobile clinics in 22 districts of the country. As patients are seen, the gospel is also shared. Ministries have been established in 16 villages. Eleven faithful brothers are involved in the ministry to the villages.

The church supports four missions projects. A correspondence school presents the gospel to unbelievers and trains those who have difficulty attending church because of persecution.

God in His power has established a strong testimony for Christ in a country known to be hostile to Him. Dr. Matt's goal, shared by the believers, is to evangelize a new village each year, and eventually to reach out in all areas of their country. They believe, as the Scriptures affirm, that nothing is too difficult for God.

Through the Fire
Rachel Metzler

Rachel and her sisters, Helene and Evelyne, served many years in Chad, where their parents had pioneered a work for Baptist Mid-Missions in the 1920s. Rachel joined Baptist Mid-Missions in 1949. After missionaries were evacuated from Chad during the country's tumultuous Cultural Revolution in the 1970s, Rachel and Evelyne began working in Haiti and established an orphanage there. Rachel went to be with the Lord in 2001.

This particular day in 1996 had been a full day of celebration for those who had received their awards for our children's Bible club in Grand Goave, Haiti. Finally, all the children in my care were in bed in the dormitory, and I retired to my room across the courtyard, weary but thankful to the Lord for such a special day.

At midnight, 18-year-old Lavisa, who sleeps in the dormitory I built for the children, came running to my window calling: "Miss Rachel—Miss Rachel! Fire! Fire!"

I jumped out of bed and ran to the courtyard, praying all the way. I could hardly believe my eyes. The children were huddled outside the dorm, trembling. We called the two older boys who sleep in another room, and they came running out too. As I ran down the dorm hallway to the back bedroom, I found a great wall of flames—roaring all the way up the ceiling and pouring out the door and out the decorative cement blocks that served as windows in the hall section.

I gave the older boys orders to turn on the generator, but the fire had burned the electrical cords. I grabbed two flashlights and ran with our oldest boy toward the room that was on fire. We slammed the door shut to try to contain the fire to one room. We barely escaped being burned from the roaring flames that were trying to leap out the door! As I saw the terrible inferno in that room, I realized again what a Great God and Protector we have. All those children were awakened and able to run through the flames and out the door without having one small burn even on the littlest, Nadia!

Using the hand pump from the well in the courtyard, the older children formed a bucket brigade. Some pumped water, some threw water on the door to soak it and keep the fire contained, and some threw water through the window into the room. One of the boys ran to the other little cottage and woke Pastor Dieupi and his teenage nephew. They helped with the water brigade. Another boy ran to wake the neighbors, who in turn woke more neighbors. Soon most of the neighborhood was helping pump water to carry to the flames. Even the witch doctor was there helping. I was really moved to see so many come out in the middle of the night to fight the fire with us. It took a good hour before the flames were subdued. Then we prayed and thanked the Lord for saving the children, and I thanked all the neighbors and gave a testimony of how the Lord takes care of His own.

Later I asked Lavisa how they had all managed to get out safely. She said, "Miss Rachel, I myself am amazed. You know how hard it is to wake me up when I'm in a deep sleep. I was sound asleep, but I kept dreaming that I had to get up and run. I kept struggling to wake up. Finally I felt very hot and kept hearing a terrible roaring in my ears and managed to open my eyes. Then I could see that we were surrounded with a wall of flames. I called, 'Lord, help us!' I jumped up and woke the other teenagers and told each to grab a child and run out. I then grabbed

Nadia under one arm and Katina under the other and ran with the others following me. I headed for the door in spite of the flames, thinking that it was better to be burned some while running out than to stay and be burned completely. As I reached the wall of flames by the door, I was amazed to see it part for us, and we all ran out and not even our hair or clothes were burned. I know the Lord led us out! Is this not a matter for praise?"

In the morning, we found enough clothes to wear to church. Everything had been burned except some clothes that had been hanging on the clothesline, and a table in the middle of a room that had a Bible and a hymnbook on it. We gave our testimony of God's goodness and greatness, and Pastor Dieupi gave a great message. People wept and we could feel the Holy Spirit working in hearts. Two stayed after for prayer and to make things right with the Lord.

Many came in the days after the fire to visit and talk—some of them were not Christians. We had many opportunities to talk to them about the Lord. Our young people in high school had their schoolmates lend or give them books and notebooks, even tennis shoes, after our young people were asked to speak in front of their class and explain what happened.

It seems that a candle that the children had thought they put out must have relighted and fallen over, igniting whatever was near it. I praised the Lord that there were no lives lost and that no one was burned. Even the smoke could have been fatal, but God protected us all.

God's Holiness

Isaiah the prophet saw a vision of the Lord sitting on His throne, high and lifted up, with His power and glory filling the temple. Mighty angels stood above Him and declared: "Holy, holy, holy is the LORD of hosts: the whole earth is full of His glory" (Isaiah 6:3). The very foundations of the temple began to shake at the pronouncement, and the temple was filled with dense smoke. At this display of immense power and glory, Isaiah cried out, "Woe is me! for I am undone; because I am a man of unclean lips, and I dwell in the midst of a people of unclean lips: for mine eyes have seen the King, the LORD of hosts" (Isaiah 6:5).

A tough fisherman named Peter had a similar reaction when he experienced the power of Jesus displayed in a miraculous catch of fish. He fell down at Jesus' knees and said, "Depart from me; for I am a sinful man, O Lord" (Luke 5:8).

The holiness of God rips through the pretenses of men and women who think they are really not that bad. "Who is like unto thee, O LORD, among the gods? Who is like thee, glorious in holiness, fearful in praises, doing wonders?" (Exodus 15:11).

In a future time, an awesome multitude of the redeemed in heaven will worship the Lord and attest,

> Great and marvelous are thy works, Lord God
> Almighty; just and true are thy ways, thou King of saints.
> Who shall not fear thee, O Lord, and glorify thy name?
> for thou only art holy: for all nations shall come and wor-
> ship before thee; for thy judgments are made manifest
> (Revelation 15:3-4).

An aspect of God's holiness is His perfection and righteousness. The apostle John wrote under the inspiration of God, "… God is light, and in him is no darkness at all" (1 John 1:5). "Righteous art thou, O LORD, and upright are thy judgments" (Psalm 119:137). "Thou art good, and doest good; teach me thy statutes" (Psalm 119:68).

The Bible is clear. God is good—all the time. If we had all the facts in any given situation, we would be convinced that God did the right thing. It inspires courage when we know that our God will never act capriciously toward us. Man's courts are fallible, but the judgment of God is pure and right. "The LORD is righteous in all his ways, and holy in all his works" (Psalm 145:17).

In faith we must acknowledge that God alone sets the standard for holiness and righteousness. As the Creator of humanity, He has exclusive right to define the terms. "For my thoughts are not your thoughts, neither are your ways my ways, saith the LORD. For as the heavens are higher than the earth, so are my ways higher than your ways, and my thoughts than your thoughts" (Isaiah 55:8-9).

It's just when we don't understand—when hurricanes destroy a city, or a drive-by shooter kills an innocent child, or even when things just don't turn out the way we thought they should—it's just then that trust needs to kick in. It's at that moment that we need to remember what the Scriptures declare about God's holiness. Then, amidst the chaos, we can have peace.

Our God is a champion of the helpless and hopeless. He defends the righteous and punishes the wicked and arrogant. In His holiness, He will cause good to prevail in the end. In this world where evil is called good and good evil, it is comforting to know that God has a standard that will never change. When it seems that evil rules, we can take courage in the knowledge that our holy God will eventually set things right. "Dearly beloved, avenge not yourselves, but rather give place unto wrath: for it is written, Vengeance is mine; I will repay, saith the Lord" (Romans 12:19).

To the non-Christian, the holiness of God is a fearful thing. Because of His holiness and their disobedience, they have no hope for anything but judgment. The righteous God is willing to forgive, but only as the sinner is willing to repent and believe on the sacrifice of Jesus Christ.

Because God is holy, He insists that His children be holy.

> Wherefore gird up the loins of your mind, be sober, and hope to the end for the grace that is to be brought unto you at the revelation of Jesus Christ; as obedient children, not fashioning yourselves according to the former lusts in your ignorance: but as he which hath called you is holy, so be ye holy in all manner of conversation; because it is written, Be ye holy; for I am holy (1 Peter 1:13-16).

However, "Be holy, for I am holy" is not a call for a do-it-yourself renovation. Oftentimes people who strive to become more holy end up focusing on a list of rules, the "dos and don'ts" of nice Christianity. They manage to conform to the standard of the church they attend, and yet inwardly their heart may be cold and filled with anxiety at trying to measure up. Joy is not evident in their lives, and they can often become judgmental of others who don't conform to their definition of holiness. Rules, rather than an authentic walk with Jesus the Righteous One, become the focus of their Christian experience. They are not happy and, frankly, neither is God.

Without the indwelling Lord Jesus Christ giving us His righteousness, we are totally incapable of being holy.

> Yea doubtless, and I count all things but loss
> for the excellency of the knowledge of Christ Jesus my
> Lord: for whom I have suffered the loss of all things, and
> do count them but dung, that I may win Christ, and be
> found in him, not having mine own righteousness, which
> is of the law, but that which is through the faith of Christ,
> the righteousness which is of God by faith (Philippians
> 3:8-9).

Self-effort is not only futile, it is an affront to God. Even in the Old Testament, it was God making men holy rather than men making themselves holy through keeping the Law. "Sanctify yourselves therefore, and be ye holy: for I am the LORD your God. And ye shall keep my statutes, and do them: I am the LORD which sanctify you" (Leviticus 20:7-8).

In Ezekiel 36:22-27, God determined to make His wayward people holy for His own name's sake.

> Therefore say unto the house of Israel, thus saith
> the Lord GOD; I do not this for your sakes, O house
> of Israel, but for mine holy name's sake, which ye have
> profaned among the heathen, whither ye went. And I will
> sanctify my great name, which was profaned among the
> heathen, which ye have profaned in the midst of them;
> and the heathen shall know that I am the LORD, saith
> the Lord GOD, when I shall be sanctified in you before
> their eyes. For I will take you from among the heathen,

and gather you out of all countries, and will bring you
into your own land. Then will I sprinkle clean water upon
you, and ye shall be clean: from all your filthiness, and
from all your idols, will I cleanse you. A new heart also
will I give you, and a new spirit will I put within you: and
I will take away the stony heart out of your flesh, and I
will give you an heart of flesh. And I will put my spirit
within you, and cause you to walk in my statutes, and ye
shall keep my judgments, and do them"

"Be ye holy, for I am holy" is God's declaration of what He is
already accomplishing, and it is a compelling invitation for us to partner
with Him in the process. God's part is the power and motivation to make
the changes. Man's part is to relinquish himself to the working of the
Holy Spirit. When a person determines to follow Jesus, the Holy Spirit
takes up residence in his or her soul and begins renovations. The indwelling Holy Spirit convicts the believer of sin and enables him or her to
choose righteousness, conforming the believer into the image of Christ.

In the following accounts, the forces of evil seek to abuse the followers of God and foolishly mock the Lord Himself. These men imagined themselves powerful until they were confronted by the Almighty
God who defends His Holy Name. Yet the Christians in these stories
triumphantly testify, "There is none holy as the LORD: for there is none
beside thee: neither is there any rock like our God" (1 Samuel 2:2).

The God Who Brings Rain
Vernon Rosenau

Vernon is the third generation of his family to have lived and served in Central African Republic (CAR). His grandparents were among Baptist Mid-Missions' first missionaries when the organization was founded in 1920. Vernon and his wife Jan joined BMM in 1975 and served in CAR until 1999. Vernon currently serves in the BMM Home Office as the Field Administrator for Africa and Europe, and Jan also serves there as a receptionist.

One of our African pastors served on the city council in Sibut, Central African Republic. The region was experiencing a severe drought, so the city council met to determine what could be done to produce rain so that the people could plant their crops.

The consensus of most of the men on the council was that the spirit of Nguerengou, who controls the rains, was miffed because the people of the town had turned from their traditional worship. Therefore they proposed that a festival be held to appease Nguerengou. The people, they said, needed to dance and to kill a chicken to appease the spirits and bring rain.

The pastor interrupted their discussion and said, "As a pastor, I can't agree with you. We have heard who God is—the Creator of heaven and earth. We know what God does. He is the One who controls the rain. My people and I will pray to the God of Heaven for rain, and you will see. It will rain."

But the council would not be swayed. "We need to appease Nguerengou," they said. So they set a date for the festival.

The pastor returned to his congregation in the village of Kanga and told them of the city council's decision. The congregation determined to petition their Heavenly Father for rain. They persevered in prayer to the True God throughout the night, asking Him to send rain so that they could plant their gardens and have food to eat, and they asked that the power of God would be known.

God rewarded their faith. In the village of Kanga, where the people were praying, it rained. It rained hard enough to soak the soil so that they could plant. But just down the road in Sibut, the drought continued—not one drop of rain fell on the town where the people were dancing and performing animal sacrifice to a heathen spirit.

Victory over Demons
James Storey as told to Bill Smallman

Jim and his first wife Bonnie joined Baptist Mid-Missions in 1986 to serve in Jamaica. After Bonnie passed away in February 1993, Jim married Becky Hales (then a BMM missionary to Scotland) in December 1994. Jim and Becky served in Jamaica for two and a half years, after which they spent six years serving in Scotland together. Jim and Becky are currently serving in Canada.

Bonnie Storey lay dying of cancer. The family had opted for home hospice care, so her husband Jim and grown daughter Heather attended her around the clock.

During her last week, Bonnie was unusually restless. She was seeing other people in the room, and this made her uncomfortable. Jim explained that her pain medication extended her transition from sleep to wakefulness. She was just "seeing" her dreams. She insisted that while fully awake she could see two, sometimes three men in the room.

Jim finally woke up. Demons? Angels? Jim told Bonnie she was close to heaven and might be seeing angels. "No," Bonnie responded, "angels don't smoke, and that one over there is smoking right now. Can't you see him?"

She described an old man dressed in yellow, with a long beard, whom she referred to as Methuselah. He was clearly in charge, ordering the other one or two around.

It was time to counterattack. Heather phoned Bonnie's mother and asked her to pray for them. Jim and Heather knelt at the sides of Bonnie's bed and prayed a hedge of protection around her by the power of the Risen Son. Heather prayed. Jim prayed. As Bonnie prayed, it was as if heaven opened and flooded the room with peace. The darkness of recent days was lifted as if the lights were turned on.

They all looked up. Bonnie said she could see Methuselah hissing at her from the corner. He vanished through the window and never returned. It was 6:00 a.m.

Bonnie's mother and sister phoned later to see how she was. Her mother told them she had been under quite a burden to pray and to wrestle for victory. Suddenly relief had come and she had peace; she felt she could stop praying. That was at 6:00 a.m.

A deacon friend visited the next day, unaware of what had happened. He came into the house and sensed such an atmosphere of tranquility that he commented, "This place feels like a great spiritual battle was just won!"

Bonnie Storey's faith in God never wavered. She knew she belonged to Christ and that nothing could take her from Him. "O death, where is thy sting? O grave, where is thy victory? But thanks be to God, which giveth us the victory through our Lord Jesus Christ" (1 Corinthians 15:55 and 57).

Bonnie died triumphantly.

(First printed in the Harvest *magazine, Summer 1993. Recorded by Bill Smallman who served as Communications Administrator, now retired.* Harvest *was BMM's main publication and is now called* Advance.*)*

Our Father's Rice
Nancy Sheppard with Pastor Emmanuel Kollie

After joining Baptist Mid-Missions in 1982, Nancy and her husband Mark served in Liberia for one term. When Liberia's bloody civil war erupted and they could not stay, the Sheppards moved to the neighboring country of Ivory Coast, where they ministered to those who had fled the conflict. After 11 years, the Sheppards were able to return to Liberia, where they currently work.

The evil men of this world think they are getting away with something, but this is only an illusion. In 1994, times were very hard for the people remaining in the interior of war-torn Liberia, West Africa. Undisciplined soldiers traveled freely from town to town, looting and demanding at gunpoint whatever they wanted. Of course, they were always after food. Only a fool would have resisted these men, who were crazed with the power that having a gun gave them.

After the rice harvest in their village, the church members of the Kpoyea Baptist Church gave tithes of their harvest to Pastor Johnson Cermu. In Liberian fashion, he stored the bundles of rice in the ceiling of his rice kitchen, a small thatched structure for outdoor cooking. Through the tithes of these church members, he and his family would have food to eat.

But one day, 11 soldiers came and found his supply of rice. Confronting Pastor Cermu, they demanded, "Who is this rice for?"

"This rice is for God," he replied. "God's people gave their tithes in rice, and we kept it in the kitchen."

The soldiers began to laugh and mock. "Ha, ha, ha. This is our Father's rice. God is our Father. So we have found our rice," the soldiers taunted as they tossed the bags of rice from one to another. "It is very fine of you to have been keeping our Father's rice. Now we have come to carry it away."

The looting of a family's provisions was a joke to them. The idea of stealing from God Himself seemed to make the matter all the more humorous. Packing the bundles into their vehicle, one of them had an afterthought. He threw ten bunches of rice to Pastor Cermu. "This is for being watchman over our Father's rice," he mocked.

They took the rice and went their way—convinced their act would go unnoticed and unpunished. They forgot about God—the Father they had so boldly mocked. Their mirth was short-lived. Soon a fight broke out among the men over the rice. Two men were shot and killed. Nine men remained.

Several days later, five of the men were killed on the battlefield. Four remained. A car accident on the way back from battle claimed the lives of those four.

A week after their theft, all 11 men were dead, facing the God they had so glibly mocked.

The Power of the Word of God
Mark Seymour

Mark is the third generation of his family to serve in Chad, Africa. His parents are Ruth and the late Dr. David Seymour, and his grandparents were Arthur and Linda Seymour. Mark and his wife Debbie joined Baptist Mid-Missions in 1979. In Chad, they were involved in church planting and theological education. Since 2009, Mark has been serving as a BMM Mission Advancement Representative.

It had been a great week ... right up until the moment when a group of men in tribal masks and grass skirts surrounded our Land Rover. Then things got a little problematic.

Earlier in the week in 1986, the new edition of the Sara Madjingaye language New Testament arrived in Chad amidst great rejoicing. Within the first week of its arrival, we took copies of the New Testament up into an area that we had not visited in awhile. We evangelized on Friday and all day Saturday, and by Sunday we were on our way back.

There were about 11 of us crammed into my Land Rover—most of them were Bible school students. It's a vehicle made for seven or eight people, and so all the baggage was on top. We were almost home when it started to rain. We needed to get the things off the top of the vehicle before the rain destroyed them, so I pulled over to the side of the dirt road. We were in the middle of nowhere.

Suddenly out of the bush came a group of men dressed in masks and grass skirts. They had just come from the camps, where they had been involved in the tribal initiation rites that included idolatrous animistic and ancestor worship. They completely surrounded the vehicle. You could sense the presence of Satan and darkness. From 1973 to 1975, when missionaries had been forced out of the country, tribal initiates had overturned vehicles and beaten people. So our situation was rather precarious.

The man leading the group came to the passenger side of the Land Rover and demanded that our African pastor give him money for something to eat. That's how these initiates live during the two or three months they are in the bush—by extorting contributions from everyone.

This Sara man was huge. We were totally surrounded and I was thinking, "What are we going to do?" I thought that we might have some stale bread or something to give them. But Pastor Machine grabbed a New Testament that had been lying on the dashboard of the car and put it through the window and right into the face of that man. He said, "This is the Word of God. This Word of God calls what you are doing idolatry—sin. We can't give you anything."

I was thinking to myself that we might want to be a lot less confrontational in this situation. For about 10 to 15 seconds, maybe longer, nobody did anything. Then this big Sara man broke into a hearty laugh and gave some secret signal to his men, and everyone disappeared again into the bush. It was the most incredible confrontation between the Word of God and sin.

The most amazing part of the story, however, was that this pastor who had just been so bold had compromised with the government back in 1973 against the teaching of God. Back then he had not had the Word of God in his hand. But now he had it, and it made him bold to stand unflinchingly on God's side. There is power in the Word of God in the hands of His people.

God's Love

The apostle John declared, "God is love." In those three words he proclaimed a truth that will take all eternity to fully comprehend. In love, God created man and his universe. He poured out every good thing on His creation. The epitome of His creation—man—He made in His very own image.

Even after man rebelled against God, the Lord continued to love His people, continued to reach out to them even though they were not so lovable. Then, when the fullness of time had come, the love of God set into motion the process that would restore that perfect fellowship between God and man.

God's greatest demonstration of His love is that He sent His Son to die on the cross for our sins. "For God so loved the world, that he gave his only begotten Son, that whosoever believeth in him should not perish, but have everlasting life. For God sent not his Son into the world to condemn the world; but that the world through him might be saved" (John 3:16-17).

Jesus did not die for us because we were worthy or deserving. Just the opposite is true. Romans 5:8 declares, "But God commendeth his love toward us, in that, while we were yet sinners, Christ died for us."

Jesus chose to love His enemies. He did good to those who hated Him. He blessed those who cursed Him and prayed for those who spitefully used Him. To those who struck Him on the cheek, He offered the other one also. When they crucified Him, He asked the Father to forgive His torturers because of their ignorance.

Our salvation was in no way based on our worthiness. We didn't deserve redemption. We couldn't deserve it. He reached out to us because of His love, because He is love.

Blessed be the God and Father of our Lord Jesus
Christ, who hath blessed us with all spiritual blessings in
heavenly places in Christ: According as he hath chosen
us in him before the foundation of the world, that we
should be holy and without blame before him in love:
Having predestinated us unto the adoption of children by
Jesus Christ to himself, according to the good pleasure of

his will, To the praise of the glory of his grace, wherein he hath made us accepted in the beloved (Ephesians 1:3-6).

When by faith we repent and receive Jesus as our Savior, we are adopted into the family of God and invited to address the Creator of the universe as "Abba, Father." The Aramaic word *Abba* means "Daddy." This term is reserved for those who belong to Him.

The believer in Jesus Christ has a new and unique connection with the Godhead. Jesus said, "As the Father hath loved me, so have I loved you ..." (John 15:9). We are united with Christ and the Father in love.

We participate in the love that the Father has for the Son. It is incomprehensible, mighty, perfect love. God is love and He Himself dwells in us. Love is not an emotion but a Person!

"Behold, what manner of love the Father hath bestowed upon us, that we should be called the sons of God" (1 John 3:1).

God's love goes way beyond what we deserve, way beyond what our performance would merit. God abides in us. He doesn't save us and then leave us to carry out the Christian life on our own. Incredible! God's love is not like the love of this world. People love us when we are lovable. As long as we live up to their expectations we are accepted.

But God's love is unconditional. God's love "... is not easily provoked, thinketh no evil; rejoiceth not in iniquity, but rejoiceth in the truth; beareth all things, believeth all things, hopeth all things, endureth all things. Charity never faileth ..." (1 Corinthians 13:5-8).

Sometimes we get hung up on this point. We know that Jesus loves dirty, rotten sinners before they are saved—before they give their lives to Him. But what about when we mess up as a believer? What about when we know what we ought to do and we don't do it because we're cowards or because we're rebellious or because we just want to pamper our flesh? What about then? Does Jesus still love us in the midst of our rebellion, in the middle of our temper tantrums? Does He still love us then? Or does He wait until we get our acts a bit cleaned up and after that shows us love again? Does His anger need to blow over? Do we need to give Him a little time to forget what a jerk we've been?

On a gut level, that's the way we act sometimes. We feel as though His love must be conditional, based on how well we are living up to His expectations, because that's the way we as humans interact with one another. If we could be rock-solid secure in the fact that God loves us as redeemed goof-ups—that would change the world.

Jesus promises, "I will never leave thee, nor forsake thee" (Hebrews 13:5).   I looked up the word "forsake" just to make sure I understood it.

> **Forsake** = to give up; renounce.
> **Renounce** = to reject, disown, to leave all together, abandon.
> **Reject** = to refuse to recognize or give affection to; to discard as defective or useless; throw away.

Jesus will never forsake (renounce, reject, or disown) us. There's no way that can mean only when we're performing well. It can't mean only when we are hitting the mark, because in all reality we're not hitting perfection all that often. We are continuously loved by God whether our performance is up to snuff or not. In our imperfectness, God loves us.

Since we did not deserve God's love in the first place, God doesn't stop loving us when we are rebellious or willfully sinning. God demonstrates His love simply because it is His character to love—whether we are lovable or not.

"The LORD hath appeared of old unto me, saying, Yea, I have loved thee with an everlasting love: therefore with lovingkindness have I drawn thee" (Jeremiah 31:3).

Are bad circumstances evidence that God doesn't love us any more? When we suffer, does that mean that God is punishing us?

> As it is written, For thy sake we are killed all the
> day long; we are accounted as sheep for the slaughter.
> Nay, in all these things we are more than conquerors
> through him that loved us. For I am persuaded, that
> neither death, nor life, nor angels, nor principalities,
> nor powers, nor things present, nor things to come, nor
> height, nor depth, nor any other creature, shall be able to
> separate us from the love of God, which is in Christ Jesus
> our Lord (Romans 8:35-39).

We fear sickness and suffering and death because we are not really sure that Christ will be there in the midst of it with us. We don't know how we could possibly handle it. And by ourselves in the flesh we can't handle it. But just as the Lord Jesus was in the midst of the fiery furnace with Shadrach, Meshach, and Abed-Nego, He will be there with us when we call.

> For ye have not received the spirit of bondage
> again to fear; but ye have received the Spirit of adoption,
> whereby we cry, Abba, Father. The Spirit itself beareth
> witness with our spirit, that we are the children of God:
> And if children, then heirs; heirs of God, and joint-heirs
> with Christ; if so be that we suffer with him, that we may
> be also glorified together (Romans 8:15-17).

Perhaps I am belaboring the point, but so often Satan uses this very lie to trip us up. He whispers, "If God really loved you, He wouldn't let this horrible thing happen to you. You've blown it too many times and so God is punishing you." It's a lie straight from the pit of hell.

Suffering is a part of life. No one escapes it. But when we suffer we can be assured that Jesus is infinitely near. Paul strives after one thing—"That I may know him, and the power of his resurrection, and the fellowship of his sufferings ..." (Philippians 3:10). The word fellowship in the Greek is *koinonia*—a partnership or participation or communion. Jesus' love draws Him especially close when His children are hurting. Our physical or emotional pain may obscure our vision so that we don't see His nearness, but we will help ourselves tremendously to hold tenaciously to the truth.

"Wherefore let them that suffer according to the will of God commit the keeping of their souls to him in well doing, as unto a faithful Creator" (1 Peter 4:19).

God loves us ... really loves us. He cannot stop loving us. He can't change who He is.

> As the Father hath loved me, so have I loved you:
> continue ye in my love. If ye keep my commandments,
> ye shall abide in my love; even as I have kept my Father's
> commandments, and abide in his love. These things have
> I spoken unto you, that my joy might remain in you, and
> that your joy might be full. This is my commandment,
> That ye love one another, as I have loved you. Greater
> love hath no man than this, that a man lay down his life
> for his friends (John 15:9-13).

The Scriptures are clear. We are loved in Christ. We have no need to wallow in feelings of being unloved, neglected, or alone. We have no need to accept Satan's lies that we are useless, unlovable, or failures. We replace the lie with the Truth by "renewing our minds" and by "casting down imaginations, and every high thing that exalteth itself against the knowledge of God, and bringing into captivity every thought to the obedience of Christ" (2 Corinthians 10:5).

In this section are those accounts that reveal the overabundance of God's love for those that are His. In these stories, God demonstrates His love simply because it is His character to love. He is not acting out of obligation or pity. In these stories, Abba Father steps in and gives His followers a blessing for no other reason than to say, "I delight in you and love you with an everlasting love. I do this just to see your joy."

May these true stories help you comprehend the great depth and height and length and width of God's love. May you be filled with the knowledge that, as a child of God, you are greatly loved by the Creator of the universe and Savior of the world.

A Changed Life
Ed and Sylvia Christy

Ed joined Baptist Mid-Missions in 1985 and Sylvia in 1987. Together they have been involved in church planting in France for more than 20 years. Ed is also integrally involved in BMM's Pastoral Baptist Bible Institute in the city of Algrange.

Isabelle came to our church one Sunday morning with her nine-year-old hearing-impaired daughter, Mathilde. She was seeking a church that talked about the love of God. She was love-starved, having grown up in a very abusive home and spending her life with very abusive men. She was following a regimen of high-powered psychiatric drugs to help her function.

Isabelle had accepted Christ and had been discipled for two years in a church near Paris. But her marital situation became unbearable, and she fled to Bordeaux to escape further abuse. She was housed by an association for the protection of battered women.

She'd been in Bordeaux for a year and had ended up in a charismatic church that talked about God's power, but she didn't hear much about His love. She wasn't really getting fed from the Scriptures. That Sunday morning, all unknown to us, she was hungry to hear about God's love. Jacques, the song-leader, had picked out Scripture and hymns relating to the theme he had felt led to use … "God's love!"

Isabelle couldn't get over it! God had answered her specific prayer. God truly did love her and was watching over her and her family.

All this happened over three years ago. But that's not all. Isabelle had been in bondage to nicotine nearly all her life, starting to smoke as a young teenager. Because the price of cigarettes was prohibitive, she began rolling her own—a very potent dose of nicotine. She could barely get through a church service without having to go outside for a smoke. Her hands shook, she had stains on her fingers, and from a distance you could smell the tobacco on her. She wanted to quit but just didn't know if she would be able to.

Our church began praying regularly for God's help in this area. Eighteen months ago, Isabelle took the plunge to quit. God has given real victory in this area ever since.

Isabelle still has a long way to go, but we're encouraged as we look back and see how far God has already brought her. We're confident that He who began a good work in her will perform it until the day of Jesus Christ.

He Loves You Anyway
Barry and Judy Byrne

After short-term service in Liberia, the Byrnes were appointed as full-time missionaries to Zambia in 1989. They have five children; the youngest two were adopted from Africa.

Angela had AIDS. All of my female missionary colleagues in our town in Zambia had at one time or another tried to witness to this young lady. But her response to them was to cut them off, saying, "Just go away and leave me alone. I don't want to hear it. When I want to hear about such things I will send for you."

The ladies had a weekly Bible study at a house next door to where Angela lived with her parents. As my wife Judy was getting ready to go to the Bible study, I was in my office working. Suddenly the Lord gave me a great burden for Angela. I told Judy I would take her to the Bible study and visit with Angela while she was with the ladies.

I entered Angela's house. She was lying on the sofa, much too weak to sit up. I sat across the room from her. After the normal greeting, I began talking with her. I said, "Angela, God loves you. He doesn't care what you may have done or not done. He loves you anyway. He loves you so much that he sent his Son, Jesus Christ, to die on the Cross for your sins." She did not tune me out or ask me to leave as she had with all the others who had tried to share that wonderful news.

As we continued to talk, she began to cry tears of repentance, and she asked the Lord Jesus to save her. I joined with tears of joy as the angels in Heaven began rejoicing.

Angela lived on this earth only a few months after that. I tried to visit her at least once a week. Sometimes when I would not show up, she asked, "Where's the Pastor?"

She would have good days and bad days physically. One day she was feeling a bit of strength, and we went outside and walked around the block. She was able to attend church a couple of times.

One day I received a call that Angela was in the hospital. I rushed there to visit her. Her mother was by her bedside. I stood at the foot of the bed silently praying. She asked her mother to help her roll over. As she turned, she saw me at the foot of the bed. She flashed me a weak smile. But in that smile I saw a thank you. Thank you for taking time to come and visit me. Thank you for coming to my home when I usually turned Christians away. And most of all thank you for telling me about the saving blood of the Lord Jesus Christ.

I never saw Angela alive again. I preached her funeral, and a number of others professed Christ as their Savior. One day Angela and I will meet again. To God be the Glory!

Patrick, a Man Touched by God
Evelyne Metzler

Evelyne was exposed to missions from birth, as the daughter of Paul and Etiennette Metzler, pioneer Baptist Mid-Missions missionaries to Chad. Evelyne also felt the call to full-time missions and joined BMM in 1958. She and her sisters, Helene and Rachel, served in Chad until the country's Cultural Revolution expelled all missionaries in 1972 (Helene had gone to be with the Lord in 1969). The next year, Evelyne and Rachel transferred to Haiti. In her final ministry before retiring in 2002, Evelyne served seven years with Campus Bible Fellowship (now called Campus Bible Fellowship International) in Miami, Florida.

Patrick Pierre Louis was born in northern Haiti in Cape Haitian. He grew up in a family that practiced voodoo, as most Haitians do. But God's hand was on him from the beginning. His wife Josette was just a school-age girl who had no family. The two of them really loved and respected each other. This is very rare among voodoo-practicing people.

Patrick and Josette had two children and lived in a small mud hut with Patrick's mother. Patrick had a job but then lost it.

While hunting for another job, Patrick met a friend who knew his problems. His friend said, "I can help you. I can take you to the captain of a big boat. He smuggles people into Florida, where they can find jobs. Then they send money back to their families, and when they get rich they return to Haiti. To go to Florida, you have to pay the captain $40."

Patrick had three cows. He sold two of them and left one for his wife. With that money, he paid the captain. The "big" boat turned out to be a modest-size wooden boat with an outboard motor. They left for Florida with nothing in their possession but a little water and food, which the passengers brought with them.

Several days later they reached a sandbar close to the Bahamas. The captain stopped at the sandbar and told the passengers that he was having problems with the outboard motor. Everyone was told to get off onto the sandbar while he tried to fix it. After a while, the captain said that he needed a new part for the motor. He instructed the people to stay on the sandbar while he went to the Bahamas for repairs. He left and never returned.

Patrick and the others suffered under the blazing sun. They had no water or food and no protection from the sun. People developed high fevers. Patrick could not endure all of this. He walked to the end of the sandbar, looked up into the sky, and said, "God, I'm sure that You see us. If You care about us, and if You would help me to get back to my wife and children, I promise that I will find out more about You and will serve You the rest of my life." He prayed that prayer several times as he paced back and forth.

Three days after being abandoned, a Coast Guard cutter picked them up and took them to Miami. They were put in jail and given food, water, and clothing. Soon they were deported back to Haiti. When they returned to Haiti, they were put in jail and beaten. Finally the soldiers released the boat people.

Now Patrick was worse off than before. He was barefoot. The only pair of pants he owned was split down the seams, held together with safety pins. His T-shirt was torn. He walked up and down the streets hunting for a job, but no one offered him one.

He was sleeping on the streets when he met Tony, an old friend from Cape Haitian. Since they had last seen each other, Tony had become a Christian. At Tony's insistence, Pastor Leo Sandgren, a Baptist Mid-

Missions missionary, had started a church on Tony's porch in the slum district of Carrefour. Tony offered Patrick a room to sleep in. Word got back to Patrick's wife in Cape Haitian that he was in Haiti. Immediately, she and the children took a bus to come be with him. They were so happy to be back together, but now Patrick had three more mouths to feed. They were having a very difficult time.

One day another friend of Patrick's suggested that he go to a certain witch doctor for help. The witch doctor demanded that Patrick give him his wife or one of his children in payment for his help. Patrick refused. The witch doctor looked at him and said, "Isn't your wife expecting?" Patrick did not understand how the witch doctor knew about his wife's pregnancy.

"If you make me a promise—and you know that you can't break a promise you make to me or to Satan—if you promise that when the baby is born you will bring it to me, then I can get you a job."

As Patrick left the witch doctor, he thought about his options. He didn't want to give this new baby to the witch doctor, but he had no choice really. He had to have a job in order to keep his wife and two children from starving to death. He dreaded the thought of telling his wife. As Patrick got near their mud hut, he noticed that there was a meeting on Tony's porch. It was Sunday.

As Patrick came closer, he saw that Tony was speaking. "Do you have a problem and you don't know where to turn?" he heard Tony say. "Turn to Jesus. He's got the answers. Just come to Him with all your problems."

Patrick thought, "How does he know? I didn't tell him what happened today and what I decided to do."

Just then Tony saw him and invited him to come in and sit down. Patrick slipped in and sat behind the others. Tony went on to tell the way of salvation. Patrick's heart was throbbing.

He said, "May I say a word?"

Tony said, "Sure."

So Patrick told his story to the group. He told them that he had just come from the witch doctor and told them about nearly perishing on the sandbar. Then he said, "I remember that while on that sandbar, I promised God to look Him up and to serve Him. But I never did. Do you think He would take a person like me now? If I go to Him, will He really take care of my problems?"

They assured Him that God would. "You come to the Lord Jesus, take Him into your heart, and you will become His child," they told him.

"Then He is responsible for you and all your problems."

Patrick said, "That's what I want."

When he accepted Christ as his Savior, Patrick cried for joy. He said, "I feel like a new person. The load has been taken away. I've got to go tell my wife right now."

Patrick went home to his wife, who was not well. He fell on his knees, put his arms around her, and said, "Josette, you don't see the same man here now that you saw this morning."

Alarmed, she replied, "Don't worry about anything, Patrick. Somehow things will work out. Just be calm."

"You don't understand, Josette. I'm happy! Things are wonderful now."

"You didn't steal, did you?" asked Josette.

"No, I didn't steal," replied Patrick. "I belong to God and not to Satan. I have a Spirit inside me who can lead us and take care of us. Now we can give all our problems to God."

Josette started to weep and said, "Oh, Patrick. How can I have that too?"

Patrick led his wife to the Lord right there.

One Sunday they had nothing to eat, as usual. Patrick learned that a fisherman, whom he had helped before, was going fishing. The man promised Patrick that if he helped him, he would give Patrick fish for his family. Patrick had a real struggle with that. "Shall I go?" he thought. "What shall I do? Do I go and get some fish so we have something to eat, or do I go to church? If I go to church, I lose the opportunity to feed my family because it will be too late afterwards."

Patrick knew what he had to do. That morning he said to himself, "I have changed masters. I have changed jobs. Today is God's day, and I have to learn more about Him. I am going to church. They tell me my problems are His, so I will leave the rest to Him." And so he went to church.

As Patrick went out of the church, he prayed, "Lord, now I am going back to my wife and children, and I have no food to take to them. We have not eaten for several days. I am not telling you I deserve food because I went to church, but I am asking You in Your love and mercy if You would just give me something for my family."

He started down the path and there on the ground was one long peppermint stick. "Praise God," he thought. "He answered my prayer." He took that peppermint candy to his wife and said, "Look what God gave us for today. Cut it in three pieces for you and the children."

She said, "Patrick, let's bow our heads first and thank the Lord for this." They ate their peppermint stick and realized that God had not forgotten them. That is all they had that Sunday, but they were happy.

Some weeks later, my sister Rachel and I invited Patrick over to our home. We gave him lunch. When the meal was over I asked, "Patrick, what work do you do?"

"Work?" he answered. "I'm hunting for a job. I'm not working now."

"Well," I said, "Praise the Lord. You are just the person we need. We are going to start camp over at Grand Goave. We have to take several loads of supplies, and we need someone to stay and watch the things and then help us during camp."

Patrick was thrilled. This was a real answer to his prayers. When he left, we gave him clothes for his wife and two children and food to take home. He could hardly wait to get home and show them to Josette and the children. They could not believe their eyes. The family rejoiced together not only for the gifts, but also for the fact that Patrick now had a job.

Several days later, Rachel and I picked up Patrick and drove to Grand Goave, where we had leased a large, wooded property by the sea. We took supplies and dropped them off, leaving Patrick to watch the supplies and start cleaning the area. When we returned with more supplies, we were amazed at how much work he had done and how clean the buildings and surrounding area were. We had 100 campers from our youth club who came from Port-au-Prince and Jacmel. Patrick was a tremendous help. He saw what needed to be done and did it. We could give him money without hesitation and send him for local supplies, knowing he was trustworthy. This was a real blessing. Patrick, eager to learn more and to grow spiritually, attended all the Bible lessons.

When camp was over, Patrick came to work for us and other BMM missionaries in our homes. Patrick became active in the church at Carrefour where he had been saved. Rachel and I continued to work there with Leo and Gloria Sandgren, but in the meantime God had led us to purchase property in Grand Goave next to the leased camp property. This was a dark place, steeped in voodoo. When we first moved there, we had much opposition.

However, we started Bible classes for the children and young people and taught the Word of God to the Haitians who worked for us.

Before long, we had a small core of Christians. They started asking for church services. We presented the need to the church at Carrefour, and Patrick and a deacon volunteered to come out by bus each Saturday to hold services. So began the small group that eventually formed Maranatha Baptist Church of Grand Goave.

About this time, the political situation in Haiti became much worse, and Carrefour was a hot spot with much violence and great danger. Patrick and Josette now had four children, all of whom were very dear to us. We feared for their safety. Each week when Patrick came for meetings we told him, "Patrick, if things become too dangerous for your family, bring them all here. There is room for you, and you are part of our family."

One morning Patrick, Josette, Theo, Daphnee, Dadie, and Caleb walked down the road to our house. They were carrying a few bundles that contained everything they owned. They looked frightened. Patrick explained that there had been so much shooting around them that bullets were flying through the house. Josette and the children had spent two nights and a day on the floor under the mattresses, praying that a bullet would not penetrate a mattress. That night we thanked God for protecting them and for giving us a safe haven large enough to accommodate them.

Patrick immediately made himself invaluable. He soon relieved us of all responsibility for the upkeep of the property and oversaw all the workers with their responsibilities.

It was becoming impossible to travel to Carrefour for meetings. The Sandgrens moved to Petit Goave, a town adjacent to Grand Goave. They worked with Patrick and us to start a church in Grand Goave. How amazing are God's ways.

The Satan-worshipping Haitians near us were filled with hate and fear of Patrick as he shared the gospel with everyone he met. These dear Haitian people had been under Satan's influence and domination for centuries. It was unbelievable how much cruelty and suffering they endured. In contrast, Patrick's heart was full of kindness and love. They were very suspicious of this kindness because they had never experienced it before.

Several times these men performed voodoo practices against us or Patrick that we might die or disappear, but of course they never worked. Little by little, some of them started to come to us, sneaking in with a sick child, a crushed thumb, or a high fever. God performed some real miracles. Those same people came to love Patrick. Because he had come out of the same slavish voodoo life as these people, God used him to reach them as nobody else could. What a blessing it was to work with a pastor like Patrick. God blessed the church and it grew rapidly.

The Lord used Patrick in a great way among the people of Grand Goave. He did love them dearly. The witch doctor's cousin was dying. He did everything he could for his cousin and saw it was to no avail. The witch doctor then said, "I know someone who can help you." He sent for Patrick, who went to the dying man's hut and told him about God. The man accepted the Lord as his Savior and rallied for a few days. Everyone was amazed because he had been on the brink of death. The witch doctor's cousin witnessed to everyone he saw during those few extra days God granted him.

The witch doctor, Willie, admitted that he had little to offer and knew God spoke and acted through Patrick. However, Willie continued his voodoo practices because this was the only way he knew to make a living.

Then Patrick became sick. He got progressively worse and was finally diagnosed with AIDS. He had received contaminated blood during an operation. All of Grand Goave was devastated, though they were only told that Patrick had a fatal illness. Had they known it was AIDS, most of them would have assumed that Patrick had been involved in immorality.

Patrick went back to his extended family in Cape Haitian to witness to them. When he returned to Grand Goave, he looked thin and haggard but had a huge smile on his face. I was so happy to see him! On the way to his house, Patrick said, "Please take me to the church first."

We had started building on the church property before he left, and now the church building was completed. As Patrick went into the building, his face was aglow. He praised God for the lovely building He had supplied.

Word got around fast in Grand Goave. People started streaming into the church, embracing Patrick and praising God. We had all thought we would never see him again on earth. The whole village escorted Patrick to his house, which was close to the church.

During the day he lay on a mattress on the porch. Many people came to talk to him, including the three witch doctors in Grand Goave. He never missed an opportunity to witness to them. When Patrick died, all of Grand Goave came to the funeral. This was a testimony to how much Patrick was loved and respected. Even in his death, he was a witness.

Gold Coffee
Beulah Pinkston

*Beulah's story recounts an event from the early days in Mexico for her and
her husband Otis. The Pinkstons joined Baptist Mid-Missions in 1961 and
served faithfully in Mexico until 2004. After her husband went to be with
the Lord, Beulah served with BMM's Spanish publications ministry, EBI,
until retiring in 2006. She continues to minister to Hispanic people through
her home church in Tennessee, a BMM church plant.*

We were living in a small village in the state of Michoacan,
Mexico, in the early 1960s. We had been in Mexico for about two years
when one day our funds ran completely out. Our household at the time
consisted of nine people—my husband Otis and I, our three children, and
a Mexican couple who had two small children. In addition to all these,
Otis went to another village on horseback every week or two and brought
a young Mexican boy back with him. That day we had only enough food
for a breakfast of instant coffee and bread for the ten of us. Of course, we
prayed, as always, that God would supply in His own time and way.

The coffee was served in clay cups, and when Daniel, the boy
from the village, stirred his coffee we heard a "clanking" noise, like metal
against the clay. With his spoon he dipped out the mysterious object,
which turned out to be a two-peso gold coin! At that time, the coin was
worth about $1.76. We took it immediately to the bank to exchange for
regular money. That money was sufficient for beans, rice, and the cornmeal to make tortillas for two to three days.

Naturally, we knew that it was God who had supplied, but we
wondered at the human element in the mystery. We noticed that the instant coffee was called *Café Oro* (Gold Coffee) and learned later that since
the coffee was new on the market, the company was putting gold coins in
a certain number of jars as a promotion.

God's supply at the precise moment and in this unusual way was
a great testimony of God's love and care for us.

Bread
Bev Kuehl

Bev began her service with Baptist Mid-Missions in 1974 and spent many years fulfilling the Great Commission in Jamaica and then in Ghana. In 2002, the Lord directed her to a very different ministry—working with Jewish people in Moncton, New Brunswick, Canada, where she continues to serve.

In April of 1981, I was a newly arrived missionary in economically deprived Ghana, West Africa. The food that was available was very expensive, and because there was so little of it, we often had to travel outside of Ghana to a nearby country to purchase food. The missionaries in Accra, the capital city, shared a bag of flour that our business manager was able to buy for us in the city. We made our own bread because bread also was difficult to find and was expensive.

One evening, about two hours before supper, information came to me that two missionary ladies from Baptist Mid-Missions were to arrive at my home for the evening meal. I was chagrined. I was glad that they were coming; but I had run out of flour, and I didn't have any bread to go with the meal. I decided that I would take this problem to the Lord. I asked Him, if it was His will, if He could please send me some bread for supper.

Ten minutes before we sat down to eat, I heard someone calling me at the gate. As I walked down the driveway, I could see the son of one of our church members. He was holding a basket. I lifted the linen towel, and there in the basket were two warm, freshly baked loaves of bread.

Carrying the basket of bread back to the house, I praised God for His love and mercy in providing what I needed. What an awesome God we have!

She'll Walk the Streets of Gold
Eleanor Brittain

In 1950, as a single missionary en route to Liberia for the first time, Eleanor met Stan Brittain, then an officer on the ship Eleanor sailed on. They married three years later, and Stan joined Eleanor in the work in Liberia. In the 1970s, they served in New Zealand, Hawaii, and finally Great Britain (Stan's home country), from which they retired in 1992. Stan went to be with the Lord in 2003.

Kara sat in her wheelchair, bobbing her head as we sang of God's love. The little girl could not walk or talk, but she seemed to delight in our little Sunday School class that met in a kitchen.

It was early 1977 and we were in Carpenders Park in north London, England. A couple who had wanted us to start a church in their neighborhood, John and Pam, had opened their home to us to hold Sunday services, since there was no other place available in the area. So our children's Sunday School class met in their kitchen, with the aroma of a chicken roasting in the oven, permeating the room.

Kara's nine-year-old sister, Lisa, had come to Sunday School first. It was nearly time for the closing prayer when Lisa had asked, "Mrs. Brittain, may I bring my sister to our class next Sunday? She is seven years old."

"Yes, of course," I said.

The following Sunday, I was looking out the kitchen window and spotted Lisa walking towards the house, accompanied by a lady pushing a little girl in a wheelchair. As they opened the gate and walked towards the front door, I could see that Lisa's sister was a "special child."

Lisa and Kara were accompanied by their mother, Jill. I welcomed them and told Jill that the adults were having a Bible study in the living room and that she was welcome to join them.

"No, that's fine," she said. "I want to stay here to make sure Kara behaves herself." Kara had a sweet smile on her innocent-looking face, and she was nodding her head. She couldn't talk, but she could make noises to let people know what she wanted. She also had a little button on one arm of her wheelchair, and when she wanted attention, she would push the button, smile, and make her noise. We were glad Jill decided to stay in our class!

Each week we had a Bible lesson, and then the children memorized a Bible verse. Kara was not left out. She actually memorized Bible verses. Jill would recite the verse, deliberately making mistakes, to which Kara would shake her head no and make her noise. When Jill finally said it correctly, Kara would produce a wide, happy smile. It was rather a sneaky way to get her mother to hide God's Word in her heart too! God has promised that His Word will not return void but will accomplish His purpose. I still pray that Jill will accept Christ as her Savior, if she hasn't already.

The children loved to sing. We had several visualized songs. Once again, Kara took part. Several weeks passed and nearly every time it was Kara's turn to choose, she would pick "The Wordless Book" song. It has blank pages, each with a different color: black, red, white, yellow, and green. I wondered why she seemed to have such a love for this particular song.

It took a while for the truth to sink in, but the Lord told me to listen to the words: "My heart was black with sin, until the Savior came in. His precious blood I know, has washed me white as snow. And in God's Word we're told. We'll walk the streets of gold. Oh wonderful, wonderful day. He washed my sins away."

I said, "Boys and girls, I think I know why Kara likes The Wordless Book song. What is it that Kara can't do now?" I asked them.

"She can't talk," some said.

"What else can't she do?" I asked.

"She can't walk!" they shouted.

Kara was really beaming by now. I asked her, "Are we right, Kara? Have you asked Jesus into your heart? Do you know you will walk the streets of gold in Heaven?"

Kara's smile was wider than ever; she was so excited. Her head was bobbing yes, and she even pushed the button on her wheelchair! That was a happy day for us all, so it was no wonder that several of us had to wipe away tears. We serve a great and faithful God. Nothing is impossible with Him.

His Tender Mercies
Nan Mosher

Nan and her husband Bill were called to vocational ministry and joined a Michigan church-planting mission shortly before their marriage. During the Vietnam conflict, God directed Bill into the Air Force chaplaincy. In 1975 they joined Baptist Mid-Missions as church planters in England. God later called Bill to the BMM Home Office, where he served as the Field Administrator for Asia and the Pacific until retiring in 2006. Using her counseling training, Nan continues to assist in their local church and in the pregnancy clinic of Faith Baptist Community Center, a BMM inner-city ministry.

Busy airports … lingering hugs … tearful goodbyes … fearful thoughts about future family times …. These are part of every missionary's experience as he or she leaves the homeland for a far-off country. The emotions crescendo as one contemplates the years expected to intervene before the next face-to-face meeting. Sometimes we fail to add the possibility of our loving, gracious God's sovereign intervention. We may be so focused on our sorrow that we forget for the moment that the Lord knows how we feel. He cares. He is able to grant exceedingly, abundantly above all that we ask or think (Ephesians 3:20).

Returning to England for our second term was particularly difficult, since we left all three of our grown children in the United States. There was never enough communication to keep up with the details of their lives. Our sons wrote infrequently; "seldom" is actually the better word to describe the frequency of their letters. Our daughter Mindy who formerly had written about her brothers who'd lived nearby, had moved several hundred miles away from them. Phone calls were too expensive, and e-mail was not yet available. It was painful to be effectively cut out of our sons' lives by the thousands of miles between us.

Two years after our return to England, my 83-year-old mother was scheduled for major abdominal cancer surgery. It seemed wise for me to return to the United States to nurse her through the post-operative convalescence. Since this was the second major abdominal surgery in nine months—the third altogether—we had doubts about her recovery period. We decided I should stay one month; however we weren't sure this would be sufficient time because of her age and previous history.

Purchasing the ticket stretched our finances to the limit. My mother's home was in Florida—far from our three children who lived in the north. My children's funds were also limited, so my only expectation was to visit with them by telephone.

Mother was one day post-op when I arrived. She looked so old and feeble with tubes flowing in and out in all directions. I was glad to be there, and I settled into her home for the month. The days were full, with several trips to the hospital daily, caring for the house and the dog, shopping, and other tasks. Within a week, Mother left the hospital. Two weeks after the operation, she was taking up some of her daily chores. Two and a half weeks after the operation, she began asking me about my plans to see the children.

"I don't expect to see them this trip," I said. "Besides, I have no money for travel," I added silently.

"You should make some plans," she said several times in the next day or two. Then she said, "I can take care of myself now … you just go ahead and buy a ticket and I'll pay for it!" It was true. Much to our amazement, she had resumed all of her normal routine. The foot-long scar had healed without complication, and she seemed energetic and capable of staying alone once more.

An equally awesome fact was that all three of our children had made earlier plans to visit their other grandparents in Texas. They would be making their way from Michigan, Colorado, and Illinois. All of them expected to be together during the final week of my month in the USA! It was incredible to me that all three had arranged with their various employers to have that very week off. Our oldest son was bringing along a young woman and was eager for me to meet her before he took the step of proposing marriage. The flight to Texas was quickly arranged. What a wonderful, unexpected reunion it was!

God wonderfully engineered the circumstances to meet the longings of this missionary mother. This made Romans 8:28 sing in my heart as I praised His glorious Name for his tender mercies and lovingkindness to an unworthy servant.

God's Grace

> And the LORD passed by before him [Moses], and proclaimed, The LORD, The LORD God, merciful and gracious, longsuffering, and abundant in goodness and truth, Keeping mercy for thousands, forgiving iniquity and transgression and sin, and that will by no means clear the guilty; visiting the iniquity of the fathers upon the children, and upon the children's children, unto the third and to the fourth generation (Exodus 34:6-7).

In the Old Testament, God chose the word *chanan* (khaw-nan') in the Hebrew to give a word picture of grace. Most of the words in the Old Testament that are translated "grace" are linked to this one word—chanan, which means to bend or stoop in kindness to an inferior.

When trying to understand the grace of God, I picture a father bending in kindness to get down on his child's level and giving that child his full attention. This is a superior person bending to treat an inferior person with kindness. This is grace.

Hezekiah was a godly king in Judah. In the first month of his first year as king, Hezekiah commanded that the temple be reopened and cleansed. He called the people back to God, reminding them of God's eternal grace. He proclaimed the grace of God to the people of Judah and even to the remnant of the northern kingdom of Israel, who had not been taken into captivity by the Assyrians. The proclamation declared:

> For if ye turn again unto the LORD, your brethren and your children shall find compassion before them that lead them captive, so that they shall come again into this land: for the LORD your God is gracious and merciful, and will not turn away his face from you, if ye return unto him (2 Chronicles 30:9).

The king's runners passed from city to city through the country of Ephraim and Manasseh, as far as Zebulun; but the people of the land laughed at them and mocked. Nevertheless, some from Asher, Manasseh, and Zebulun humbled themselves and came to Jerusalem. A great revival followed.

Throughout his reign, when Hezekiah remained humble before the Lord, God blessed him. Later in life, Hezekiah's wife gave birth to a son. They named him Manasseh. This son eventually became Hezekiah's successor.

The wickedness of King Manasseh was legendary. Although his father had been a righteous man and a follower of Yahweh—the one true God—Manasseh would have none of it. As soon as his dad was dead and the kingdom was his, he rebelled against his father's religion. He rebuilt the shrines and idols that his father had destroyed, and Manasseh took idol worship a giant step farther. He placed despicable altars and statues inside the Temple of the Almighty God, thereby desecrating it completely.

He practiced witchcraft and divination and even burned his sons as human sacrifices to the god Molech. He guided the people of God into all the same evil that he himself practiced. In this he provoked Yahweh to great anger.

God sent prophets to warn him and his people of severe judgment if they did not repent. But in his pride, Manasseh refused to be intimidated and remained unrepentant. Tradition says that he killed God's prophet Isaiah, a friend and advisor to his father. Scripture records that he shed much innocent blood until he had filled Jerusalem with blood from one end to the other.

So God in His holiness judged Manasseh and the tribe of Judah. He sent the king of Assyria to Jerusalem to capture Manasseh. The Assyrians put him in chains and carried him off to Babylon. In his Babylonian prison cell, Manasseh came to his senses and realized all the evil he had done. He humbled himself greatly before the Lord and repented of all the wickedness that he had committed. Manasseh had been extremely wicked. He did not deserve to be forgiven. Over and over he had mocked and ridiculed the Lord God Almighty. But when Manasseh humbled himself before God, he opened the door to God's grace.

That day God forgave Manasseh, son of Hezekiah. He took away his sin and made him a new man. God even restored Manasseh to his kingdom in Jerusalem. That's grace—the unmerited favor of God.

> The LORD is merciful and gracious, slow to
> anger, and plenteous in mercy. He will not always chide:
> neither will he keep his anger for ever. He hath not dealt
> with us after our sins; nor rewarded us according to our
> iniquities. For as the heaven is high above the earth,

so great is his mercy toward them that fear him. As
far as the east is from the west, so far hath he removed
our transgressions from us. Like as a father pitieth his
children, so the LORD pitieth them that fear him. For
he knoweth our frame; he remembereth that we are dust
(Psalm 103:8-14).

When God forgave Manasseh, He already knew what it would
cost Him. Because of His holiness, He couldn't simply dismiss all the evil
that Manasseh had done. Someone had to pay for that sin and for the sins
of every other human that God the Father had purposed to forgive.

None of us is worthy of forgiveness. Although few of us will
commit the heinous acts of a man like Manasseh, the Bible is clear that
from God's perspective all humankind has sinned and fallen short of His
holy standard. "There is none righteous, no, not one" (Romans 3:10). Every one of us is guilty and every one of us must humble himself or herself
before the Lord as Manasseh did. God cannot give grace to the proud.

When God forgave Manasseh, He knew it would require that Jesus, the Son of God, leave Heaven in all its perfection and come to earth,
a cesspool of sin, sadness, and misery. God would be required to stoop
in kindness to the inferior level of man and live among evil and imperfect
people for more than 30 years.

Jesus made Himself a common man—not a king with servants
to care for all His needs. He became the son of a poor carpenter from
the despised region of Galilee—a man of no reputation. He walked from
place to place, mixing with all manner of sick and needy people. Our
holy, perfect, spotless God lived in the midst of dirty, smelly, profane humanity. He stooped to our level and loved us. He chose to be gracious to
us. "For ye know the grace of our Lord Jesus Christ, that, though he was
rich, yet for your sakes he became poor, that ye through his poverty might
be rich" (2 Corinthians 8:9).

But the sacrifice that Jesus made for sinful man went so much
further than that. There is no remission of sin without the shedding of
blood. Men like Manasseh and people like you and me could not be freed
from our sin without a sacrifice. And so Jesus took grace to its ultimate
extent and voluntarily went to the cross. He allowed Himself to be beaten, tortured, and crucified so that His grace could be poured out on those
who did not deserve it. As He hung on the cross, the incredibly vile sins
of the entire world were placed on His shoulders. His Holy Father could

not look on Him in His sinful state. Jesus cried out, "My God, my God, why hast thou forsaken me?" (Matthew 27:46). In that awful moment, Jesus was separated from His Father and then ... it was finished. The sacrifice had been made. Jesus had given His life for unworthy sinners.

Gloriously, three days later He rose from the tomb where He had been buried, and the shout rang out: "He is alive!" With the resurrection of Jesus Christ, mankind now had the opportunity to be forgiven of their sins through faith in Christ. All those who came to God in repentance and humility would be accepted, forgiven, and transformed. The message was preached everywhere, and it turned the world upside down.

That message is still turning the world upside down in our time. This section of true stories reveals God's grace in the salvation and transformation of lives around the globe. "Unorthodox Methodology" and "New Beginnings in Dekalb County, Georgia" reveal that God's grace is not dependent on our righteousness.

Nor does God ignore those who have embraced a false religion. "From Idol-Maker to Disciple-Maker" gives testimony to the fundamental truth that no one is beyond God's redeeming grace. "Not Beyond His Reach" reveals that God's love penetrates to even the remotest parts of the earth. No matter where God finds us, we can be assured that as we turn to Him in faith and repentance we will be accepted. His grace is sufficient.

God is in the business of saving the unrighteous. The Apostle Paul proclaims in Ephesians 2:4-9:

> But God, who is rich in mercy, for his great love wherewith he loved us, even when we were dead in sins, hath quickened us together with Christ, (by grace ye are saved;) and hath raised us up together, and made us sit together in heavenly places in Christ Jesus: that in the ages to come he might shew the exceeding riches of his grace in his kindness toward us through Christ Jesus. For by grace are ye saved through faith; and that not of yourselves: it is the gift of God: not of works, lest any man should boast.

In our natural selves we are unacceptable to God. But grace makes us accepted in the Beloved (Ephesians 1:6). God's grace sustains the believer in Jesus Christ. It is by grace that we can take our requests into the very Holiest of Holies—the very presence of God.

> Seeing then that we have a great high priest, that
> is passed into the heavens, Jesus the Son of God, let us
> hold fast our profession. For we have not an high priest
> which cannot be touched with the feeling of our infirmi-
> ties; but was in all points tempted like as we are, yet with-
> out sin. Let us therefore come boldly unto the throne of
> grace, that we may obtain mercy, and find grace to help
> in time of need (Hebrews 4:14-16).

God's grace is sufficient for our every need. The Apostle Paul had a thorn in the flesh—either a physical infirmity or perhaps a persistent persecutor. He described this thorn as a messenger of Satan. He pleaded with the Lord three times that it might depart from him. The Lord's answer in 2 Corinthians 12:9 was "My grace is sufficient for thee: for my strength is made perfect in weakness." Paul then testifies:

> Most gladly therefore will I rather glory in my
> infirmities, that the power of Christ may rest upon me.
> Therefore I take pleasure in infirmities, in reproaches, in
> necessities, in persecutions, in distresses for Christ's sake:
> for when I am weak, then am I strong (2 Corinthians
> 12:9-10).

When Paul exhorts the believers to sow bountifully, he speaks with assurance that God's grace will be sufficient. "And God is able to make all grace abound toward you; that ye, always having all sufficiency in all things, may abound to every good work" (2 Corinthians 9:8).

God's grace is enough. Perhaps that is why Paul's letters start with "Grace be unto you, and peace, from God our Father, and from the Lord Jesus Christ" and end with "The grace of our Lord Jesus Christ be with you all." He wants the believers to never forget the great gift that they have at their disposal. God's favor cannot be earned, and it is not a reward for our perfectionist, prideful efforts to be better than everyone else. It is a gift of God. And it must be received in humility.

Grace is entirely dependent on the kindness of the giver and the humility of the recipient. Proverbs 3:34 declares, "Surely he scorneth the scorners: but he giveth grace unto the lowly." If we want more grace, the way to receive it is to be more humble. There is no other way. "And the grace of our Lord was exceeding abundant with faith and love which is in

Christ Jesus" (1 Timothy 1:14).

       Grace is ours to receive. As you read these testimonies, "Grace and peace be multiplied unto you through the knowledge of God, and of Jesus our Lord" (2 Peter 1:2).

I Was Blind, but Now I Can See
Tim Reiner

As the son of BMM missionaries Harold and the late Ruth Reiner, Tim has been a firsthand witness of God at work in Brazil. In 1976, Tim and his wife Vicki were appointed with Baptist Mid-Missions. Entering Brazil as full-time missionaries, they joined Harold and his wife Joan as well as Tim's aunt and uncle, and numerous cousins serving with BMM in Northeast Brazil.

In the 1950s, Baptist Mid-Missions missionaries attempted to evangelize the city of Barbalha in northeast Brazil. They met with fierce opposition from the Catholics in the area. One evening a mob came to disrupt the Baptist meeting that was going on. After two hours of bombardment, the crowd broke down the gate and entered the house where the meeting was being held. Furniture was smashed and people were injured. In the months following, the Catholics in Barbalha waged a crusade against Protestantism. Men painted a sign on the wall of a building near the entrance to the city. The sign said, "Halt, Mr. Protestant! Barbalha of St. Anthony is already evangelized!"

I didn't know the connection at the time, but in 1997 I met the son of the man who had chosen the slogan for that sign at a meeting of the city fathers. The son, Dr. Ricardo, owned the construction firm that was selected out of four other contractors who had bid on the construction of Baptist Mid-Missions' new ministry complex in Fortaleza, Brazil. When completed, the complex would house the national headquarters of BMM in Brazil, the regional offices, radio and television studios, 10 small apartments for guests, and the Fortaleza Academy for missionary children.

Pastor Mauro Clark, an engineer and pastor of a church in Fortaleza, and I were heavily involved in the project. After much delay waiting for the proper documents to be approved, we broke ground on October 6, 1997. From the very start of this large project, the missionaries and national believers prayed for the salvation of Dr. Ricardo. Pastor Mauro and I, as well as the other missionaries involved in the project, took every opportunity to present to Dr. Ricardo and his workers the plan of salvation through Jesus Christ. Free Bibles were offered to the workers, and many accepted the gift. During the 11-month construction, special meetings were held on the construction site. Dr. Ricardo authorized the work to stop an hour early so his men could attend the evangelistic meetings on company time. In many instances, up to 140 bricklayers, carpenters, foremen, engineers, and other helpers listened attentively to a clear presentation of God's plan of salvation.

For almost a year, the workmen labored. The complex was finally ready for the inauguration ceremony in July 1999. At the ceremony, there was much rejoicing and giving of praise to God. After several people delivered messages, I returned to the platform to recognize those who had labored on the project. I called them up to the platform and handed them a small gift of appreciation. I then presented the construction firm of WR Engenharia with a framed letter of appreciation from Baptist Mid-Missions. Dr. Ricardo accepted the letter on behalf of the firm. Then all those receiving gifts of appreciation returned to their seats, but Dr. Ricardo remained standing at my right. I quietly asked him if he wanted to say something. Despite his intense dislike of speaking in public, Dr. Ricardo asked to say a few words.

He stepped to the podium before an audience of over 300 and leaned toward the microphone. Breathing deeply between phrases and with a trembling voice he said, "This is not the largest construction that WR has built nor is this the construction that has produced the greatest profit ... But this is the most important construction that WR has ever built ... It was through this project that I met Pastor Mauro and Pastor Timoteo. They have spent much time in the Bible with me. Through them, my wife and I heard about Christ and salvation. Almost two months ago, my wife came to know Christ as Savior. I am here before you tonight to tell you that I was blind but now I can see. I was dead, but now I am alive!"

I sat there in my front row seat listening to Dr. Ricardo—surrounded by all those brand new beautiful buildings—and none of it seemed as important as the salvation of the man in front of me. Eternity has a lens all its own, and I got to see through it for a moment that night. What a night to remember! I don't believe there was a dry eye in the auditorium.

After Dr. Ricardo finished speaking, missionary Russ Gordon stepped to the podium and led us in the final song: "To God Be the Glory." I don't know if Russ asked us to stand or not, but we did—and gave God a standing ovation that night.

Unorthodox Methodology

Stan Boelman

Stan and his wife Paula were appointed with Baptist Mid-Missions in 1977 to serve in England. They continue to serve in Luton, where this story takes place.

In the mid-1980s, Murray was a teenager living near Luton, England. Like many other young people of his day, he had lived a fairly worldly life. He had attended expensive, private schools but had also dabbled in recreational drugs and even helped to distribute some of them. One night, he and a friend who sold drugs to him were driving around the countryside just outside of Luton. It was an evening with nothing to do, and they were bored. At some point, Murray's friend "Jim" (name changed) told him about a man Murray just had to see to believe. This man, Dave, had been aggressively telling Jim about Jesus Christ. The amazing thing was that Dave was also buying his marijuana from Jim.

Dave, a converted Jew from Australia, had moved to England with his wife to try to witness to family. He had settled into our church while we were on furlough and was very aggressive about his witness for Christ. Dave would go to his local pub and spend all night playing pool and looking for someone to witness to. He would buy a half a pint of beer and set it on the pool table. That made him a purchasing customer, and therefore the pub owner couldn't kick him out. The problem for Dave was that he still had some old habits from his life before he became a Christian. He still smoked marijuana. So at the same time that he was witnessing to people in the pubs, he was also looking for someone to buy marijuana from. During one of these nights at the pub, Jim had met Dave.

Dave started buying from Jim and at the same time began witnessing to him about Jesus Christ. Dave would say things like "I'm a backward Christian; don't do what I do." These efforts were slowly having a response with people from this background. Dave and his wife Carol invited Jim and his girlfriend over to their house for a meal and then followed that with intensive witnessing in what Dave called his witnessing room (complete with table, chairs, and a Bible). They would talk until about two or three o' clock in the morning.

With that going on, Jim insisted that Murray had to meet Dave. So they went to Dave's house, and Dave began his high-pressure witness to Murray. Dave and his wife spent hours witnessing to Murray, explaining the gospel story and answering Murray's questions. This was high-pressure salesmanship.

Murray was the first to receive Jesus as His Savior. He then shared Christ with his brother Aidan, who also accepted the Lord. Eventually Jim and his girlfriend made professions of faith too. Finally both Murray's and Aidan's girlfriends received Christ. All of them began to attend the church that we'd started in Luton.

By the time we came back from our furlough in 1986, the nature of the congregation was vastly different. As opposed to the usual dress styles and backgrounds of Luton, I found myself preaching to a congregation that looked more like the crowd that hangs out at the train station. They were wearing army jackets and had odd and striking hairstyles and ear piercings to match. And they were all lighting up cigarettes between Sunday School and church (although I am not sure it was tobacco!)

At that time, we had no idea if we would keep any of them. The odds were against it, since these folks had been so deeply involved in the world's culture and vices. But God is greater than our doubts. We continued to encourage as many of these people as we could, and some moved forward in their spiritual lives.

Murray continued to grow and was very interested in learning more of the Scriptures. He was one of the first students at the Bible college our field team started, and he finished three years later. He also began a friendship with Marjorie, a young lady who had joined the Luton work back in 1983. She was also in the college, so they spent a lot of time together, and they were eventually married. When we organized as a church in 1989, Murray was one of our first deacons and served with distinction for some years. He and Marjorie were like a pair of Timothys in the faith and became solid members of the church family.

In the mid 1990s, another BMM church was looking for a pastor. Hatfield is a town north of London and about 30 minutes driving time from Luton. The church had been started in the '80s, and one of the founding missionaries was leaving the field, so the church was looking for a pastor.

The church issued a call to Murray, and he began serving there. Eventually, Murray and Marjorie moved to Hatfield and threw their heart and soul into the church. The work is still small, but Murray has been teaching, leading, and working with the congregation and is a faithful servant of the Lord. He is fully engaged in the ministry and lives by faith via support from the Hatfield church and others. He and his wife have adopted four children and are rearing these children in the faith and offering a sound role model to other families.

From a human perspective, it could be argued that none of this would have happened if a drug-using Jewish convert had not moved from Australia and met Jim, who knew Murray. One could argue that this was absolutely the opposite of how evangelism is to be handled. (For one thing, it isn't recommended to buy drugs in order to witness!) And yet God is greater than our ideas of what should happen. He can, and often does, use unorthodox methodologies to transform lives.

A Christmas to Remember
Charles Nichols

Charles and his wife Joan were appointed to serve in Brazil in 1965. Twenty years later, Charles accepted the assignment of Baptist Mid-Missions' Latin America Field Administrator. In 1994 Joan also joined the Home Office staff as secretary of the Audio-Visual Department. The Nicholses retired in 2000. Charles went to be with the Lord in 2010.

It was Christmas Eve of 1978. Maranatha Baptist Church in Fortaleza, Brazil, was nearly packed with parents and friends eager to see the children and young people present their program. We were thankful to see many there who rarely attended the church. Of course, our members and friends who were always in attendance were there as well. Among this second group was a young father who had not yet received Jesus Christ as his Savior. If you had visited one of our services, you might have thought that Francisco was one of our members, because he was nearly always in attendance. For six years, we had been praying for his salvation. That night, his four little daughters were part of the program.

Francisco was seated way down front with a flash camera so he could get pictures of his girls as they performed. At the conclusion of the program, I brought a simple gospel message and invited anyone who wanted to receive Jesus Christ as Savior to raise a hand. My eyes were focused toward the rear of the auditorium as I hoped to see some of the visiting parents respond to the invitation. To my surprise, I noticed that someone near the front was making some movement.

Francisco had raised his hand. What a delight it was to review with him Scripture passages relating to salvation and to listen as he prayed to receive Jesus Christ as Savior. How we all rejoiced in this answer to our prayers. Among the believers, there was hardly a dry eye as we closed that very special service.

A few weeks later when Francisco entered the baptismal waters, he whispered, "Pastor, can I say something?" I granted permission, and he proceeded to speak. He said, "Folks, you know that I delayed a long time before I trusted Christ. Many of you also know that I had a problem with alcohol. I had made a vow to myself that I would only become a believer when I could stop drinking. I could never quit, but on Christmas Eve I had such a desire to trust Christ that I forgot about my vow. The amazing thing is that, since that night, I have never taken another drink."

Francisco went on to become one of the leaders in the church. As nearly as I know, now 30 years later, he has never again been enslaved to alcohol. That was truly a Christmas to remember.

Give Me This Water!
Ward Harris

Ward was appointed in 1951 with Baptist Mid-Missions. In 1955, he married missionary colleague Lucille Hukill in Bangassou, Central African Republic (CAR). Fifteen months later, Lucille went to be with the Lord following an automobile accident during their first furlough. The Lord later brought Sarah Jane Cornett into his life, and they married in 1962. Together they served in CAR until 1986, when they took up ministry in North America. The Harrises retired in 1992.

Some Central African preachers and I were holding meetings in the villages of the Birao area. Birao is a small city near the Sudan border.

We had already preached in a half dozen villages that day when we pulled into a large center where there was a school. The schoolteacher was friendly toward the gospel and offered us camping space for the night. He then sent word to the village people to bring us some pots of water. But the Muslim leaders instructed the people to have nothing to do with us.

After we unloaded our belongings and set up camp for the night, we debated where we might go to find some water. We asked where the spring was located. Just then a young businessman of the village rode up on his bike with a five-gallon can of clear water strapped to the back of his bicycle. He said he had heard we were asking for water, so he had gotten on his bike and pedaled to the spring and filled this can so that we could have good drinking water. I thanked him for being so kind to us and invited him to the meeting we planned to have that evening.

We hung up a kerosene pressure lamp and started singing gospel songs to alert the people of the village that we were meeting. Our Good Samaritan came and sat right up close to where I was speaking and listened attentively. I spoke in Sango from John 4:15 on the subject, *"Mou Na Mbi Ngou"* (Sir, give me this water). He did not receive the Living Water that night, but he never forgot the message or the invitation.

Some months later, he took his inventory of merchandise to a large mining camp and set up a store there to sell his wares. While there, he became deathly sick and very weak. He begged his Muslim friends to get him on a truck and take him to the hospital in Bria.

One Sunday afternoon, some of the Bible school students were doing visitation among the sick at the hospital. They came to this man, and he asked them, "Do you know the missionary—I think his name is Harris. Is he home today? Will you please go tell him that the man who brought him water at Salamaka is calling for him to come and see him?"

The Bible school students came immediately and very excitedly explained to me about the fellow in the hospital. "He is very sick," they said, "and he is calling for you to come to him."

I got on my motorcycle and sped up to the hospital. The Muslim men who had brought him into the hospital heard that the Baptist missionary was coming, so they gathered around his bed in a tight circle and attempted to prevent my talking with him.

Nevertheless, I pushed by them and stood up close to his bed. I started talking to him about the Lord and his need of being saved by receiving Christ as his personal Lord and Savior. His response was *"Mou na mbi ngou ni!"* Give me this Living Water!"

The Muslim men said, "No! Have nothing to do with this man. Do not listen to him!" But he cried all the more insistently, "Give me the Living Water! Give me the Living Water!"

They put pressure on me to leave, so I went outside, thinking they would leave and I could go back later. Instead they surrounded his bed in such a way as to make it impossible for me to speak to him again.

The next day when I went back, the nurse told me that he had passed away the previous night and that the Muslims had taken his body to bury in a shallow grave.

I believe I will see this man in heaven. I believe his urgent and insistent cry of "Give me this water!" was his confession of his need to be born again. I praise the Lord that He allowed this man to live until he got to Bria and could make public his confession of Christ.

The Other Woman
Ernie and Carol Mason

Ernie and Carol have been serving with Baptist Mid-Missions since 1990. The Masons started the first independent Baptist work in the southern half of Cordoba, Argentina, where they continue to serve.

Evelinda is an elderly lady we met in our first days in Argentina. She would visit the neighborhood, frequently asking for food. That's how she got to know us, the "rich" foreigners! In the early days of our ministry, she faithfully attended the church we started, and within six months, she was saved. Her constant look of worry was replaced by a smile.

Twelve or so years earlier, her marriage had broken up. Although they were not officially divorced, her husband went to live with the next-door neighbor. Yet, he still worked in the garage of Evelinda's house, where he had a car painting shop. One day "the other woman" came to our church services, and Evelinda was greatly disturbed. She left as soon as the service ended but then came back about 30 minutes later and declared, "This is the only place I have found peace, and now SHE comes here to ruin it! She is trying to ruin the joy I have found!"

We counseled Evelinda to pray for the other woman's salvation. The next time the "other woman" came, she sat right next to Evelinda in the Sunday School class. The other woman didn't know where anything was in the Bible. God gave Evelinda the grace to help the woman find the verses. In the sovereignty of God, we were studying the Ten Commandments, and that day the lesson was about adultery! God had the perfect word for the perfect moment!

Sadly, the other woman did not come back to church after that. A few years later, after having evicted Evelinda's husband, she died of cancer.

Years later, the husband became ill. Here in Argentina, public hospitals do not have the nursing staff to attend to the needs of patients around the clock, so a family member or friend stays to care for them. For over a month, Evelinda sat with her husband day and night in the hospital. When asked about it, she said simply, "It was my duty." That is the power of God to remove bitterness and to provide enduring joy.

Surrender
Robert Meyer

In 1953, Bob and his wife Lena began serving with Baptist Mid-Missions, appointed to the Dominican Republic. The Lord gave them a fruitful ministry there, but in 1988 they were challenged to open the field of Ecuador for BMM. This they did, and many other missionaries joined them. The Meyers retired in 1999. Their three children, Richard, Jeannie, and Anita, and their spouses serve with Baptist Mid-Missions.

In the capital city of Santo Domingo in the Dominican Republic, we pioneered a work among the upper class of people. I consider this group to be one of the most neglected peoples on earth when it comes to the gospel.

One day Mitzi, a Spanish lady, walked past our church building, saw the sign, and decided to start attending our services. She had come to know the Lord Jesus Christ as her Savior while living in Cuba. Her husband had been a military officer under the Italian dictator Benito Mussolini. He was a captain in World War I and a major general in World War II. When Mussolini's fascist government crumbled, they fled to South America. Things did not work out well there, so they moved to Cuba and started over. When Fidel Castro took control, they again lost everything they had, and so they moved to Santo Domingo.

Mitzi's husband allowed her to attend church services, but he forbade her to be baptized. The old general said, "If you get baptized, you get divorced."

Mitzi waited 20 long years before she finally obtained permission from her husband to be baptized. She was so happy at her baptism that she forgot to close her mouth as she went under the water and came up spouting like a whale but with a big smile on her face.

The next day she called me and said, "Pastor, my husband has been terrible to me today."

I said, "Well, what do you expect? He just lost a major battle yesterday."

He had to surrender in the First World War. He had to surrender in the Second World War. He wasn't about to give in to his wife's religion. But a year later, the old gentleman at age 74 stepped into the aisle and walked forward in a Sunday morning service and received the Lord as his Savior. It was hard for him to surrender again, especially to "his wife's religion."

Mitzi heard him praying a few days later, "Lord, help me. I don't want to sin any more. I've sinned so much in my life, Lord. I don't want to sin any more."

He lived another ten years, with real joy in his life.

Accidental Evangelism
Mark A. Swedberg

Mark and his wife Anita are both second-generation Baptist Mid-Missions missionaries (the children of John and Karen Swedberg and Robert and Lena Meyer). The Swedbergs joined BMM in 1990 to serve in Brazil, the country in which Mark grew up.

In this day and age of creative evangelistic techniques such as Evangelism Explosion, friendship evangelism, and power evangelism, here in Brazil we discovered one more. We call it accidental evangelism.

Sérgio was drunk and wobbling his way home one day when he was accidentally hit by Jair, a member of our young church plant, Central Baptist in Olímpia, Brazil. Jair took such good care of him that when Sérgio's sister-in-law, Áurea, needed help, she asked Jair. Jair brought her to us, and she made a profession of faith. Áurea then brought her niece, Denise, who trusted Christ. Denise brought her boyfriend, Edmilson, and he got saved.

Edmilson's brother, Evandro, was a hard case. He loved parties and getting drunk. And he hated believers. He told Edmilson that if I ever showed up to talk to him, he was going to punch my lights out. Luckily, I never did.

But one day, Evandro showed up at my office with a lot of questions. I answered those questions and shared Christ with him. Later on, he did a Bible study with my assistant and was saved as a result.

Evandro turned out to be an aggressive evangelist. He was concerned for his parents, Pedro and Bela. One day I visited them in their home. They seemed close to Christ, but Bela had a hang-up: she was unwilling to give up her faith in the Virgin Mary. She said that she had always believed in Mary and wasn't going to stop now. Pedro acted like he was ready to trust Christ but would wait for Bela so they could get saved together.

That was a Sunday. On Thursday I was back in their home. I keyed on Bela, thinking that if she came to Christ, Pedro would too. At one point I said, "Can't you see that salvation is only through Christ, since He was the one who died for our sins? Can't you see that Mary can't save us?" At that point Pedro interrupted and said, "I can, which is why I trusted Him last Tuesday."

Bela came to Christ several weeks later. After that, Edmilson and Evandro's younger brother, Eder, also trusted Christ. And that is how the Central Baptist Church of Olímpia was founded.

Better than Diamonds

Ward Harris

Ward was appointed in 1951 with Baptist Mid-Missions. In 1955, he married missionary colleague Lucille Hukill in Bangassou, Central African Republic (CAR). Fifteen months later, Lucille went to be with the Lord following an automobile accident during their first furlough. The Lord later brought Sarah Jane Cornett into his life, and they married in 1962. Together they served in CAR until 1986, when they took up ministry in North America. The Harrises retired in 1992.

Many years ago, my wife and I were led of the Lord to take a trip to some of the outlying churches in the Yalinga area of the Central African Republic. It was right in the middle of the rainy season. Generally, missionaries do not hold these types of meetings during the rainy season, because the roads are all but impassable. Many times the bridges are washed out. Nevertheless, I believed that the Lord wanted to save souls in these villages in the rainy season as well as in the dry season, so we ventured to make the trip.

We had a four-wheel-drive Jeep station wagon. We loaded camping equipment, food, and other necessities in a two-wheel trailer. I had contacted the pastors to let them know we were coming, and I explained what we planned to do while we were with them.

We drove to one large village. The pastor welcomed us, and the chief of the village came to greet us. As we stood talking, I asked if they had prepared a place for us to set up camp for our stay in the village. Apparently they had not thought about that. The chief said that there was an old guesthouse that hadn't been used for quite some time. The elephant grass had grown over the road leading to it. It could hardly be seen from where we were standing.

The chief called a group of young men to come and cut the grass with their machetes so that we could drive our Jeep back to the guesthouse and unload the trailer. It had rained hard, and the thick mud of the dirt floor built up on the soles of our shoes.

Later in the evening, we called the people of the village to come to our meeting. Instead of a church bell, we used "talking drums" to alert the villagers of the meeting. We had a good, lively song service, and then I preached an evangelistic message, stressing the need of personal salvation.

Each day, we had an early morning prayer meeting, followed by some messages from the Bible for the believers of the village. A young couple from another area had come to this village to hunt diamonds. Some of the local congregation had invited them to attend the meetings, and they came to each of the evening services.

As they listened to the Word of God preached in the power of the Holy Spirit, they were convicted of their sin. Also, they were convinced that the wages of sin is death. After listening to several messages, they felt compelled to step out and receive Christ as their Savior. The young man came forward, followed by his wife. I dealt with them, showing them from the Bible that all have sinned and come short of the glory of God. The wages of sin is death, but God so loved them that He sent His only begotten Son, Jesus, to seek and to save them. I explained to them that Jesus lived a perfect life and died a sacrificial death, and if they would receive Jesus as Savior and confess Him openly as their Lord, they would be saved. They would be possessors of eternal life.

Right then and there, they bowed their heads and asked Jesus to come into their hearts and save them.

Several years later, we had come back from a furlough in the United States and had moved from Yalinga to Bria, a larger center 100 miles to the southwest. There we established an evening Bible school to train young men whom God had called to preach. We held the classes at night in order that the men could work during the day and provide for the needs of their families. Generally, the men worked at the mission, helping with building projects and the like. One day a couple of men were with me in my Chevy pickup truck. As we were riding along in the cab, one of the men said, "Mister, you have forgotten me."

I asked, "How is that? You are Antoine and your wife is Louise. Both of you are in classes in the evening Bible school, and I am your teacher."

"Yes," he replied, "but you have forgotten when we first met. Do you remember holding meetings in 1963 at a village where Pastor Manton had a Baptist church? Do you remember how it rained in between the meetings? Do you remember that young couple that came each night? The young man had a package of cigarettes in his shirt pocket. I was mining diamonds and had money. So I thought, since all the white men carried a pack of cigarettes in their shirt pocket, that was the thing that people of means did. Your preaching from the Word of God convicted me of my sin. After listening to you preach, both my wife and I felt compelled to come forward, and you showed us from the Bible how to be saved."

Antoine continued, "We moved back to Bria and started attending church here, and as we listened to the Word, the Lord spoke to me about presenting my body as a living sacrifice, and He called me to enter Bible school to train to be a preacher."

What a blessing it was to hear this man's testimony and that of his wife. They finished Bible school and have been used of the Lord to win others to Christ.

Jean-Pierre
Ed and Sylvia Christy

Ed joined Baptist Mid-Missions in 1985 and Sylvia in 1987. Together they have been involved in church planting in France for more than 20 years. Ed is also integrally involved in BMM's Pastoral Baptist Bible Institute in the city of Algrange.

A couple of weeks before Christmas of 2004, we were driving back from the first of two cantata performances given during that special season by our church and two sister churches in the Bordeaux, France, area. On our way home, we were dropping off one of the newer members of our church, Jean-Pierre, at his apartment.

Jean-Pierre, sharply dressed in his choir outfit, including dress shirt and tie, looked over at us and commented, "Who would ever have believed it? A few years ago I was just a homeless drunk. Look at me now, dressed up and singing in a choir for the Lord!"

It came home to us with great clarity: That's what it's all about—transformed lives! Jean-Pierre is not just the fruit of the ministry of our church here in Floirac. Many Christians have played a part in his spiritual life. While wrongly imprisoned in another city in France for a crime he didn't commit, Jean-Pierre heard of Christ's love for him and accepted

God's pardon for his sin. For a while, he floated in and out of churches, including ours.

But little by little, he became more stable and grew. He was baptized in 2003 and is now one of our most faithful members. He arrives early each Sunday to unlock the church. His favorite role is that of greeter at the door. His presence is a joyous testimony to the power of Christ to change lives.

His Chosen People
Frank Hoover

Frank and his wife Marjorie both had tender hearts toward Jewish people. In 1950, they began serving with Baptist Mid-Missions to reach this people group, first in St. Louis and later in Washington State. Despite times of intense opposition, they shared God's truths with kindness and perseverance. Marjorie went to be with the Lord in 2007, and Frank in 2009.

I spent most of my adult years endeavoring to introduce God's chosen people to their Messiah. Throughout all history, God has sought to woo the Jew to Himself. It is written in Deuteronomy 7:6, "For thou art an holy people unto the LORD thy God: the LORD thy God hath chosen thee to be a special people unto himself, above all people that are upon the face of the earth." Jesus loved the Jews and brought His message of redemption to the Jew first. I have sought to follow in His footsteps.

It hasn't always been this way in my life, though. I was born in Canada and raised in North Dakota. I came out to Washington State in 1937 and stayed with a cousin who was quite anti-Semitic. He gave me a great deal of anti-Jewish literature to read, and that had a profound effect on my thinking. I really knew nothing about the Jewish people, because back in North Dakota there were none. So I believed all the anti-Semitic lies I was reading and started hating the Jews too.

Then in 1939 in Atlantic, Iowa, I had a minor operation, and a lady witnessing in the hospital handed me a tract entitled *Why All Good People Will Be Lost*. Through reading that tract, I accepted the Lord as my Savior.

I came back to Washington and was drafted into the army and served 17 months. Because of a physical problem, I could not go into combat, so I served my time in the military police force at Fort Lewis. While I was in the service, I went to the Christian Servicemen's Center in Tacoma. One evening at the Servicemen's Center, I heard a Hebrew Christian speak on Jewish evangelism. Right then and there, the Lord spoke to my heart and said, "This is where I want you, Frank."

I met my future wife Marjorie there at the Christian Servicemen's Center. After a time of dating, I proposed to her, but she turned me down. She felt she'd been called to Africa. But when the Lord closed the door to Africa, she agreed to marry me. We spent several years at the Bible Institute of Los Angeles and then finished at Simpson Bible College. We contacted Baptist Mid-Missions and were accepted in 1950 for Messianic Ministries.

Our first assignment was in St. Louis. We learned how to approach Jewish work under Carl Anderson, a veteran missionary. He told us, "If you're easily discouraged, don't go into Jewish work." It is a long process to bring a Jewish person to the point that they will even consider the claims of Jesus. There are not a lot of avenues for evangelism. Most of the time you just have to be out there, beating the sidewalks, going calling house to house. We would go through the telephone book looking for Jewish names, searching out contacts.

After St. Louis, we served nine years in Spokane, Washington, before coming to Seattle. We served in Seattle from 1962 until we retired. On three-by-five cards, we kept track of the people we contacted. Over the years, we accumulated 12 shoeboxes full of cards representing the Jewish people that we had tried to witness to for Christ. I praise God for His goodness to us and especially for giving me a love for His chosen people—the Jews.

Francisco Carlos
Jim Leonard

Jim and his wife Julie came with Baptist Mid-Missions in 1986 to serve in Brazil, where Jim grew up as the son of BMM missionaries Jerry and Frances Leonard. They serve in the city of Crato, where they are involved in church planting and theological education.

Francisco Carlos was saved in 2000 through our Source of Light Bible Correspondence School lessons. He faithfully came to our church, Igreja Batista da Graça in Crato, Brazil, bringing his four children with him. Fátima, his wife, however, resisted the gospel and would never come to church with the family. Finally, she came to church for a Christmas dinner in 2001 and attended occasionally after that. On Easter Sunday of 2002 she, too, received Christ as Savior.

Both Francisco Carlos and Fátima worked at a large factory in town where beach sandals of the "Ryder" brand were made. Francisco Carlos became our missionary to the workers in this factory, where over 3,000 people were employed. He personally delivered lessons from our Correspondence Bible School and brought the tests back for grading. Every Sunday, they had several visitors with them in the church service.

Five years later, Francisco Carlos and Fátima were both laid off from the sandal factory by godless foremen who did not like to see them witnessing to their fellow workers. Francisco Carlos, by this time a deacon at the Igreja Batista da Graça, was appointed by his church to help us with the development of a new church plant in another part of Crato where there was no evangelical church. He and his family of six walked 30 minutes one way, several times each week to get to the Parque Grangeiro, where this new church plant was being developed. While we were on furlough, he assumed the leadership responsibilities and his wife taught the junior Sunday School class.

One Sunday, he was not feeling well because of an intestinal flu, so he did not make it to church. On Monday morning he went to the hospital, hoping to see a doctor and then go home. Instead he was hospitalized and kept there for the whole week. On Monday, he was too sick to get out of bed. On Tuesday, a man who used to work with him and was sick in the ward just down the hall recognized him and asked him to bring a message from God to his ward. Francisco Carlos gladly took his Bible down to the ward and preached the gospel to the six men in that hospital room.

The word quickly spread that there was a pastor in the hospital, and for the remaining four days, several times each day, Francisco Carlos was called on to preach in the various wards of the hospital. Even though he felt well enough to go home on Tuesday, the doctors did not release him until Friday night. Dozens of people who otherwise would not have heard the gospel were evangelized.

Desert Deliverance
Sam and Jamie Hornbrook

Sam and Jamie joined Baptist Mid-Missions in 1988 to serve in Mexico. Sam is following in the footsteps of his missionary parents, Sam and Ellen Hornbrook, who also serve with BMM. Sam and Jamie work in the Mexico City area.

Sylvester was one of 60 people from Mexico who had paid $1,500 dollars to an experienced guide who would help them get across the Texas border and on their way to jobs in various cities in different parts of the United States of America. To get the money to pay the guide, Sylvester borrowed most of it from friends and family members. He was a gate-keeper making $150 dollars a month in a middle-class neighborhood in Mexico City. The promise of work that paid six dollars an hour was very attractive. His plan was to work in Miami, Florida, for as long as necessary in order to pay back everyone who had loaned him money for his trip, and after that to buy a pickup truck. Then he would come back home to his wife and two children in Mexico City.

The guide took the group of 60 people across the Rio Grande River near Laredo, Texas. It was close to midnight. The river came up to Sylvester's chest, and the current was stronger than he expected, but he made it safely across. As he was climbing the bank on the other side, he heard the screams and then the sobs of a woman. He heard that the woman's four-year-old daughter had been swept away by the current, and no one had been able to help.

Sylvester was beginning to have second thoughts about this adventure that promised a better future. He thought of his eight-year-old son and five-year-old daughter that he had left behind. He had never been separated from them for more than a week before. Would it be worth the painful separation from his family in order to buy a truck? But he had already come this far and decided it was too late to go back.

After walking through the night for three hours, the group of illegal immigrants came to a small house where they spent the night sleeping on the crowded floor. At this point, the group was split up into many smaller groups. The guide promised that the next day a van would take Sylvester and five other people to another town where they would take a bus to Miami. When they were getting ready the next morning, however, the guide said that they would have to walk another three hours to get to the place where the van would pick them up.

They were soon walking through the Texas desert, and the three hours turned into all day long. The guide said something about the van breaking down so they would have to continue on foot. They spent the night in the cold desert, and the next morning, the guide was gone. The group of six was totally disoriented and did not even know how to go back.

The small group decided that they should look for a road that would hopefully lead them out of the desert. They began making their way through open desert, occasionally climbing through barbed wire fences. They ate what little food they had, and their water soon ran out. As thirst and hunger grew, Sylvester thought about his family and wished he had never left them. He also remembered the small Christian church he had been attending for the past three months with his family. Even though he was convinced that the Bible taught the truth about his need to accept God's Son as his Lord and Savior, Sylvester had not made that decision yet.

He was not sure that he wanted to give up his self-sufficiency and independence. At the age of 11 he had left his home in a village in the state of Michocán in southern Mexico, with the plan to find work in Mexico City. His father neglected and abused his mother and five younger siblings. His mother never had enough money or food for everyone's needs, so Sylvester's plan was to help his mother by sending money to her. His life had been very difficult in the big city, but he had survived, worked, and sent money home whenever he could.

Years later, his father had become a Christian and was making great changes in his life, but Sylvester was still angry and bitter about all the years of neglect and abuse. When he traveled home to visit his parents, he would not let his father talk to him about the Lord or the Bible. Yet God was working in Sylvester's heart. His eight-year-old son had been asking him questions about God and asking why they never went to church. Then a Christian family that lived in the neighborhood where Sylvester worked invited him to go to their small church where we were starting our second church plant.

Sylvester's wife Irma had been raised in a very traditional Roman Catholic family with a shrine to the Virgin Mary in their home. She was very afraid of going to a Protestant church, but Sylvester had said, "Either we all go or nobody goes. I have decided we are all going." His son liked going to church right away, so they kept attending.

Sylvester's hurting stomach and dry mouth reminded him that he needed to continue pushing forward, knowing that their only hope of survival in the desert was to find a road where they would run into people. By this time, he was stepping on the bones of what he could only assume were people who had been abandoned in this awful desert like he and his companions had been.

They saw a person sitting on the ground in the distance and decided they would offer help, even though they were practically carrying one of their own group who was already too weak to continue on his own. As they approached the person sitting on the ground, they were horrified to find that the man was dead. He could not have been dead more than a day or two, due to the condition of his body. They all knew they were in great danger of facing the same fate.

On the eighth day after they had set out on foot, Sylvester addressed the rest of the group. He said, "I don't know if I will live through this day, and the rest of you are not doing much better than I am. If I die, I know I am not ready to meet God, so I am going to take care of that right now. The rest of you should do the same." Right there, in the presence of the others, Sylvester asked God to forgive him of his sin and trusted His Son Jesus Christ as Lord and Savior.

Later that day, Sylvester and his companions stumbled upon a highway. To this day Sylvester has no idea where they were or how far they had gone. Not long after coming to the road, a Texas Border Patrol came along in a big Suburban and picked them up. They were taken to a holding cell for a few hours, where they were given water and some crackers. Later they were driven across the border, where they were released.

Sylvester bought a sandwich and a bus ticket home. His stomach was so constricted from not having eaten for an entire week that he was able to eat only half of the sandwich during the 10-hour bus ride.

On a Sunday in June 2005, Sylvester arrived at New Life Baptist Church with his family to give testimony of how God had softened his heart and then rescued him in the Texas desert. He now talks to everyone who will listen about all God did to bring him to Christ.

Unlike others who continue trying to get to the United States to find work, Sylvester learned that all the money in the world is not worth losing your life and your family. A few months after Sylvester's adventure in the Texas desert, his wife Irma received Christ into her heart as well. Sylvester and his family are faithful members of New Life Baptist Church.

Three Breakfasts
Joanne Richter

Joanne and her husband Don joined Baptist Mid-Missions in 1970 to serve in Alaska. The Richters served 30 years in church planting before Don went to be with the Lord in 2001. Joanne served six more years with missionary colleagues before retiring in 2007. Her daughter, Lisa (Armstrong) Wils, and Lisa's late husband, Jesse Armstrong, served with BMM in Russia.

It was a typical morning in the Alaskan bush. My husband, our two daughters, and I lived in the village of Iliamna, 200 miles southwest of Anchorage. We were serving the Lord doing church planting under Baptist Mid-Missions.

Our family had just finished eating breakfast when we heard a small plane "buzz" our home, which was located on the shores of Slopbucket Lake and Lake Iliamna. Company was a common occurrence living in the bush, even though we were accessible only by air. My husband Don drove to the dirt airstrip to pick up our visitors. It happened to be a pastor friend from Anchorage. He'd brought along a guest who was visiting from one of the southern states. We chatted and enjoyed the fellowship as I made a second breakfast, for our guests this time.

After a couple of hours, we all noticed the weather was getting very windy, and it had started to rain. Our guests decided to leave before the weather deteriorated even further. Don drove them back to their airplane.

On his return trip home, he couldn't help but notice the poor man sitting beside his kayak on the shores of Lake Iliamna. The driving rains and wind were thoroughly drenching the man. Don stopped our truck and invited the man to come to our home for some shelter and a hot meal.

As they entered our home, Don said, "Joanne, would you mind making our friend some hot breakfast?" So as I started cooking the third breakfast of the day, I listened to this stranger's story. Evo was from Czechoslovakia. He had ventured across Cook Inlet with his kayak and a small motor. He got in a storm and lost his map. When he started across Lake Iliamna, his boat motor developed mechanical problems. When my husband picked him up from the beach, he didn't know where he was. He just knew he was cold, wet, hungry, and lost.

Like most storms on Lake Iliamna, this particular one lasted for several days. Evo stayed with us those stormy days, and there was opportunity to speak to him regarding his spiritual needs. Evo could see that God had spared his life for a special reason. In the living room of our home, he trusted Christ as his Savior.

Aren't God's ways interesting! He brought Evo all the way from Czechoslovakia to a small village in the Alaskan bush to hear the gospel of Jesus Christ. Yes, bush hospitality was a great ministry. We had many opportunities to share the gospel with strangers while we lived on Lake Iliamna, but I shall always remember the day that I cooked three breakfasts!

Tied to a Tree
George Norton

*During his years in the Amazon region of Brazil, George picked up the nick-
name of "George of the Jungle." He and his wife Elizabeth were appointed
with Baptist Mid-Missions in 1950 and planted churches there until retiring
in 1997. Elizabeth went to be with her Lord in 1998. In 2003, George married Doris Griffin, a widow who had also served in Brazil.*

About 200 miles from the mouth of the mighty Amazon River
and far back in the jungle, there is a little group of people, where I,
"Jungle" George Norton, went nearly every week. We had to cut away
a lot of trees so that our boat, the Blessed Hope Launch, could get just
halfway there. We had to do the remaining miles on foot. The name of
this quaint place was Guajara Mirim. The people living there were very
sociable, so we soon became great friends. They came to our services and
sat on logs or rocks to hear the message of salvation.

In Guajara Mirim, there was a man who was often tied to a tree.
His name was Julio. He would get so drunk and crazy that the people
would capture him when he became violent. Julio had a large, sharp machete. When he was drunk, he took his machete and went around trying
to kill people. He was big, ugly, and strong, so all the people were afraid
of him with good reason. The people didn't want to have an arm, leg, or
even a head cut off, so they tied him to a tree.

Well, Julio came to our meeting one night only half drunk. He
paid unusual attention as I spoke. When all the people were asked to tell
me if they wanted to take the Lord Jesus into their hearts, half-drunk Julio
stood and said, *"eu quero"* (I want to). We didn't know what to think.
Was he sober enough to understand what he was doing? Sitting down
with him, I explained about sin, hell, righteousness, and heaven. After I
read certain Scriptures to him, he said, "I want to take the Lord Jesus into
my heart."

The people did not immediately believe that he had been
changed, but the next day Julio cut down the tree that they used to tie him
to. Eventually, he became one of the staunchest Christians in that place.

About three weeks later, I met Julio on the path to Guajara Mirim
but did not recognize him. When I asked him if he was a Christian, he

looked very surprised and said, "Pastor, I was saved. I accepted the Lord in the meeting that we had."

Embarrassed, I said, "Julio, I did not know it was you, for now you are shaved, cleaned up, have a smile on your face, and you walk like a very happy man."

As time went on, he brought others there for me to lead to Christ. He became one of the best leaders in the group and a good husband and father. He is a mighty testimony for the Lord and a real leader. He helped me to realize that God can transform anyone—even a crazy man that they used to tie to a tree.

New Beginnings in Dekalb County, Georgia
John Kennedy

A native of Scotland, John and his first wife Catherine served many years in Brazil with another agency. They joined the Baptist Mid-Missions Family in 1972. The Kennedys felt burdened to reach the United Kingdom for Christ, and they opened BMM's ministry there in 1973. After Catherine went to be with the Lord, John married Rillie Mae Leach, and they served throughout the United Kingdom. Even after retirement in 1993, John has continued to pursue multiple avenues of ministry. John's daughter Ruth is a BMM missionary in Africa.

The Dekalb County Jail in metropolitan Atlanta is a huge, crowded facility. For most men it is a dead end, but for some prisoners it has been the place where they have found new life, joy, and peace. I witnessed many miracles of God's grace in this jail since being led by the Lord to begin a ministry there in early 1997.

The jail ministry was indeed an unexpected opportunity after a lifetime of church planting in Brazil, England, Scotland, and Ireland. I could not imagine that, at age 72, I would start out on another ministry, but that is how the Lord led. My wife Rillie Mae and I retired from Baptist Mid-Missions in 1993 and moved to the Atlanta area. Like Paul in Acts 9:6, we asked, "Lord, what wilt Thou have me to do?" He laid it upon our hearts to learn Spanish and minister to the large Hispanic population in Atlanta. This we did.

Then in the spring of 1996, I received a letter from an English-speaking inmate in the Dekalb County Jail. He expressed concern for the Hispanic prisoners who spoke very little English. About 20 percent of the inmates in the jail are Hispanics. I visited this man and the chief chaplain, and the result was the beginning of the jail ministry in early 1997 that lasted until health issues forced me to step out of this service in 2003. Matthew 25:36 was being fulfilled in our day and age—"… I was in prison, and ye came unto me."

I conducted four services a day, four times a week. Hour after hour was also spent in one-on-one counseling with many men who had hit bottom in their lives. Many came to their senses spiritually and made things right with the Lord.

From the very beginning, God drew inmates to Himself. In 1997, 138 inmates recognized their need for a Savior and repented of their sins. Each year more than 100 inmates came to Christ.

God transformed lives. I was making the rounds one day and met Jose. He asked me if I knew his brother Mario, who was incarcerated on another floor.

"Mario knows more of the Bible than I do," Jose said. When I finally met up with Mario at one of the weekly services, I told him what his brother had said. When we reached the part of the service reserved for preaching and teaching, I asked, "What truth or doctrine would you like to deal with today?"

Mario's hand went up. "I would like to know more about the Resurrection," he said.

What a great opportunity to compare the resurrection of the believer with that of the unbeliever! At the end of the service, Mario was one of those who trusted Christ as his Savior. Praise the Lord! Later Jose also believed on the Lord Jesus Christ for salvation.

The Lord Jesus Christ commanded His disciples to go into all the world to preach the gospel. In our case, He brought the world to us. On Sundays, we went to the floor of the jail where illegal immigrants were housed prior to being deported—a unique foreign mission field. Through the ministry that the Lord gave me in the jail, I was privileged to see the Lord call to Himself men from North America, Latin America, Africa, Europe and Asia.

Men from Mexico, Honduras, Guatemala, Columbia, Venezuela, Ghana, Italy, Puerto Rico, Albania, and China have gone back to their countries with the Lord Jesus Christ in their hearts, a Bible in their hands, and with some teaching regarding the living out of the Christian life.

We encouraged those who accepted the Lord as their Savior to contact us from their country of origin so that we could help them by correspondence or put them in contact with a missionary in their part of their country.

We rejoiced at the letter we received from Jonathan, a man who was deported back to his home in Ghana after having accepted Christ as his Savior. He wrote, asking us for Bibles and literature and to assure us that he was continuing on for the Lord.

One time, a group of 180 young Chinese men, who were brought to the United States illegally, were incarcerated in the jail. There was an older Chinese prisoner who had lived in South America and spoke Spanish. So I preached in Spanish, and the Spanish-speaking Chinese prisoner translated the message into Chinese. Some of these prisoners accepted the Lord.

The Lord answered the prayers of Christian family members of inmates who, in days past, undoubtedly agonized as they saw their errant loved ones committing crimes and straying far from the Savior. One example of this is Artur. He was an Albanian who spoke English and Italian as well as his native language. I conducted a special Bible study class for four Albanian men—Artur, Fatmer, Ndreck, and Artan—with Artur serving as the interpreter. Artur accepted the Lord as his Savior. Ndreck came to know the Lord as well. After all four men left the jail, I received a letter from Artur's father in Albania. He knows the Lord as his Savior and rejoiced when he learned that his son is now also a believer.

As one "congregation" was deported, another one moved in, and we had the opportunity to see others saved and taught the Word of God, so that they, too, returned to their homelands as true believers in our Lord Jesus Christ. We could not possibly visit all the countries represented by our "congregation." But the Lord made it possible for us to see souls saved so that they, like the Ethiopian eunuch in Acts 8, might take the gospel back to their own people.

All told, more than 800 men who had hit bottom at the Dekalb County Jail have instead found new life and a new beginning in Christ. Praise the Lord!

A Weak Vessel in the Potter's Hand
Eleanor Brittain

In 1950, as a single missionary en route to Liberia for the first time, Eleanor met Stan Brittain, then an officer on the ship Eleanor sailed on. They married three years later, and Stan joined Eleanor in the work in Liberia. In the 1970s, they served in New Zealand, Hawaii, and finally Great Britain (Stan's home country), from which they retired in 1992. Stan went to be with the Lord in 2003.

The month of January 1950 started out cold and snowy in Grand Rapids, Michigan, as I and two other young single ladies began our missionary careers. I, Eleanor Van Houten, was the youngest at 22. Carolyn Hovingh, 23, and Joan Peckinpaugh, 25, completed the group. We were all graduates of the Baptist Bible Institute. Carolyn and I were members of the first Day School class and graduated in 1946, Joan in 1949. The train depot was crowded with family and friends who came to give us a big sendoff. There was much talking, singing of hymns, and then a quiet time of prayer for our safety and blessings as we started on our journey to Liberia, West Africa via New York City.

The weather at the end of January was quite the opposite from when we'd left. It was extremely hot and humid as the ship docked in Monrovia, Liberia. There were many unfamiliar faces on the dock. Unexpectedly, there was no one from our mission to meet our ship. Captain Kingen was appalled and said, "I will not leave these young girls in this God-forsaken country unless someone comes to take care of them. I will take them on to the next port." The next port was Accra, Ghana, and … what then?

What were we new missionaries doing? Oh no, we were not on our knees praying, instead we were sitting on deck on our footlockers singing, "Here we sit like birds in the wilderness, waiting for Uncle Harlan!"

Rev. Harlan Rahilly was the business manager for the Mid-Liberia Baptist Mission and lived 125 miles interior on the SuaKoko mission station. He was supposed to meet us and take us upcountry. The captain was about to set sail, and by now we were definitely praying, when a "matronly" lady appeared on the scene. Please remember we were young! We looked at each other and said, "Is that how we will look in a few years?" This lady turned out to be Emma Wisser, business manager and hostess for the W.E.C. Mission. Harlan was delayed and somehow got word to Emma to rescue us!

We soon found out that Emma was a lovely lady, and she became a dear friend for many years. Our first Sunday in Liberia, Emma drove us the 30-some miles interior to the Firestone rubber plantation. It was a bumpy ride over rough dirt roads in a rather dilapidated vehicle. Every Sunday, Emma made this trip to bring the gospel message to camps where groups of men lived while they worked tapping rubber trees.

Emma decided we should start being missionaries as soon as possible, so she assigned each of us to speak at a camp. I don't have a clue what I said that day, except I know that I presented the gospel in a simple way and told them Jesus loved them and invited them to accept Christ as their own personal Savior. I do remember I was very scared and certainly a very weak vessel in the Potter's hand.

Now the story skips forward about 17 years. I was now a more seasoned missionary, with a husband, Stan Brittain, and four children—still serving the Lord in Liberia. We were attending a Bible conference on the Tappi Station. Liberian Christians had gathered together from all around Tappi to fellowship and listen to God's Word.

The second afternoon, a smiling young man (they always looked young to me) came up to my husband and me and was very excited. He greeted us and then asked, "Missy, you don't know me? You don't remember me?"

"I'm sorry, oh, I don't know your name," I had to admit.

"Oh Missy, you don't remember! You came to my camp at Firestone many years ago. You told us about Jesus. You said Jesus loved me. I gave Jesus my heart. I gave Jesus my life. I study God's Word. I go back to my village and preach. Now we have church there and I am pastor. Oh Missy. I thank God for you coming to Firestone!"

We rejoiced together, and I was humbled to think God had used a frightened, weak vessel like me—BUT—God has promised that His Word will NOT return void. We never know how or when God might use us to fulfill His purpose. We need to be faithful and willing servants. God takes care of the results. Praise His Name!

Twice Unshackled
Jim Johnson

Jim and his wife Rosie were appointed with Baptist Mid-Missions in 1983 to serve in the Central African Republic. Civil war and political turmoil forced the Johnsons to relocate twice: first to Ivory Coast and then to Ghana, where they currently serve.

A man came to our clinic in Ivory Coast wearing a handcuff. He had broken away from the police in Liberia, and somewhere along the line—probably in breaking away—the handcuff had injured his wrist. The wound had become infected, and his wrist was in pretty bad shape by the time he came to us.

The first time he appeared at the clinic, we couldn't get the handcuff off, so he went someplace else and had it removed. Then he came back to the clinic. That's when I first saw him. His wrist had been bandaged. I treated the infection again and put on a new bandage. While I was doing this, a Liberian talked to him about the Lord. They were conversing in English, and so I understood everything that was being said.

After I was finished caring for his wound, I sat down with him and talked to him a little bit. Then I went into the next room and got a tract that Baptist Mid-Missions had used at the Olympic Games in Atlanta in 1996. I went through the tract with him and led him to the Lord. We did not see him after that. He may have gone back to Liberia. But I will always remember him as the man who was twice unshackled—once from the handcuff and once from the shackle of sin.

Thank You for Never Giving Up on Me
Ray and Annette Ronk

In 1988, Ray and Annette joined the Baptist Mid-Missions team in Brazil. Over the years, the Lord has used them to change many lives for Christ. Their current work is in the city of Japurá in Brazil's Paraná State.

The salvation story of Jethro is one that passes through our first two terms of service in Brazil. We first met this young man when his mother began attending services at Maranatha Baptist Church in Recanto das Emas. This church began in May of 1994 in the front yard of a lady in the neighborhood. God blessed this new work, and the church grew enough to move to its own property. The shack that had been standing on the lot became Sunday School space. We needed much wisdom and creativity to stretch our meager building funds. Jethro often stopped by to talk as I was working on repairs or planning different outreach ministries.

Jethro's mother and younger sister became members of the church. They were faithful to witness to all of their family, which included seven other brothers and sisters! Jethro was addicted to drugs and alcohol, but he frequently stopped by to discuss religious topics.

I will never forget the night he came into the church screaming, "They're going to kill me, Pastor! They are going to KILL me!" Almost everyone had left after the evening service, but a few were still there. They helped to calm him and try to understand what was bothering this young man. Finally, we discovered that he owed money to the local drug lord. There was a contract out on his life. The total that he owed was equivalent to $18.00.

I was not going to pay for his drug habit, but we also decided that his soul had a greater value than $18.00. Those who remained after church joined together for prayer, and I went with Jethro to speak to the drug lord, Adilson. What a surprise was waiting for me when I walked up to the gate of this man's house. Two little girls came barreling out of the door shouting, "Pastor, Pastor, are you here to see us??" Christina and Fabiana regularly attended our Sunday School and children's Bible club! When I explained that I needed to see their father, they grabbed my hands and pulled me into the house to meet him.

So, over a cup of coffee, we discussed the money owed and Adilson's need for salvation. He was very polite and called off the contract on Jethro's life. He did not accept Christ as his personal Savior that night. But Adilson was gloriously saved several years later during a teacher training seminar at Maranatha Baptist Church.

Jethro helped me at the church for several days to pay back the money he owed me, and then he disappeared. We crossed paths again a few years later while he was recovering from gunshot wounds he had received during a fight at a local bar. The family had asked me to break the news to Jethro that his two brothers had been killed during the fight.

Jethro was an alcoholic and realized that he needed help beyond his own strength. He heard of a Christian center in a town six hours from his home, and he checked himself in. The church family committed to pray and help as we could with his basic necessities. During the first few weeks, Jethro tried to run away several times but ended up staying.

He participated in the Bible studies, and very soon he clearly saw his need to give his heart and life to Jesus Christ. Jethro was saved in June of 2000. What a joy it was to see Jethro and his mother enter the front door of the church during his first visit home that August. He walked to the front of the church and gave me a hug that I will never forget, all the time saying, "Thank you for never giving up on me—for always remembering to pray for me."

The church service that followed was one of great victory for all of us. Jethro returned to the small city where he found Christ. There, he is helping others who were in the same condition as he was before his salvation.

One Step Closer
Janet Stinedurf

Janet and her husband Jim previously worked with another agency in Puerto Rico before joining Baptist Mid-Missions in 1972. They continued their service in that country and have been involved in church planting and theological education.

I had never yet met anyone before who believed in reincarnation. So this conversation while on a plane headed for Puerto Rico was rather an eye-opening experience for me.

I had been in the United States for the birth of our 14th grandchild. On the plane home to Puerto Rico, I was seated by a young man who was probably in his 20s. He was kind and helpful, and it wasn't long before we were talking. He was born and raised in the States, but his family was from India, and he was following the religion of his ancestors.

Knowing very little of their beliefs, I asked him to explain his religion to me. I was quite taken aback when I learned that this all-American man believed that he would reincarnate one day—for better, if he lived a good life, and for worse if he didn't.

I had many questions that he was more than happy to answer. When it was my turn to share my beliefs, I felt speechless. I wanted to share Jesus with him, but we had no more in common than our citizenship. I groped for words and prayed harder than I ever have while witnessing.

"I just don't know what to say to you," I admitted. "Our beliefs have nothing in common. You see, I am a Christian. I worship the Creator God."

God had surely given me that phrase. Every time I used God's name, my hand lifted to about as high as my head, emphasizing that the one true God was over all. We both knew without saying it, that God, the Creator, was over his gods too.

He was open to listen. In fact, he shared that he had looked up something on the internet about Christianity. So we continued talking. I could feel my face shine with the joy of knowing that I was headed for heaven. I also knew that he could sense the peace that this knowledge brings to a believer in Christ. Yes, I was praying hard, and it was a beautiful conversation. God surely was leading.

At one point he said, "Christians really propagate their beliefs."

"Yes," I said, "we have so much to share. Really, and I say this kindly, you don't have hope ... you have nothing to share."

He got more and more into the conversation as we talked, and I encouraged him to receive Christ as his Savior. When we had shared about as much as we were going to, I encouraged him to go find those empty seats that he had planned to take a nap in. When we said goodbye, I asked his name.

"Simon," he said.

I said, "I'll pray for you, Simon."

He thanked me and left. It is wonderful to see someone get saved, but I don't have to see people come to the Lord to feel satisfied. I know that God used me to bring Simon one step closer to Him.

From Idol-Maker to Disciple-Maker
Carolyn Nuss

Carolyn Hovingh joined Baptist Mid-Missions in 1949 to serve in Liberia. After marrying in 1964, she continued serving there with her husband, Arthur Washburn. They later worked in North America. After Arthur went to be with the Lord, Carolyn married Carl Nuss, a widower who had also worked with BMM in North America. Carolyn went to be with the Lord in 2001, and Carl in 2004.

Taa was an idol-maker who lived in one of the Mano villages of Liberia. He made a good living by selling the idols that he carved out of wood—until he contracted leprosy. The disease began to destroy his fingers, then his hands, and then ulcers began to consume his feet. He could no longer support himself, because he couldn't make idols with the stubs that had replaced his once artistic fingers. Taa didn't know what to do. He couldn't stay in his town much longer.

Finally he decided to come to the Yila leprosy colony. But he couldn't walk there, and he didn't have the money to be carried. So Taa slowly, painfully crawled as far as he could on his knees, rested, then crawled some more. Big ulcers formed on his knees as he crawled and hobbled 10 strenuous days to get to Yila. At last he arrived at the leprosy colony. I began to treat his wounds as well as his leprosy. Taa not only received treatment for his physical body, he also received healing for his soul. He came to receive Christ through the testimony of the workers in the leprosy colony and through the ministry of the church there.

Eventually Taa's leprosy went into remission, and he began to think of going back to his town to tell the people there about Jesus Christ. So after five or six years of living at Yila, he prepared to leave. Taa asked for some of our Sunday School papers, with their colorful pictures. He reasoned that he could use the pictures to tell his village the Bible stories about the true God. So he and the local pastor, Enoch, came to me for a few days, and we went through many of the pictures, telling the stories. We had a good time getting him ready to go back to his town. Taa couldn't read in English, but the pictures helped him to remember each story.

He went home with a big stack of pictures. He was very happy when he left. His happiness wasn't just because his leprosy was in remission but because he was free from his sin. We didn't hear from Taa for awhile. Finally, one day Enoch came to me and said, "You have a visitor."

It was Taa. I asked him how he was doing. He told me that he had been using the pictures to teach the lessons in his town. The town did not have a preaching center, so he was used by the Lord to minister in a totally unreached area. He enjoyed it very much. But the people in his village were so tired of the same stories—he had been having church services every morning and evening. So they sent him back to Yila to get more stories. We gave him another pile of Sunday School papers, and Pastor Enoch explained the stories to him. Then Taa, the former idol-maker, returned to his people to carry on the work of telling them of the true God and Savior, Jesus Christ.

The Tale of Two Brothers
Doris Youmans

In 1950, Doris began her service with Baptist Mid-Missions, appointed for the field of Japan. For nearly 40 years, the Lord used her to change lives for the glory of Christ in that country.

One spring day, a young Japanese high school student went in search of a place where he could obtain free help with his study of English. A poster had said the classes were in the Watari district, but Osamu couldn't find the address. So he decided to ask for help.

"Could you tell me where the Mormons have their classes?" he asked a lady in the neighborhood.

"Oh, if you need help with English, you had better go to the American missionaries who live on the other side of the city," the lady kindly suggested.

Osamu was directed to the Gospel Book Store and was soon knocking on the door of Baptist Mid-Missions missionary Miss Evelyn Regier. Miss Regier welcomed him in, and soon a time was set up for Osamu to begin his weekly studies in English, along with some introductory studies in the Bible. He was also invited to attend Fukushima Baptist Church. From the beginning, Osamu had a keen interest in Bible study and soon became a regular attendee at church.

After attending a special evangelistic meeting and hearing the way of salvation, he later testified, "I couldn't believe right away, but I couldn't get away from the question, 'If you should die today, would you go to heaven?' By the Word of God in 1 John 5:5-13, I was led to a clear decision, and in April 1981 I was baptized at the Fukushima Baptist Church."

Shortly after he began studying with my coworker, I returned to Japan from furlough. The first time I met Osamu, he told me that he had a twin brother, Takashi, but that his brother was not interested in Christianity, church, or the Bible. I promised to pray for him.

Several months later, Osamu's duplicate appeared at my door. Takashi also requested help in English but made it clear that he didn't want to attend church. "Alright, we'll study English!" I thought. At the time, both brothers were studying for university entrance examinations. The older (by just a few minutes) said to his younger sibling, "Osamu, you are crazy to be spending so much time attending church when you should be cramming for the upcoming exams." Exam time came. Guess who passed. Yes, it was Osamu, the Christian.

In the spring of the following year, Osamu went off to university and soon became an active member of one of our churches near Tokyo. Takashi enrolled in a preparatory school and continued studying with me. We also began some basic Bible studies, and he started attending our Saturday afternoon youth meetings at church. Inwardly, his struggle continued.

As the older son in a Japanese family, he faced some serious questions as to the future. He would become heir, and therefore was expected to carry on the family traditions and religion. He wondered if he could fulfill his responsibilities as firstborn if he became a Christian. One day in class he said to me, "If I become a Christian, it will be like cutting myself off from the rest of my family." He asked, "If I become a Christian, will I have to be baptized, will I have to go to church, will I have to … etc, etc?" I could tell he was doing some serious thinking. Fellow missionaries, church members, and prayer warriors back in the USA were praying for this young man. God answers prayer.

One day an evangelist spoke to our youth group. Takashi was visibly touched by the speaker's testimony. The speaker's struggle before he believed sounded so much like what Takashi was going through! Yet, Takashi was still not ready to believe. Another incident happened, which caused him to think of life eternal. Riding home on a bicycle, he fell and was within inches of almost certain death.

One day in class he said something which upset me, and tears came to my eyes. Years later I heard him testify, "When I saw tears in my teacher's eyes and realized she cared for me, I decided I had better do some rethinking."

One day in October, he came to class. His troubled look and argumentative spirit were gone, and he wore a pleasant smile. I said, "Oh, have you made the right decision to accept the Lord Jesus Christ as your personal Savior?"

He answered, "Yes, how could you tell?" He had made his decision the previous evening while he was alone in his room. What a time of rejoicing and thanksgiving we had in class that day!

The following spring, Takashi followed his brother's footsteps and entered the same university. His growth as a Christian was not as fast or as dramatic as his brother's, but it was a joy for me to watch the Yuasa brothers grow in faith and knowledge of the Lord Jesus Christ!

Praise the Lord He loves each and every one of us, whether we are someone with a submissive, gentle spirit like Osamu or someone who is more argumentative, contemplative, and resistant like Takashi. God loves us all! I praise the Lord for letting me have a part in the lives of the Yuasa brothers. I felt like a proud mama one morning in church when a young lady whispered to me, "Which brother is here this morning, Osamu or Takashi?"

More than 20 years later, Osamu is married and has two daughters. He is now pastor of the Megumi Baptist Church. Takashi is married and has one son and is a faithful member of the Nihonmatsu Baptist Church.

Unexpected Fruit
Richard McMillen

Richard and his wife Dorothy started their service with Baptist Mid-Missions in 1950. The first half of their ministry was served in Central African Republic. In 1970, they transferred to North America and served there until retirement in 1994. The McMillens tell their ministry story in their book To the Praise of His Glory.

"Therefore, my beloved brethren, be ye stedfast, unmoveable, always abounding in the work of the Lord, forasmuch as ye know that your labour is not in vain in the Lord" (1 Corinthians 15:58).

In these days of fast food, the average American often expects instant results. In the realm of the Spirit, believers often long for instant answers to prayer. It is soon discovered that the Lord may not answer as quickly as we would like.

In the Lord's work, as we witness for Christ and teach God's Word, we remember Galatians 6:9: "And let us not be weary in well doing: for in due season we shall reap, if we faint not."

In June 1970, we moved from Silver Spring, Maryland, down to 599 Southern Avenue, Washington DC. Our goal was to see a Bible-believing Baptist church planted in that area of the Lord's great harvest field. To begin the process, we had a rubber stamp made with this statement: "Available for a Bible Study in your home" along with our name, address, and phone number. Many gospel tracts with this message were distributed. It wasn't long before a couple who lived near us invited us to their home. They had many questions, and we soon had a nucleus for a local church plant.

As we waited on the Lord to add to our number, we began a Bible club in the lower level of our home. Children from the neighborhood came. At first the number was small, but it soon grew, and the children seemed to enjoy the time very much. There were as many as 25 children who came regularly.

One boy of around seven years of age seemed to enjoy coming along with his two older sisters. He was a lovable child with a bubbly personality, but he was also determined to use the class as a time to have fun and pick on other children. He continually caused a commotion, which kept others from concentrating on the Bible lesson being presented.

My wife Dorothy taught this age group, and she had to scold Kevin over and over again for causing disorder. She warned him on numerous occasions that he would have to leave if he did not behave. One day she had to give a final warning that if he did not settle down, he had to leave. Sure enough, the time came and she had to lead him to the door. His plea to her that day was something like this, "I know you just don't want me to be in class where I can hear about the Lord and be saved." How could a teacher with a compassionate heart refuse such a cry?

A number of times he promised to settle down and be good, and she permitted him to come back in. However his promised good behavior never lasted, and finally she had to tell him that he could not return. We really did not know how much spiritual truth he had absorbed.

When the adult Bible class outgrew our home, we found a public meeting hall suitable for Bible studies. Our number grew to the point that we ultimately started having Sunday School and regular morning and evening church services.

Eventually we were able to buy the property on 940 Owens Road in Oxon Hill, Maryland, just one block off the District of Columbia line. This is where Beracah Baptist Church now stands.

One evening about 15 years later, a car came up our driveway and a handsome young man got out, came over, and gave Dorothy a giant hug. He was aware that she did not recognize him. He said, "Mrs. Mac, you don't recognize me, do you?"

"No, to be honest, I don't," she replied.

"I'm Kevin Gentry. Remember, I was in your class years ago at 599 Southern Avenue?" How could Dorothy ever forget? He then called his wife to come over with their two little girls. What a happy reunion after all these years! His testimony thrilled our hearts.

He now knew the Lord. He said, "You didn't think I was listening back there, but I was." He was now active in a church.

Man witnesses. Man preaches. Man teaches, but we need to keep in mind the clear testimony of the Apostle Paul. "I have planted, Apollos watered; but God gave the increase. So then neither is he that planteth any thing, neither he that watereth; but God that giveth the increase" (1 Corinthians 3:6-7).

Oh, how it pays to be faithful in sowing the seed of the Word of God. Our labor is not in vain in the Lord as we witness to the grace of

God in salvation. The Word of God is living and powerful. The gospel is still the power of God unto salvation to every one who believes. Therefore, let us be steadfast in the work that the Lord has given us to do. Yes, "… Salvation is of the LORD" (Jonah 2:9). May we never forget that He alone deserves all the glory!

The Garlows' Trail

Rev. H. C. Stephens

Representative of the New Testament Baptist Churches Association
Manipur, India

The subjects of Rev. Stephens' story, Jim and Joyce Garlow, joined Baptist Mid-Missions in 1938 to serve in India and worked with Asian nationals all their lives. Jim went to be with the Lord in 2004, and Joyce in 2006.

"How beautiful upon the mountains are the feet of him that bringeth good tidings, that publisheth peace; that bringeth good tidings of good." (Isaiah 52:7). How lovely and true it is! What a noble adventure it is to participate in the cause of Christ and His Great Commission. Jim and Joyce Garlow, missionaries with Baptist Mid-Missions in India, became the uncle and aunt to the hill people in India and Myanmar and especially to my Simte people in Manipur State.

What a joy it is for me to retrace their trail. I rejoice and praise God for the wonderful things He has accomplished through these pioneer missionaries in the jungles of Northeast India. The paths of the Garlows and the Simte people crossed each other in the late 1950s. Earlier in that decade, a handful of the Simte people had embraced Christianity. However, that was by choice and resolution—not through conversion and regeneration. There was no Bible, no hymnal, and no Bible teachers or spiritual leaders. But God, in His providence and in His own time, brought the Garlows to our people.

Jim Garlow and his team took a hazardous journey of a week or more to reach the Simte, who are mountain-top dwellers. They took a ferryboat and then went on foot for many days. His first visit and preaching resulted in mass regeneration, which was followed by believers' baptism. There was a great joy among our people, which was followed by a great feasting ceremony. In his evangelistic trips, Rev. Garlow covered most of the Simte villages in the hills and valleys. As a result of his effort, the New Testament Baptist Churches Association came into existence in the late 1950s.

Rev. Garlow did everything he could to build up this association. He took young people for Bible and nurses' training. He helped us to translate the Bible into our mother tongue. He helped us to start and run Bible schools and Christian day schools. In short, he was behind us in everything.

Today as we look back, we have a million reasons to be thankful to the Lord for sending His brave soldier to us. Jim Garlow has since gone home to be with the Lord, but the work he started and built up is growing by God's grace. During the past five decades, the New Testament Baptist Churches Association grew from 20 small local churches to 46. The whole Simte tribe has been reached and won for Christ.

Now we have the complete Bible in our own language. We have our own hymnal. We run a Bible school and 10 Christian day schools. The Lord enables us to send out missionaries who are actively involved in planting churches. When the Garlows retired, their work continued to grow and reproduce after its own kind. Their colaborer, Dr. Paul Versluis, carried on the good work. With Dr. Paul Versluis' vision and untiring effort, churches were planted in Asian countries. Many projects have been adopted and funded to evangelize and to reach the lost for Christ.

We praise God and plead His grace to bless Baptist Mid-Missions to enlist and send out more brave soldiers and heroes like the Garlows to conquer the world for Christ. They have poured their lives into us and have perpetuated their names in our hearts. In fact, we are the crown of their rejoicing, and only eternity will reveal how much we are indebted and thankful to the Lord and to them. We also praise God for all those who supported and labored with the Garlows. We give glory and honor unto the only living, wise, and eternal God. Hallelujah, Amen.

With Stammering Lips
Nancy Knopf

Nancy was appointed with Baptist Mid-Missions in 1966 to serve in Chad. Civil unrest in the early 1970s forced many missionaries off the field, including Nancy. She served six years in neighboring Central African Republic before transferring to North America. She has been serving with Baptist Youth Ministries since 1980.

In November of 1968, as a new, very green missionary, I arrived in Chad, Africa. In January of 1969, the Lord led me to Kyabé to work with the Robert Vaughns. I had spent a year and a half learning French; now I needed to learn the local language, Sara Kaba. That very month I began language study, which is a slow process because Sara Kaba is a tonal language. It isn't just what you say but how you say it that determines the meaning of the word.

When Bible school began later that year, I was asked to teach one course in French and one in Sara Kaba! Often I wrote out every word and went over the lesson first with Banga, my Chadian tutor. It also helped that the students were accustomed to "missionary Sara Kaba," and that they really wanted to study the Bible!

One day, after teaching in the morning and having a language lesson in the afternoon, I decided to take a break. I rode my bike past the dispensary and the "sick huts." As I did, I felt the Holy Spirit wanted me to stop to talk with the patients. I began making excuses in my mind. People staying at the sick huts might not understand my fledgling Sara Kaba. They might (and often do) speak a different dialect. I might not understand them. So I rode by.

But to return home there was only one path, the same one I came on—the one going past the dispensary. I felt the same need to witness to someone at the sick huts. Well, I could get my Gospel of John and read some verses. Romans had not yet been translated into Sara Kaba, so I could not use the Romans Road or the verses that go with it.

Returning to the sick huts, I first came upon a man and two women sitting outside on a grass mat. I greeted them in Sara Kaba and they responded. They actually understood what I said! I asked where they were from and who was sick. (Usually family members come to cook food for the sick person, and it was not apparent which one was ill.) In short order, I exhausted my conversational Sara Kaba, so I asked if they were believers. They all said, "Yes," and told me where they attended church. Ah, they undoubtedly had heard missionary Sara Kaba before.

I left them and walked over to a young girl sitting outside on some old bed springs. I greeted her. No response. I asked her name. No response. I asked the name of her village. No response. She was either very bashful or was not understanding my words, or both.

By this time, the man I had spoken to earlier took pity on both of us and came over. He spoke to the girl and she responded. But I could not understand a thing she said! So the man turned to me and interpreted her words in simple Sara Kaba. I asked her if she knew Jesus as her Savior. The man took my words and put them in her dialect. She answered, "No!"

She told him that today, when the morning message was preached at the dispensary, was the first time she had heard about Jesus. Just now she had been sitting outside, wondering what that message was all about. That day, God saw a young girl who needed Christ as Savior but could not wait until I spoke good Sara Kaba. He brought me to her because, as a missionary, I knew how to lead someone to Christ, even if I could not speak good Sara Kaba. And He placed nearby a fellow believer, who knew good Sara Kaba but did not know how to lead someone to Christ, to act as an interpreter. God brought the three of us together, and on that day this young girl prayed to receive Christ.

I had the joy of leading other Sara Kabas to Christ, but I shall never forget that first convert. That event convinced me again that God saves and that He will direct people and circumstances to see that it happens. "Not that we are sufficient of ourselves to think any thing as of ourselves; but our sufficiency is of God ... But we have this treasure in earthen vessels, that the excellency of the power may be of God, and not of us" 2 Corinthians 3:5; 4:7.

Our Little Missionary
Eugene E. Williams

Eugene joined Baptist Mid-Missions in 1955. On his way to a BMM confer-
ence, he met another single missionary, Enid Alber. The two married in
1956. Their years in Ghana had many struggles, but they kept a good spirit
and focus on the Lord. After retiring from the field in 1971, the Williamses
served in a pastorate in Maine. Enid went to be with the Lord in 2006.

The excitement started the day before our daughter Beth was
born in 1957. My wife Enid and I had come to Ghana as missionaries
and were staying in Teshie with our best friends. My wife started to have
contractions in the middle of the night, so we woke our friends early in
the morning. A few minutes later, we were on our way to Agogo Hospital—150 rough miles away. As it turned out, there was no hurry, as Beth
did not arrive until 3:00 p.m.—bright and happy and all smiles.

We stayed in Agogo two weeks. Then our missionary colleague
Mr. Hayes came and took us to Tumu, about 250 miles north. In Tumu,
Beth enjoyed the hot, dry weather. Every day, we would read the Bible to
her, sing, and pray. She liked the singing the best. Some mornings, Enid
would go over to town to teach the ladies in different compounds about
Christ. Sometimes Beth would go with her mom, and the African ladies
and children would touch her arms and her blond hair. In the evening, I
would go to different villages and preach the good news.

While we were in Tumu, our twins were born. When they arrived, there were no twins in the Tumu area. One of the twins always
died at birth; it was a curse to let them both live. We lived in Tumu a year
and a half after the twins were born. We received many curses and were
not permitted to return for our second term.

We were in Ghana two and a half years when my wife got sick.
Then I became very sick and never really got over the illness. We were 85
miles from the closest doctor, and he came to Tumu only once a month.

So when Beth was almost three years old, we went on furlough
back to the United States. Then it was little Beth's turn to get sick. The
first hospital we took her to couldn't help her. She was just too ill. We
took her to the best doctor and the best hospital in Cleveland, Ohio. They
diagnosed Beth with leukemia.

At the time of Beth's diagnosis, I succumbed again to the African diseases that I carried around in my body. They put me on the third floor of the Cleveland Clinic and Beth on the seventh floor. Beth just kept getting worse. Our pastor came and prayed for her and told her that people all over the world were praying for our family.

One day the doctor told Enid that Beth would die that night. She was just skin and bones—an awful sight to look at. My poor wife left Beth and came down to tell me the sad news. She did not know how to tell me that Beth had only a few hours to live, but God gave her the words to say. We prayed together, and then she went back to be with Beth. I cried and prayed the best I could, asking God to let me see my daughter once more before she died. Then I went to sleep. My wife was so exhausted that she had to go home to bed as well.

A friend from our church, Dr. Yevon, volunteered to stay all night with Beth. She sang and prayed and quoted Bible verses all night. That day Beth's body had refused to accept any more blood through the tube in her leg, but about 3:00 a.m. Dr. Yevon said she saw a drop go into her vein and then another. The blood began to flow into Beth's body again!

God heard the prayers of all our family and friends in Cleveland, Ghana, and around the world. Beth started to get better. The doctors could not believe it when she started to get cantankerous and began asking them to let her go home. At that time, Beth was one out of 1,000 that experienced remission from leukemia.

I was released from the hospital, and my family and I stayed with my friend Ben McGrew. Beth joined us there and spent her recovery listening to Christian records. The one she liked best was a song about Jesus and the children. It said, "Even the little children can believe."

One time while the record was playing, Beth said, "Dad! Stop the record! Stop the record!"

"What is it?" I asked, alarmed.

"Can I be saved?" asked Beth.

"Yes!" I said with a big smile. "Just tell Jesus that you believe He is God and ask him to save you from your sins." Beth did just that, and then we went right off to tell her Mom and Mr. and Mrs. McGrew and everyone else the good news.

Beth was three years old when our daughter Adissa was born. She looked just like Beth, and Beth loved her. We taught all our kids how to sing, memorize Bible verses, and talk to God.

Every so often, Beth had to go back to the hospital for painful tests. Once in December, she went for tests and asked the nurse if she was saved (just like her Dad did). The nurse replied, "No, but I would like to hear about Him." So Beth sang "Gospel Bells" to her and quoted John 3:16. The nurse asked Enid if Beth could sing to all the other doctors and nurses. Enid agreed. It took them about 45 minutes to make the rounds. Beth was a little tired, but she loved every minute of it.

About every six months or so, Beth got really bad headaches and we would find ourselves back in the nearest hospital. One day I went to see her at the hospital, and Beth told me that none of the nurses there loved Jesus. I asked, "How do you know this?"

Beth replied, "I asked them." So we prayed for them.

When Beth was five, we all moved to Ashtabula, Ohio, to stay with Grandma Williams. Beth started kindergarten. About this time, she told her mother that she and Great-grandma were going to go see Jesus. Beth enjoyed kindergarten, although she couldn't run and play with the other children. A few months went by before Beth got sick again. This time she did not get well. At Christmas, she memorized Luke 2:1-12, sang, played quiet games, and studied at home because she was too sick to return to school. She just kept getting worse until one day she asked me, "Dad, how long before I see Jesus?"

During her last week, she couldn't eat very much or tolerate anyone touching her. One day in May, I took her outside to pick violets. The man next door gave her a piece of candy, and she thanked him. She had a good sleep that night, and the next morning she saw the Son in Heaven. We have had many trials, but all for the glory of the gospel of Christ.

After Beth's death in May 1963, the Lord called us to return to Accra, Ghana, and serve Him there.

God Be Merciful to Me a Sinner
Gordon Katsion

Gordon and his first wife Rosemary joined Baptist Mid-Missions in 1965 to serve in Jamaica. In 1976, the Katsions transferred fields to Great Britain and then to Bibles International in 1979. The Lord took Rosemary home to be with Him in 1998. The following year, Gordon married Virginia Wilterink, and he continues to serve with Bibles International.

In 1970 I witnessed the power of the Holy Spirit to convict a man of his sin without much human intervention. We were holding a prayer meeting at Hillview Baptist Church in Montego Bay, Jamaica. We had our normal time of Bible study and preaching but nothing particularly evangelistic. It was for believers. In attendance that night was a sergeant in the Jamaican police force who had come with one of the church members.

After we had the Bible study, we divided up into men's and women's groups to pray. I, of course, went with the men. We went into one of the rooms in the church and began praying in turn around a circle. As we prayed one after the other, I assumed this visitor would just nudge the fellow next to him and not pray. To my surprise, the sergeant prayed the sinner's prayer of repentance! It was so beautiful—just like from the Scriptures. He was a man asking God to forgive him of his sins and to save him. After the prayer meeting was over, he excused himself and left. I chatted with the man he had come with.

"No, he hasn't been here before," he said, in response to my question. "This was his first time."

"I'm amazed," I said.

Sunday morning, the sergeant and his wife were in church. During the closing hymn, he came forward with his wife. Then he said, "Wednesday night I got saved. My wife is a Christian. We want to come and be baptized and join Hillview Baptist Church in Montego Bay." Such is the power of God to transform a life.

Not Beyond His Reach
Doris Youmans

In 1950, Doris began her service with Baptist Mid-Missions, appointed for the field of Japan. For nearly 40 years, the Lord used her to change lives for the glory of Christ in that country.

Many years ago now, my coworker Evelyn and I received a letter from a young lady who lived way over in the mountains of Japan. Although it was still in the same prefecture, her village was quite a distance away from us. She wrote that she was not a Christian but had acquired a

Bible and would like some more information. So I started corresponding with her and sent her Christian literature. Eventually this young lady came to believe in the Lord Jesus Christ.

But how did this woman way over in the mountains in a village with no Christian witness come to hear about us? It's wonderful how the Lord brings circumstances around so that those with hungry hearts meet someone who can help them.

It happened like this. One year, I went by train to the coast to help my fellow missionaries, the Zinkes, in their work. On a Sunday afternoon, I was returning from Iwaki over to Fukushima, and I got into a conversation with a woman on the train. Amazed that I could speak Japanese, she asked me how long I had lived in Japan.

The next morning, I received a telephone call from a young reporter, and he said, "You met my wife on the train yesterday, and I hear you have been in Japan a long time. May I come and interview you?" I agreed and he came over. Evelyn was with me at the time, and so he took our pictures and interviewed us. The interview appeared in the newspaper. And that's how the young lady way over in the mountains heard about us.

Later I came to realize just how far away her village was. I had to take three trains and two buses to get there. But I was able to meet her. She's continuing with the Lord now, and she writes to me. She doesn't get to church very often, because the nearest church that preaches the gospel is about two hours away by public transportation. But I'm glad for her salvation, and I praise the Lord that He created a way for her to hear the gospel and be saved way out there in the mountains of Japan.

Jun
Sharon Keller

Sharon and her husband Mike have a special heart for the national and international students with whom they work at Florida International University in Miami. The Kellers have been serving in Campus Bible Fellowship International with Baptist Mid-Missions since 1999.

We have many names written in our guest book, and each name has a story to tell … a story of God's love and providence. The students who visit our home, we believe, do not come by chance. While we like to entertain and welcome them, we understand that each has come by a divine appointment by the loving hand of God. It gives us great joy to serve with Campus Bible Fellowship International in Miami, Florida, and to be a part of their stories, even if for only one evening.

Reading through our guest book, you will find some of their names easy to manage, such as Ana, Apple, Yolanda, Fawn, Monica, Miguel, and Maria. If you are not a linguist, others present a small challenge such as Yuanyuan, Swapna, Supna, Snigdha, Smitha, Sreepat, and Srividya. But each one was told the sweet news of the gospel in our home, and many of these have put their faith in Jesus Christ. Others have come dozens of times to study the Scriptures, but we still wait to see what God writes in the next chapter of their stories.

When I see the name Jun, a beautiful story echoes through my memory. Jun came to our home every Saturday morning for Bible study. While working on her PhD, Jun felt the need to explore the Bible with me while she was here in America from China. From the very first day, I saw that God had more to add to her story.

My introductory lesson to the Bible typically lasts an hour, but Jun was thirsty beyond my comprehension. The more we talked, the more she wanted to know. Even though this was her first time to see a Bible, she was very receptive. The lunch hour passed, but I sensed she was ready to hear the entire plan of salvation. Jun said she had heard of the name "Jesus" once in China but was visibly shaken when I told her Jesus was God.

When I neared the end of the gospel story, Jun's eyes were full of tears as she said, "So, should I trust in Jesus from this day on?" As we talked a little further, she felt she needed to think on it a little more. Then Jun asked, "If I put my faith to Jesus, should I tell you?"

"You should tell God first," I said, "then you can tell me."

I gave Jun her own Bible—a simple leather one with gold-edged pages. She stroked it with awe and tenderness. She took it home to her husband, who proclaimed, "It is all glory!"

Over the next 12 months, Jun and I rarely missed a Saturday morning together over the Word of God. She brought me questions such as: "How can I know these are God's words He gave so long ago? What commands does He have for me? How can I know where to find them in the Bible? How can I know Jesus is really alive? Can we compare Communism with God—just another idea to believe in to better one's life on Earth?"

One morning she seemed a little miffed at me. Finally she blurted out, "Why does God look like you?" After puzzling for a moment, I realized she wanted to know why God was "American" and not Chinese.

"He doesn't look like me," I said.

Jun squinted, "He doesn't? But I went to that museum in Washington DC last month and saw that painting. He looks like you."

Jun continued to grapple with truth. When I taught her more about sin and salvation, I mentioned that we either belong to God or we belong to Satan. Jun cringed over the little diagram I had drawn and wrinkled up her tiny nose. "I really don't consider myself to belong to the Devil; I don't want to belong to him. Is there a third option?" After more Scripture, explanation, and discussion, she picked up her Bible and stroked it carefully. "I believe this Bible book."

"You do?"

"Well … most of it," Jun replied. Given that she had read only the first 27 chapters, I saw that God was deep at work in her story.

About eight months after we began our studies together, I saw her heart was very heavy with the weight of sin. After two and a half hours one Saturday, "digging through the deep things," as she called it, Jun asked me, "Why do you always have to use the word 'sin'? It's such an ugly word." The same day she asked me if it was normal for people to struggle with belief as she was struggling.

Then one day Jun shared with me that her mother in China was very ill. Even though Jun did not yet believe, she wanted to know how her mother would find out about God. I told her I would pray that God would send someone to tell her mother about Jesus. In the coming days, God laid it upon my heart to tell her myself. I asked Jun if I could write a letter to her mother and have her translate it for me. Jun began weeping and readily agreed to take a letter I would write in English and translate it word by word and mail it to her mother, along with a Bible in Chinese.

During our translation preparation, another young lady from China, whom God had saved through our Bible studies, called me. "Grace" was making an emergency trip to China because her father had suffered a heart attack. She called to ask me if I knew where she could get a Bible in Chinese to take to him. I had two on my shelf. As God would have it, Grace volunteered to take both Bibles and the translated letter to China to deliver them. Jun, Grace, and I were all deeply moved with emotion when we discovered in the days ahead that Grace's father and Jun's mother lived in the very same town!

Jun e-mailed me and wrote, "I can feel Grace is the right person to send the Book ... she and I came from the same city, U____. I doubt she knows me. Sharon, what an amazing it is! I think it is the time to let my Mom to know the God."

God allowed Grace to hand-deliver both Bibles, the translated letter, and an oral message of the gospel without incident. I was so thankful that God knew where the city of U____ was located! I had no idea it even existed.

In the following weeks, my husband Mike went to hear Jun's husband defend his thesis in Chemistry. Mike did not understand a single word of it, but Jun's husband David was greatly moved that he would attend. I also had opportunity to include Jun in some church activities such as the ladies Christmas tea, where she heard once again the beautiful truth God had prepared for her before the foundations of the world. As I continued to develop our relationship outside of Bible studies, I watched while God moved His perfect pen in writing the story of Jun's life.

A few months later, Jun came for her usual Saturday Bible study. She was noticeably without her usual barrage of questions. When we finished, I asked her if she had any questions or comments.

"Yes, I want to tell you that I have put my faith to the God."

"Can you tell me about it?" I asked.

Jun's eyes filled with tears as she waved her hand helplessly, "Can I have a towel?" I got the box of tissues, and she wept for a few minutes even before she could speak. Jun told me that a few days earlier, she had come to the end of herself and realized she needed God. Jun was sure that she was a sinner and believed that Jesus is God. Jun said she believed that Jesus rose from the dead, and she now wanted to follow Him. Jun went on to say that she had immediately told her husband and then called her mother in China. "I will now be telling a lot of people," Jun said.

My husband was home that day, so she wanted to tell him also. When Jun told Mike what she had done, she ended her story with, "... so I realized I needed a new life." I responded with a quiet, "Amen."

Jun looked at me and asked, "What is that word?"

Ah, yes, one chapter entitled "Salvation" finished by God and the next one entitled "Discipleship" begins with His perfect hand and a fresh page. It was one year to the day that I had labored with Jun over the "deep things," as she likes to call them. Her husband has since been gloriously saved, and his life transformed—truly a new man.

When I see a name in our family guest book, I cannot help but wonder at what the Master Author has waiting to be penned for each one. I may not always be able to pronounce their names correctly, but Jesus knows each name, as well as every little word and letter of their story.

The Life That Does Not Satisfy
Robert Meyer

In 1953, Bob and his wife Lena began serving with Baptist Mid-Missions, appointed to the Dominican Republic. The Lord gave them a fruitful ministry there, but in 1988 they were challenged to open the field of Ecuador for BMM. This they did, and many other missionaries joined them. The Meyers retired in 1999. Their three children, Richard, Jeannie, and Anita, and their spouses serve with Baptist Mid-Missions.

Young ChiChi ran with the fastest crowd of playboys in Latin America. His buddy's dad was Generalisimo Rafael Leonidas Trujillo, the dictator of the Dominican Republic. The dictator's fortune was worth about $800 million, and the boys liked to help him spend it. But in 1961, Trujillo was assassinated, and his son fled to Europe with the family's wealth.

ChiChi had to find some new companions. He lived across the street from our church and started attending Bible studies. He eventually came to know the Lord as His Savior. When I preached on the book of Ecclesiastes in which Solomon laments the vanity of all that the world has to offer, ChiChi testified, "Pastor, that book was written about me. I tried it all, and it did not satisfy."

Another time he testified, "I used to think that I was living the life, but now I've found what satisfies."

ChiChi led the song service in that church for nearly 30 years— radiating the joy of the Lord. He's an example of a transformed life from being in one of the fastest crowd of playboys to being a godly servant in a Baptist church.

From Bitterness to Joy

Alice Smith

Neal and Alice Smith served with Baptist Mid-Missions in Brazil from 1952 to 1992. After retiring in 1993, they returned to Oregon. Neal went home to be with the Lord 10 years later in December of 2003.

Maria was a Brazilian woman filled with bitterness and hatred for everyone. She was especially bitter towards the men in her life—her father, who had abandoned her when she was just a child, and her husband, who drank too much. She had much of what life could offer—social status, a teaching career, and two lovely daughters. Yet her life was empty, bitter, and without purpose or joy.

Maria envied her sister-in-law, Aline. Lately, a great change had come into Aline's life. In the past she had abandoned her Catholic faith for spiritism. But now she was reading the Bible, attending a little Baptist church, and even doing Bible lessons with her neighbors and friends. She radiated happiness and fulfillment.

Aline encouraged Maria to read the Bible and study the lessons entitled, "What Does the Bible Say About Salvation." After much persuasion, Maria began to read the Word of God. She couldn't understand what she was reading but kept at it because she longed for the joy and peace that Aline had.

One day, Maria became convinced that she was a sinner and needed the Savior. When she accepted the Lord Jesus Christ as her Savior, a great change came over her life. She was amazed at how peace and harmony now reigned between herself and her husband and her two daughters. Her family and neighbors were shocked when she greeted them with a cheery, "Good morning." She began attending Aline's church regularly and grew rapidly in the Lord.

Maria repeatedly knelt before the Lord in prayer, asking Him to remove the bitterness and hatred that had so long consumed her life. The Lord heard and gave her sweet relief. What peace and joy swept through her being! She had a desire to forgive her father and to tell him the good news of salvation. With one of her sons-in-law, she made the 12-hour trip by bus to present her father with a Bible and to ask him for forgiveness for shutting him out of her life. She encouraged him to receive the Lord.

Over time, she became a sought-out speaker for women's groups. After her retirement from her teaching career, she offered to teach Portuguese at the Parana Regular Baptist Bible School in south Brazil. She taught there without pay for many years. Only upon the school's insistence did she accept remuneration for her traveling expenses.

Maria's husband accepted the Lord on his deathbed. Her two daughters, along with their husbands and children, have all given their hearts to the Lord. Maria and Aline continue faithfully serving the Lord Jesus and reaching out to those who need the Savior.

She Just Did Not Give Up
S. David and Geri Smith

David and Geri have been with Baptist Mid-Missions since 1987 and have served their entire career in Brazil. The Smiths are currently planting a church in the city of Londrina in Brazil's Paraná State.

Lica's desire in life was to see her parents saved. Ever since she had received Christ 11 years before, she had been praying for her parents' salvation. While in Bible college, Lica witnessed many times to her parents but always to no avail. She prayed and prayed for them. Lica graduated from our Bible college in 1997.

In January of 1998, Lica began a simple Bible study with her mom, Mônica, and after a few weeks her mother accepted Christ as her Savior. Mônica's biggest excuse for not coming to Victory Baptist Church in Curitiba, Brazil, was that she did not want to leave her invalid husband, José, at home by himself.

In July, Lica's 80-year-old father's health began to deteriorate, and José was taken to the hospital several times. The church began to pray in earnest for his health and salvation. Lica, concerned about her father's spiritual condition without Christ, went to the hospital and witnessed to him. José heard the gospel from his 24-year-old daughter, but he willingly rejected it.

Two hours later, José went into a coma. The doctors said he would never awake from the coma. Four days later, he came out of it and was conscious for about a week before he died. Two days before he passed away, they sent him home from the hospital. His health only deteriorated, and he was rushed to the hospital about an hour before he went into eternity. Thus died José.

The next day, as the family members were collecting his personal items from the hospital room, they met one of the male nurses that had helped take care of José. A few days before, while the family was visiting, this nurse had asked them if José was a Christian. They had responded no. Wondering why he might have asked that, they questioned him about it. In response, the nurse said that before José had left the hospital, José had told him that he was a "Christian."

After the funeral, José's wife said that 24 hours before he died, he had told her in a weak, whispering voice: "I ...... accepted ...... Christ ...... as ...... my ...... Savior." We did not know about that until after the funeral.

For 10 years, Mônica had taken care of her invalid husband. After his death, she did not know what to do. She was 60 years old and was not in good health. She became depressed, and two months later she also died.

God answered a daughter's prayer after 11 years of praying diligently for her parents. Did she ever get discouraged? Did she ever get hurt that they rejected the Christ she loved so much? Did she ever wonder if God was going to answer her prayers? Did she ever wonder if she was just wasting her time? The answer to each of these is "Yes." But did she let that stop her? No!

Since 1999, Lica has been serving the Lord as a missionary in the northern part of her state of Paraná. She has served in the cities of Weissopolis, Londrina, and Japurá, Paraná. Her brother is now a pastor—all because Lica would not give up praying and sharing the love of God with her family.

Saved out of the Hills of Missouri
Ken Moon

Ken and Lynne Moon joined Baptist Mid-Missions in 1987. They oversee Missionary Acres, Baptist Mid-Missions' retirement village in Silva, Missouri. Lynn is the daughter of retired missionaries Leon and Marvilyn Williams.

Down one of the rough boulder-strewn roads in rural southeast Missouri, where Missionary Acres is located, lived a little second-grade boy by the name of Jason. Every Sunday and Tuesday night I went by his house to pick him up for church and Bible Seekers Club. Time and again he said he wasn't interested, but I kept going back. When I knocked at the door of his house, chickens came flying out of the windows. There was no glass in the windows and just cardboard on the door. The house would have made a small garage in the city—but they had a satellite dish out in the yard.

Finally, Jason came to church with us. He began to come to Bible Seekers off and on when he was home. One night at club, Jason and another boy named James raised their hands, indicating that they needed to be saved in response to the Bible lesson that night. I led James to the Lord during game time, but Jason didn't respond to the invitation. As club drew to a close, the Lord seemed to really impress on my heart that I needed to talk to Jason.

When I took kids home after club, Jason's house was usually my first stop. But that night I decided to take him home last. On the way back around those gravel roads, I pulled up next to an old barn and said, "Jason would you like to receive the Lord Jesus as your Savior?"

"I sure would, Mr. Moon," he said. I had the joy of leading Jason to the Lord. What a thrill it was to hear him receive Christ as Savior. He prayed the sweetest and most sincere prayer I have ever heard anyone pray. He was so excited afterwards.

Jason moved three weeks after that, and we haven't seen him since. I still go by that old house every week as I pick up other kids. As I drive by, I often think, "What if I hadn't stopped at that house to visit that little boy? What if I had not obeyed the Lord's leading that night?" I thank the Lord that I took that opportunity to share Jesus Christ with Jason and that as a result he is now a child of God.

Persecution in Rakusy

LeAnne Waite

LeAnne Muhr grew up as a BMM Missionary Kid in the Central African Republic (CAR). She was appointed with Baptist Mid-Missions in 1992 to serve in the land that she grew up in. Two years later, she married Don Waite, who shared her calling. However, political tensions in CAR made it impossible to conduct ministry there. The Waites served briefly in Ethiopia before transferring to Slovakia, where they are church planters.

My husband Don and our coworker Michael had been seeking to bring the gospel of Jesus Christ to the Gypsy village of Rakusy since October 2007. With Michael and Sarah Stevens, we had added an afternoon Gypsy service to the ministries of Independent Baptist Church of Kezmarok, Slovakia. We had seen several Gypsies receive Christ as Savior, including a number of young men from Rakusy, about eight kilometers from Kezmarok.

A Gypsy couple from Podhorany, Marian and Maria Pista, had been saved and baptized in February 2008. They were anxious to help in the outreach to Rakusy. So in May 2008, we decided to try to hold several days of Vacation Bible School for the children of the village.

From the beginning of the men's visits to Rakusy, there had been a problem with the children in the village. Often the children threw mud at the men and spat upon them. They'd scratched the vehicles and broken a headlight. Several things had been stolen. In spite of the harassment, we saw God work in the lives of several young men who had been saved in the Sunday services.

We left home at 2:30 in the afternoon in two vehicles: my husband and I and our son David; the Stevenses with their toddler Olivia; Marian and Maria; and a man from Ohio, Justin Brenenstahl. Along with us was a translator for Justin. We arrived at Rakusy a couple of minutes after 3:00 and parked the vehicles at the end of the village beside the soccer field. It was the first time Sarah, Olivia, David, and I had been to the village.

As soon as the vehicles arrived, kids started coming and coming and coming. There were lots of adults and teenagers hanging around too. We had quite a time getting any semblance of order. These kids are highly undisciplined.

When we finally had a good number sitting on the ground and the rest in the vicinity, Justin did a magic trick or two. After the tricks— and getting everyone halfway quiet again—Sarah and Michael taught them a chorus in the Gypsy language. After that, Justin did a short Bible lesson on Noah. During this whole time, things went much more smoothly than any of us anticipated. At least five or six of the young men who had been coming to church on Sunday and who had accepted Christ as their Savior were there to help with crowd control. Marian and Maria were also helping.

After the Bible lesson, the kids were divided into two groups to try to play a game involving two soccer balls. Things began to unravel at this point. There were just too many kids to control, when they don't know what control means.

After the game, Justin wanted to pass out balloons and candy. He asked the kids to wait at one of the soccer goals while he gave the bags of balloons twisted into different shapes to the young men that were there to help pass them out to the kids. We were standing at the vehicles at this point. As soon as Don opened one door of the vehicle to get the first bag of balloons, the kids mobbed the van. The balloons in the bag were broken.

The men decided that we needed to leave before things got more out of control. We put everyone in our van except Justin and Michael. They got in the Stevens' vehicle and pulled out in front of our van. As soon as we started moving, the van was mobbed and the back window was shattered. Don kept driving. David and Maria were in the back seat. Thankfully, there were no serious injuries. Maria had a minuscule cut on her elbow, and David had a sliver of glass on one of his fingers but no cuts. I have to admit that all of us were a little shaken. David had really looked forward to going. He was a pretty scared 11-year-old. He'd been harassed some before the window was shattered, and that was the straw that broke the camel's back, so to speak.

When we got a distance from the village, Don and Michael pulled over, and we transferred several people to the Stevenses' vehicle, as the glass was falling out of our window with each bump we hit.

When we got back to the church, one of the first questions Marian asked was, "When are we going again?" Maria's initial reaction was, "I'm not ever going back to that village again." However, within a very short time she was offering to speak with her brother, who lives in Rakusy, to see if we could have a children's program in his home. We had a time of prayer before everyone dispersed.

On Wednesday, Don, Michael, Justin, and Marian visited Rakusy again. The visit went well. At the end of their visit, they met a man who teaches in the school out there. He offered to arrange a place for us at the school the next time we want to do a children's program. Several said they would be in church on Sunday.

On Sunday, the men left at 1:00 p.m. to go pick people up for the service. At 1:30, two young teenage boys came into the auditorium and sat down. Sarah and I asked them if they had come with the men. Don had led one of the boys, David, to the Lord the week before. David said that they hadn't seen the men. They had come in by bus just for the service. We waited and waited and waited. The men didn't return until 2:20 p.m.

Honestly, we had been getting a little nervous. When they came in, there were several new faces in the group, including a man named Yullow and another middle-aged man named Mirro. At the end of the service, Mirro accepted Christ as his Savior.

Yullow talked to Don after the service. He told him that the Catholic priest had been telling people they shouldn't come to our church. He told Don, "I came today to see for myself. I like what I saw. I like the singing and I like the message. I am going home to tell my wife and family that it is okay. I will bring them next week. I am Catholic. I am not ready to accept Christ, but I will bring my family next week."

Later, we learned that the reason the men were late was because they met an elderly man who invited them into his house to ask them about salvation. He, too, had accepted Christ that afternoon. On Tuesday, Michael and Justin went back to visit this elderly gentleman in his home. He understood the decision he had made and was very happy to see them.

Marian and Maria had not been in the service on Sunday, which was very unusual for them, so on Friday afternoon Don, Michael, and Justin decided to visit them. When they arrived, Marian wasn't home so they spoke with Maria. She was visibly shaking. Maria told Michael they couldn't come on Sunday. She said she didn't feel well. Michael said, "Maria, it is Friday. How can you know if you will feel well on Sunday? What is really the matter?" She then broke down and said their family had been pressuring them not to come to the services. It was so typical of the way the Catholic Church operates to put pressure on the family in this way. They were withholding baptism from Ivan, their oldest son's child, because Marian and Maria were attending services at the Baptist church. Their son, who owned the house they were living at, told them to move out. As the persecution persisted, Marian and Maria dropped out of the Gypsy Baptist church.

We were a little apprehensive about the afternoon service the next week. It was pouring rain when the men left. In the past, that has been fuel for the kids in Rakusy to cover Don and Michael with mud. We have also found that when it is raining, few people come. We weren't anticipating much ... shame on us! There were 17 Gypsies in the service. Don had to go back to the village for a second carload of people. Yullow was there with his wife, daughter, and son-in-law. Mirro was there at 1:00 so that he could go with the men and make sure the people that he had invited came. There were at least six new faces in the service. At the end of the service, Don had the privilege of leading Yullow and then his wife Ruženka to the Lord. Michael led another young man and Yullow's daughter to the Lord. Yullow wore a huge grin as he walked back to his seat.

So, in spite of the difficulties, God blessed. We have been studying through the book of Acts with the kids in Kids' Club on Friday afternoons. One of the things they are learning is that God often uses persecution as a means of growing His church. It is a comfort to know that God's work will go forward, that Satan has already been defeated. How thrilling to see God at work in the hearts and lives of people. How thrilling to have the privilege of allowing God to work through us to love these people. Our prayer is that God would help us to see these people the way He sees them and that they may see the love of God in us and that God would use us to lead them to Him. We pray that God would give us this village as a shining testimony in this region of His love and power to save and change people.

Tell Us About Jesus
Bill Brown

Bill and his wife Clara began service with Baptist Mid-Missions in 1955. Their early ministry was in Central African Republic and Chad. In 1969 Bill pastored a church in Iowa, and he and Clara worked with Campus Bible Fellowship (now known as Campus Bible Fellowship International). The

Browns returned to Central African Republic for several years before retiring in 1999. Bill went to be with the Lord in 2009 and Clara in 2010.

The two men had bicycled for days with one objective in mind—to find someone in Chad who could tell them about Jesus. In God's amazing providence, they came upon our Bible conference at a village on the main road to Fort Archambault, which is now called Sarh.

My wife and I were stationed in Goundi, Chad, and I often made trips into the surrounding areas. On this particular trip, I was only about a day away from home. Several pastors were with me, and several more had come from the surrounding area for this conference. While I was speaking on Sunday morning, these two fellows rode up on bicycles. We could tell that they had been on a dusty road for quite a while, because they were very dirty. As they approached the church, I wondered who they were. They sat right in front, in the place usually reserved for children. It was obvious that they were not accustomed to being in a church, but yet they listened intently.

I was preaching in the Sara Madjingaye language at the time, but the message was also being translated into Arabic because on that road there were many who did not know the Sarh languages. These men knew both languages, so they got the benefit of both translations. I invited those who wanted to know how to accept the Lord Jesus Christ as their Savior to remain after the service, and these two stayed.

I listened as Jacob, one of the pastors with me, dealt with them personally. They said that they had been on their way to Fort Archambault because they had heard that there were missionaries there who could tell them about Jesus. They had been traveling three or four days by bicycle when they had come upon our conference. Fort Archambault was still another day by bicycle. When they stopped at the conference, they were so excited that they were able to hear about Jesus without going all the way into Fort Archambault.

That day both of them received Christ as their Savior. The conference went on for a couple more days, and they stayed and had fellowship with us and learned more about the Bible.

They invited us to come to their village, which was way up in the north, toward the Sahara Desert, in a part of Chad that is predominately Muslim. At a later time, missionary Leo Sandgren and I took a trip up there, along with some Christian college students from our school in Fort Archambault. When we finally got to their village, we discovered that these two men had been faithfully and courageously telling everyone in their village about Jesus.

God's Mercy

Jesus' life on earth was characterized by mercy. In between teaching and preaching to the multitudes, He paused to meet the needs of individuals. He healed the blind, the lame, and the mute. He cleansed lepers and raised the dead.

A particularly powerful display of His mercy occurred outside the city gates of Nain. As a funeral possession passed by, Jesus observed the grieving mother, and compassion welled up in His heart. The woman was a widow, and the dead man was her only son. Approaching the sobbing woman, Jesus said, "Weep not." Then He touched the coffin and commanded, "Young man, I say unto thee, Arise." The dead man came back to life, sat up, and began to speak! (Luke 7:11-15). Jesus saw the sorrow of one woman and was compelled by His mercy to remove her pain. Even though crowds witnessed this miracle, Jesus did not do miracles to draw attention to Himself. Compassion is simply a part of His nature that has to be expressed.

The New Testament records several times where Jesus was "moved with compassion."

> And there came a leper to him, beseeching him, and kneeling down to him, and saying unto him, If thou wilt, thou canst make me clean. And Jesus, moved with compassion, put forth his hand, and touched him, and saith unto him, I will; be thou clean. And as soon as he had spoken, immediately the leprosy departed from him, and he was cleansed (Mark 1:40-42).

In His mercy, Jesus reached out and touched the leper, the outcast. Nobody touched lepers for fear of contamination, but Jesus did. He touched him and made him clean.

> The LORD is merciful and gracious, slow to anger, and plenteous in mercy. He will not always chide: neither will he keep his anger for ever. He hath not dealt with us after our sins; nor rewarded us according to our iniquities. For as the heaven is high above the earth,

> so great is his mercy toward them that fear him. As
> far as the east is from the west, so far hath he removed
> our transgressions from us. Like as a father pitieth his
> children, so the LORD pitieth them that fear him. For
> he knoweth our frame; he remembereth that we are dust
> (Psalm 103:8-14).

The Lord is merciful. He has a deep awareness of the suffering of people and is compelled to show compassion to the hurting and helpless. "Who is a God like unto thee, that pardoneth iniquity, and passeth by the transgression of the remnant of his heritage? he retaineth not his anger for ever, because he delighteth in mercy" (Micah 7:18).

God delights in reaching out in compassion to help. The Hebrew word *chesed*, often translated "mercy" or "lovingkindness," is used approximately 250 times in the Old Testament. The focal point of Israel's worship was the Tabernacle and the Ark of the Covenant. The covering of the Ark of the Covenant was called the mercy seat. The mercy seat was located in the Most Holy place in the Tabernacle.

> And there I will meet with thee, and I will
> commune with thee from above the mercy seat, from
> between the two cherubims which are upon the ark of
> the testimony, of all things which I will give thee in com-
> mandment unto the children of Israel (Exodus 25:22).

Man met with God and God met with man on the basis of mercy. Even under the law, God could not be something less than merciful, because it is His nature to be merciful. He is incapable of being indifferent to pain and suffering. Many of the psalms speak of this attribute of God. "But I will sing of thy power; yea, I will sing aloud of thy mercy in the morning: for thou hast been my defence and refuge in the day of my trouble. Unto thee, O my strength, will I sing: for God is my defence, and the God of my mercy" (Psalm 59:16-17).

God bestows mercy on the undeserving. Daniel writes,

> O my God, incline thine ear, and hear; open
> thine eyes, and behold our desolations, and the city
> which is called by thy name: for we do not present our
> supplications before thee for our righteousnesses, but for

thy great mercies. O Lord, hear; O Lord, forgive; O Lord,
hearken and do; defer not, for thine own sake, O my
God: for thy city and thy people are called by thy name
(Daniel 9:18-19).

He does not tell God all the good things that Israel had done in
order to be worthy of God's mercy. He admits their unrighteousness but
presents the need, fully convinced because of God's compassionate nature,
that He would indeed hear, forgive, and act on their behalf.

If God were not merciful, we would be without hope. Praise be
to God that His mercy is abundant and full and endures forever. "It is of
the LORD's mercies that we are not consumed, because his compassions
fail not. They are new every morning: great is thy faithfulness. The LORD
is my portion, saith my soul; therefore will I hope in him" (Lamentations
3:22-24).

The death of Jesus and the rending of the veil between God and
man opened the way for mercy to flow unrestricted to men.

Having therefore, brethren, boldness to enter
into the holiest by the blood of Jesus, by a new and living
way, which he hath consecrated for us, through the veil,
that is to say, his flesh; and having an high priest over the
house of God; let us draw near with a true heart in full
assurance of faith, having our hearts sprinkled from an
evil conscience, and our bodies washed with pure water
(Hebrews 10:19-22).

"For we have not an high priest which cannot be touched with
the feeling of our infirmities; but was in all points tempted like as we are,
yet without sin. Let us therefore come boldly unto the throne of grace,
that we may obtain mercy, and find grace to help in time of need" (Hebrews 4:15-16).

We cannot exhaust God's mercy. For as long as time exists and
man is on this fallen earth, God's mercy will be there to get us through.
Just as a father has compassion on his children, so the Lord has compassion on those who reverence Him.

He does not delight in our pain, although He knows that sometimes pain is necessary to produce Christlikeness. In His perfect kingdom, pain will be absent. "And God shall wipe away all tears from their

eyes; and there shall be no more death, neither sorrow, nor crying, neither shall there be any more pain: for the former things are passed away" (Revelation 21:4).

In a foretaste of that perfect kingdom, God in His mercy sometimes removes pain. In "Arrested," missionary Jennie Adams suffered for many years with back pain. But when she was arrested and was forced to sit all day in a prison cell, God healed her back in a rather unusual way.

God's children can look to the Father for deliverance in times of illness, sorrow, and danger. When deadly "Blackwater Fever" attacks five-year-old Paul Jeunnette in Africa, the doctor gives up hope for his survival. But the African believers beseech God for Paul's life, and in faith declare that God has heard.

God has a special place in His heart for strangers, orphans, and widows—the most helpless of any society.

> Thou shalt neither vex a stranger, nor oppress him: for ye were strangers in the land of Egypt. Ye shall not afflict any widow, or fatherless child. If thou afflict them in any wise, and they cry at all unto me, I will surely hear their cry; And my wrath shall wax hot, and I will kill you with the sword; and your wives shall be widows, and your children fatherless (Exodus 22:21-24).

> The righteous cry, and the LORD heareth, and delivereth them out of all their troubles. The LORD is nigh unto them that are of a broken heart; and saveth such as be of a contrite spirit. Many are the afflictions of the righteous: but the LORD delivereth him out of them all (Psalm 34:17-19).

In times of deprivation, the Lord will have mercy. In times of danger and disease, God will have mercy. He cannot help but be moved by compassion.

The stories in this section are evidence that Jesus continues to respond in kindness to the sorrows of mankind. In "Delivered from Fear," Rene Street shared that, as a young missionary, she was consumed by fear of the very people to whom God had called her to minister. So ashamed was she of this, she would not admit it to anyone. She could only turn it over to the Lord and beg Him to remove it from her. His mercy was sufficient.

God's mercy is abundant and full. Our sorrows and concerns are not lost on God. He cares about our needs and weeps with us in our adversity. God cares about our relationships with family and friends. In "Grandma Kawabata's Prayer" and "God Has the Solution," it is clear that God hears our prayers for our family members and is not insensitive to the longings of our hearts. The Lord asks us to cast all our cares on Him because He cares for us (1 Peter 5:7).

High Adventure in Brazil
Andrew Comings

In the 1990s, Andrew served short-term in Brazil with Baptist Mid-Missions. During this time, he met Itacyara Bezerra, and they married in 2000. Full-time missionaries since 2002, they are church planters in Itacyara's homeland of Brazil.

My trips with our Cariri Baptist Seminary students to visit their practical ministries have typically been anything but boring. I have crossed precarious bridges, had encounters with exotic wildlife, and met a host of interesting people. None of this, however, came close to the sheer adrenaline level I experienced one night.

That weekend, we had an evangelistic campaign in the city of Exu, about an hour from the seminary in Crato. People were saved, and God was glorified. Fresh from this exciting event, I piled into the truck with four young people (three seminary students and a girl from one of our local churches) and my son Mikey.

Between Exu and Crato there is a gigantic plateau, called the Serra do Araripe. To get home, it was necessary for us to climb the ridge, cross the plateau, and go down the other side. The roads on either side are steep and winding. The road on top is straight as an arrow, and desolate.

As we began our ascent, I noticed that the truck was not showing its usual "oomph." I attributed this to the fact that we were loaded to the gills with people and supplies. We eventually made it to the top and stopped at a gas station—the last outpost of civilization before the other side of the plateau. There we encountered the other members of our team in another pickup. The driver of that truck asked me if everything was OK, and I—not even thinking about the slight trouble I had just experienced—assured him that we were fine. Then we took off, the other vehicle in the front.

As the gas station faded into the background, I noticed that we were having trouble keeping up with the truck in front of us. I had the gas pedal to the floor, and still our companions were disappearing into the night. Soon they were gone. At just that point, the truck completely lost power. The engine was running, and would accelerate when I touched the gas, but somehow this was not being translated to the wheels, no matter what gear I tried.

Coasting to a stop and getting out of the car, we evaluated our situation. Simply put, we were stuck. Our options were limited to two—wait for someone to come back looking for us, or go get help. The first option was not attractive at all, considering the fact that we were alone in one of the more dangerous patches of road in the area and had no idea when people would figure out we were missing. The second option, while equally unattractive, did seem to be the lesser of the two evils. After all, looking back, I could still make out the green glow from the sign of the gas station we had just passed.

With this in mind, I gave instructions to Daniel—the only male student with us—to stay with the girls and Mikey while I walked back to get help. I placed an iron pipe in his hand—which I carry in the car at all times and affectionately refer to as my "security system"—and solemnly charged him with the protection of the women and child. Then I struck out in the direction of the light.

There being no streetlights and absolutely no houses anywhere nearby, the only illumination I had was provided by the stars. And what illumination! The night air caused them to appear much closer and bigger than normal, and I reveled in their beauty.

As I continued to walk, I would look at the stars and then at the greenish light in front of me. "Wouldn't it be funny, I thought, if that light in front of me were just another star?" That train of thought brought me up short. The same principle that made the stars appear closer than normal was also making the sign appear nearer than it actually was. Much nearer.

Suddenly, the prospect of a long walk in the dark caused fear to well up within me. The stories of assaults in that area returned to my mind in all their gory detail. I remembered at that point that every snake I have ever seen in the wild here in Brazil had been dead on the side of the road—and made the assumption that at one point they had been alive on the side of the road.

My ears became alert to even the slightest noise. Just about then, I saw the distant growing lights of a car. The possibility that they would stop and help was slim to none. Nobody stops on that road, and for good reason. As the headlights grew in front of me, I moved over to the side of the road to get out of their way. Just as the car passed, I stepped off the curb and onto some dried grass, which crackled under my feet. A dog barked somewhere nearby, and I ran like I had never run in my life.

As I strained my legs to get from them every possible ounce of speed, I listened intently for the sound of canine panting behind me. The only panting I heard came from me. Relieved, I slowed down to a walk.

Looking up, I saw the green glow of the sign in front of me. Looking back, I could no longer see the blinkers of the car. How far had I walked? How far did I still have to go? I had no idea. I continued to put one foot in front of the other, always looking toward the sign, which never seemed to grow bigger. The starry skies stretched in an endless circle around me. I began to lose all sense of distance and perspective.

Suddenly a light appeared, no more than 50 feet in front of me, and stayed there. I slowed my pace and listened for some sound. There was none. The light bobbed a little, and I got the distinct impression that it was a flashlight. I could not make out anything behind it. Glancing behind me, I saw another light—this one a little further off but still too close for comfort. Still no sound.

"Who's there?" I called out with a shaky voice. There was no answer. My heart began to race wildly, and I waged a desperate war against panic. My palms were sweaty and my tongue was dry. Faintly in the distance, I heard the sound of an engine. "If I can wait until the oncoming vehicle passes, I will be able to see what is behind the lights," I thought, "and if they are bandidos, I can make a run for it."

I stopped and waited. Slowly the sound of the motor grew louder. Suddenly, the light in front of me grew and divided into two. I jumped to the side of the road just as the large dump truck—whose lights I had seen long before I had heard the motor—passed by. I stood there for several seconds breathing hard and wiping gobs of sweat from my forehead. I could now see that the lights behind me were also from an oncoming truck.

I began to fervently pray that this truck—or any truck, for that matter—would stop and offer me a lift. Disappointment flooded me as the eighteen-wheeler roared past ... and then hope sprang anew as it stopped and began to back up! I ran up to the cab. The driver rolled down the window and looked at me.

"Are you the owner of the Hilux I saw back there?" he asked. I assured him that I was. "Hop in," he said. "I'll take you to the gas station." The only sweeter sound I have ever heard was when I asked my wife Itacyara to marry me, and she said yes.

I climbed into the cab of the truck, silently blessing all truck drivers everywhere. It was amazing how quickly the soft-green glow of the sign in front of me grew as we approached the gas station. The truck driver stopped, and I thanked him profusely before getting out.

Of course the gas station had no phone, but there was a weigh station across the street operated by the state police. I walked over there and went up to the window. As I put my hand on the counter to explain my situation to the officer, I was stung by a bee. So great was the amount of adrenalin pumping through my system that I barely felt it.

The officer invited me to come into the station, where he and his coworkers were watching TV and checking the scores of their favorite teams on the internet. After spending what had seemed an eternity in the middle of nowhere (actually about an hour and a half), I felt like crying at the sight of computers and telephones.

Especially telephones. I called Itacyara to let her know I was okay and then called one of our missionaries in Crato to see about getting help for the car. He assured me that he would arrange everything, and we hung up.

I chatted with the guards for a while and then walked back over to the gas station to wait for the missionary who was coming to pick us up. I prayed that he would come quickly, and I prayed for the safety of the people back at the car.

After buying a Coke and talking to the gas station attendant for a while, I sat down on the curb and waited for help to arrive. After what seemed like another eternity, I saw the familiar headlights of my colleague's SUV.

As we started back toward my car, I asked him to set his trip odometer so I could see how far I had come. "Oh, I already clocked it," was his reply. "You came 7.4 kilometers." That is about 4.6 miles. I estimated that I walked about three miles of that before the trucker picked me up. As I sat resting comfortably in the front seat of Jim Leonard's SUV, I breathed a sigh of relief. I thought, "The adventure was over." Boy, was I wrong.

Back at the car, Daniel had taken his job of protecting the women and Mikey very seriously. Fortunately, they received no threats. When Jim and I arrived, we had some decisions to make. His car had room for seven with no luggage. We had six people, and lots of luggage.

Then there was the question of what to do with the truck. On his way to pick us up, Jim had phoned a towing company that advertises "25-hour service." Nobody answered. Between us, we had no ropes or chains suitable for towing.

We decided that Jim would take the girls and Mikey back to the seminary, and Daniel and I would wait with the car. Jim would then return with a rope, and we would tow the truck somewhere secure. We were not quite sure where that would be.

For the second time that night, we watched a car pull away from us. This time, however, there was the promise that they would be back. Daniel and I settled back for the wait. In order to save on the battery, I turned all the lights off. Once again the night enveloped us. We gazed at the stars and marveled as the red crescent moon rose in front of us. We talked of ministry, plans, and various inconvenient experiences we had encountered while traveling.

It didn't seem like too long before Jim pulled up again. In reality, it was about an hour and a half. He had stopped by a police post in town, and they had loaned him some sturdy ropes.

There in the darkness, we concocted our plan. Jim would tow us to a nearby IBAMA (the Brazilian version of the Environmental Protection Agency) outpost, where we would park the truck for the night, and return for it in the morning. The outpost was about 20 kilometers away. The most important advantage that it held was that it was before the steep incline that leads down the other side of the plateau and into town. I shuddered at the thought of having to try to navigate that treacherous stretch of road in neutral.

Jim got into his truck, and Daniel and I got back into ours. We watched nervously as Jim slowly pulled out and the ropes went taut. Then we began to move slowly. The ropes held! Hallelujah!

Our praise service was cut short as I realized that I had only about eight feet of "buffer space" between my front bumper and the rear of Jim's SUV. Once again the adrenaline began to flow. I gripped the wheel so hard I probably left prints. As my engine was turned off, the steering wheel and brakes worked very hard.

Daniel and I began counting the kilometers. After an agonizing half hour, the IBAMA outpost appeared. We pulled over, and Jim got out of his vehicle and walked up the gate. As Daniel and I got out of the truck, Jim was walking back to us, shaking his head.

"Closed," he said. "It was open when I came by just now."

"Where is the next safe place we can leave the truck?" I asked, fearing the answer.

"At the police outpost halfway down the mountain," was the reply. It was a bad option, but it was our only option. We drove on for another couple of kilometers until we came to the beginning of the long descent. Then we stopped and undid the ropes. Jim would ride ahead of us. We would coast in neutral to the police station.

Daniel, my faithful copilot, volunteered to ride with me. Jim took off, we gave the car a little push, and down we went. Under normal circumstances, the trip down the mountain at night is one of my favorites. The forest gives way, and the traveler is treated to a breathtaking panorama of lights as three cities spread out beneath him. These were not normal circumstances.

Once again, my fingers dug into the steering wheel. My lights were very dim, and it was hard to see the road in front of me. Daniel kept up a running commentary: "Pastor, you are getting too far over to this side. You are almost over the edge. Now you are too far the other side. Watch out, there is a curve up ahead."

Believe it or not, I appreciated his input at this juncture. I have never been so focused on driving. It was an unnerving feeling as the car picked up momentum. Every time I put on the brakes, I silently breathed a prayer of thanks when they held. In this manner, we negotiated the perilous curves and incline of the Serra do Araripe.

Up until now, I have viewed the police outposts with some irritation, knowing that they can mean inconvenient stops, document checks, fines, and even the occasional bribe attempt. However, this particular post, on this particular night, was one of the most welcome sights I have ever laid eyes upon. I gave thanks to my merciful God who had kept me safe from all the many perils that night.

I arrived home at 3:30 am. Daniel lives off campus, so he bunked at our house for the night, then took off in the morning. As for me, at first I was too tense to even think about sleeping. Soon exhaustion caught up with me, however, and I slept like a baby.

The next day I was sore. My hand ached where the bee stung me. I spent the whole day on car-related issues. But I thought, "I am ALIVE! I am in my home with my loving wife and adorable son. There is really nothing more I could want."

I did have one final adrenaline attack that day. After we had retrieved the truck and deposited it at the repair shop, the mechanic diagnosed a burned-out clutch. He handed me the estimate—R$700 (about US $325). All in all, it could have been worse.

Delivered from Fear

Rene Street

Rene and her husband Howard served a decade with another agency before joining Baptist Mid-Missions in 1948. The Streets began in Belgian Congo but later served in Liberia. In 1966, they moved back to the US to serve with BMM's Home Office. Their final assignment was in the administration of BMM's retirement village, Missionary Acres. Howard has been with the Lord since 2003, and Rene since 2005.

When we went to the Belgian Congo as missionaries in 1938, I was 22 years old, and my husband Howard was 23. We had just graduated from Trinity College in Florida and wanted to conquer the Congo for the Lord.

We were stationed in the south at the Panzi station, as the missionaries there had not had a furlough in many years. We had not learned any of the language. The naked village people were fierce to look at. I was not afraid of their color. But the paint on their bodies, the animal horns and fetishes hanging around their necks, the machetes and small knives tucked in their cord belts frightened me. Hearing stories of their savage behavior scared me nearly to death. I was ashamed that I had this fear inside—so ashamed that I would not even share it with my husband. God had called me to serve in this land among these people, and I must not fear them. Yet the fear was there.

After several months at Panzi, we had learned some of the language, and Howard thought it was time for us to go into the villages to get acquainted with the people and the preachers and teachers there. We made preparations for both of us to go. Our means of transportation was a chair woven from bamboo, mounted on bamboo poles to be carried on the shoulders of four men. Food, sleeping gear, clothing, and supplies had to be taken along as well. But it was impossible to find sufficient men to carry us both. So I told Howard that I would stay home. He did not know of my great fear, and I was not about to tell him.

It was late afternoon when he left. I sat on the porch in the swing, watching him disappear into the forest. No other missionaries were there. I was the only white person left on the station. I was afraid, yet somehow I knew I would get through the weeks ahead.

With the sun going down in the west and darkness soon to follow, I sat on the porch too afraid to go inside and light the kerosene lamp. Kerosene lamps cast shadows on the walls! It is customary for an African to "sleep" sentry just in case of an emergency. In Howard's haste to get away before dark, he forgot to leave a sentry to watch over me. But just before dark, I saw Mwemba Kebeya coming through the forest. My heart rejoiced because I knew Howard had sent him back to watch over me. Sure enough, he came walking down the long trail to the house and informed me that the missionary had asked him to come "sleep" sentry. I thanked him and told him I was glad that he was there. He said that he needed to go to the village to get his blanket and to eat supper. Then he turned to walk away.

Had he kept going, things would have been different, but he turned around again and asked me, "Madam, why are you afraid of us?"

I lied and said, "Mwemba, I am not afraid!" Yet there I sat on the porch, too afraid to go inside.

"Madam," he said, "we love you as our missionary and would never let anything happen to you. If a stranger came on the mission station, we would be the very first to intercept him and find out what he wanted. We are so happy to have you here to teach us the Word of God. So, please, do not be afraid of us."

Right then and there I knew this fear had to be conquered, so I said, "Mwemba, I don't need you to come back tonight." He replied that my husband had sent him back for this purpose and that he would return soon. I knew in my heart that if my ministry was ever to amount to anything at all among these dear people, then fear must be conquered, and this was a good time to do it. So I insisted that Mwemba not return that night.

Finally, I braved the darkness, went inside, and prepared to retire. My only protection was the mosquito netting around my bed. I prayed, rolled, and tossed all night. Fearful? Yes! I continued to pray for the Lord to take away that fear. The Congolese believe that if an owl sits on your roof at night and hoots, someone in that house will soon die. About two in the morning an owl got on our roof and hooted and hooted.

"Lord, I am the only one in this house, and if I am to die, please let it be soon," I said. I continued to roll, toss, and pray for deliverance. About four in the morning, I fell asleep and slept soundly until six a.m. When I awoke, I felt refreshed. I had not died, and the Lord had answered prayer! That fear was gone, gone, gone! In reading my Bible that morning I came across a verse in Psalms 4:8, "I will both lay me down in peace and sleep, for Thou, Lord, only makest me dwell in safety."

What peace flooded my soul! To be delivered from fear was a whole new way of life. What God does, He does completely. From that time on, for the remaining 27 years in the Congo and one year in Monrovia, Liberia, I never again feared the dear people to whom the Lord had sent us. That fear was gone. Praise the Lord! From then on, my ministry bore fruit among the women and in the school. As I ministered, great joy replaced fear. Congo really became our home. The language of the people became our language. The people became our people.

Angels Sing
Ray Ronk

In 1988, Ray and Annette joined the Baptist Mid-Missions team in Brazil. Over the years, the Lord has used them to change many lives for Christ. Their current work is in the city of Japurá in Brazil's Paraná State.

One of the special blessings of moving often is that our family has a lot of memories from each place where we have lived. Early in our missionary ministry in Brazil, we rented a rather rundown house in the heart of Ceilândia, one of the older cities in the Federal District of Brasília. There were many things that needed to be fixed in that house, but one thing that was constantly in need of repair was the front door.

No matter how many times we fixed it, something new came up each month! This door would open at all hours of the day or night. When we left for church, three or four of us would make sure that it was fastened securely.

On one particular Sunday, we were delayed returning home after the morning service because we went to visit someone. When we arrived back home in the afternoon, our front door was standing wide open. Since our house had already been vandalized twice the previous month, we were preparing ourselves to find our home empty. However, after a quick check around the house, we found that everything seemed to be in place.

Later that afternoon, we found out that the door had been open since before 10 a.m. One of the neighbor boys came by to ask me how my wife was doing. A bit bewildered by his question, I answered that she was fine. Ronaldo told me that he knew that Annette must not be too sick because she was singing most of the morning. Now I was really bewildered, because no one had been home that morning. I even called Annette to the gate to talk to Ronaldo, because he would not believe that she had not been at home singing all morning.

He told us that word had quickly spread on the street that the "Americano's house" was open, so he and his brother went there to keep an eye out for us. When they called out, no one appeared, but they said that the lady was singing hymns, so they figured she was all right.

When we finally did convince Ronaldo and his brothers that we were all at church that day, they said that God must have protected us and sent His angels to sing and scare away the bad people.

Kidnapped
Sam Hornbrook

Sam and his wife Jamie joined Baptist Mid-Missions in 1988 to serve in Mexico. Sam is following in the footsteps of his missionary parents, Sam and Ellen Hornbrook, who also serve with BMM. Sam and Jamie work in the Mexico City area.

On May 26, 2009, while running an errand for his father, Allan was abducted and forced to get into a car with several men. This 19-year-old is a faithful Christian who attends Peniel Baptist Church in Mexico City, where I have been preaching on Sunday nights. The church had been started years earlier by Baptist Mid-Missions missionaries Dan and Peggy Whitcher.

The kidnappers communicated with Allan's family via phone, demanding $300,000 US in exchange for him. A special police force tapped the phone lines of Allan's home to try to trace the calls but to no avail. Two weeks after the abduction, the kidnappers sent a video to the family showing mistreatment of Allan to increase the pressure for them to pay the ransom. The parents tried to negotiate for a lesser amount that they could actually come up with, but the kidnappers demanded "all or nothing."

Peniel Baptist Church held times of prayer in the home of Dr. Julio, a church deacon who lives next door to Allan's grandmother. On Friday evening, June 12, I sent an e-mail to my supporting churches and friends asking them to pray for the situation. The prayers of God's people from several countries ascended to the Throne of God, and God heard. Many prayed specifically that Allan would be able to escape.

From the time of his kidnapping, Allan prayed like he had never prayed before. He prayed day and night, knowing that the Lord was watching over him. Even after his captors cut off part of his earlobe for the video that was sent to his parents, Allan's confidence in God's provision and protection remained strong. Though his hands and feet were tied at all times, Allan believed that if his captors would fall asleep, he would have a chance to escape. That is what he began to ask the Lord to do. Early Sunday morning, June 14, sometime between 2:00 and 3:00 a.m., Allan realized the Lord had answered his request.

After drinking and consuming drugs, all the captors in the house were fast asleep. Allan was able to crawl and scoot himself out of the house. After finding objects to scrape the ropes off his hands, he untied his feet. He recognized the area where he had been held and ran all the way home, arriving around 3:30 a.m. The police special agents were there and immediately Allan led them to the kidnappers' place. They surprised seven of the kidnappers, who were still unaware that Allan had gotten away, and arrested them. Later that day, eight more arrests were made.

Perhaps the most special thing God accomplished through this was that Allan's father accepted the Lord. Although he had never been willing to go to church before, he had attended the prayer meetings since his son was abducted. He memorized Psalm 16:8, "I have set the LORD always before me: because He is at my right hand I shall not be moved." For many weeks after gaining his freedom, Allan and his parents visited churches in Mexico City that had prayed for him, testifying to God's faithfulness and inviting those who had not yet done so to believe on the Lord for salvation.

Yes, the Lord shows Himself strong on behalf of those who put their faith in Him.

A Rude Awakening
Helen (Hall) Jones

Helen's story takes place a year after she joined Baptist Mid-Missions as a single missionary (Helen Rowe). She served nearly 15 years in Brazil before leaving BMM to marry Hugh Hall in 1967. After she was widowed, Helen married a missionary from Brazil, Robert Jones, in 1999.

The year was 1952 in Fortaleza, Brazil. It had been a long, hot day. My coworker Alice Holmquist and I decided, since we were living on the second floor, that it would be safe to sleep with our windows open. Earlier in the day, I had withdrawn $700 from the bank in order to buy plane tickets. I carefully placed the money in the stand beside my bed and then settled in for a good night of sleep. Alice went through her little routine of climbing into her hammock and then placing her alarm clock and glasses on the floor beneath her.

The wonderful ocean breeze coming in the windows was a blessing, and we soon were asleep. The next thing we knew, the alarm was ringing and it was time to get up.

"I'm awake, Alice, you can turn off the alarm."

With a bit of irritation in her voice, Alice replied, "Where is the alarm? Why did you move my clock? I can't find it or my glasses."

I was a bit indignant as I answered her, "I didn't touch your clock or your glasses." Then climbing out of bed, I waltzed dramatically toward the window, saying, "I think someone came in the window."

I froze in my tracks! By the time I had said those words, I was at the window and there, leaning against the outside wall, was a ladder coming right up to our ledge!

The $700? I rushed to the night stand. Praise the Lord, the money was there. Instantly Psalm 121:4 flashed into my mind, "Behold, he that keepeth Israel shall neither slumber nor sleep."

The thief had taken Alice's billfold containing $3 and her glasses. He was caught later in the day trying to sell the glasses. We learned the hard way that even the second floor windows should be closed when sleeping or away.

Being young and very curious, I wanted to see this thief who had sneaked around in my bedroom while I was sleeping. I changed my mind, however, when I learned he had been carrying a machete.

We had slept—oblivious to the danger—but our merciful, faithful Lord never sleeps. He had been on guard, watching over His own.

God Has Not Given a Spirit of Fear
Debbie Seymour

Debbie and her husband Mark joined Baptist Mid-Missions in 1979 to serve in Chad, the country where Mark grew up as an MK. There, they were involved in church planting and theological education. Since 2009, Mark has been serving as a BMM Mission Advancement Representative.

My husband Mark had a real burden to work with our Chadian young people who oftentimes do not really know the Scriptures or how to interpret them properly. Because they come out of an animistic background where evil spirits must be appeased, even the Christians are often controlled by fear. We started with a small core group of about seven young people in their early 20s and began a course in hermeneutics (biblical interpretation).

Mark came to the lesson about how God is no longer directly communicating with man except through the Word of God. The subject of dreams came up. When the Chadians have a dream, it plays into their animistic background. They are consumed by fear.

"Well, what if I dream something, and it seems like some of the things come to pass?" asked one student.

"No, it's not the Lord," said Mark, "God has given us His Word."

"I had a dream that I was in an accident. When my boss asked me to drive across town to do something, I told him that I couldn't because of this dream that I had," one of them admitted.

He had been totally controlled and consumed by fear. Mark told the young man that he needed to be controlled by the Holy Spirit and not by fear. Mark shared 2 Timothy 1:7, which says, "For God hath not given us the spirit of fear; but of power, and of love, and of a sound mind."

"Satan often attacks Christians through fear," my husband said.

It was a wonderful Bible study. These young people were realizing that they could no longer be controlled by fear but needed to be controlled by the Holy Spirit. They were beginning to understand that God's love and grace could overcome fear.

We got up from our Bible study at about nine p.m. Mark and I usually try to leave the table first to go and shake everyone's hands and say goodnight to them at our door. I got up and walked to the end of the table, and there was a black spitting cobra slithering across our dining room floor. It was a small one, but nonetheless it was a poisonous snake.

I screamed in fright. The guys at the end of the table saw the snake and stomped it to death right there on our dining room floor.

I was really shaken up. I asked our night guard, "Do you think that this snake was just recently hatched or was it simply a small snake?"

"Oh, no, I think it was just hatched," he said.

Then I started to panic with the thought that there might be another snake that was going to hatch in my house. I think I could have easily been consumed by fear at that point and not been able to function normally. I would have been looking at everything, expecting to see a cobra.

Then the Lord reminded me of the Bible lesson we had just completed. It was just amazing. I thought this Bible lesson was to challenge the Chadian young believers in their fear. But God had so prepared my own heart that I could commit this to the Lord and say, "Lord, I will not be consumed by fear. I know You have protected me before, and You will protect me again." It was just a thrill to see how God not only worked through His Word in the Chadians' lives to strengthen them in their belief but also how He worked in mine.

God's Guiding Hand
Gene and Doris Stockton

The Stocktons have served in a number of Spanish-speaking countries since joining Baptist Mid-Missions in 1961. Their story is an account from their first field of Venezuela. The Stocktons later worked in Puerto Rico, Argentina, and North America before retiring in 2002.

"Everything is under control," I boasted, confident of my ability to expertly care for our two little girls and our jungle home while my wife and five-year-old son, Sam, were in town attending a ladies' conference. Our first term of service in Venezuela was with the Warao Indians, who live in the remote delta region of the Orinoco River. I envisioned my wife being so proud of me and my ability to take care of the house while she was away. Upon her return, the house was going to be immaculate, with everything picked up and in its place. My little girls would be all dressed up and so pretty when mommy came home. It was already 5 p.m. and, so far, my plan was working well.

While my wife and I were talking via two-way radio, two Warao Indians came up to the house. I knew them both, and I saw right away that Bejerano had suffered a serious accident. His left hand was bandaged, and the bandage was soaked with blood. He told me that he had been cutting vines in the jungle, and as he struck the vine with his machete, it had ricocheted and cut his hand. As I questioned him further, I learned that he had severed the tendon that controlled the movement of his hand.

I went back to the radio to tell Doris what had happened. As a nurse, she immediately realized that the problem needed the attention of a surgeon. I hurriedly told her goodbye and arranged that we would talk again the next day at 8:00 a.m.

I told Bejerano and Diego, his nephew, that I would get the boat ready and that we would go to the clinic in Pedrenales. They knew that it took about an hour to get there. They said, *Yakera* ("That's good"). We left about 6:30 p.m. When we arrived, I went to the police station to inform them why we had come and that I needed to take my friend to the clinic. The clinic wasn't that far from the waterfront, so the policeman told me I could use their wheelbarrow. No, I'm not kidding. Diego told Bejerano to get in, and off we went to the clinic.

At this little clinic, there was only one doctor and one nurse on duty. The doctor put Bejerano on the table, and the nurse administered the chloroform. Diego and I were in the same room. The doctor worked and worked, and the nurse kept giving Bejerano more chloroform. I could tell things weren't going well. At about 9:00 p.m. he told me that he was not able to find the tendon because it had receded too far up into the arm.

He said that I would have to take my friend to Tucupita. I couldn't believe my ears! From where we were to Tucupita was a trip of about six hours, even in the daytime.

The next step was to put Bejerano back into the wheelbarrow and get him to the boat. He was still under the effects of the chloroform. I tried to laugh. We made it back to the boat okay, but we almost lost him as we were headed back on the river. He started thrashing around as he was waking up, and Diego had to restrain him to keep him from falling overboard.

We arrived back at our house around 10:30 p.m. I told Esteban, a young teacher who was living with us, what had happened. When I told him that I needed to take Bejerano to Tucupita, he told me not to worry; he would take care of Susan, our two-year-old, and Kathy, who was one. We ate a quick meal, and Esteban packed a lunch for us.

When we left to go to Tucupita, it was almost midnight. On this trip, Bejerano's son, Monagas, went with us. By this time, Bejerano had recovered from the effects of the chloroform. In the daytime, if all went well, I could make it to Tucupita in four hours. However, this was the exception and not the rule. On one trip, the motor had lost power in one cylinder, and I didn't get home until the next day.

On that middle-of-the-night trip, God revealed to us just how great He is. Truly He guided us with His hand that dark night. Monagas and I had our flashlights, but God's light was showing us the way. His power and mercy are infinite! Believe it or not, from the time we left our house until I pulled into the dock in front of the hospital at 5:00 a.m., the motor purred like a kitten. I didn't have to stop even once to clean trash off the propeller. God guided us around all the floating logs, debris, and other dangers. "So he fed them according to the integrity of his heart; and guided them by the skilfulness of his hands" (Psalm 78:72).

We took Bejerano to the hospital and left him under the doctor's care. As we were going back downriver to our home, we looked up and saw Ken Johnsen, the missionary pilot, in his Piper Cub. He circled and then landed near us. He had just taken Doris and Sam back home. After greeting us, he said, "Esteban called us this morning and was in a panic. He said that he couldn't understand the girls, and they couldn't understand him. He said to tell Doris that she had to get back home as soon as possible." Laughing, he continued, "You won't believe what we found when we arrived at your place. The inside of your house looks like a tornado went through it. Susan and Kathy were in one crib, and both were naked."

I'm glad that all is well that ends well. My wife didn't divorce me, and my children came through it unscathed. Later, we were told that Bejerano's surgery was successful and that he would be able to use his hand. What a blessing and what a relief! Not too many months later, we saw Bejerano going to his garden plot. His hand was whole again.

Aa Po Nyosoa Sgo
Elaine Schulte

A registered nurse, Elaine joined Baptist Mid-Missions in 1975 to serve in medical ministry in Africa. She served in both Chad and Ivory Coast (Côte d'Ivoire) before coming back to the US to care for her elderly parents. In 1998, Elaine became part of the Bibles International team in Grand Rapids, Michigan.

It had been a typical day in the little village of Péhé, Côte d'Ivoire, West Africa, with no indication that the miraculous was about to occur. I'd spent the morning and early afternoon seeing patients in the dispensary, where I worked without the aid of a doctor. The clinic was just a stone's throw away from my home. Now I was studying the tribal dialect with one of the Ivorian Kaowlu speakers.

"Tantie," (Auntie) one of the national dispensary workers, Baïbo, called to me through my screened window.

"Oui."

"Do you hear the sound of the death wail?" I had heard it and knew it probably meant that another Guéré national had gone out into eternity without the Lord. It might mean death had already occurred, or it might mean that it seemed unavoidable.

Some villagers chose not to call the Toubaboo (the White Thing—the name the nationals used for Caucasians) when the death of a relative seemed imminent. No one had asked for my help.

"Tantie," Baïbo continued, "a pregnant woman in the village just finished preparing her food, sat down to eat it, and fell over. Tantie, she wants to die." I had been there long enough to understand that this phrase was not to be taken literally but was an idiom meaning death seemed inevitable. "Can you come quickly?"

Rushing to the dispensary, I picked up a blood pressure cuff and stethoscope. I began jogging to the village, following the sound of the wailing to determine which hut housed the comatose patient. I prayed as I jogged. How could I possibly diagnose the condition of a comatose woman with only the few crude tests available here in the village? And since she was pregnant, if I could not treat her successfully, the baby would surely die when she did. If I couldn't make a correct diagnosis, it was unlikely I could treat her effectively. It seemed apparent that I was about to witness the death of two individuals—the mother and her un-born baby.

Silently calling out to God, I begged Him for wisdom, reminding Him that it was He who had led me to this primitive little village and that His reputation was at stake. Once again, I was in over my head.

Nearing the hut, I could distinguish the cries more clearly. *"Jay-oh! Jay-oh! Jay-oh!"* (No! No! No!) The cries were always the same. I had not grown used to them. There was total desolation in the voices of the people.

I pushed my way through the crowd of wailing villagers, many of whom were immediate or extended family. As was typical of that culture, the husband waited outside the hut, choosing to leave his wife to the care of female family members. Other village men waited with him.

Giving my eyes a few minutes to adjust after entering the dark hut, I found exactly what I had anticipated. On a low platform-bed, made from split pieces of bamboo covered by a thin straw mat, lay an obviously pregnant woman. She was surrounded by what appeared to be all the females in the village, including the young girls.

As I approached the primitive bed, I tested the patient's level of consciousness by digging my nails into the soft tissue on the inside of her wrist. My heart sank when that simple, preliminary test showed she was deeply comatose. There was no response to pain. A quick check of her vital signs demonstrated nothing unusual. When I questioned the women surrounding the patient, I found that they had no additional information beyond that already given to me by Baïbo.

Seated beside the woman on the uncomfortable bed, I silently prayed once again for wisdom. In fact, I had not ceased my silent suppli-cations ever since Baïbo had given me the alarming news.

Rising from the bed, I spoke to the women, "I'll go back to the dispensary and get a *piqure* (injection)." Piqures are viewed in that culture almost as if they have some magic. Any serious illness always demands a piqure or a series of them to satisfy the people there.

I silently pled with the Lord on my way back to the dispensary. "Lord, show me how to treat her," I begged. "What kind of an illness would make an apparently healthy woman drop over in a coma?"

As I passed the home of my coworker, she called out to me through the window. "What's wrong, Elaine?"

"I don't know." When I described the woman's symptoms, my coworker's response surprised me. "The only disease I can think of that causes those symptoms is cerebral malaria." Was this the answer I'd been seeking?

Arriving back at the dispensary, I pulled my dusty tropical medicine textbooks off the shelf. I'd studied cerebral malaria in the tropical medicine course I'd taken in Belgium. But I'd never before seen the disease, or at least I'd never recognized it.

"So what is the treatment?" I asked myself. Of the several medications listed, I had one. Breathing a sigh of relief and a prayer of thanksgiving, I read further to determine the dosage. Imagine my dismay when I read in bold print: This medication is not to be administered to pregnant or nursing women.

Again my heart sank. "What should I do, Lord?" I was praying audibly now. After a few minutes, the answer seemed apparent to me. If I used the medication, thereby saving the mother's life, at least one life would be spared. If I chose not to use it, both mother and child would probably be lost. I made my decision, believing the Lord had led me.

With shaking hands, I found the medicine. Drawing it up into a large, sterile syringe, I then retrieved the other supplies I would need in order to inject this medication directly into a vein.

Back at her bedside, I hastily prepared the woman's arm for the piqure. My hands continued to shake as I began pushing the medication into one of her rope-like veins. Inject a bit; pause. Inject a bit more; pause. The process continued as I pushed the large amount of medication into the vein.

Suddenly my heart skipped a beat. Amazement washed over me as I thought I detected a tiny movement. In a matter of minutes, the pregnant patient was forcefully struggling to sit up. Hard, calloused hands of family members reached down to restrain her so that I could continue injecting the final medication into her vein.

Before I finished, she began pleading. "Please, let me up; I need to go relieve myself." As soon as I removed the needle from her arm, the woman sat up with the help of family members. Slowly, and with even more help, she rose clumsily to her feet.

By this time, the wailing had ceased and expressions of amazement were heard inside the hut. The milling crowd outside began to detect the changed atmosphere within.

"What's happening in there?" shouted someone from outside. When female family members called out the amazing news, wailing changed to rejoicing.

"Aa po Nyosoa sgo! Aa po Nyosoa sgo!" (We thank God! We thank God!) Shouts of joy rang out, replacing the death wail! As I exited the hut, the thankful husband grabbed my wrist pulling it up in the air repeatedly, thanking me in the traditional Guéré way of expressing gratitude.

A few weeks later, my joy was immeasurable when this woman walked into our little church-hut on Sunday morning. On her back, attached with a brightly colored piece of African cloth, was a small lump. A tiny head, covered with tightly curled black hair, could be seen. Not only had God spared the mother's life, He had also given her a healthy baby! "Aa po Nyosoa sgo!"

Arrested
Jennie Adams

Jennie was a remarkable woman who served as an Army nurse during WWII before joining Baptist Mid-Missions in 1954. She had helped carry wounded soldiers off Normandy beach during the D-Day invasion. She was a humble servant and applied her skills wherever needed on the mission field. "Aunt Jennie" as she was known, served 40 years in Peru. She has been with her Lord since 2005.

It's not too often that the Lord puts a missionary on the inside of a jail to be a witness for Him—unless, of course, they are imprisoned for preaching the gospel. But that is how the Lord chose to use me in Peru. For five years I was in and out of various jails until I was finally cleared of the charges against me.

It all started rather innocently. For about two years, I had been doing itinerant teaching in drug country in the mountains of northern

Peru. Because I held Bible classes in several different locations, I was able to get to each place only once a month. I had walked everywhere I went for my first 20 years in Peru so I could empathize with the Peruvians who had to walk to market. But then I was given a Dodge van and later a Chevy Blazer, which allowed me to go farther up into the mountains of northern Peru to hold Bible classes. On my way down the mountain after my classes, I usually picked up passengers until my vehicle was full. Some of these people I knew and others I didn't.

One particular time, I drove up to the guard station, and the barrier was down across the road. There were two trucks ahead of me. The policemen were new and they were searching everything. If they had been ones who knew me, I would have been motioned around the barrier; but this time I had to wait my turn.

There were probably a dozen people in the first truck, and each of them had fruits and vegetables and chickens and goats and whatever else they were carrying to market. The police dumped all this stuff behind the truck and searched through it. They couldn't find what they were looking for, so finally they told the people that they could collect their belongings and get back into the truck. The same thing happened with the next vehicle. Finally, it was my turn.

"Where did you come from?" queried the guard.

"Compin," I replied.

"What were you doing there?" he barked.

"I was teaching Bible classes."

Then he proceeded to look through my bags, under the hood, in the gas tank, everywhere. Nothing. Motioning with his gun, he invited all my passengers to get out and go up to the guard station with their belongings. I was told to park the car and then join them. As I entered the building, the guards were opening a red one-gallon Shell oil can. People in the mountains carry things in whatever container they can find. The policeman had asked the man what was in it, and he said, "Honey." They opened it up and sure enough it was honey. But there was a little corner of blue plastic sticking out. So they poured out the honey and opened the blue plastic bag. It contained a wet, gray powder.

The officer looked at me and said, "See, it's cocaine."

"Cocaine's not like that," I argued. "Cocaine is a white powder." I had never actually seen cocaine before, but I had heard it was a white powder.

"This is cocaine. It's not refined, but it's cocaine," he said triumphantly.

We were under arrest. They put all eight of us in a little room with two cots that had no mattresses on them. Then they took us out one at a time to question us and then returned us to the cell.

The next day they took us women to a different jail. This was on a sugar plantation off the main road. All the regular jail cells were already full, so they put us in the room where the police officers normally stored their bicycles. This was to be my new home. The other ladies decided to sleep on the floor, and that left me a bench about ten inches wide and about fifteen feet long for my bed.

During the day, I was required to sit all the time. Prisoners weren't allowed to stand or walk around because it made the guards nervous. But it was very painful for me to sit for any length of time. I had undergone back surgery about 10 years before, but with traveling on such rough roads it had kind of worn off. I had to sit when I taught, because I always taught men. A woman couldn't be above a man. And I had to sit when I drove, of course, so that meant that my back hurt most of the time.

Night finally came on that first day in jail, and so I lay down on the bench. During the night I must have tried to change position, because I turned over and fell off the bench and landed flat on my back on that cement floor. And that's how the Lord cured my back! It hasn't hurt since. It was the most wonderful thing. It was just like the Lord saying to me, "Jennie, I'm not mad at you. But I just need you to be here for awhile, and so I've fixed your back so you'll be more comfortable."

After I had been in jail for a while, I received a letter from one of the mountain men I had been teaching. He thanked me for teaching them and then wrote, "When you came, we had class once a month. But now that you can't come anymore, we are having class every week."

I hadn't seen that they had advanced enough to go on their own. But the Lord had seen it and knew they were ready, so He just put me away for awhile so that they could go on their own. I really appreciate the Lord's ability to get His point across, no matter how hard of understanding we may be.

Well, when I realized that I would be in jail for awhile, I decided to find out what the Lord wanted me to do there. One day in the penitentiary, I was sitting in my little space reading my Bible. Another inmate came up and asked me what I was doing. When I told her I was reading the Bible, she insisted that I couldn't be reading because I was a woman. I convinced her that I really could read and then asked her if she would like to learn. She was elated at the opportunity. So we asked around to see if there were others who wanted to learn, and then on Monday we started a class.

Isn't the Lord marvelous? In a Catholic country, you couldn't teach Bible in jail. But teaching reading was considered very noble. In the book bag that I had with me were some Bible Society leaflets—all in color—and just perfectly suited for teaching reading. There were a series of leaflets; the first ones started out with just two rows of words in big letters under a colored picture on each page. As you progressed through the series, the letters got smaller and there were more rows of words.

So that first week we went through and learned the vowel sounds. The next week we started on Monday with the consonants. Most of the important words in Spanish are short, so I picked consonants that would combine to make words quickly. By the end of the second week, they were recognizing words. They were delighted! They could read. We went on using those Bible Society leaflets until we had learned all the consonants and the women could read. Of course, we had to talk about what they read to be sure that they understood and weren't just reading without comprehension.

I discovered that I had a greater influence with the women prisoners because I was one of them. There were people from outside the jail that would come once a week and hold worship services. But then they would leave and go about their lives on the outside. So their words did not carry as much weight with the inmates. There were limits to what I could say to anybody in jail in the hearing of anybody else, but eventually I could get my point across.

After about five years in and out of several different jails, I was finally declared innocent of any wrongdoing. How merciful the Lord was to work in and through me during my time in that penitentiary.

God Has the Solution
Judy Gordon

Judy and her husband Russell were appointed with Baptist Mid-Missions in 1968 and served their entire career in Brazil. Since retiring in 2008, they have been helping with BMM's retirement care ministries by offering special care for the needs of missionary retirees in North Carolina, Virginia, and South Carolina.

Some years ago, we were struggling with some needs in our family. My mother needed to have someone to take care of her because she was 86 years of age. Our daughter was graduating from Cedarville College and was going through an unsettling time in her life. We came home from Brazil with the plan that my husband would spend six weeks in the States and then go back to Brazil and that I would follow as soon as we had a solution worked out for Mom.

Many people were praying for us, because my husband can't cook and he would be hard-pressed to take care of himself in Brazil without me. We knew that God had the solution. After our daughter's graduation ceremony, my husband left to go back to Brazil on July 16. His parting words were, "Please, hurry back."

"I'll come as soon as I can," I replied.

We had decided that my mom would come to live with us in Brazil, and so I began the process of obtaining a visa for her. Although my daughter had graduated, she still lacked her student teaching. She was scheduled to go back to Cedarville on September 21. I told my husband that I would set my sights on returning to Brazil on the first plane after our daughter returned to school.

Our son, who lives in Washington DC, was helping us with all the paperwork for the visa. In the middle of August, he called the consulate in Washington to inquire as to whether the visa was ready. They said, "No, this process takes time. We just got it sent down to Brazil."

In the meantime, my husband was calling and saying, "Come as soon as you can."

My son called the consulate around the first of September. The man said, "Nothing yet. Call again next Wednesday." My son called back the next Wednesday, and they said, "Nothing yet. Call again next Wednesday."

The next Monday, I called my son and asked, "Son, have you called the consulate yet?"

He said "No."

I said, "Why don't you call them again?" My daughter was scheduled to go back to Cedarville on that next Thursday, and I was anxious to be on my way back to Brazil.

My son called the consulate again and they said, "You know, the visa for your grandmother came in last Wednesday after I talked with you. It's here and you can come and pick it up."

So my son picked it up and mailed it to us. My daughter left for Cedarville on Thursday, and my mom and I left for Brazil on Friday. We just praise the Lord for His timing and all His mercies to us. My mom spent two years with us in Brazil. She was never sick, and we brought her back to the United States safe and sound.

Attack on the Bangui Station
Knute Orton

In 1956, Knute and his wife Lillian joined the Baptist Mid-Missions Family to serve in the Central African Republic, then a region of French Equatorial Africa. In their nearly 50 years there, the Ortons weathered periods of political unrest. In this story, Knute describes a time of great upheaval and the faithfulness of God, who got them through it.

The Central African Republic (CAR) had long been building up with labor, civil service, and military discontent. Many had gone months without their salaries. Schoolteachers were months behind in getting their pay, and the students were constantly calling for strikes because they were not getting their student subsidies. Strikes did take place, and along with the strikes came riots and violence and demands for the government to resign.

My wife Lillian and I found ourselves in the midst of this cauldron of discontent in May of 1991. We had just returned to the Central African Republic for our ninth term of service with Baptist Mid-Missions. We had seen our second daughter finish high school and get settled, and we were returning to the field without our family.

Normally, we would have returned to Kaga Bandoro, which was the station where we had worked for many years. However, because of a shortage of personnel in Bangui, we were asked by the field council to fill in there until another couple could arrive. We readily agreed, though we might have thought twice about it if we had known what the next months would bring!

Upon our arrival in May, things seemed to be coming to a more critical stage. One ominous difference was that the rioters began to attack previously untouched areas of the population, e.g. private enterprises and homes, especially those that were owned by foreigners such as the French, Portuguese, and Lebanese.

As May moved into June, the attacks came dangerously close to us when a coffee processing plant belonging to a Lebanese company was destroyed just a quarter mile down the road! Then one week later, on June 25, at two o'clock in the morning, we were awakened by much shouting, yelling, and the noise of stones landing on our aluminum roofs. My colleague Bill Brown and I went out to meet an angry, riotous crowd of about 150 teenagers between 15 and 20 years old. They were supposedly all students, though we recognized some among them who were not. All were shouting and demanding coffee, tea, beer, and money.

When one particularly vocal young man, who called me by name, demanded cases of beer, I replied, "Young man, if you know me well enough to call me by name, you also must know that we do not have any beer here!"

At that, they all stooped to the piles of rocks each had brought for the occasion and began throwing them at us and our African guards! But then, a strange thing happened—not one rock hit us or any window of the house that was just a few feet behind us! Here were 150 young people who are normally quite adept at hitting birds or knocking down fruit from trees, standing no more than 25 feet from us, and yet not one rock connected with its target. "Thou shalt not be afraid for the terror by night, nor for the arrow [nor the rocks] that flieth by day" Psalm 91:5.

When they did not get their tea, coffee, money, or beer, they spent the next two hours ransacking every garage, storeroom, and toolshed they could break into. When no one answered our calls to the central police station, we finally telephoned Brent Bohne, a Christian friend who was the security officer at the American Embassy. Brent soon arrived, accompanied by a truckload of African policemen. Upon their arrival, the "students" vanished into the woods behind the mission. But they had already stolen many tools, demolished two cars, and did much more structural damage.

Violence had entered a new phase in the CAR. Churches and mission stations which had previously been off limits to such actions could no longer enjoy that immunity. We were soon to learn that this attack by "students" was just a foretaste of things much more sinister.

July 3, 1991

The Baptist Mid-Missions station in Bangui was located on the extreme northern edge of the city along the main road heading out of the city to all points north. That station was in a somewhat isolated suburb called Gobongo, which had in recent years become a hotbed of violence.

Following the students' raid on the Bangui station, violence around the city increased almost daily. The city and most of the country soon became virtually paralyzed by continual strikes. The days of July 3-4 were normally a festive time for the American community. On the evening of July 3, we were usually at the American Ambassador's residence for an official US government reception given for dignitaries from various embassies, businesses, etc. For some reason, that year we were not invited. Had we been there, the events of that evening might have been very different!

All afternoon on July 3, various individuals came to us to report rumors that our mission was to be attacked that night by bandits. At first, we did not take these reports seriously, mainly because there did not seem to be any substance to them. Where did they originate? And just when do bandits spread word far and wide that they are going to attack some particular named victims at such-and-such a night and hour?

As the day went on, however, these stories persisted until finally a good friend came to warn us. He was a new Christian, one whom we viewed as a responsible person, not given to spreading such reports if they were without foundation. He came expressing genuine concern and said that from his sources, he felt that this was no empty threat. We began to believe that indeed something ominous was afoot.

By late afternoon, virtually all traffic had stopped on the main road heading northward out of the city. This was due in part to a countrywide curfew soon to take effect and partly because of fear by the general population to be moving about. That day had been declared a "dead-city" day, meaning that if a person was seen moving about, rioting gangs might give him a very rough time. The bandits threatened to beat up pedestrians, smash the bikes of bicyclists, stop motorists, beat up occupants of the vehicles, and even burn their cars. It was best to stay home. We did!

Just as the early darkness of the tropical evening began to descend upon the city, I sent word to the commandant of the local army brigade temporarily stationed in an outdoor marketplace just a quarter of a mile away. He and his lieutenant came over immediately, and upon hearing of these threats, assured me that we need not worry, for he would send his soldiers to surround our mission station. So a little later, while we missionaries were having a prayer meeting, soldiers were walking around shooting their guns into the air. Under any other conditions, this would have been disconcerting to say the least, but this particular night it was a welcome diversion!

However, our sense of security soon vanished when the shooting suddenly stopped at about 10 p.m. I sent one of our station guards over to the marketplace to ask the commandant what had happened. The guard returned to tell us that the entire brigade, officers and all, were gone. No one was there! Not good! We had previously been instructed that if there ever was any trouble and we needed military help, to phone the French Embassy. But when I called them, the only advice I got was, "If you are attacked, when you actually see them coming, call us." With the French Embassy located about 10 miles from us at the other end of the city, it would have been difficult for them to reach us in time!

While we were praying, a station guard motioned for me to step outdoors. He told me that he had just been informed that a gang of rebels were meeting in a schoolhouse not far away, and that they planned to attack us at 1:30 a.m.

We had visitors on our station that day. Paul and Karla Gault had just come from their station some 300 miles east with a niece and nephew who were flying back to the States the next morning after paying a short visit to the CAR. I didn't know how exciting their visit had been to this point, but if they had lacked excitement before, this night was going to make up for it! One of our veteran missionary ladies, Miss Mae Allen, had accompanied them to do some shopping in the city. A young Canadian motorcyclist traveling across Africa was spending a few days in our house recuperating from a bad case of malaria and was still quite weak. But feeble as he was, he pitched in the next two days and was a big help before he bade goodbye to the CAR.

Two of our resident missionary ladies, Miss Polly Strong and Mrs. Ruth Rosenau, who had just lost her husband the previous November, lived in their own homes. In view of the threats that we all faced that night, we felt that no one should be alone, so they came over to our house.

At about 11:00 p.m., most of the missionaries had gone to try to rest while Bill and I remained up and circulating around the station.

Then by the glow of the churchyard light about a block away, much to our surprise and horror, we saw a large group of men approaching the mission and starting to fan out. As Bill ran for the phone in his house to call the French military, one of the approaching rebels climbed the telephone pole. Bill came back with the alarming word that the phone lines had already been cut! We couldn't call anyone! It wasn't 1:30 a.m.—it was 11:00 p.m.! Had that been a deliberate diversion?

Bill's wife Clara asked to go over to our house to be with the other ladies. I told Bill I would take her and rouse everyone in that house as well as everyone in the guesthouse. After leaving Clara with the others, I spread the alarm to the other guests. Leaving the guesthouse to cross a short, dark area where the light from the yard lights did not penetrate, I was suddenly accosted from behind with a strong arm around my neck and a long knife held threateningly close to my throat!

One man held my arms while yet another held a long truck tire iron over my head. The man holding me in a headlock said menacingly, "If you cry out, you will be dead!" His tone of voice and the firmness with which he held me were adequately convincing. In fact, he held me so tightly I doubt that I could have cried out had I tried to! Soon they had emptied my pockets and had taken my wristwatch. They then forced me into the guesthouse with the Gaults and Mae Allen and told me to shut and bolt the door. After following his instructions, I went to the back window which faced our house and saw my wife Lillian standing in the open doorway trying to see what was going on. She could hear the shouting but in the dark areas could not see. By the light from the porch light, I could see bandits coming from behind the house to attack her and enter the house. I called to her to tell her that we were all okay, but she must get in the house and lock it immediately! She did, just in time. As bad as it appeared, strangely, it seemed that they were being careful not to hurt us.

During the following two hours, the bandits broke into all the garages and storerooms again. This time, though, they had crowbars, axes, and other tools to help them in their thievery, which they continued until 2:00 a.m., when two truckloads of armed, helmeted police arrived! The bandits scattered. The lieutenant in charge asked some questions, then they all began to search through the nearby woods for the things we had watched the thieves steal—many items of furniture, all kinds of appliances, even large, heavy items such as refrigerators, 50-gallon barrels, etc. After the initial investigation was finished and the police prepared to leave, I asked the lieutenant if he could leave one or two armed policemen for the rest of the night. He replied that he could not, because these kinds of attacks were going on all over the city, and they were woefully short of men. So at about 3:00 a.m., we were left alone.

There was no more sleeping for anyone that night. We walked around the station, appraising the damage. We could hear the bandits in the woods and deep grass around the station. It did not take long for them to regroup for another attack.

About 4:00 a.m., we watched as they gathered again under the yard light of Gobongo Baptist Church. They were noisy and brazen now, confident that they could pull off another attack before daylight, this time uninterrupted by the police. What would happen now? Would they be as careful not to harm us as they had been before? At the first raid of the night, I had not experienced any great fear, perhaps more anger than fear. But now as they approached, noisier than before, I grew more apprehensive. I knew there was no way to call for help. All we could do now was to call upon the Lord! "Call unto me, and I will answer thee, and show thee great and mighty things, which thou knowest not" Jeremiah 33:3.

Just as the bandits reached us, down the lane again came two big truckloads of police! And again the intruders promptly dispersed! The lieutenant approached me asking, "Where are the bandits? You called saying they were attacking you again." I told him that they had fled when they saw his trucks coming, but I reminded him that I could not call him as our phone lines had been cut. "But if you did not call, who did?" he asked.

Then on his walkie-talkie he called police headquarters and asked who called saying that the American mission was being attacked again. I heard the response: "The American ambassador!" I was thankful but mused, "How did he know?" "The angel of the LORD encampeth round about them that fear him, and delivereth them" (Psalm 34:7).

Later that morning, another rumor reached us, "Anyone who remains here tonight will die!" I had decided by now that I didn't like rumors, and in view of the events of the past night, I thought it best to do all that I could to respond to this one. I went into the city to see Col. Biamba Philippe, the top gendarme of the country and a longtime personal friend and a Christian. Both he and his wife had been my dental patients. We had been in their home and they had been in ours. When I told him of the events of the past night and the threat we had received that morning, he spent some time on his phone. Then in tears and with his arm around my shoulder, he told me to get everyone out of the mission station immediately. He could not help us! Bewildered, I thanked him; we prayed, and I left. That night we all stayed at other mission stations in town while our homes were being broken into and much was being stolen.

With the help of missionaries from other mission agencies in the city and our own Baptist Mid-Missions coworkers from our nearest station, Sibut, some 120 miles away, we worked all the next day evacuating as many of our belongings as we could. That night no one was on the station when bandits and looters took what was left and set fire to whatever would burn. Fortunately, a steady rain kept most of the fires to a minimum. The library of the former MK school was a total loss.

A few days later, the American ambassador asked Lynn Muhr, our mission field president, and me to his office for a sort of debriefing of all that had taken place. During the interview, he asked me, "By the way, how were you able to call me on my security phone at 4:00 in the morning to tell me you were being attacked? That line is a direct line between my office in the embassy, or my bedroom at the residence, and the US State Department in Washington, DC! No one can make calls on that line. It's a secure line!"

"Mr. Ambassador," I exclaimed, "I did not call you on ANY line! My phone lines were cut. Believe me; I would have called you if I could have!"

"But it was YOUR voice," he insisted.

The ambassador never figured out who made that call. But we remembered those reassuring words that we had read just before the attack: "He shall give His angels charge over thee, to keep thee in all thy ways." Psalm 91:11.

Christ Calms His Child

Ricka Butler

Ricka and her husband Steve felt God's call to missions during their time in a pastorate and joined Baptist Mid-Missions in 1984. They spent nearly a decade as church planters in Australia before Steve accepted his current assignment of BMM Field Administrator for North America.

We had been on deputation for about five weeks in 1984 and were living in Memphis, Tennessee. One Sunday, we were supposed to go to a church in one of the suburbs of Memphis. Our six-year-old daughter, Amy, was sick all day Saturday. I thought that maybe she had the stomach flu. Sunday morning she was still very sick, so Steve went to church by himself. As the morning went on, I started to suspect that she had appendicitis. She was really in pain. She was just writhing. She lay on the couch and then rolled on the floor.

She begged me, "Mother, please take me to the hospital." I assured her that as soon as her dad got home, we would take her to the hospital. Over and over she asked me, "Where is he? Where is he?"

Finally, my husband came home about 1:30 in the afternoon. We got into the car and went to the emergency room. The first emergency room we went to refused us because we didn't have insurance. We had just started deputation, and so we didn't have enough money for health insurance yet with Baptist Mid-Missions.

They told us to go to Le Bonheur, a children's hospital in downtown Memphis. They said Le Bonheur would accept us even if we didn't have any money.

So we took Amy to Le Bonheur. It was just terrible to see her suffer that way. She was writhing in pain and crying and screaming. The doctor did some x-rays in the afternoon, and they determined that she needed an operation.

When Amy was settled in a room, I stayed with her while Steve went and called Willow Park, our commissioning church in Memphis. He got in contact with our pastor just before they had prayer meeting. It's a Southern church, and so they have prayer meeting before the evening service every Sunday night for about 20 minutes. Pastor Vincent said, "Yes, we'll pray for you."

By the time Steve got back to Amy's room, it was like someone had drugged her. She was completely calm, completely quiet. She hardly spoke. Amy barely moved until about an hour later when they took her to the operating room. One of the nurses came in and noticed that she was so quiet and calm and asked if someone had already given her the pre-operative medication to calm her. But no one had.

I couldn't believe what had happened to her. I leaned over and whispered, "Amy, do you still hurt?" She was completely placid and calm and said she didn't hurt. We knew that it was the Lord who had calmed her in response to the prayers of His people.

My Mouth Shall Praise You, Lord
Lisa (Armstrong) Wils

Lisa and her late husband Jesse became missionaries with Baptist Mid-Missions in 1994, appointed to the field of Russia. After two terms of church planting, they had to return to the US when Jesse was diagnosed with ALS (Lou Gehrig's disease). The Armstrong family saw many evidences of God's faithfulness throughout their years as missionaries, which helped sustain them through Jesse's illness. He passed away in 2009. Shortly thereafter, God in His goodness brought a widower, Barry Wils, into Lisa's life, and they were married in 2010.

We were on deputation preparing to be missionaries in Russia. I had known for some time that I needed to have my wisdom teeth pulled before we left the United States. The problem was that my dentist refused to do the job. He wanted to send me to an oral surgeon and have the procedure done under anesthesia. He also insisted that only two teeth should be removed at one time, thus requiring two separate procedures. The cost was going to be high. And it was likely that I would feel miserable after each procedure. I had seen people whose faces had turned black and blue after having their wisdom teeth removed. Others had their cheeks swell up like chipmunks and were in significant pain during the healing process. My husband Jesse and I were in the midst of language classes and deputation travels. So we opted to put off the needed dental work because of the cost and inconvenience.

During the course of our travels, we were in a missionary conference in Minnesota. On Tuesday night of the conference, a dentist in the church approached us and invited our family to his office the next day for checkups. He had set aside his schedule for the morning to accommodate any needs that our family might have.

As he checked my teeth he commented, "You really should have your wisdom teeth pulled before you move overseas." I explained that I was aware of the problem but had delayed the procedure because of cost and inconvenience. After a few moments of conversation he said, "You know, I could probably pull all four of those teeth in about 30 seconds and get the job done for you. Of course, you might be miserable afterwards when the novocaine wears off."

The offer was inviting, so I asked Jesse about it. He remembered his own experience with wisdom teeth and looked at me rather skeptically. He reminded me that we had a dinner appointment in three hours and an evening service right after that. We were to leave early the next morning to drive back to Seattle and arrive home just in time for our next scheduled language class. There was no break in our schedule to allow for a three-or four-day recovery from having wisdom teeth pulled. Jesse finally decided to let me make the decision.

I accepted the dentist's offer and sat in the chair for another hour or so while he did x-rays, filled a tooth, and proceeded to pull all four wisdom teeth. One of the roots was a bit hooked and stubborn, so the extraction took about 15 minutes instead of just 30 seconds. But soon it was over, and the problem teeth were gone. I stayed in the dentist's office for another half hour, biting down on gauze to stop any bleeding. My biggest challenge was trying to answer my son's persistent questions while at the same time keeping my mouth tightly closed. He finally asked, "Mom, why are you talking that way? Are you speaking in Russian or something?"

Once we were allowed to leave the dentist's office, we headed back to our host's home for a short rest. Then we were off to our dinner appointment. I wondered how I was going to eat spaghetti with a numb mouth, but just about the time we started to eat, the novocaine wore off completely. I made it successfully through dinner. Then we rushed off to the Wednesday evening service at the church. I took some ibuprofen just in case I might feel some pain, since the novocaine had worn off. But I felt nothing except the odd feeling of four gaping holes in the back of my mouth.

The next morning we began the drive home. We had been on the road for about eight weeks, and we were like horses headed toward the barn. We stopped only when a bad snowstorm prohibited us from getting through a mountain pass at night. After a few hours of sleep in our trailer, we continued on our way home to Seattle. The Lord spared me from all the potential complications and discomfort. I experienced no swelling or bruising and felt very little pain throughout the healing process. We continued on with our language classes as scheduled.

The kind services of that Christian dentist and his staff as well as the problem-free recovery were a direct provision of the Lord. No one can convince me that God is not concerned with the little things in our lives.

Blackwater Fever

Esther Jeunnette

Esther and her husband Clarence were among Baptist Mid-Missions' early missionaries, having joined in 1924. They served on BMM's first field, Central African Republic. After Clarence died in 1958, Esther served the Lord there for another decade before retiring. She went to be with her Lord in 2002, at the age of 101.

Our five-year-old son, Paul, got sick in October of 1936 while we were missionaries in the Central African Republic. Very early one morning, he got up and went to the bathroom, and there was blood in his urine. Right away I told my husband Clarence and he said, "That shows he has blackwater fever." We didn't recall Paul having had malaria, but he must have because blackwater fever is the result of malaria.

Clarence got the car ready, and before sunup he was on the road down to Bambari, 50 miles away, to get a doctor. He got to the ferry, but the ferry wasn't running yet because it was too early. The sun hadn't even come up. But he called out, and they brought the ferry over. The doctor came to stay with us. He kept giving Paul injections of saline solution in his abdomen. When Paul saw that needle coming, he just yelled. It was very difficult for him. Yet even with those injections, he kept losing blood.

After three days the doctor said, "There is nothing more I can do. I might as well go home. I can't do anything else. If your God doesn't intervene, this boy won't live."

So the doctor left. Clarence and I went into the other room, and we got down on our knees and we prayed. We committed Paul to the Lord. That was all we could do. The doctor was gone, so it was up to the Lord if He wanted him to live.

The Lord did intervene. When we came out of the room after praying, Paul looked a little brighter. That was Saturday morning. Our houseboy just loved Paul, and he took care of him all the time. He had gone to the village and told the people that Paul was very sick and that they should pray. So they all went up from the village to the church to pray. They were praying all morning, and at noon Paul passed the crisis. At about three o'clock in the afternoon, we heard singing in the chapel.

I said to the houseboy, "What are they singing for? This is Saturday. There is no meeting in the chapel today."

"Haven't they been praying all morning? Now they are assured that Paul is going to get better," he said.

It was just marvelous the way the Africans applied their faith like that.

Paul started getting better, but it took a long time for him to get his strength back. We weren't able to go to the conference of our missionaries in November. We didn't dare take him up there because even then he really wasn't strong enough.

We started home for furlough in March of 1937. As soon as we got home to America, we took Paul to a doctor for an examination. The doctor said there was nothing wrong with him. God had completely healed our son, and we gave Him all the praise.

Grandma Kawabata's Prayer
Joyce Oshiro

Joyce's parents, Roy and her late mother Kimiko, and stepmother Kiyo served the Lord as missionaries in Okinawa, beginning in 1950. Joyce joined Baptist Mid-Missions in 1982 and continues to serve in Japan.

In 2002 Grandma Kawabata celebrated her 98th birthday. Even at that age, she continued to be faithful in attending morning worship services at Gushikawa Baptist Church in Okinawa, Japan, where she was an encouragement to many. Grandma Kawabata consistently rejoiced in the Lord.

However, it was not always so. Her husband left her with three children to raise and ran off to Brazil. Then she contracted Hansen's disease and was forced to leave her home and enter a leprosarium on a remote island.

But it was there she heard the gospel and accepted the Lord Jesus Christ as her Savior at the age of 53. From then on, she began to pray that the Lord would send a gospel witness and provide a church in her home village. After her release from the leprosarium, she returned home. Soon thereafter my father Roy arrived in Okinawa and was led of the Lord to start a church—in her very village.

Mrs. Kawabata became a faithful member and was one of the first people baptized in the ministry. When her husband returned to Okinawa after 25 years, she accepted him back and continued to be a gentle witness to him and to pray for his salvation. When he was hospitalized with cancer, she was able to lead him to the Lord three days before he passed away—40 years after she had started praying for him! Her third son and grandson followed and also became part of God's family.

Mrs. Kawabata never refused an opportunity to praise the Lord and was an amazing example to us of perseverance in prayer. In 2004, after her 100th birthday, the Lord called this faithful servant Home, having honored her desire to be faithful to the end.

Augustin
Evelyne Metzler

Evelyne was exposed to missions from birth, as the daughter of Paul and Etiennette Metzler, pioneer Baptist Mid-Missions missionaries to Chad. Evelyne also felt the call to full-time missions and joined BMM in 1958. She and her sisters, Helene and Rachel, served in Chad until the country's Cultural Revolution expelled all missionaries in 1972 (Helene had gone to be with the Lord in 1969). The next year, Evelyne and Rachel transferred to Haiti. In her final ministry before retiring in 2002, Evelyne served seven years with Campus Bible Fellowship (now called Campus Bible Fellowship International) in Miami, Florida.

"One of our second-grade boys died last night."
"He did? Who was it?"
"Francois."
"What was wrong with him?"
"We don't know. He was absent only two days."
"Who has him for chapel?"

"Mr. Simon."

"Simon, do you know if he was saved?"

Simon answered, "The last day he was in school, I gave an invitation after the Bible story. I asked, 'Which one of you knows when he's going to die?' Francois raised his hand. I thought he had misunderstood, so I repeated the question. Again he raised his hand. I said, 'Francois, do you know when you're going to die?' He answered soberly, 'Yes, sir. I am going to die in two days. But I am ready. I have accepted the Lord Jesus as my Savior.' I still thought he didn't know what he was saying, so I dropped the subject. I guess he did know. Praise God, he was saved."

This discussion took place at the teachers' prayer meeting that we had every morning before school at the Balimba Primary School in the Republic of Chad. That day, school was dismissed early. All the teachers and the school director went to the home of the deceased to pay their respects to the parents and to talk to them about the Lord Jesus.

When we arrived in the family concession, we sensed right away that something was wrong. Usually there would be a group of people sitting in the concession of a family who is in mourning. This day there were only two men sitting alone in the burning sun, and we could sense a tension that did not have anything to do with mourning or sorrow.

We were given benches far apart from the two mourners and left to ourselves, something else that was very unusual. We should have been seated right with the mourners. After sitting in a group for half an hour, Rachel Metzler (the school director) and Michel Kanago (the head African teacher) took their stools and went over to join the mourners.

They found out that the two men were Francois' father and uncle. But where was the rest of the family? Slowly and bitterly, the father spoke. They were members of a tribe up north at Kyabe. They had been living here for several years but had no friends. Several months earlier, they had lost a small boy with rabies. When the boy was bitten by a rabid dog, they took him to the hospital. There, the father was told that if he bought the antirabies vaccine at the drugstore, that they would give the child shots. The vaccine cost about $5.00, and the father had no money. So they had to sit and watch their little son die a horrible death.

Then another son became sick. In spite of the care from the dispensary and much home remedy, he grew continually worse. This son, Augustin, was in the first grade in our school and had been absent for four months. It was recorded that he had dropped out of school.

Francois had come home from school Friday in perfect health.

He had eaten supper and gone to bed. In the night he became violently ill with stomach cramps and vomiting. In the morning, they carried him to the hospital, where he died two days later. We think he died of blood poisoning from a sliver.

The father was deeply embittered and had lost all faith in nurses, doctors, and hospitals. He did not even want to talk to Rachel anymore.

"But what about the first grader who is so sick?" Rachel asked.

"Nothing can be done for him now; he's dying," the father responded.

"Maybe we can do something. Let me take him to the hospital myself and have the doctor check him and see what can be done," she said.

"No! No one can do anything for him!"

"Then let me try!" said Rachel, emphatically. "I am his teacher, and I want to see him. God can help him."

"No! He's dying, and you can't do anything to help him," said the father despondently.

We teachers were all listening to the conversation, and by this time we were praying fervently, "Dear God, soften this man's heart and let us help the child who is dying. We cannot just go home and let him die. Oh God, help us!"

Finally, the father very reluctantly and bitterly said, "All right, you can see the child. Then you will see that it is too late."

On one side of the concession was a small, lonely hovel. He led us there and pushed back the grass mat that hid the doorway. When we entered the dark, sweltering hut we could not see anything at first, for we had stepped out of the dazzling sunlight. When our eyes became accustomed to the darkness, we could hardly believe what we saw. It didn't seem possible that the little heap on a grass mat in the corner was a person. We all felt sick to our stomachs, and just could not believe it was true.

Two big eyes stared at us from an emaciated face. All we could see was a skeleton, covered with skin. We had heard of such things before but had never seen it. It was like a nightmare, and we had to keep telling ourselves, "That is a person!"

Now we knew what the father meant. It was too late! That little skeleton could not possibly live much longer. In fact, we could not understand why he was still alive. But we didn't feel we could just go home and forget about him.

"Oh God, show us what to do!" we prayed. If we took him home and he died on the way or while there, we could get in a lot of trouble—especially since his father did not want us to take him in the first place.

Rachel told the father that she would take the teachers home and then come back. She brought us back to Balimba and then returned with Michel and our African nurse, Jacques Djimassibe. We prayed that God would direct them, and that His will would be done. When they returned, the father was more determined than ever that they should not take the child. When Jacques saw that pathetic little pile of bones, he also felt that there was not much hope.

However, Rachel felt that she could not leave him to die, so she called on the Lord to change the father's heart. At the same time, she prayed for someone who could come along to care for him, for the child would need full-time nursing. Much as we would like to, we could not possibly spare the time, with school still in session and 12 children in our home.

When Rachel finished praying, the father said, "I would let you take him, but he can't go without his mother, and she doesn't want to go."

All this time the mother had been sitting silently next to the poor, little form huddled on the ground. Eagerly she spoke, "Yes, I want to go. I want to take my son and go with Miss."

The father was chagrined. He had not expected that response and now did not know what to do. Finally he said in exasperation, "All right, take him!"

Rachel thanked God but prayed fervently that the child would not die. They brought him to Balimba. A toolshed was cleared out to make a home for the boy and his mother. We had a prayer meeting and asked the Lord to heal that poor, little body if He would. We also asked Him to bring this child into His fold and work in the hearts of his parents.

The first few days were touch and go. Only a miracle of God could save him. We kept praying, and Rachel and the nurse treated him for parasites and malnutrition. They gave him serum intravenously. It was a while before he could keep anything down. Of course, we cared for the mother's needs also.

Augustin's father came to see him every day. After several days had passed, he told Rachel that he wanted to talk to her.

"Miss, when you brought my boy to your home, you didn't save one life, you saved two. After what had happened to my family and many other disappointments, I had given up," he said. "I was waiting for Augustin to die; then I was going to slit my throat and die, too. That's why I didn't want you to take him. I was resolved to my fate and didn't want it changed.

"I didn't want Augustin to get better. I wanted him to die, so I could die too. But you took him and my wife. You gave them a room and have been feeding them without asking for anything in return. I don't even have five francs to give them for food. I'm a stranger here. I have no job or land on which to plant. I have no way to get money. I thought nobody cared, but now I see that you do. I am a Christian, Miss, but I have strayed a long way from the fold. I want to ask God's forgiveness now and come back to Him."

He bowed his head right there and prayed to the Lord. Then he called his wife and said, "You have been out of fellowship with the Lord, too. It is time to ask His forgiveness and come back." She was very happy. She bowed her head, and another prodigal returned to the arms of the loving Father.

Then the father said, "My son Francois was ready when the Lord took him home, but Augustin is not ready to go. We must lead him to the Lord right now; then if he dies it will be all right."

He knelt by the mat of little Augustin and quietly led him to the Lord. After the child had accepted the Lord Jesus as his Savior, a peace came over his countenance. How thrilled we were to see God's answer to our prayers!

Very, very slowly, Augustin started getting better. By this time, many people were praying for him at Balimba and in America. God heard our prayers and worked a miracle. Three months later, Augustin and his mother returned to their home. His cheeks were full and his strength and vitality had returned. As he neared his home, he jumped up and down with joy and excitement. The most wonderful thing is that Augustin returned to his village a new creature in Christ. His whole family is changed now. There is no more bitterness and sorrow, but real joy and happiness. God does answer prayer! "Call unto me, and I will answer thee, and show thee great and mighty things, which thou knowest not" (Jeremiah 33:3).

Psalm 91
Jack McKillop

Jack and his wife Doris began their service with Baptist Mid-Missions in 1951. They ministered in Jamaica until 1976, when they began serving at Missionary Acres, BMM's retirement village in Silva, Missouri. The McKillops retired in 1991 and continue to live at Missionary Acres.

We lived at Anchovy, seven miles southwest of Montego Bay in Jamaica. It was the day before Christmas in the late 1960s. Shortly after breakfast, we heard of a terrible tragedy that had happened in town near Hillview Baptist Church, where we ministered. A Syrian couple and their seven-year-old daughter, who lived about a hundred feet from the rear corner of the church building, had been murdered.

Their hired man had stolen some money from the couple, and the little girl had seen him do it. She told her parents and the man was fired. He came back a couple of weeks later and killed the little girl in her bed with a machete, and then killed her parents.

The incident was heavy on our hearts all day. That night, as we were having a snack in the back of the house, we attempted to listen to Trans World Radio. It was not coming in clearly, so we decided to go to bed. I went through the living room and locked the front door before going into our bedroom. Before we went to bed, we especially prayed for the Lord's protection through the night. As we knelt there, we were unaware that a burglar was already lying under the bed.

Our four young children were sleeping on bunk beds in a small room on the opposite side of the bathroom. I enjoyed rising at night to look after the children. I reasoned that if my wife could give birth to our little ones, surely I could care for them through the night.

I heard one of the children tossing and turning and decided to get up and check on him. As I put my feet out on the floor, I touched a bare foot. I turned on the light. It was 3:20 a.m. I pounced over the foot of the bed and looked under it. There, I saw a pair of brown legs. I reached for a four-foot metal level standing in the closet. I swung hard at him, first one side of the bed and then the other.

My wife woke up and wondered if I was crazy. I pointed and she understood. She then reached for the telephone and called the neighbor to bring his gun. In a few seconds, out from under the bed came the 17-year-old young man. He raced through the bathroom and into the children's room. I recognized him because he had robbed our house in August. His name was Maurice.

I followed Maurice with my level and cornered him between the bunks. I was not attempting to kill him but rather to beat him to the floor and maybe knock him unconscious, to protect my family. He pulled open the bolt on our French-style windows, climbed over a bunk, and sailed out the window headfirst. He was bleeding, because we found blood on the windowsill.

About five minutes later, the neighbor arrived with his .38 revolver. But Maurice had already fled. Earlier, Maurice had escaped from prison and after robbing the local post office had come to our home. We think that Maurice slipped into the house while we were trying to listen to the radio. When he heard us coming, there was nothing to do but get under the bed.

The following morning, which was a Sunday, a farmer happened to go to a small hut at the back of his property and found Maurice with a dirty bandage on his head. The farmer asked, "What happened?"

Maurice answered, "You know I was 'in' (meaning in jail). I wanted to come home for Christmas, so I rode the train, and when I jumped off I hit my head on the rails." The farmer asked if he would come with him to get his head cared for properly. He led him to the center of the village, where the police were dealing with the post office robbery. They took charge of Maurice. How sad it was to see a young man headed in that direction.

We prayed not only for the Lord's protection from physical danger and harm but also for His protection from the evil one. The entire 91st Psalm was so precious to us.

My greatest fear in going to the mission field was not crime nor lack of funds nor breakdown of health. Rather, I feared that I would somehow do something that would put me on the shelf, ruin my ministry, and be a blot on the cause of Christ. It was my ardent desire to always be a great testimony for my Savior, the Lord Jesus Christ. To this end we prayed, and the Lord has been faithful.

Guardian Angels Watching Over Me
Joy Spieth

Joy is a second-generation missionary serving in Brazil. Her parents, Albert and Naomi Spieth, began their service with Baptist Mid-Missions in 1941, and Joy joined in 1967. As did her parents, Joy serves in Brazil's Amazon region.

We have guardian angels all over Manaus, Brazil. When you drive in Manaus, it's good to know that you have the Lord's angels on your side. One evening I was driving to church, and when I came around the corner, there was a man in my lane coming head-on toward me. He was trying to go around two illegally parked cars. I stopped to give him room to pull back into his own lane.

But instead of doing that, he decided to block the road. He got out of his car with a revolver in his hand. His wife hollered at him, "No, no, don't go." Ignoring his wife and swearing profusely, the man came towards my car with the revolver pointed right at me.

A lot of different thoughts went through my head at that moment. I thought about asking him why he was calling me all those names when I didn't know what they meant anyway. The other thing I thought of saying was, "You can kill me, because I know where I am going." But I didn't think I should incite his emotions any higher, so I didn't say anything at all.

Finally, he went back to his car. But by this time, there was a whole line of cars behind me, and the drivers started calling the man names for blocking traffic. So he came back to my car—thinking I was the one calling him names.

I stuck my head out the window and said, "Mister, I don't want to fight with you. I'm just trying to get out of your way." When he saw that I was a lady, he calmly went back to his car. I got to church really shaky and crying—just the nervous reaction of having someone pull a gun on me. But I also could testify that the Lord and His guardian angels had protected me once again.

God's Faithfulness on the Side of the Road
John Proios

John was appointed to serve with Baptist Mid-Missions in Brazil in 1994. While raising support, he met his future wife, Robin Emel, and they were married in 2000. The Proios family serves in Brazil's Amazon region.

Jonathan Teachout, my former Bible college classmate, and I were both candidates for missionary service with Baptist Mid-Missions in 1994. We attended the BMM Triannual Conference in Lapeer, Michigan, in order to complete our doctrinal oral examinations. By God's grace, we both passed. We thought the next step in our candidature was Candidate Seminar in Cedarville, Ohio. We were unaware that the Lord first had a little faith test for us on the side of the road.

We teamed up in Jonathan's car to drive down to Cedarville College. Right before we left, the pastor of the church in Lapeer advised us to take a different route than the one we had planned, in order to avoid construction traffic. We hopped in the car and started driving south to Cedarville, Ohio—about a four- or five-hour drive. About an hour into the trip, I noticed that Jonathan's oil light was blinking on and off. I asked him about it, and he said that his car always did that. A little voice in the back of my mind was saying, "We should pull over and check the oil." But then I said to myself, "No, it's his car and he knows what he's doing."

A couple of hours later, we were driving through Ohio on the interstate, talking about our days at Piedmont Baptist College and what had happened to our classmates. We didn't have air conditioning, so our windows were down. It seemed like the noise from the trucks around us was getting louder and louder. Then I realized that the noise we were hearing was not from the trucks but was coming from Jonathan's engine. Then I noticed his oil light come on.

I yelled, "Pull over! Stop the engine."

He pulled off the interstate onto the shoulder as fast as he could and then stopped the car. It was a blistering hot July day.

"Did you turn the engine off?" I asked.

"No, it stopped before I could turn it off," he replied.

So we went to the front of the car, popped the hood open, and looked at the engine. It was sizzling. We stared at the engine and Jonathan said, "Let's pray."

So we both bowed our heads along the side of the interstate and Jonathan prayed, thanking the Lord for His faithfulness and begging Him for His help. At first I thought, "The Lord is going to take care of us." But then as I thought about our situation, my faith evaporated in the heat. I thought, "We're doomed. I'm 1,500 miles from home. It's over 100 degrees out here along this interstate, and we've seized the engine. We're doomed out in the middle of nowhere."

After he finished praying, Jonathan went to the trunk of his car for some oil. I turned around right then, and Carl and Selma Barton— also missionaries with Baptist Mid-Missions—pulled over to help us. The Bartons and I had stayed at the same home during the Triannual Conference, so they had recognized me standing on the side of the road. The Bartons came along within five seconds after Jonathan had prayed!

Then another man in a YWCA van pulled over to help, and he took us to the first exit. There was a AAA station there. We ended up riding the rest of the way to Cedarville College in a wrecker truck with the car on the back. Through this incident, the Lord taught me about His faithfulness and His ability to take care of His children in times of need.

Thirteen years later, I was driving on a parkway in New York City when my full gas tank almost broke off the car and the strap securing the tank was dragging on the road! My father was behind me, but he usually took another expressway home. I did not have my cell phone with me, but I knew that we always have a cell phone with prayer! I asked the Lord to send my father my way after he crossed the bridge. Five minutes later, my father came along and stopped to help me. He told me that he never took the parkway. I used his cell phone to call the fire department (I was leaking fuel) and to get a tow truck. I praise the Lord that the gas tank did not drop off when I was on the interstate with my family. God answers prayer!

Journey to Japan
Eulalie Zimmerman

In 1957, Eulalie and her husband Charles joined Baptist Mid-Missions after previously serving in Japan with another agency. They spent most of their service in Fukushima City but later were caretakers of a camp until retiring in 1986. Eulalie has been with the Lord since 2007 and Charles since 2008.

After much preparation and waiting, my husband and I and our 18-month-old daughter were finally ready to go to Japan as missionaries in September of 1951. We stood on the dock in Oakland, California, watching the loading of our freight.

The ship was a very unimpressive freighter—the Edgar Luckenbock. I have always been afraid of great expanses of water, yet here I was on the deck of that little tub on the ocean. We were shown to our stateroom and were informed that the trip would take about nine days. As I began to unpack and make things a little homelike, the rolling movement of the sea became apparent. In a short time, it was evident to me that this was not going to be a pleasant cruise.

The ship was transporting supplies to Korea for the military. It was during the Korean War. Not only was our freight tucked in between military things, but the deck was also stacked with large containers and telephone poles. They told us that trees were so scarce in Korea that it was necessary to import poles.

After several days of lovely weather and a somewhat settling of my stomach, the wind began to rise. As we sat at a meal, the rocking of the ship was so violent that any liquid on the table would splash out of its container. After the third roll that emptied all the soup bowls, the first mate gave up and left. Just about that time, a real roller came along, and our daughter, strapped in her highchair, took a great bound across the deck, to be rescued by one of the men. Eating was virtually impossible.

We made our way back up to our rooms to tie the baby down and roll on our bunks with the ship. Skitter. Skitter. Bang! Our army footlocker danced across the floor and banged into the wall. Crash! The door of the medicine cabinet flew open, the contents breaking in the sink below.

With each roll of the ship, it seemed impossible but to think that this was the end of us. How could we ever be righted? But slowly, after scudding on its side for what seemed like an eternity, the ship begin to recover and right itself. It was a fantastic, awesome feeling. But immediately the ship began the opposite roll, and we experienced the same thoughts and feelings. This just has to be our Waterloo, we thought as we prayed. Yet our confidence was in the One who commanded the sea.

This scenario continued for several days. By this time, although greatly hindered in speed, we were approaching our destination—Japan. When we were finally able to get up and walk about, we were surprised to see those great, heavy freight containers lying helter-skelter on the deck and not one telephone pole remained. The great chains had been snapped, and every pole was gone. This was our introduction to cruising the mighty Pacific.

We arrived in Japan a few pounds lighter but for all that, quite well and very excited to set foot on this land. Our first port was Yokohama. Today it is a noisy, crowded place. We arrived on a Sunday. All was quiet. Not a soul was on the street. War devastation was still evident, although the people had worked to erase as much of the results of the war as possible.

Finally, we met a man. The look on his face was one of dismay, but his curiosity was greater. He stopped and stared at this foreign family. What could we say? How much we wanted to communicate, but couldn't.

We thank the Lord for the years He gave us there in Japan. We thank Him that we were eventually able to communicate the wonderful love of the Lord Jesus to the Japanese after they had suffered such a devastating defeat in World War II.

God, Africa, and the Leopard
Mary Lee Teachout

Mary Lee's story comes from her growing-up years in the Central African Republic, where her parents, Richard and Oril Teachout, had served from the 1930s until the 1970s.

Squawk! Squawk! My mother awoke with a start because of the noise in the night. Something or someone was after the six chickens that we kept in a rabbit pen. My dad was away from our home in Bambari, Central African Republic, at the time. So Mom, thinking a fox was after the chickens, bounded out of bed, grabbed the flashlight, and dashed out onto the porch. She hesitated and then turned back for her slippers to protect her bare feet from scorpions or centipedes. She arrived in the backyard too late to save the chicken.

In the moonlight she saw a large animal, much bigger than a fox, disappearing into the darkness with the squawking chicken in its mouth. The next morning, Mom discovered leopard tracks. The Lord had sent her back for slippers and kept her from danger. Had she cornered the savage beast in the shed, she could easily have been wounded or killed.

My parents had only recently returned from furlough in the United States, where they had left two sons, Dick and Don, for school. In August of 1950, my folks had written from the mission station: "The nationals came bringing bundles of grass on their heads to fix the roof of the house—it leaked badly! They also brought about eight dozen eggs, nine chickens, rice, peanuts, etc. About 100 people gathered, so we had them sit down and we had a praise and prayer service. How our hearts rejoiced to hear their testimonies and prayers. They have been faithful in continued prayer for our return. God has answered. They praised Him, and we did too." Little did my parents know then how dangerous Bambari was about to become.

It was on September 24 that Mom had the first near miss with the leopard. Dad was on a trip to the outstation of Kwango. For 10 days, people carried lights if they went out after dark. Most leopards stay in the wild, but an injured one will often come to a village for easy prey. One night, the beast was chased off by villagers as it tried to catch a goat.

My brother Arnie and I were in boarding school in Crampel, blissfully unaware of the danger facing my parents and younger brothers, Robert and Cliff. Crampel was about 188 miles away from Bambari over extremely bumpy dirt roads.

One night after Dad's return, Mom awakened him, whispering that something was pushing on the tub under which the chickens were sleeping. Whoosh! Whoosh! Dad went out with a flashlight and his rifle. He shone the light on the long shadowy figure of the leopard as it pushed on the stone-weighted tub.

Dad raised the gun with a shaky hand. It was impossible to see the leopard clearly through the gloomy darkness. What if the first shot only wounded the leopard? Would he have time to shoot again if the beast pounced? Slowly, Dad pulled the trigger. God guided that bullet right into the heart of that deadly leopard, killing it instantly! To make sure, however, Dad shot again. But this time the bullet missed the leopard completely and hit Mom's tub.

Even before the sun rose the next day, villagers began coming from all around to see the animal. "Many thanks for killing our enemy," they said. The Bible school students and their families enjoyed a marvelous feast. Mom regretted having the challenge of replacing the bullet-holed tub, but she was very thankful she no longer had to face the leopard.

Friends that prayed in America, my brothers in Pennsylvania, and Arnie and I at Crampel were oblivious to our parents' near disaster. But God knew and cared and watched over them. "Fear thou not; for I am with thee: be not dismayed; for I am thy God: I will strengthen thee; yea, I will help thee; yea, I will uphold thee with the right hand of my righteousness" (Isaiah 41:10). He preserved their lives by His all-powerful hand guiding bare feet back to slippers and directing a bullet from a shaking gun to the precise spot to kill a deadly foe for His glory. "That they may see, and know, and consider, and understand together, that the hand of the LORD hath done this …" (Isaiah 41:20). "Now unto him that is able to do exceeding abundantly above all that we ask or think, according to the power that worketh in us, unto him be glory in the church by Christ Jesus throughout all ages, world without end. Amen" (Ephesians 3:20, 21).

Crisis in the Air
Elaine Schulte

A registered nurse, Elaine joined Baptist Mid-Missions in 1975 to serve in medical ministry in Africa. She served in both Chad and Ivory Coast before coming back to the US to care for her elderly parents. In 1998, Elaine became part of the Bibles International team in Grand Rapids, Michigan.

"Please, if there is a doctor or nurse on board, would you identify yourself?"

I could not believe my ears! It had been a stressful first term of missionary service in Côte d'Ivoire (Ivory Coast), West Africa, and I was on my way home for furlough. Just before boarding the plane in the city of Abidjan, I had visited with other missionaries I had met while serving my first four-year term. We chatted a bit. When we boarded the plane, they were seated in the center section of the same row as I.

It was to be an overnight flight to Belgium. We had been served an evening meal before people began settling down for a few hours of sleep. I was sitting next to the window and had found a pillow and blanket. With the pillow cushioning my head against the window, I was trying to drift off to sleep.

Just as I was beginning to doze, the announcement came over the plane's PA system. Since the plane was full, I couldn't believe I was the only doctor or nurse on board. Although my carnal nature wanted to continue to doze, there were two things that kept me from doing so—my conscience and knowing the other missionaries on this flight knew I was a nurse.

Then the announcement came the second time: "Please, if there is a doctor or nurse on board, would you identify yourself?" The same announcement, by the same voice, held a bit more urgency this time.

Opening my eyes, I glanced at the missionaries sitting a few seats over from me. The man was staring at me. "You'd better go," he mouthed the words.

With pounding heart, I stood to try to decide where I might be needed. It took only a few seconds to assess the situation. About 10 rows in front of me, a group of airline crew members huddled together in the aisle. Climbing over the passenger beside me, I walked toward the huddle, praying for wisdom as I went. What would I face when I arrived on the scene?

Upon arrival, I asked if they were still in need of medical personnel. When one of the female attendants responded affirmatively, I identified myself as a nurse. She indicated to me that one of the passengers was in crisis. The flight crew had already brought a small oxygen canister from which they were administering oxygen to a male passenger.

The man was a Caucasian—a European, I surmised. He had been clad in dress clothes, but by the time I arrived on the scene, his coat had been removed, the knot in his tie had been loosened, and his belt and shirt collar were opened. Looking at him, I felt certain he had done none of this for himself. His wife, seated beside him, was hovering over him, anxiety clearly written on her face.

The color of the man's face matched his shirt—white! When I questioned him about his symptoms, there was neither verbal response nor any other kind of reaction. Bending down, I tried to check his radial pulse (in his arm) but found it was too weak to count.

"Do you have an emergency kit on board?" I spoke to the flight attendant in French, since that was the language they were using.

"*Oui, Madame,*" she responded and rushed to get it.

While she was away, I continued visually assessing the man. It seemed clear to me that he was suffering from a heart condition of some kind. Since he was unable to communicate, I spoke to his wife.

"How did his symptoms start? Did he complain of pain?" I asked.

"*Non, Madame.*"

"Did he complain of nausea?" I asked.

"*Non, Madame.*"

"What did he complain of?" I asked, becoming ever more puzzled by his condition and her answers.

"He only complained of weakness, Madame. He said he felt very weak, and then he quit talking. He doesn't respond in any way."

When the flight attendant returned with the emergency kit, I searched inside. As I had hoped, I found a blood pressure cuff and stethoscope. Pulling them from the kit, I began putting the blood pressure cuff around the man's upper arm. He made no effort to help me.

As I suspected, his blood pressure was very low—80/60. Listening to his apical pulse was not comforting either. Even with the stethoscope poised directly over his heart, I could hardly pick up a heartbeat.

There were a few emergency drugs included in the meager supply. Although I did not want to do so, I began considering which of the medications I should give him. To my relief, I found a list of medications with a brief list of indications, or reasons they should be given. It seemed as if the explanation of the uses for the medicines had been given for nonmedical people. Among those medicines was only one that I felt was appropriate—Neo-Synephrine. The indication read, "To be given in the case of shock due to hypotension (low blood pressure)." Reading that, the thought came to me, "If this isn't shock due to hypotension, then I don't know what is."

I turned back to the patient to reassess his condition. When I rechecked his blood pressure, my heart sank. It was now 60/0! I no longer had any doubt. If I did not take action, death seemed imminent. The chief flight attendant had been watching my expression as I rechecked his blood pressure. When she read my expression of grave concern, she turned and walked away.

With shaking hands, I began searching for the vial of Neo-Synephrine. I did not want to administer any medication to this patient, because I had no idea if my African nurse's license covered me in this situation. In Côte d'Ivoire, I was licensed to do anything I felt was appropriate for a patient. We were flying over the continent of Africa, but we were being transported by a Belgian plane. So whose laws were in effect five to six miles above terra firma? I was not sure I had the legal right to treat this man.

I felt fairly certain, however, that if I did nothing, he would not live long enough to arrive in Brussels, which was our destination. The decision was made with many silent pleas to the Lord.

Once I found the vial of medicine, I was faced with another dilemma. What was the appropriate dose? If I gave him too much, I assumed I could kill him. If I didn't give him enough, the medicine would probably be ineffective.

Continuing to pray for the Lord's direction, I decided I would give the entire contents of the ampoule of medication. With hands that were trembling so violently I could hardly fit the needle through the tiny opening in the top of the ampoule, I drew up the medication. I hesitated only a moment more. I might be setting myself up for a lawsuit and the loss of my professional license, but I felt as if the Lord was directing me to do this. So, I steadied myself and determined to follow through with my plan of action.

Finding a place to inject the medicine was not easy. The passenger was wearing a long-sleeved dress shirt. My attempts to get the sleeve high enough were ineffective. I next tried slipping the shirt down over his shoulder in order to reach the deltoid area of his arm. Just as I succeeded in doing that with the aid of the patient's wife and a couple of flight attendants, the chief flight attendant returned.

"*Attendez!*" (Wait!) She commanded me. "What are you doing? Do you have the right to do this? What is that medicine?" She hurled the questions in my direction.

I was almost speechless! She, who had pleaded for medical help, was now questioning me? Truthfully, I was asking myself some of the same questions in my heart.

"Madame," I began hesitantly, "I've been treating patients for the past four years in Africa. But if you don't want me to give him this injection, I won't."

Looking down at the patient and back to me, she gave her reluctant assent. (I had almost hoped she would not.) Once permission was granted, I gave the medication with a sinking feeling.

Giving her the needle and syringe for disposal, I told her, "I'll go back to my seat for a few minutes before checking on him again." Once back at the row in which the other missionaries and I were seated, I turned to them before reclaiming my seat.

"There's a man up there who looks like he's going to die. I've just given him an injection and may have implicated myself. Please be in earnest prayer," I explained.

Once seated, I poured out my heart to the Lord. I felt certain that if He did not intervene, the man would die. And I had no idea if he was a believer. After spending a few more minutes in prayer, I got up to recheck the patient's condition. Glancing at the missionaries, I think my face told the story—they had an assignment, a mission. They were expected to be pleading with the Lord as I was.

Seeing the patient, my heart sank. He had no more color than before. I again lifted his flaccid arm in order to check his blood pressure. There was no improvement. I walked away from the patient, asking the chief flight attendant to accompany me.

In a few concise sentences, I expressed my concern to her. "If we don't land and take this man off the plane, I'm afraid he's going to die. Can't we land someplace and get adequate emergency care for him?"

"I'll ask the captain," she answered.

Going back to my seat, I prayed all the more earnestly. I had no peace. The situation appeared dire. As I continued praying, the flight attendant came to my seat.

"The captain wants to talk to you," she said.

Despair washed over me! Why would the captain of the plane want to talk to me? Following her toward the front of the plane, I was amazed to see that she was heading for the cockpit. Surely she didn't intend to take me into the cockpit!

"What's wrong?" inquired the captain, standing in the doorway of the cockpit.

I explained my concerns. "I don't even know where we are, but if we're near a city, could you land to take him off? If not, I'm afraid he's going to die."

"We're flying over Algeria. We could land in Algiers if it's absolutely necessary, but I'd rather go on at least as far as Nice on the southeastern coast of France. Do you think he can make it that far?"

"How long will it take to get to France?" I asked.

The captain turned back toward the cockpit. "Let me see …"

At that moment, one of the male flight attendants came rushing to the cockpit. "He's awake! He's talking! He's asking for a glass of water." I knew exactly of whom he spoke!

Turning toward the captain, I excused myself quickly, explaining that I needed to check on the patient. What a relief it was to find the man responding appropriately, with his clothing arranged as one would expect. When he saw me, he tried to thank me. I brushed off his thanks as graciously as I could and rushed back to my seat. I needed time to thank the Lord for what He had done on behalf of the patient and, to a lesser degree, what He had done for me. And I wanted to thank the other missionaries for their prayer support.

As we landed in Brussels, there was the usual rush to deplane. I didn't join the rush, wishing to speak to the man and his wife before leaving the plane. As the missionaries joined the others who were preparing to deplane, they told me goodbye, commenting on the Lord's goodness in preserving the man who had been so critically ill. As I had done before, I thanked them for their prayer support.

Once the plane was empty except for the patient, his wife, the flight crew, and myself, I rose to leave. I stopped by the row where the two were seated. As the man tried to thank me, I reminded him, as I had done before, that it was not I who had saved his life; rather, his life had been spared by God. I spoke with him a bit longer and then encouraged him to see a doctor as soon as he could. Then I walked on toward the front of the plane.

As I approached the door, the flight crew, including the captain and the copilot, were lined up near the exit. As I prepared to walk through the open door, I was stopped by the nearest crew member. With hand extended, she thanked me cordially for my help. I explained that I felt no need to be thanked. To my amazement, as I continued toward the door, each flight crew member repeated the same action. In spite of my lack of knowledge, the Lord had chosen to use me on that flight. He had once again worked through me, a very weak vessel, to accomplish His purpose.

Angel Watching Over Me

Martha Fogle

Martha joined Baptist Mid-Missions in 1937, the year after her husband Lester was appointed. They served in Africa until retirement in 1978. Lester went to be with the Lord in 1994. Their son Larry and his wife Sallie serve with BMM in the Pastoral Enrichment Program, and Larry and Sallie's daughter Janine serves with BMM in Zambia.

Having been missionaries for 40 years in French Equatorial Africa, now known as Chad and Central African Republic, I and my husband Lester have experienced God's watchcare and comfort time after time. There is one time in particular, however, that stands out in my mind.

My husband was gone on an outstation trip, and I was alone in our house on the mission station. These trips could take days or even weeks. That night, after the light plant was shut off, I went to bed, prayed, and went to sleep.

Sometime during the night, I awoke very frightened. To this day I don't know what woke me up, but everything within me screamed, "DANGER!!!" I sensed that danger was very real, very evil, and very close. I was extremely frightened. It was a very dark night, and I couldn't see two inches past my face. I was so scared. I lay very still, not moving a muscle, only moving my eyes around the room, trying to get accustomed to the darkness. But it was too dark. I couldn't see anything. I tried to calm my fast-beating heart. Something was desperately wrong, and I didn't know what.

I began to silently pray and recite verses, calling on the Lord for deliverance from evil and for comfort and freedom from fear. Suddenly, I sensed a calming presence with me there in the bedroom, and looking up I saw an angel floating above my bed. He was large—about the size of a full-grown adult male or larger—and his white robes were fluttering as he looked down toward me. The moment I saw him, I was filled with peace and quietness. I cannot describe to you what a glorious peace enveloped me.

Where I had felt fear, I now felt complete freedom from fear. The angel of the Lord brought me such a feeling of protection and comfort, and all sense of danger and evil fled. I was left feeling the peace and presence of God. The angel stayed with me—visible and comforting. I watched him until I fell into a peaceful, restful sleep. "The angel of the LORD encampeth round about them that fear Him, and delivereth them" Psalm 34:7.

Still in His Service
Charlie and Gai Jewell

The Jewells were appointed to serve in the Central African Republic in 1986. For Charlie it was a return home, because he grew up there as the son of missionaries Doug and Elizabeth Jewell. Charlie and Gai are stationed in the capital city, Bangui, and they assist national pastors and leaders.

In 1996, during our second term of service, there was a coup in the Central African Republic (CAR), and all missionaries and Peace Corps workers that were in CAR were evacuated by the French and then by US military C-10 jets. They came and picked up our family of five as well as our coworker Edith Wotherspoon and other expatriates at the Bangassou airport without problems. We stayed out of the country for over a year, but we knew that the Lord wanted us in CAR so we returned in late 1997. We finished our term, had a regular furlough, and then went back again to CAR.

It was October 25, 2001, and Charlie was moving some of our things to Bangui from Bangassou, where we had served for 14 years. We would be filling in for John and Paula Dannenberg in Bangui while they went on furlough. That trip for Charlie was one that none of us will ever forget.

Charlie was on a very bad stretch of road, in our white pick-up truck, between the towns of Bambari and Sibut. He was traveling very slowly so as not to tip the truck over. Suddenly, up ahead in the middle of the road, a man wearing an Arab garment stood pointing a rifle at the truck.

Charlie stopped, and soon about eight of them surrounded the truck, all with weapons. They pulled him out of the truck and immediately became rough with him and his passengers. His passengers were two pastors who needed cancer checkups in Bangui, one young lady, and one young man. The bandits spoke French badly and little Sango, but their Arabic was very good. They made Charlie and his passengers take off their clothes so that they could look for money. They began to rip open mail to look for money, too.

Charlie and his passengers were forced to lie face down on the ground for almost two hours. Money, food, and their travel bags were all stolen. The bandits went through everything on the truck. Each time someone passed Charlie, they would kick him or hit him with the butt of their gun on his body and face. They kept asking where all the money was hidden. During the entire ordeal, Charlie continued to pray for the safety of his passengers and for Gai and our daughter Lynda at Bangassou.

One of the Arabs said, "You think that bin Laden's followers are only in Afghanistan?" With the terrorist attacks of 9-11 still fresh on all of our minds, this was a very unsettling message.

About one and a half hours into their ordeal, another white truck came along. We learned later that this was the truck that the bandits had heard was carrying a huge amount of money.

Seeing Charlie and his passengers face down in the road, the antiterrorist soldiers in the other truck realized there was trouble and sprang into action. Charlie and his passengers moved to a safer position—Charlie in front of the truck and his passengers in the ditches along the road.

A gun battle ensued. One bullet went through the back fender, the tire, and the rim, before it kicked up gravel at Charlie's feet. Hundreds of bullets flew back and forth. The sound of it rang in Charlie's ears for days. After about 10 to 15 minutes, the soldiers were able to chase away the bandits. For Charlie and his companions, those minutes seemed like hours.

We praise the Lord for His protection of Charlie and those who were with him. None of them were injured in the gun battle. After the bandits fled, Charlie and his passengers collected the baggage that was left. Praise the Lord that the bandits had not taken the truck battery. They found the truck keys in the grass at the side of the road. They were then able to drive to the next little town for help and to report what had happened. Although the town provided some safety, Charlie and his companions felt compelled to press on to the Sibut station. They arrived there about 9:30 p.m. Charlie didn't sleep well that night.

When Charlie spoke to Gai on the shortwave radio the next morning, the news hit her and Lynda hard. Fortunately, two pastors were there, along with our houseboy. They immediately called our coworker Edie to come to be with Gai. Gai and Lynda and Edie were surrounded by pastors, students, and friends who prayed with Gai and Lynda for peace of mind and for strength. Edie stayed with Gai and Lynda all day.

Three and a half months later, on February 11, 2002, at our home in Bangassou, we were robbed at gunpoint. Charlie heard noises on the porch and intended to prevent their quick entrance by placing a metal dresser up against the door and bracing it with his body.

The bandits forced the door open a little and then realized what Charlie was doing. They shot into the ceiling through the glass window-panes in the door. The falling glass made Charlie flinch, and this gave the bandits the advantage they needed to push open the door enough to hit Charlie in the head with the butt of their gun.

When they entered, they tied him up and threw him on the office floor. They demanded the combination to the safe and the location of any other money. When they didn't find much money, they kicked him and hit him. Then they came back to the bedrooms of the house and broke into Lynda's bedroom first and then Gai's. They did not hurt Lynda or Gai, but they looked for money in our bedrooms.

The students were having a wake at the student village that night for a student who had died. There were over 200 people in the village. When they thought they heard shots, some of the students came up to the station and turned on the light plant, which scared the bandits away. While Charlie lay down on the sofa, Gai and Lynda went to check on the student guards. The two students were roughed up and shaking from the experience of being tied up, thrown down on the cement, and having guns planted in their ears. Gai and Lynda ministered to the student guards and read Psalm 18 to them and then prayed with them.

We praised the Lord again and again for His protection for us and our friends in these situations. Now the question in our minds was—what was God was trying to teach us in these things?

In November of 2002, we experienced a military coup where we had to drive out of CAR to Cameroon. The Lord was with us every step of the way. Even then, our hearts' desire was to return to the people of CAR as soon as we could. We knew that there would be a great many needs when we returned.

Later in 2004, when we came back to CAR after the evacuation, we were able to talk to, encourage, pray, and share God's Word with lay leaders and pastors and their wives, who went through terrible situations of beatings and robbings. We understood their fear, their pain, and their needs. We knew that the Lord was not finished with us here in CAR. The love and the care that the people here have shown to us make us so thankful that we could understand what He was doing in our lives and theirs.

When we read or think about the first few chapters of Genesis, we learn that God is a God of order and a God who loves us. He never lets those that are His out of His sight. God has a plan and His plan is perfect. He knows why things happen, and we are to rest in that. Some verses that come to mind about God's perfect plans are: "I will say of the LORD, He is my refuge and my fortress: my God; in him will I trust" (Psalm 91:2), and "This is my comfort in my affliction: for thy word hath quickened me. … Let, I pray thee, thy merciful kindness be for my comfort, according to thy word unto thy servant" (Psalm 119:50, 76). He is our Savior and our Friend, and we must never forget that He is God and He is in control, even when we cannot see it.

As of 2010, we are still living, ministering, teaching, and writing in the Central African Republic. Our hearts and our lives are here with these dear people who still need teaching and encouragement to be faithful in their ministries. There are, also, still so many who do not know of the true gospel. We are thankful every day that the Lord has us here in CAR to preach and to teach His word to a very loving but needy people.

Strokes from the Master's Brush
Bill Smallman

In 2009, Bill retired as Baptist Mid-Missions' Vice President and Director of Global Training. He and his wife Doris came with BMM in 1968 and served two terms in Brazil, where they worked in church planting and theological education. In 1980, Bill became director of BMM's Candidate Department, a position he held 24 years.

"Adversity is a magnet which draws people together." This is the opening line of my *Diary of a Stroke,* which began the first week of a medical adventure for my wife Doris and me. Now, I can look back over that fat memoir as the logbook of a voyage into uncharted waters. What makes it bearable is the certainty that the Captain at the helm knows exactly where He is taking us, even if we do not.

July 20, 2002, was a normal summer Saturday for us. I was three hours away from home in the early days of Baptist Mid-Missions' annual orientation program for incoming missionaries, Candidate Seminar, and Doris was at home. Earlier in the day, she had been out running around our town of Medina, Ohio, in her project of getting an elderly friend resettled in her new assisted living quarters. Doris had just walked in the kitchen door at home in the afternoon when lightning struck. She was floored by a massive stroke that left her fully paralyzed on the entire left side and left her dazed, unable to move for a couple of hours. Our adult daughter Margie came home early and found her mom floundering on the floor. She called an ambulance, left word for me to call home, and called a nurse friend. Ambulance sirens soon shattered the silence of our peaceful suburban neighborhood.

When I received the devastating telephone message, I quickly left the direction of Candidate Seminar in the very capable hands of the other men on the Mission administration. We are accustomed to covering for one another when one is out or down sick, and now it was my turn to accept such assistance from the team. For the next two weeks, I did not have to worry about whether my work was getting done properly. At home and around the world, we were quickly surrounded by supportive friends and family praying for us, sending cards and e-mails, and offering whatever help was possible.

A new era of life began for us with shocking suddenness. I drove home imagining the worst and the best, with the phrase "The Lord is in His holy temple; let all the earth keep silence in Him," echoing through my mind. Getting into Medina before nine p.m., I headed right to the ICU at our fine county hospital just a mile from home. Dr. Gary Anderson, our Mission president, had been there for much of the evening, still a pastor at heart.

Once I could get into the ICU to see Doris, I reminded her that nearly 40 years before, I had promised to be true to her "for better or for worse." This was definitely that "worse" part, and the promise stood firm. This was our stroke, not just hers. For whatever terrible days lay before us, she would never feel abandoned or alone.

We need not rehearse the technical details and treatments here beyond the basics. The best hypothesis indicates that Doris was a classic case of a stroke waiting to happen. After childhood rheumatic fever, and later 30 years of irregular heartbeat, despite all due precautions, a blood clot apparently moved from her damaged mitral heart valve to her brain, where it blocked blood flow to the right frontal lobe for long enough to cause serious and permanent damage.

The first few days were critical. The swelling of affected brain tissue produced a severe headache and the danger of worsening conditions. The medical team later revealed that they had feared that Doris would not survive Sunday night. Our son Dave brought his family home from their missionary work in Brazil for the couple of weeks when it meant the most to all of us. Emergency measures, quick testing, competent doctoring, and effective medications reversed the edema by the grace of God, and we relaxed a bit. Still, there was no quick fix available. This was a major change in our whole lives, and we would all be permanently affected by whatever the outcome would be.

The ICU staff members were amazed at how many church folk stopped in to see Doris and appreciated the caring Christian atmosphere they created for all of us. Our neurologist later commented on how helpful it was to have people praying for us and that it really does make a difference. (We knew that.)

The next move was to Edwin Shaw Hospital in nearby Akron, a high-quality rehabilitation hospital less than an hour from home, which specialized in post-stroke rehab processes. Thank the Lord for such help, previously unknown, and for excellent health insurance in Baptist Mid-Missions!

But only a few days after we got Doris settled in at Shaw, she needed to return to Medina for emergency abdominal surgery only peripherally related to the stroke. That ICU was getting all too familiar! During those hospital days, Doris took comfort in 2 Timothy 1:7, "For God hath not given us a spirit of fear; but of power, and of love, and of a sound mind."

As Doris was on the gurney 10 days later to return to Shaw, Margie lifted Doris' limp left hand and said, "Give me a squeeze, Mom." And she did! There was just minimal movement of her fingertips, but she had made her first voluntary muscular movements a full month after the stroke. That was a happy day. Recovery was underway.

Your perspective changes when you have been under the clouds, so that even a tiny ray of sunshine brings the joy of a sunny day. We were already well beyond any complaint like, "Hey, we're serving the Lord, so everything is supposed to go well for us." No, we knew that God's grace is most visible under adverse circumstances. We wanted to display God's grace, but the adversity was not at all welcome. We had come to be thankful for a gift from God that we did not want.

In the typical post-stroke recovery process, most of the significant rehabilitation will take place in the first four months or so, with lesser progress through the first two years. Virtually every day now brought a new "first" experience in the restoration of normal movement on Doris' left side. This second period in the rehab hospital lasted only 44 days but allowed a transformation back to a degree of normalcy, whatever "normal" would become.

We remember celebrating her first time to grip an object, to take her first step in the parallel bars, to lift a sheet of paper, and to let go of something she had struggled to pick up. We remember her first car ride outside the hospital when we got to park right at the edge of the prep field for a hot air balloon festival and be surrounded by these gentle giants stirring from their slumber to rise triumphantly into the air in a riot of color. It was a real lift for us!

For our 40th anniversary, Margie set our own table in the hospital dining room with a checkered tablecloth and flowers, and a basket of BBQ ribs for the three of us from a favorite restaurant. When Doris expressed her amazement of how I had risen to the occasion to be such a caregiver, I told her I just had to imagine how she would have cared for me if our roles were reversed. I took my lessons from her.

The rehabilitation exercises were hard work. Hours were spent each day in both physical therapy and occupational therapy. The therapists worked with diligence and patience and tenderness and drive that kept pushing Doris toward improvement. Of course, her hard-headed Dutch nature now became a major asset as she determined to recover as fully as would be possible.

She would not be stopped. We reveled in the flood of encouraging cards and e-mails from around the globe. There were some times of deep depression, and we walked through a normal grieving process, but she found comfort in the Scriptures as we read and prayed together, and as she encouraged her roommates at the rehab hospital.

During her rehab routines at the hospital, I was able to return to partial days at the Baptist Mid-Missions office. We wondered with some trepidation how Doris could later manage at home when there was so little she could do for herself. We could not bring one of the fine nurses' aides or therapists home with us; that was my job, with Margie's wonderful help. We were now very thankful for Margie's experience and training during her college summers as a nurses' aide in a rest home, as well as her natural attributes as a caregiver.

The daily hours of rehabilitation training were having their intended effect as Doris recovered more dexterity in her hand and was increasingly able to get around with a walker and cane, needing a brace for her lower leg and foot for lift. By the time those six weeks had passed, and we had made some necessary modifications at home, Doris was actually looking forward to the challenges of life back in her own home. Earlier, it had been a source of dread.

We came home in our van at the end of September, fully 10 weeks after Doris had left by ambulance. The license plate on her van says BZY LADY, but now she would be dependent on the help of other busy ladies for quite a long time. She was used to giving help, not needing help, but it was clearly our turn to be on the receiving end for a while.

Families from First Baptist Church were eager to help by bringing meals, driving Doris to the continuing outpatient therapy for several months, occasionally cleaning house or taking her shopping. Life at home was a new adventure that was often hard to face. Margie and I accepted new shares of housework while we waited to see how much Doris could later take back as her welcome part at home.

I got a copy of the rich little book *A Promise Kept* by Dr. J. Robertson McQuilkin, who chronicled his care for his beloved wife as she drifted into Alzheimer's disease. He shared how he did not have to care for Muriel but got to care for Muriel as a ministry of privilege. He said that she had cared for him wonderfully for over 40 years, so if he got to care for her for 40 years, he was still in her debt. I knew I needed to drink deeply of that caring spirit.

Doris and I both cried as I read the book aloud, and we reveled in their beautiful love story and how the love of Christ flowed through each of them to each other. I had a few other models before me of our own friends who provided loving care for their wives in disabilities or advancing MS. This was a foreshadowing of a whole new way of life for us all. This was still our stroke, not just hers. My life was changed along with hers, from present activities to planning our retirement ministries. This arresting of physical activity has led to more concentration on the spiritual facets of life, with more time in the Word and in uplifting books like Joni Eareckson Tada's sensitive work, *When God Weeps*.

Doris came to be quite independent at home, with a diminishing list of things that she simply cannot do for herself. She had the options of walking with the cane, using the walker when more tired, or whipping around in her wheelchair for kitchen work or longer distances.

The normal post-stroke depression was faced head on with feeding on the Word of God and with a return to getting back to First Baptist Church regularly. Isaiah 43:1-3 and 10-13 comforted her with the concept that she could pass through deep waters and not worry about drowning, and that her life was a witness of God's faithfulness. The largest issues now related to acceptance of how things are going to be for the rest of her life. She will not wake up one morning and discover that it was all a nightmare. For most Americans, 9-11 marks a major turning point. For us, it was 7-20 when life changed.

Still, home life was a wholly new adventure. Doris had plenty to do and did not mind being alone at home while Margie and I got back to some semblance of our normal schedules. Since more help was needed in the morning, I gravitated to a regular plan of going off to the Mission office an hour later than usual and working an hour later. Some of my tasks can just as well be brought home. Our administrative team continued to be supportive and understanding over the long haul. My administrative assistant, Dorothy Roduner, took on additional duties related to our work with incoming candidates to allow me more flexibility. We were deeply grateful to all who helped us manage this crisis and its aftermath, by the grace of God.

Doris' progress allowed us to enjoy a wonderful trip to south Brazil in August of 2003 to enjoy our son Dave, his wife Val, our three grandchildren, and the fine ministry they have in the land we still love. All this was possible despite severe anemia that kept Doris feeling weakened and slowed down. Folks in the church there had prayed for us for the past 13 months, so they happily embraced Doris as a living answer to their own prayers. The visit was all we had hoped for.

Two years after the stroke, Doris had recovered most of what she will ever get back, though she continued therapy in the exercise of daily living and occasionally returned to physical therapy at the hospital. While she could control and use her left hand, there is no feeling in it (apart from deep heat or cold or pressure) so she could use it only to do things she could see it do. The same pertained to her left foot. Her brace became a friend rather than a burden, giving her freedom to walk about with a cane.

She was able to run her own kitchen again, having simplified some recipes and procedures, and even went shopping alone. She was able to legally drive her van again and be on her own, at least around town. She is back to helping other people as strength permits, more in prayer and telephone encouragement than getting out and about.

Are we thankful for the stroke? Are we glad it happened? Not really. We are thankful for the lessons that accompanied it, and for the people and their loving care it brought into our lives, and for the impact that we have unwittingly had in others' lives.

We're thankful that when we are driven to the Father in desperation, we find Him to be loving and lifting and longsuffering. But, given the choice, we would gladly rewind the tape and delete that whole traumatic episode. It's not fun—yet.

God gives grace for acceptance of His unwelcome gifts, and that is part of the message that we incarnate. Jesus accepted the unwelcome burden of the penalty of our sins and turned it for good on the Cross. His crushing load was a path of redemption for us, in ways we can hardly understand. His resurrection to new life promises our new life in Him, whether or not our specific sufferings are relieved here and now.

So if God gives us heavy loads which we cannot understand, we leave it with Him to turn it into something good for His glory, to weave a tapestry that reveals His own image in us. God is good, even when life is not. That makes life good.

God's Faithfulness

When the Lord promised Abraham that his descendants would inherit the land of Canaan after 400 years in slavery, Abraham knew that it was as good as done. Abraham knew that what God promised to do, He was faithful to complete. At the appointed time, God freed the Israelites from bondage in Egypt and led them to Mount Sinai, where He gave them His law. At that point, the nation of Israel proved that they had not yet learned to put their trust in God's faithfulness. While Moses was on the mountain speaking with God, the people got anxious. They made a golden calf and began to worship it, thus breaking their covenant with God.

In His anger, God threatened to consume them, but Moses begged God for mercy, appealing to His faithfulness to fulfill His promise to Abraham. God Almighty relented and promised to accompany the nation of Israel into the land. Soon the Israelites approached the border of Canaan and sent in 12 men to spy out the territory. Ten of the spies came back with a fearful report. The people were too big, they said, and the cities were too well fortified. In fear, the people complained against God and appointed a leader to take them back to Egypt and slavery.

The Lord God Almighty viewed their unbelief as an affront to His character. Had He let them down even once since they had left Egypt? God had proved Himself faithful by providing water from a rock and food from heaven. He had parted the Red Sea and allowed the nation of Israel to walk across on dry land and, in the process, utterly destroyed the powerful Egyptian army. He had caused them to triumph over the army of Amalek. What more did they need to see in order to believe that He would enable them to conquer the land of Canaan?

God sentenced the Israelites to 40 years of wandering in the desert until all those who had refused to trust Him lay buried in the sand. He would take the next generation of Hebrews into Canaan. But even in His bitter disappointment with the nation of Israel, God continued to meet all their physical needs. For 40 years He provided water and manna without fail. The clothes of the people did not wear out and their feet did not swell. God constantly led them with the pillar of cloud in the day and the pillar of fire at night. He gave His Spirit to instruct them. After 40 years, He took them into the land that He'd promised to them. At the end of his life, Joshua, then the leader of the nation of Israel, testified, "There failed not ought of any good thing which the LORD had spoken unto the house of Israel; all came to pass" (Joshua 21:45).

All that God has declared to do He will bring to pass—guaranteed. And since the Bible is His Word, we can be assured that it is a true and faithful expression of what God intends to do. Young believers often doubt that God answers prayer. In the story "Lost and Found," God proves to a group of Russian teenagers that He really is listening. And in "Trek to Goatoi," He confirms that "So shall my word be that goeth forth out of my mouth: it shall not return unto me void, but it shall accomplish that which I please, and it shall prosper in the thing whereto I sent it" (Isaiah 55:11).

God's faithfulness is exhibited to believers on a daily basis. It is that quality in God that causes Him, day in and day out, moment by moment, to provide for us, protect us, enable us to have victory over sin, and produce fruit for Him. His faithfulness finds expression in His constant, consistent care for us that we often do not recognize or notice. He is the unseen Presence that keeps us out of harm's way and provides for each need.

God has committed Himself to meet the temporal needs of Christians. Jesus declared,

> Therefore take no thought, saying, What shall we
> eat? or, What shall we drink? or, Wherewithal shall we be
> clothed? (For after all these things do the Gentiles seek:)
> for your heavenly Father knoweth that ye have need of
> all these things. But seek ye first the kingdom of God,
> and his righteousness; and all these things shall be added
> unto you (Matthew 6:31-33).

Jesus taught that Christians should have an attitude of acknowledged dependence on God.

Of paramount importance to God is our focus. He wants our focus to be on Him—not on our need. We are not to fret and worry about where the next supply is coming from. At the onset of trouble, He desires that we turn to Him in faith rather than quickly implementing half-baked solutions of our own design.

God won't do for us what we do not depend on Him to do for us. If we think we are capable of doing something in our own strength, God will let us try … and may let us fail. But if we are dependent on Him like a child is dependent on his father, our Heavenly Father will never abandon us. He will meet every need because the provision will not be for our glory but for His.

This attitude of depending on God does not exclude work. It is not a lazy approach to life. But it does put God in the driver's seat. God often provides for our needs by providing gainful employment. Such was the case for the Armstrong family in the story "Just Enough, Just in Time." No need is beyond His ability to provide. A well in the middle of Africa? No problem. Food for a family of seven and a houseful of guests? No sweat. He delights in providing money for church property, buildings, and renovations. If a child of God has a need, the Father will meet it.

> Ask, and it shall be given you; seek, and ye shall find; knock, and it shall be opened unto you: for every one that asketh receiveth; and he that seeketh findeth; and to him that knocketh it shall be opened. Or what man is there of you, whom if his son ask bread, will he give him a stone? Or if he ask a fish, will he give him a serpent? If ye then, being evil, know how to give good gifts unto your children, how much more shall your Father which is in heaven give good things to them that ask him? (Matthew 7:7-11).

The Lord invites the righteous to lay their burdens upon Him and promises that they will not be forsaken. Our Lord is faithful. "Let us therefore come boldly unto the throne of grace, that we may obtain mercy, and find grace to help in time of need" (Hebrews 4:16).

God Provides a Meeting Place in Finland
Tom and Linda Ruhkala

*In 1978, Tom and Linda were appointed to the challenging field of Finland.
For 30 years, they have served as BMM's only missionaries on that field.
In recent times, they have begun to see a harvest in Finland and now have
several young men who are interested in Bible training to one day become
pastors.*

On January 1, 2007, Linda and I received an unexpected New
Year's message from the owner of our church meeting place. She announced that we needed to vacate the premises. We had been renting her
modest storefront near the center of Tampere for seven years, and it had
served our purposes well. We had negotiated a reasonable rent of 700
euros per month (about $1,000), but now she issued a deadline of March
31 for us to move out. The neighboring business had made an offer to
buy that she could not refuse.

At first Linda and I were discouraged at the news but confident
at the same time that our Lord had given us this "setback" for our good
and for His glory. That previous fall we had been led, with a lawyer's
help, to organize Baptist Mid-Missions of Finland as an officially registered nonprofit association in Finland. Our church isn't registered, since
registration requires a membership of at least 20 adults. We have not met
that criterion yet. But an association can register with as few as three
members. We thought it prudent to be officially recognized by Finland
as a legitimate religious entity. We were concerned about the European
Union's desire to standardize even religious activity within its member
states.

The prospect of having no place to meet put our little congregation into a panic. We called an early business meeting and discussed
our options. We could seek another location to rent, or we could try to
buy our own place. Rental costs were high, and bank interest rates were
low. With the new BMM of Finland association officially registered in
Helsinki, we could legally buy real estate. Our big problem was that we
had no money. Our church was barely able to meet the rental expenses
from month to month, and often the largest share was paid out of our

personal/field funds. We are the only BMM missionaries serving in
Finland, so there are no others to share ministry expenses. A few wanted
to start meeting in private homes again. This, in effect, would mean going
"underground" and giving up any credible public presence. Some of our
group did not even attend the business meeting—assuming the discussion would be too stressful.

I began checking the real estate agencies and searching the
internet for a public place to rent or buy. Market costs for renting had
climbed, and there were no suitable places within our budget. Purchasing
our own place seemed to be wiser, since a mortgage would be no more
expensive than renting, and the church family would begin building equi-
ty. But buying would require securing a loan—a seemingly insurmount-
able obstacle for a small, unregistered group of believers and a brand-new
association with no credit history. For several weeks we gathered real
estate information and made copies for the congregation to consider.

To our dismay, almost nobody was interested to even look at the
options we presented. Very few properties were available, regardless of
whether we rented or bought. For the most part, they were all far too expensive. We visited local banks to talk about loans and were turned down
without hesitation.

All this activity with no results began to irritate some in our congregation. All along we had urged everyone to pray for God's leading and
direction. I preached from Haggai about putting God first and sought to
obey it myself. I urged people to trust the Lord, so that we might enjoy
the blessing and joy of obedience.

Unfortunately, the challenge from God's Word led to accusations
from a vocal few that my wife and I were persecuting them out of hatred.
Some even threatened to leave the church if we decided to buy our own
meeting place. We discovered that in an affluent country like Finland,
many have never had to risk doing what was right and to depend on the
Lord for His provision. If they didn't have tens of thousands of euros in
their own pockets, how could God want them to take on such financial
responsibility?

They wanted nothing to do with any of it. About this same time,
I was hospitalized for five days for prostrate surgery. It was a real time of
testing. Yet it was a time of experiencing that sweet place of rest in God's
care and protection.

Providentially, while driving by a new housing development
near the city center, Linda noticed a building nearing completion, with

a 700-square-foot business space for sale on the ground floor. The price was much less than any other alternatives that we had found and only 125,000 euros (about $180,000). My wife and I believed that this could be the solution to our problem. But would the others see this as a God-given opportunity or as another unworkable, upsetting proposal? Could we raise a down payment?

We presented this option to the congregation at another business meeting. This new option was met with both heated opposition and cold indifference. Only one man was even interested enough to visit the property with us. The threat of destroying church unity over a meeting place drove us to our knees in prayer and fasting. Emotionally, we had come to the brink of giving up. If the Lord didn't intervene soon, our ministry of 27 years in Finland would likely be at an end.

After much prayer and soul searching, Linda and I were confident that God would provide for the costs if we as a church were willing to walk through open doors and do what we could financially—be it only two mites—to do His will. I made a chart showing what we needed to raise for a down payment and put it on the wall. In the beginning, that empty thermometer wasn't very encouraging. My wife and I contributed to the fund to get it above zero. We made the project known to our faithful supporters in the States. Gifts from churches and individuals began to appear on our monthly statement.

But time was running short. We had only one month before we had to move out, and the promising location would not stay on the market long. Other buyers had bought up the neighboring business spaces already. We prayed and fasted. Then one man, another foreigner living in Finland, whose family was attending our services, gave 1,000 euros to the fund. This man's declaration of faith in God's ability and willingness to help our church through his sacrificial gift may well have saved the day. For the most part, many still had a wait-and-see attitude, some were ungracious in their opposition, and one family even left the church, never to return.

A couple of smaller gifts came in from nonmembers who attended our services. Then one couple who had strongly opposed the project had a change of heart and gave 2,000 euros. My wife and I felt led to give all our savings to the Lord for this project. We knew that He expected us to walk with integrity and trust Him. With the gifts coming in from our supporters in the States, we had accumulated over 20,000 euros. We arranged another meeting with one bank and presented our application to the loan officer. Amazingly, the bank decided to take a chance on us and grant our association a loan. This was the sign we had been praying for. We rejoiced, and the association's members accepted the terms. We would be in debt for 20 years, but we would finally have our own meeting place—a place where no landlord could make us move out.

There were still many unbelievers in our midst, and those who were the most able refused to give anything out of principle. One family decided to relocate to another city. But we have learned that it is better to trust in God rather than in people. He commands us to be strong and courageous because He will never leave us or forsake us.

On the very day we had to move out of our rented facilities, we had everything ready to go and the move was completed in record time with many helping hands. Our new place had just been readied for occupancy, and we moved our church furnishings into place and made ready for Easter. It was truly the work of the Lord. Our monthly mortgage payments were only a little more than our rent had been. The Lord had given us a place of our own!

As months passed by, new gifts continued to come in from praying friends in the States. Twice our church was actually able to pay several thousand euros off our loan ahead of time. The loan officer was impressed with our progress, knowing how small our congregation was. We told her that it was our good Lord providing for us.

Then that same year in August, Linda and I received shocking news from our home church in Alaska, that they were dissolving and selling the church property. It was necessary for us to seek another supporting church to accept us as their missionaries and become our sending church. The Lord provided for our needs once again, and a sister church took us on. Our supporters at our original sending church knew about the purchase of our new meeting place and had been praying for us. Just before Christmas, we received word that they were giving our little church a check for $100,000 from the proceeds of the sale of their property.

This was totally unexpected! This gift almost paid off our entire loan. Now the whole congregation recognized the hand of the Lord in our midst, and everybody rejoiced. Our total outstanding debt stood at only 3,000 euros. Two church families who had remained neutral or disagreed with the purchase gave significant gifts. The church was able to pay the loan off completely on December 17, 2007, less than a year after purchasing the property.

Today we see new people coming into the church and replacing those who left. Our monthly expenses are far less than if we were renting comparable property. But the Lord was not finished blessing us in this project to go forward in faith. In April 2008, a Christian friend in Helsinki who is a lead tenor in the Finnish National Opera wanted to help. He hadn't been in a position to give previously, so he asked if he could hold a public concert in Tampere for my 60th birthday and give all the proceeds to our church. He did, and we were blessed by his brilliant singing and his kind generosity. We used those funds to buy a small but much needed additional storage unit for our literature and materials. God has done great things for us. To God be the glory!

Onyame Bekyere
Ken and Arlene Updyke

Ken and Arlene came with Baptist Mid-Missions in 1954. The Updykes served nearly 30 years on their first field, Ghana. In 1983, they began a second phase in their ministry, working in North America. Ken and Arlene retired from BMM in 1995 but Ken continued as pastor to the seniors at their home church for another 12 years.

We were scheduled to travel from Accra, the capital of Ghana, north 500 miles to Wa for a mission meeting. A Ghanaian pastor and two of his deacons were to accompany us. The trip on bone-jarring dirt and asphalt roads would probably take about 12 hours of hard driving. Our trusty French Peugeot sedan was good for the trip, but our two back tires were as smooth as ripe mangoes. The spare tire was even worse. Unlike in the United States, it was not a simple matter to go out and buy tires. They were just not available in the shops. New tires on the black market often sold for $363 each; used ones could be had for $110. So we set out on faith, trusting that the tires we had would make it to Wa and back.

After just 50 miles, one of the tires blew out and the Peugeot came to an abrupt stop. We were on a country road about 20 miles from the town of Nkawkaw. After putting on the spare tire, we discussed what we should do. Should we go ahead and trust that the spare would take us to Wa, or should we turn around and go back to Accra? Going ahead seemed almost impossible and perhaps foolhardy, because the roads would become even rockier further on. But the prospects were not all that good for going back either. After prayer, we decided to continue on to Nkawkaw. Perhaps there another tire could be found. Pastor Abraham summed up our hopes by saying, "Well, God can do wonderful things."

After another 10 miles, we heard the familiar thump-thump-thump sound. Another tire had gone flat. After patching up the inner tube, we proceeded to Nkawkaw. As we drove, we discussed whether we should head back to Accra if we were able to get an old spare tire in town. Accra was only 70 miles from Nkawkaw, but Wa was still 430 miles to the north.

On the outskirts of Nkawkaw, we saw a big red and white sign. It read "Onyame Bekyere—Firestone Tire Sales." This was as good a place as any to inquire about a spare tire. When we pulled into the lot and got out of the car, someone noticed that the patched tire was going flat again. But a tire repairman was set up just in front of the Firestone place. He came over and immediately started to jack up the car. We went into the shop to make inquiries. The owner grinned and said that he had a consignment of new tires the exact size needed for the Peugeot, and that he was willing to sell two for the government-controlled price of $72 apiece! We were thrilled at how God had met our urgent need. By this time, the repairman had fixed the flat tire. The two new tires were put on the rear wheels, and with great rejoicing and praise to God, we headed north—to Wa.

As we looked back at the providential tire station, we noticed again the words *Onyame Bekyere*. We asked, "Pastor, what does Onyame Bekyere (Own—yah—me Bey—chey—rey) mean?"

"God will provide," said the pastor, smiling. With praise and wonder in our hearts, we continued on our way, having learned once again that—yes, God will provide.

An "Impossible" Situation
Todd Daily

Since 1989, Todd and his wife Dawn have served on Baptist Mid-Missions' Germany team. Their primary ministry has been theological and ministry training of church leadership in Ingolstadt and Bad Heilbrunn.

When we arrived in Germany after our last furlough in August 2002, we could purchase one euro for one dollar. At that time, they were predicting that the euro would get stronger against the dollar, and it has been doing exactly that.

In simple terms, with $3,000 in August of 2002 we could purchase 3,000 euros. In November of 2007, that same $3,000 purchased just a little over 2,000 euros.

Although our rent was not raised during that time period, instead of us paying $725 per month, the exchange rate caused the rent to effectively go up to $1,075. A gallon of milk in 2002 cost us $2.20, increasing to $3.90. And we love the American gas prices! We pay $8.30 a gallon for unleaded.

A recalculation of our finances in the fall of 2007 showed that we were $1,500 short of what we needed to stay here in Germany. We had drained our financial savings over the last years and had ended the previous six months in the red. It looked like the only solution was to return to the US for a year-long furlough to raise more support.

In October we informed our church and our coworkers of our situation. I preached about the crossing of the Red Sea. God had led His people to an impossible situation—soldiers on one side and the Red Sea on the other. God's answer? Moses was to lift up his staff, and God would deal with the problem. And God performed a miracle!

During a previously arranged trip to the United States, I traveled to the Midwest for a month of reporting to churches and speaking on Bible college and seminary campuses. I spoke with many of our supporting pastors, and the pastor of our sending church in Iowa, Slater Baptist, sent out a letter to all our supporters. Our weekly e-mail update kept thousands of prayer warriors informed and on their knees. After my month in the US, I returned to Germany, where my family and I continued to seek the Lord about what we should do.

By this time, we as a family were in the position that we were ready to go or ready to stay. We had set a deadline of the first of March for determining our plans. If the needed support was committed by then we would stay; if not, we would recognize that God had other plans for us, and we would start making arrangements for moving back to Iowa in August 2008. You can imagine the questions that were going through our minds about housing, transportation, and school if we were to move. And how would we get our ministries finished up here and everything packed up and stored by August?

Some increases in support had been coming in from churches and individuals. Special gifts built our reserves back up. But it still looked like we would be leaving Germany in August. We had plane tickets on hold and were working to get rid of our ministry responsibilities here. In our January 27 update, we asked our prayer partners to pray that the Lord would make His will clear to us in the following week. We felt like we needed to know whether we should stay here or start making concrete plans for returning to Iowa. That update said that we needed $1,200 more monthly support. By Friday afternoon, that $1,200 was reduced to $0! Amazing! What a week of answered prayer!

Since the first of January, a new supporting church and three new families took on our support. Seven churches and two families increased the amount of support they were giving. And then an adjustment in the amount of government subsidy that we are receiving added up to meet the need! It was exciting to keep the family posted throughout the week as the changes kept coming in. When the last amount came in, we shouted, "Yeah!" God parted the Red Sea for us, and we're looking forward to the next miracle!

God Supplies a Well
Margery Benedict

A missionary nurse, Margery came with Baptist Mid-Missions in 1950 and served in the Central African Republic. She ran a clinic and dispensary and handled cases ranging from midwifery to dental work. She loved working with youth, and several of her students went on to Bible school. Margery went to be with her Lord in 2007. Her life's story is told in her book I'd Do It Again.

In March of 1993, at the start of our Bible school year, I was distressed when I saw some of my students' wives nodding off in class. I knew why they were sleepy. Some of them had risen at 2:30 a.m. in order to get water for their families. The mission well that was only three blocks from our Bible school village was empty, as this was toward the end of the dry season in the Central African Republic. This meant that the women had to walk over a half a mile to the community well and back, balancing their heavy water basins on their heads. They had to go very early, because well before daybreak people lined up to get water. Too many people were dependent on this one well.

A drilling company had come to our mission in 1990, but there hadn't been enough water where they first drilled, and they abandoned the project. They promised to come back and drill again, but these were just empty promises. Every time missionary Lynn Muhr went to their headquarters in the capital city, they said they would return sometime. But more than two years had passed, and we were desperate.

So I cast this problem on the Lord. He reminded me of Ephesians 3:20, "Now unto him that is able to do exceeding abundantly above all that we ask or think, according to the power that worketh in us."

Then the Spirit reminded me of 1 John 5:14-15. "And this is the confidence that we have in him, that, if we ask any thing according to his will, he heareth us: and if we know that he hear us, whatsoever we ask, we know that we have the petitions that we desired of him."

"Lord, I know that it is Your will for the students to be here, for You have called them, the husbands with their wives, to come here and go to school so that someday they can serve you as pastors. And since we know that it is Your will, we have the right to ask you for a miracle to meet our need for a well," I prayed.

The next morning, I began my first class by asking the women, "How many of you believe that God answers prayer?" Of course, everyone's hand went up. So I gave them an assignment for the next day. "I want all of you to come to class with a verse on either faith or prayer," I said.

The next day all the students shared the verses they had found. Then I explained the motive behind the assignment. "Would you believe with me that by faith we can ask the Lord for a well?" I challenged. "Come, leave your desks and join hands with me in a circle around the room and let's pray."

After many of the African women prayed, I asked them to start thanking the Lord for the well that He was going to give us. We could sense the presence of the Lord around us as we prayed. Then we broke forth into singing and praising the Lord with thanksgiving. It was a precious time!

Two weeks later on a Friday evening, Lynn Muhr's wife Margo burst into the room where I was preparing to teach. With excitement in her voice she asked, "Margery, do you know a family named Gwinn?"

"Of course, I do, "I replied. "They are a couple that has supported me since I left the United States for my first term in Africa."

"Well, word has come through that $6,000 has come in from them for a well!" she exclaimed.

I had written home to ask my friends to pray that God might provide a well. Hallelujah, the Lord had supplied the money! But where in the middle of Africa could we find a well-drilling outfit?

But God had it figured out! Shortly thereafter, we heard that a well-digging rig from a Swedish mission located 600 miles away was right then in our town digging a well for the Catholic mission just two miles from where we stood! What a miracle! Six hundred miles may not seem like much in the United States, but coming over the rough, potholed roads of the Central African Republic is quite a different thing.

Lynn Muhr immediately went to the Catholic mission to talk the well-digging crew into coming to our mission and digging a well for us. Three days later, the truck with the crew and equipment arrived at our mission village. The crew picked a spot right in the center of the village and started drilling. Everyone was so excited, praying that they would strike water.

They did! What a celebration! The women let loose and danced like the biblical King David did before the Lord. Their joy on that day is imprinted on my mind for forever.

God Even Uses TWA
Deborah Rowland

Debbie and her husband Doug began serving in England after their appointment with Baptist Mid-Missions in 1982. In 1996, they began ministry with BMM's Campus Bible Fellowship International. They currently serve in Boise, Idaho.

"What are we going to do about a car?" my husband Doug asked. I had lost count of how many times that question had been asked over the course of the summer. We had come home from England on a two-month furlough. The furlough had been fun and rewarding but failed to produce the needed funds for a new vehicle. Our previous car had been given up for scrap. Three years previously, our family increased overnight by the adoption of two teenage children. Therefore, we could no longer fit in the typical five-passenger British car.

A week before our return to England, Doug's frustration was apparent. "What are we going to do about a car?"

"Listen, honey, God will provide something." I probably sounded more defensive than spiritual.

"I'll remind you of that when we're walking all over England," said Doug, half in jest and half in exasperation.

"I'll remind you, when God provides a car," I teased back.

We didn't doubt God's provision for our needs, but the timing was making us nervous.

On our last Sunday in church in America, a couple handed Doug a check for our car fund. Thanking them gratefully, Doug slipped the check into his coat pocket without looking at the amount. Later while driving home from church, Doug asked our then 16-year-old daughter, Paula, to hand him the check from his coat, which was in the back seat.

"Dad, who is this from?" exclaimed Paula.

"Never mind," said Doug. "Just tell me how much it is for."

"$2,000!"

For a moment it was silent. Then we all started talking at once.

"I won!" I said, laughing.

"OK," my husband said, grinning. "But just remember that it won't transfer to much in English pounds." Our spirits, however, were definitely up after that. Although the exchange rate between US dollars and English pounds had never been on our side, there was a glimmer of hope that all would be well. A few other gifts from family and friends came in. I was sure that God had something special in mind.

Then it was time to return to England. As we flew to Baltimore on the first leg of our trip, our heads ached and we had puffy eyes from the emotional goodbyes. Doug asked the question again, "What are we going to do for a car?" The $2,000 was a great start, but it wouldn't be enough to purchase a vehicle in England.

"Wait and see," was all I said. He gave my hand a reassuring squeeze.

When we arrived in Baltimore, it was announced that our TWA flight to England had been overbooked by six seats.

"Great," I complained. "I bet I know who the lucky six will be who get asked to stay behind."

"Deb, do you want an adventure?" asked Doug, who had been listening intently to the announcement.

"What? No, I just want to go home," I said.

"We'll get a free motel and meals and also upgraded to Ambassador class," Doug continued enthusiastically.

I hesitated and then looked at my kids' faces that were willing me to say yes.

"Debbie, listen. They are also giving $400 each."

"You're kidding," I exclaimed.

"No."

No wonder he looked so excited.

"Each of us $400?" I asked, incredulously.

"That's what they said."

"But that's," urging my tired brain to work the sum, "$2,400!"

Doug went to sign us up, and then we gathered our family of six together and prayed, "Lord, let them pick us!"

And they did! We can truly say we saw the blessings of God unfold on us. We had a fantastic family adventure that still remains a special memory.

As we landed in London, we couldn't contain our excitement. All six tired bodies, twelve suitcases, six carry-ons, a guitar, and umbrella crammed on a train for the two-hour journey home. Our friends greeted us joyfully, even the fellow we'd woken up at 3 a.m. to inform him that we would arrive at a different time.

The Lord graciously provided a van for us for the exact amount of money raised that summer. It served our family and the church for five years. There was another benefit to this incident. Three years later, on another short furlough with just two of our kids, we were able to use all the TWA air miles as payment for our trip home. The previous trip was during their anniversary special, and we were given triple air miles. The four of us were able to have our international flights as well as two domestic US flights for a total of just $400. The money that we had set aside in our account for airline tickets was instead able to be used to pay a debt at BMM's Home Office. It is always exciting to see how God will provide for us. And we are always thankful for the many people and means He uses to bless us in unexpected ways.

Windows of Heaven
Richard Teachout

Richard and his wife Nancy first served in Central African Republic after they were appointed with Baptist Mid-Missions in 1969. Then they served in France from 1978 until 1985, when they went to Quebec. In 2004, they became Stewardship representatives of Bibles International, BMM's transla-tion division. Richard is an MK, the son of Richard and Oril Teachout, who served with BMM in Africa.

Several years ago my wife Nancy and I were church-planting missionaries in the greater Quebec City area. The church in which we were working had gone through difficult times before we came to min-ister there. The church had very few members—with limited financial means—and our building was old and large. We had a real crisis one win-ter when the price of heating oil spiked and our heating bill doubled in one month. Unless something was done, the heating bills would certainly break our budget.

We had a couple of meetings with the members and discussed what we should do. The building was drafty. We decided that we needed to add insulation to the auditorium and change several windows and doors that were letting in a lot of cold weather. We have winter tempera-tures in Quebec City as low as -40 degrees F.

The trouble was that the best estimated cost of the needed reno-vation was $12,000. We did not have the money, and borrowing it did not seem wise. With varying degrees of faith that God would provide an answer, we decided to pray about the need.

The next morning was a Monday. I received a call from a retired Baptist pastor in California. He was a good friend who had been the pas-tor of one of our supporting churches before retiring. He prayed for our ministry earnestly and regularly.

"Hi, Richard," he said.

"Hi. It's good to hear from you," I responded.

"I am praying for you," he said.

"I know it." I replied. "You always are, and we appreciate it very much."

"Do you have a special prayer request?" he asked.

"Well, yes I do … a rather urgent request," I said, and then proceeded to tell him about the gas bills and the need to renovate.

"How much do you need?" he said, after listening to my explanation.

"What did you say, Pastor?"

"How much do you need to complete the project?" he said, a little louder.

"We need $12,000," I answered.

"Are you sure that would be sufficient?" he asked.

"That's what we estimate," I said.

"I'll put a check in the mail today," he replied, confidently.

"Whaaat??" I couldn't believe what I had just heard. The pastor explained that the Lord had blessed him and his wife with an inheritance, and that they wanted it to be used on the mission field. I thanked him profusely.

He sent the check, and soon we had the auditorium well-insulated and new windows and doors put all around. The Lord permitted the work of the church to go on. Our people (and we, ourselves) were really touched that God answered our prayers so dramatically and so quickly! Many times God answers prayer by communicating through His Word, "Trust me, wait, and see what I will do." This time He opened the windows of heaven and poured out a blessing. We could almost hear Him say, "Your faith was so small."

After Ten Years, God Answered My Prayer
S. David and Geri Smith

David and Geri have been with Baptist Mid-Missions since 1987 and have served their entire career in Brazil. The Smiths are currently planting a church in the city of Londrina in Brazil's Paraná State.

When we began our first church in Brazil, a lady named Josefa attended. She lived nearby and had two sons, ages 8 and 10. That first night, she was beaming from ear to ear and just seemed so happy to be there. We figured she would get over it. She came the next night and was the same way: smiling. That night, she even brought a visitor. She came four days the first week and then five days the second week. She was smiling almost every time she came.

Then on the second Sunday evening service, she came forward with joy on her face and asked if she could give a short testimony.

Josefa told the congregation that when she was 17 years of age, she had attended a church near her house, heard the gospel, and accepted Christ as her Savior. A few months later, she married a Catholic and moved from one side of the city of São Paulo to the other.

A few years passed and she had a son named Hugo. After Hugo was born, Josefa began praying: "God, put a Bible-believing church in my area where I can send my son to hear the gospel of Jesus Christ." Two years later, she had another son and named him Edwardo. She continued praying: "God, put a Bible-believing church in my area where I can send my sons to hear the gospel." She continued praying this for eight more years.

The week before we began our first service, she had received a flyer inviting her to the inaugural service of the Esperança (Hope) Baptist Church. She said that for 10 years she had prayed that God would put a Bible-believing church in her area so that she could send her children to it.

With tears running down her face, she concluded her testimony: "God has answered my prayers. Not only am I going to send my two sons to this church, but I am going to bring them here and attend with them."

Two weeks later, her sons, Hugo and Edwardo, received Christ as their Savior. She did not quit, and God answered her prayer.

A Ten-Millimeter Bolt in the Road
Glenn Kerr

In 1995, Glenn and his wife Becky joined Baptist Mid-Missions to serve with Bibles International (BI), the Bible society of BMM. Glenn's work as the Chief Translation Consultant takes him around the world. Becky works in BI's Home Office as an editor/journalist.

The road up the mountain was the worst I'd ever seen, but then I'd never been on such an adventure before. This trip to India and the foothills of the Himalayas was my first experience overseas. A year before, I had begun helping Bibles International as a volunteer, preparing translation helps for the Old Testament. Now I was on a short-term mission trip, experiencing firsthand a dramatically different culture and dramatically different work from my usual occupation of repairing musical instruments. My unique preparation in Greek and Hebrew years before had given me this remarkable assignment.

I came to India to attend a workshop to help native translators correct and complete their translations of the Bible. Several times our bus had crawled past other buses and trucks on narrow curves and in crowded villages. But reaching our destination and accomplishing our goals had more than made up for the difficultly in getting there. My three-and-a-half-week session in the foothills of the Himalayas proved life-changing; while there, I told the Lord that I would commit my life to Bible translation.

After much work, many unforgettable experiences, and many sad goodbyes to newfound brothers and sisters in Christ, we left the northern India mountains for the first step in our long journey home. The first leg was the most dangerous. Though the roads were paved, the rugged mountains were not particularly tamed. On many curves, I could not see the road beside the bus, only the steep drop-off. The bus driver was careful, but we had to maneuver around road repair crews and other buses and trucks coming up the other way.

Then, when we had reached the village of Haldwani at the foot of the mountains, it happened. I heard a loud bang and felt the bus shudder toward the edge of the road. We'd blown a tire. There were wide shoulders in this village, and we got off the road relatively easily. We found ourselves stopped within a hundred feet of a tire shop! There, the large rear dual wheel was pulled off and repaired.

I got out of the bus to see what had caused the flat. Protruding into the tire and still lodged securely in its tread was a ten-millimeter bolt, about five inches long. The bolt had entered headfirst, even though the hex head of the bolt was about an inch across!

I realized that the bolt was an example of God's providence and protection. He does not keep the "bolts" of life from sticking into our tires. If he did, people would become Christians just to get the "accident insurance." But God works all things together for the good of his children. Our tire hit the bolt—not on the treacherous mountain curves—but on the plains, in the town, just up the road from the tire shop. It doesn't always work out that smoothly, but God's care is always evident. We can trust him with our lives.

I have reflected often about friends and acquaintances, pastors, missionaries, church leaders, and other dedicated saints who have gone through the fire in the course of God's service. Sometimes what they and I have encountered was definitely much more than a bolt in the road—such as the day we laid my younger sister, a missionary in France, into the loving arms of her Savior.

Sometimes we think God should pick up all the bolts that lie in our way, but God's plan is to put us on the road—with the bolts. The fact that there are bolts in the road makes it no less the road of God's purpose. And even if the bolt should prove the end of the road, God's purpose for the saint will be fulfilled. Peter said that the testing of our faith is much more precious than gold, and that it is the testing that shows the genuineness of our faith, and the genuineness of God's faithfulness.

The start of my journey to be a full-time Bible translator was not without a "bolt in the road," and yet I knew God would lead me every step of the way and accomplish His purpose.

Just Enough, Just in Time
Lisa (Armstrong) Wils

Lisa and her late husband Jesse became missionaries with Baptist Mid-Missions in 1994, appointed to the field of Russia. After two terms of church planting, they had to return to the US when Jesse was diagnosed with ALS (Lou Gehrig's disease). The Armstrong family saw many evidences of God's faithfulness throughout their years as missionaries, which helped sustain them through Jesse's illness. Jesse passed away in 2009. Shortly thereafter, God in His goodness brought a widower, Barry Wils, into Lisa's life, and they were married in 2010.

After God called us to be missionaries, we felt the need for my husband Jesse to go back to Northland Baptist Bible College in Wisconsin for the Master of Arts in Biblical Studies program in August 1993. For that entire year, we had no regular income. Jesse attended classes and worked on campus, but any money that he earned was applied directly to his tuition. I stayed at home with our son Christopher and took any babysitting jobs that I could find. But these were scarce. We survived for the whole year on a small savings account that we had built up over the first two years of our marriage and through an occasional monetary gift sent by a friend. That summer of 1994, we were appointed as missionaries to Russia under Baptist Mid-Missions.

After the joy of being accepted subsided a bit, we saw the predicament that we were in. There we were, facing deputation with all the preparations for it, with basically no income and little savings. When our second son, Corey, was born in October, there was just enough in our savings account to pay off the hospital bill in its entirety.

We were living in my hometown of Petersburg, Alaska—a small island community in the southeastern part of the state. Jobs were very scarce on the island in the winter. But the Lord provided a two and a half week job for Jesse that stretched into two and a half months. We lived with my parents and saved what money we could.

A month before we were supposed to start our first conference— a five-week whirlwind tour of Baptist churches in Alaska—it became apparent that our van was in need of a new engine. With all the miles of deputation travel before us, we knew we could not ignore this pressing need. Almost all of the money we had saved from Jesse's winter work was sent to the car dealership for a new engine. The churches involved in the round-robin conference paid for Jesse's travel, but we were responsible for paying for the ferry and plane tickets to get the family up to Juneau and then on to Anchorage. There was just enough money left over after the engine was purchased to buy the needed tickets and pay for small expenses along the way.

Once we were off the island, we could not expect to be able to get back on during the week. Our van became our home base for the first several months of deputation. During that first five-week conference, we spoke in 17 different churches. We were constantly on the move from home to home and church to church.

At the end of the first conference, we did a week of pulpit supply in Soldotna, Alaska. By this time we were in urgent need of a break.

We were exhausted and sick with a flu bug and longed to have some time alone with just our family. Thus, a two-week respite from meetings was a welcome prospect. Jesse arranged with a church in Palmer to let us use a small room in the back of their church for sleeping quarters and the church kitchen to fix our own meals.

Although delighted at the prospect of a rest, I began to wonder how we would survive on our own. Up to that point, meals and housing had been provided along the way. I made a small grocery list of some basics that I knew our family would need. Then I counted the money that we had left—six dollars and a few cents. With a two-year-old and a baby, I knew that six dollars of grocery money wouldn't go far in an Alaskan supermarket. As usual, we turned to our Heavenly Father in prayer and asked Him to meet our need.

Then we packed up the van and began to say our goodbyes to the pastor's wife in Soldotna. Just then the telephone rang. It was the pastor who was calling from the church office. A packet of mail for us had just arrived. He asked us to stop by the church and pick it up on our way out of town. So we stopped by the church, picked up our mail, and headed on our way.

Jesse drove while I settled the boys in their car seats with books and toys. Then I opened the packet of mail. I thumbed through a number of items before I noticed an envelope from the IRS. I opened it and found a tax refund of nearly $2,000! God's timing was perfect. If the telephone call had come just five minutes later, we would have already left town. The refund check provided for the needs of our family for the next five months until we moved to Seattle and Jesse was able to find part-time work.

In one of our general prayer letters, we had mentioned that we would be relocating to the Seattle area at the end of the summer to continue our deputation. At just that time, a church in Burien was fixing up a little house on their property as a home for missionaries. After reading our prayer letter, the pastor contacted us and asked if we'd like to be the first occupants. We had no previous contact with this church except that Jesse had phoned them to set up a meeting. We prayed about this possibility and determined that God was using this church to meet our housing need. There was no way that we could have paid rent anywhere in Seattle at that point.

When we arrived in Burien, the house was completely furnished, and the church people had put some food in the cupboards. Then Jesse came home from a week of speaking at a camp in eastern Washington with all the leftover food. They had expected more campers than had actually attended, so there was quite a bit of food left over. They sent it all back with Jesse.

The Lord provided just enough, just in time to always meet all our needs!

Can Do
Elizabeth Mayner

In 1981 Elizabeth McDonald joined Baptist Mid-Missions to serve with Campus Bible Fellowship International (CBFI) in Cleveland, Ohio. She married David Mayner in 1988, and they spent two years in Ecuador participating in BMM's ¡Arriba! missions internship program. They have been serving with CBFI in Binghamton, New York, since 1994.

I began the 2006-07 school year feeling completely overwhelmed. The demands upon me were more pressing than I had ever experienced before. It might have seemed a little more doable if I had not had to complete it all in less than the 10 months a school year normally takes. Surveying the situation, there seemed to be NO WAY I could possibly get it all done on time.

Nevertheless, God encouraged me to trust Him and give it my best shot. One September morning, in the middle of a conversation with a friend about the impossibility of my circumstances, I glanced up and read these words written on a blackboard: "We are all faced with a series of great opportunities brilliantly disguised as impossible situations."

Through those words, the Lord showed me that my perspective was all wrong. I had to admit that I was certainly faced with great opportunities: training the next generation as I homeschooled my two sons; influencing future leaders through Campus Bible Fellowship International; editing *Disciples In Deed*, a 76-lesson discipleship course to impact lives of spiritual leaders yet to come. Adjusting my attitude, I realized that these were indeed awesome opportunities, in addition to my normal responsibilities of ministering to the needs of my family as a wife and mother. If

I could learn to view these daily impossibilities as great opportunities to serve God, maybe I would be able to make it through the year.

That same night, I attended a ladies' Bible study at church: the first session in a video series by Beth Moore, *Living Beyond Yourself.* The title said it all. God was encouraging me to believe that, although I couldn't do it all by myself, with His help I could do all that He wanted me to do.

It was not an easy year. Looking back, I realize that it was undoubtedly the most difficult year of my life thus far. Many times I had to make a conscious choice to trust the Lord to get me through seemingly impossible situations. He always did. In February, God gave me an encouragement directly from Scripture when our pastor quoted from John 15:5, "Without Me, ye can do nothing." The words of Philippians 4:13 flashed across my mind, "I can do all things through Christ which strengtheneth me." For the first time I noticed the identical words in those two verses I had memorized years earlier. Without Christ I CAN DO nothing, but by His strength I CAN DO everything He wants me to do—even what seems humanly impossible.

Reaching the end of May 2007, I looked back over the year in amazement. The boys had successfully completed another grade in school. I had fulfilled my CBFI responsibilities at Binghamton University. The discipleship course was finished in time for our annual CBFI conference in June, except for a small section which I completed after the meeting. I made it to most of the *Living Beyond Yourself* studies, and I even managed to start a discipleship group with three other ladies at church, which served to encourage me in each of the other areas as well. With God's help I had done it all, and even on schedule! I give the Lord all the glory for getting me through that year by His grace and power.

The Check's in the Mail
Verna Friesen

Verna is the manager of Baptist Mid-Missions' Canadian office, a position she's held since 1996. Her husband Tim formerly served as BMM's Canadian representative and is now a member of BMM's General Council. In addi-

tion to pastoring Emmanuel Baptist Church, Tim is president of Emmanuel Baptist Bible Institute in Moncton, New Brunswick, Canada.

We were waiting for our monthly paycheck from Baptist Mid-Missions. It usually came a certain week of the month, and we had arranged with the bank to automatically pay our mortgage and bills by a certain date. But the check didn't come!

I waited for a few days and thought, "I'm not going to panic! I'm going to trust the Lord to take care of it." I waited and the check still did not come. The day came when all our bills were to be paid from our account, but the money was not there! The bank called to inquire about the lack of funds to cover all the automatic payments.

"I know," I said, "it hasn't arrived yet. We are waiting for it. It should have been here at the latest on Monday." This was now Wednesday.

"Well, we will go to the end of the week, and I hope the funds will be in by then," said the bank clerk.

"I hope so too," I said. I called the Home Office to see when the check had been sent. They said it had been sent as usual.

"Oh, Lord," I prayed, "this is not a good time for it to be lost in the mail."

Thursday came and went. No check!

Friday morning arrived, and I felt quite confident that this would be the day when my concerns would be put to rest. The usual time for the mail to come was between 9:30 and 10:00 a.m. and, as I expected, it was on time. I rushed to open the mailbox, and the mail was there. I made a point of looking to make sure I'd gotten everything in the mailbox. Then I went into the house and looked through the envelopes. It wasn't there! This cannot be!

Oh, my, I was just devastated. This was nearing ten o'clock, and around lunchtime I was expecting my husband Tim to return from a trip as a Mission representative. I was thinking, "Maybe he will know how to handle this. He could go to the bank and make some arrangements." My mind was racing a million miles per hour.

Tim didn't come home for lunch, and it was now after one o'clock. The bank was open until three. Again, I prayed and asked the Lord for wisdom. For some silly reason, I went back to the mailbox and opened it. I don't really know why. After all, I had already removed the mail and made sure the box was empty. But when I opened it this time—the check was there! How was that possible?

The Lord reminded me again of Philippians 4, verse 6, "Be careful for nothing; but in every thing by prayer and supplication with thanksgiving ..." Verse 19 says, "But my God shall supply all your need according to his riches in glory by Christ Jesus." I had to confess my lack of faith to the Lord and seek His forgiveness. This incident has been a reminder to me of God's faithfulness and His infinite ability to meet our every need.

A Stranger to the Rescue
Randy Laase

Randy was appointed with Baptist Mid-Missions in 1986 and served several years in Chad, where this story takes place. During Randy's language studies in France, the Lord led him to Patricia Hébert. They married in 1992 and worked in Chad as a couple. Since 2001, they have served as church planters in France.

One of my responsibilities working in the capital of Chad is to meet our mission teams at the airport and to help them through customs and on to their final destination in the south of the country, where most of our mission stations are located. Getting through customs is rarely a pleasant experience. Customs agents in Chad are practically their own bosses and can seize taxable goods for as long as they choose until they get the bribe that they want.

Our difficulties, however, are merely opportunities for God to prove His faithfulness. This was most evident when a team of workers came out to do electrical work on one of our mission stations. They came with lots of equipment and parts—things that make customs officials here drool. The customs officers opened one suitcase and saw all the spare parts inside. When they put the suitcase to one side to seize it for customs charges, I knew we were in trouble.

While they were searching the next suitcase, a well-dressed Chadian man with a radio walked up to me and asked me for one of the team members' passports that I was holding in my hand. He looked at the cover and handed it back to me without opening it. Then he turned to the customs agents working on our baggage and said, "All of this comes in free." In spite of their arguments about the taxable items in the luggage, he insisted and they were obliged to let us go.

The man waited for us to get our bags together and then silently accompanied us to our car. All the time I was thinking, "Oh no, this guy saw the American passport and saw a chance for big bucks. He's going to ask us for a bribe for helping us once we get out into the parking lot." When we got to our car, the man turned away without saying a word and got into the car parked right in front of us. It was a big black Mercedes that had a Chadian government license plate. Then he drove off! I was stunned. No one else was with him. It was as if he had come especially to handle our case and then left.

I had never seen that man before and have never seen him since, but apparently the customs officers knew who he was, because they obeyed him. I can't even say that he must have been a well-placed believer who knew who we were, because he was a Northerner and, almost without exception, all Northerners in Chad are Muslim.

Was he an angel sent from God? I don't know. All I know is that God sent him to help us. When I got back into the car, I asked the team if they had been praying about this trip. When they asked me why, I explained to them what had just happened. Big tears rolled down the team leader's cheeks out of thankfulness to God. I have seen God intervene many other times to get materials in without cost or hassle, but none in a more mysterious way! We serve a great God!

(First printed in Harvest *magazine, Winter-Spring 1999-2000.* Harvest *was BMM's main publication and is now called* Advance.*)*

Deputation Dollars
Anna Beth Wivell

Appointed in 2006, Anna is the third generation of her family to serve with Baptist Mid-Missions. She grew up in Australia as the daughter of Steve and Jan Wivell. Her grandparents, Claude and Anna M. Wivell, were missionaries in the Belgian Congo and North America. Anna is preparing to serve in Chad, Africa.

I was a young missionary appointee on deputation to go to Africa with Baptist Mid-Missions' translation division, Bibles International. I joined BMM in 2006 and started deputation part-time while finishing up my studies at Faith Baptist Theological Seminary in Ankeny, Iowa. One of the greatest lessons God was teaching me on deputation was simply to trust Him. One of the first lessons in trust that I learned on deputation was in the area of finances. Even though I am an MK, I never realized just how much money goes into missions, especially during the early parts of deputation. Candidate School alone cost at least as much as one of my seminary classes, and then I had to get prayer cards, equipment, and display items, and I had to pay for all the additional travel costs and phone bills ... it added up fast! And at that point I didn't have any financial support. In addition to the cost of deputation, I was also finishing up seminary, and after nearly eight years of college and seminary, I didn't have much saved up.

I did a real battle with the sin of worry during those early months of deputation. February and March of 2007 were especially difficult, as every week I wondered if I would have enough money in my bank account to pay the next bill. One week I had less than $8 in the bank, but I knew that within the next few weeks, I would have bills amounting to several hundred dollars. I learned what it really meant to trust God with something huge that was beyond my own control. I had no other human resources to draw on. I had to ask God to help me trust in the promises of Matthew 6:24-34—God knew what I needed and He would provide.

I began to wonder if it would work out like the missionary stories I had read, where the poor, desperate missionary receives a check in the mail from someone who had no idea of his need, for the exact amount that was needed. Well, sometimes God works like that, and it is great cause to thank Him when He does. But so often He works much less dramatically.

There was no last-minute check in the mail or anything of that sort, although once I did receive an anonymous cash gift. My needs were provided through more ordinary means—paychecks at the right time, love offerings from deputation meetings, and so on. Once when I was ready to panic because I didn't have enough money to pay a bill that was nearly due, I balanced my checkbook and discovered I had simply forgotten to record a paycheck. I actually had enough money all the time.

Through those months, I began to learn (I'm still learning it) just how foolish I was to worry about my finances. Of course, God wanted me to be wise in how I used my money, but to worry about whether my needs would be met was foolishness. When I look back on those months, I didn't really have any cause to worry anyway, because He had it all in control.

I am learning what it means to pray the prayer of the writer of Proverbs 30:7-9: "Two things have I required of thee; deny me them not before I die: remove far from me vanity and lies: give me neither poverty nor riches; feed me with food convenient for me: lest I be full, and deny thee, and say, Who is the LORD? or lest I be poor, and steal, and take the name of my God in vain."

When I first prayed that prayer some years ago, I didn't know what it would mean when God answered it. Well, now He is answering it, and I have found it is no light thing to pray, because it means you really have to learn how to trust God. But it's worth it, because God doesn't let you down—He keeps His promises!

The Customs Officer
Rachel Metzler

Rachel and her sisters, Helene and Evelyne, served many years in Chad, where their parents had pioneered a work for Baptist Mid-Missions in the 1920s. Rachel joined Baptist Mid-Missions in 1949. After missionaries were evacuated from Chad during the country's tumultuous Cultural Revolution in the 1970s, Rachel and Evelyne began working in Haiti and established an orphanage there. Rachel went to be with the Lord in 2001.

I dreaded the ordeal of going through customs with all the boxes and suitcases and parcels of supplies for the children in Haiti that I take care of. I did not have the funds to pay the exorbitant fees that are often charged by the customs officials. So I told my faithful helpers who met me at the airport to pray, and then I turned to face the two frowning officers standing behind the customs table.

The one who was the senior officer looked at me as I approached, and then he waved toward the great pile of suitcases, totes, and garbage cans. He said, "All these things that have 'Metzler' on them, are they yours? Are you Metzler?"

I laughed outwardly but inwardly groaned and said, "Yes, sir, but you see, they are really for the children at Grand Goave." As I talked I reached into my purse and pulled out pictures of the children.

But he cut me short, saying, "I don't need any other explanations, just start taking them." I understood him to mean to start taking the baggage through for inspection, so I motioned for the men to start bringing the things to us at the table. I told the officer that I had been sick, but that the Lord had answered prayers and healed me and made it possible for me to come back to Haiti.

The officer answered, "Yes, I know." Then, directing his instructions to the men he said, "Go ahead and take everything to your pickup truck, and let's hurry so she won't have to stand too much. Don't forget she's been sick."

Then he said to me, "The porters and workers here have told me that you are a good person who loves God and the people of Haiti and bring these things for the children in your home. Well, I am a pastor who works as a customs inspector during the weekdays because my church can't fully support me. As a pastor who is a servant of the Lord and a Christian brother, I certainly would not think of making a fellow servant and a sister in Christ pay any customs on these things."

The junior officer wasn't very happy at all. After my helpers filed by with five or six containers he said, "We can't just let her go off with everything! We've got to open at least some for inspection!"

So the senior officer said to one of the fellows going by with a suitcase, "Hey you, put that on the table and open it." So I opened the suitcase, and the junior officer started to put his hands in it and the senior officer shut the cover on his hands and said, "Zip it shut. Now we've opened something, okay? Let's get on with this so we can go home. Hurry up guys, take them out!"

So we hurried out. I said to the officers, including the junior officer so that he would not feel too ruffled, "Thank you so much on my behalf and on the behalf of my children. I know the Lord will bless you for what you have done for one of the least of His servants."

We separated with a great handshake. Even the junior officer ended up smiling and shaking my hand.

With God's Interest
Gordon Katsion

Gordon and his first wife Rosemary joined Baptist Mid-Missions in 1965 to serve in Jamaica. In 1976, the Katsions transferred fields to Great Britain and then to Bibles International in 1979. The Lord took Rosemary home to be with Him in 1998. The following year, Gordon married Virginia Wilterink, and they continue to serve with Bibles International.

Grace Baptist Church in the town of Andover in Hampshire, England, had been able to purchase a 20-foot by 40-foot church building that had been abandoned. It was just a frame building, but it was adequate for the needs of the church. After a while, however, we decided as a congregation to add on a new front to the building, which would give us restrooms and a more attractive entrance. We got the superstructure up and the roof on so that it was dry. But we had no windows or doors installed when we suddenly ran out of money.

I didn't feel we should go into debt to carry on construction, so it sat that way for 10 months. During that time, one of our missionaries was on furlough, and he met a fellow in his home church who was out of work because his union was on strike. This man said, "Boy, I wish I could do something for the Lord."

My coworker asked him, "What can you do?"

He told him all the things that he could do, and it turned out that he was really a jack-of-all-trades in the area of building construction. My coworker contacted me, and I said that we could sure use a man like that. Well, to my surprise, a couple of months later this couple called and said that they were coming and would arrive on such and such a date.

Now I really was in a jam, because we didn't have any money to do the construction. The fellow and his wife were paying their own way to England, and it wouldn't be a problem to put them up in our home, but what could we accomplish with no money for building materials?

The very day the couple arrived from America, while everyone was still sitting around the kitchen table getting acquainted, I received a telephone call from a sister church in Basingstoke. Two years previously, we had sent the church $300 as an incentive to help them get going on their building program. We were both small congregations, so we sent the money to encourage them.

The pastor on the telephone said, "Brother, we're going to give you back the money you gave us, because our building program has fallen through, and we don't want to hold on to this money with false pretenses. The church voted last night to send you the money with God's interest."

"I didn't know God had a banking business," I said.

"Well, God does," he replied. "We're sending you $3,000." That three thousand dollars paid for all the materials that were required to finish the construction. Isn't God wonderful?

Hector's Stroke
Marilyn Pitzer

Marilyn spent many years translating the Old Testament into Venezuela's Warao language. Appointed in 1969 with Baptist Mid-Missions, Marilyn lived among the Warao tribe from May 1974 until November 2005. She then worked with the Baptist Bible Institute of Venezuela in its Warao Ministerial Training Center and presently helps a local church in its Warao outreach.

"Something is the matter with Hector!" exclaimed Leví into the phone.

Moments before, I had been quietly working at my computer entering the translation work that Hector and I had just completed the previous week. One week out of each month, the Warao Indian church leaders from El Pajal and Las Morochas had been coming to our Warao Ministerial Training Center for instruction. Hector was one of the leaders from El Pajal. During time outside of class, Hector and I labored at translating the Old Testament into the language of the Warao Indian tribe of Venezuela. From the sound of Leví's voice, it was obvious that something was seriously wrong with Hector.

Leví continued, "He got up this morning, and then he fell, and now he can't move his arm, and his mouth is crooked. Do you think we should try to take him to the doctor?"

From my limited medical experience, I suspected that Hector had suffered a stroke. "Yes, get him to a doctor immediately!" I answered.

Leaving El Pajal "immediately" took several hours, as Hector's family first had to arrange for a boat, motor, gasoline, and a driver; get clothing and money together; and find someone to take care of the children. Hector's wife Alicia would be needed to care for Hector in the hospital in the event that he would be admitted. Finally ready, they headed for Boca, a town about half an hour away by boat. In Boca there is a small medical facility where an ambulance is sometimes available. The ambulance could then take him to the small hospital in Temblador.

I left my home in Ciudad Guayana by public transportation to rendezvous with them in Temblador. Serious cases that arrive in Temblador are normally taken on to the big hospital in the city of Maturin. But if I was going to be able to help Hector, he would need to be in a hospital in Ciudad Guayana where I lived. For this to be possible, he would require transportation and a doctor to admit him when he arrived.

Now this is the way the Lord worked. When Hector and company arrived at Boca, the ambulance was there! Hector was placed inside and whisked off to Temblador. Hector's teenage daughter, Mairilys, was employed in Temblador in the home of a lady who was a government official. When the official heard of Hector's arrival in Temblador and of the family's desire to have him sent to Ciudad Guayana, she came personally and gave the necessary orders for him to be taken there. I even got to ride with them in the ambulance!

Upon arrival at one hospital in Ciudad Guayana, we experienced what we thought was a complication, but it later turned out to be God's superintending of the situation. That hospital was doing some construction and therefore was not admitting anyone who could potentially be there more than a couple of days. Rather crossly, they sent us on to a different hospital close by.

Now we needed a doctor to admit Hector. I was acquainted with Dr. Owen Martinez, a member of my coworkers' church, but found out he was on vacation! However, with the help of another believer, he was contacted by phone (a miracle). He contacted one of his colleagues who, at that very moment, was in that hospital where we were (another miracle). She sought us out, and shortly thereafter Hector was admitted to emergency. When an MRI was performed, all was completely clear. Whatever blockage had caused the stroke had completely disappeared.

Later Dr. Owen, a noted cardiologist, gave Hector various heart exams free of charge. He was able to determine the heart problem that had led to the stroke and was able to prescribe the proper medication to prevent another. In a little over a week, Hector was released from the hospital. His leg had regained strength, his speech was nearly normal, and he had regained partial use of his arm and hand. He returned to El Pajal.

At the very next class of the Warao Ministerial Training Center, Hector was in the front row. Absolutely no one could have engineered all that but the Lord! Hector continued to improve. Except for a little weakness in his hand and a slightly crooked smile, he is back to normal. He faithfully takes his medicine and continues working with me in the translation of the Warao Old Testament. He graduated from WMTC in May of 2009. Praise be to our wonderful Lord!

Praying Beyond Belief
Marilae Golike

Marilae and her late husband Bob joined Baptist Mid-Missions in 1953. After a long and fruitful career in Central African Republic, the Golikes retired to their hometown of Bunker Hill, Illinois. There, Bob continued writing Bible School material until he went to be with the Lord in 1995.

Back in 1987 my husband Bob broke his leg while he was at the Sibut station in the Central African Republic. Because of Bob's previous war injury, the doctor sent us home on medical furlough. When we got to the United States, we received many letters assuring us that people were praying for us. Word from Bangassou, where we had been stationed, was that the Africans were praying continually for Bob. After eight months, God enabled us to go back to the Central African Republic.

When we got there, we had a steady stream of Africans coming to the door—most of them bringing chickens. They told us, "We were praying for you all the time, asking God to let you come back. But we really didn't think we would see you again until we saw you in heaven."

At that time, we reminded them of Acts chapter 12. This passage tells how the believers were praying earnestly for Peter's release from prison but then didn't believe it when God actually set Peter free. We told them that they must have been praying like the people prayed for Peter, because it seemed like they really weren't expecting God to answer prayer and to bring us back to Africa.

We wondered why we were getting so many chickens from our African brothers and sisters in Christ. Then one pastor explained it to us. "People bring a chicken when someone has come back from the dead," he said.

We saw how our return became a real lesson to many, many Africans that God does answer prayer.

Lost and Found
Mary Amesbury

Mary joined Baptist Mid-Missions in 1992 and served first in the Far East of Russia. Since 2000, she has been serving with Campus Bible Fellowship International in Cleveland, Ohio.

My desire was to see the youth of Vanino Baptist Church of Vanino, Russia, mature in their faith. I wanted them to experience God and have evidence for themselves that He cares for the details of their lives.

One Saturday after Christmas play practice, the teens and I decided to go on a hike. It was a cold day but not overly so. The blue sky made it a good day to be together. Even though it was only the 16th of November 1996, the Cheestavodnaya (Clean Water) River was already frozen. From the trail that we were on, we could see the river down below. Looking for some adventure, we hiked down the hill, crossed the highway, and hiked down to the river's edge.

Cautiously scooting on his belly across the thinner ice near the shore, 14-year-old Anton tested the strength of the ice. Satisfied that it was secure, he stood and walked over to an abandoned ice-fishing hole. "It's plenty thick," he yelled back. "Come on. Let's go for a walk." With some trepidation, the teen girls and I followed him out onto the ice.

I was fascinated by the blue and green hues of the frozen expanse. We wandered here and there over the ice, climbing over ice boulders and skirting ice-fishing holes. Laughing and joking, we described the various ice formations. One looked like a turtle. Another looked like a rabbit.

Then the ice began to make cracking noises. Some of the girls decided they'd rather not be out there. I readily agreed. "Let's go, guys. I don't like the sound of this ice," I said.

Nobody argued with me and soon we were trudging back up the hill to the trail. I'd just made it to the top of the hill with about half of the group when Tanya yelled from below for us to come back down.

My half of the group opted to wait at the top of the hill while I went back down to Tanya and the group with her. She'd lost her keys, she said, probably out on the ice. "We have to go look for them. My mom's going to be so mad if I don't find them," she exclaimed, starting down the hill.

"Wait a second," I said. "Let's pray first."

Somewhat reluctantly the group waited until I prayed, asking God's help in finding the keys. Then they ran back down the hill and stepped gingerly back onto the frozen river. We all began to look but it was much like searching for the proverbial needle in a haystack. We had covered quite a bit of territory while we were exploring the first time.

I prayed silently. "Lord, please show them that You are worthy of their trust. Please show them that You do answer prayer—even in the little things in life."

A few minutes after I had finished the second prayer, I heard Tanya shout: "I found them!" Her keys were nestled in a little depression under an overhang of ice.

I gathered the group together, and we thanked God for helping us find the keys. "Let's go home," I said, grinning.

Exactly eight months later, on August 16, 1997, the youth and I were again on an outing. We were at the beach, although it wasn't really "beach weather"—mostly overcast but dry. We'd waited most of the summer for a good day and decided to go to the beach anyway despite the less than ideal conditions. The hardiest among us swam a little in the ocean, but mostly we sat around a campfire or played soccer on the sand. A few went exploring along the shore and nearby trails.

Late in the day Pastor Dan Pollard, my missionary coworker, realized that he'd lost his black wallet containing important documents. The back pocket of his cutoffs was torn clear through. The group split up and began to search along the shore and trails. After about 20 minutes of fruitless searching, 13-year-old Tanya approached me and said, "Wait a minute. We are going about this all wrong. We haven't prayed. Don't you remember when we were looking for my keys on the ice?"

"Yeah, you're right," I said, feeling foolish for not having thought of that myself. "Let's get everybody together and pray."

So we gathered together and I prayed, and then we began looking again. About five or ten minutes later, when we had retraced Dan's steps to the top of a knoll, we found the wallet. It had fallen open and thus was easier to spot alongside the trail. Tanya was jubilant. "Just like I thought! I knew we'd find it (after we'd prayed)."

(First printed in Harvest *magazine, Winter-Spring, 1999-2000. Harvest was BMM's main publication and is now called* Advance.*)*

Trek to Goatoi
Marilee Ostrander

Marilee Seewer joined Baptist Mid-Missions as a single missionary in 1953. She married Albert Ostrander in 1967, and he joined BMM that year. They served as a couple in Liberia until 1980 when they transferred to North America. The Ostranders retired in 1989, and Albert went to be with his Lord in 1991.

I first went out to Liberia in 1954. I was stationed at Tappi Ta, where I studied the Mano language and headed up the mission school for Liberian children. I taught Bible each day and supervised our Liberian teachers, so I didn't often get the opportunity to go on trek into the villages. The only time I could go out into the villages to take the gospel and to teach flannelgraph lessons was during school vacation time.

My missionary friend, Doris Porter, also wanted to go on trek. Doris and I were both from Emmanuel Baptist Church in Toledo, Ohio. When I returned to Liberia after my first furlough, Doris came out with me. She was a missionary nurse stationed at Yila. We often talked about how nice it would be for the two of us to go on trek together. Finally we decided we would go to a place called Goatoi, a village across the St. John River from Yila.

So our missionary pilot flew me over to the Yila station in our little mission plane. I spent the night there. The next morning we packed up, and some of the Liberian Christians helped us to get our things down to the river. We loaded everything into a dugout canoe and crossed the river. There were Christians on the other side who came to meet us and to help us up the steep bank. We spent the first night in their town by the river. Then the next morning we trekked to Goatoi.

Shortly after we arrived in Goatoi, Doris got called back to Yila because a man had been shot and she needed to go treat his wounds. So I had to decide whether to go back with Doris or stay alone in Goatoi. This was very hard for me because I have always been kind of a fraidy cat. But I talked with one of the Bible school students who had gone with us and he said he would interpret for me, so I decided to stay.

The Christians told me about a Mandingo teacher who came to their village quite often to talk to them about the Muslim religion. They, in turn, had been trying to tell him of Jesus Christ.

The day after Doris left, this Mandingo teacher came riding into town on his bicycle. The Christians introduced us and we began to converse. One thing led to another and we began talking about spiritual things. He asked me questions and I answered them the best way that I knew how. Then I would ask him a question and it went back and forth like this for two hours. As we talked, a crowd gathered around us. They all wanted to hear what we were talking about. The Lord brought to mind verses of Scripture that I had learned as a child as well as verses that I had memorized later while in Bible school. It was wonderful. I could just feel the Holy Spirit working and helping me to answer his questions with verses of Scripture that someday could help him come to know the Lord.

At the end of those two hours he said, "It would be so nice to have a Bible in Arabic. I wish I had one."

"When I go Monrovia the next time, I will see if I can find an Arabic Bible and send it to you," I promised.

So after I had spent my time in Goatoi, I returned to Tappi Ta. When I had an opportunity to fly to Monrovia, someone suggested that I might find an Arabic Bible at the American Bible Society bookstore. So I went there and they had just one Bible in Arabic. I purchased it and took it back to Tappi Ta. I went to the pastor of our church, John Demey, and told him my story about talking to this Mandingo teacher.

"Do you think you could find someone who could take this Bible to the Mandingo teacher in the town of Goatoi?" I asked. "It would be a long trip for them."

"I don't know, Missy, but I'll try," he replied.

So I left the Bible in Pastor Demey's care and prayed much that this man would eventually receive it. I didn't hear any more about it until the next term. I had married by then, and my husband and I came to Liberia together and we were stationed at Yila. I was in charge of the mission school there. One day a man from the village of Goatoi came to Yila to register his child in our mission school. When I learned he was from Goatoi, I said, "Oh, I remember being in Goatoi one time. Were you there when I was there?"

"Yes, Missy, I remember you," he said.

"There was a Mandingo teacher who came into town when I was there and we had a long talk together. Were you there then?" I asked.

"Yes," he replied.

"After I got back to Tappi I went to Monrovia and bought him a Bible and sent it to him. I never heard if he ever got it. Do you know anything about it?" I asked.

"Oh, yes. He got the Bible, Missy," the man declared. "He reads it every day."

My Jehovah-Jireh
As told by Helen Jean Zwyghuizen

Helen Jean Moose served as a single missionary from 1946 until retirement in 1986. Her first ministry was in China shortly before the Communist takeover. From there she served in Indonesia, Canada, and Hawaii. In 1995, she married a widowed pastor, Hilbert Zwyghuizen. He went to be with the Lord in 2004.

I did not have the privilege of serving a lifetime in China. The Communists took care of that. But in those few years, I learned that God is my Jehovah-Jireh, the Lord who provides and who makes the impossible possible.

I was accepted by Baptist Mid-Missions for work in China in 1946. I first went to linguistics school in Oklahoma and then on to Yale to study Chinese. My coworker, Louise Marqueling, also studied Chinese at Yale. When we completed our language training, we wanted to leave immediately for China, but we were delayed because of the civil war there between the Nationalists and the Communists. Figuring that the war would soon quiet down, we headed for California. There we were told that the longshoremen were on strike and that we would have to wait again. With all the delays, we could have given up and done something else, but we were assured that God had called each of us to China. Finally on Chinese New Year's Eve of 1949, we arrived in Hong Kong.

Baptist Mid-Missions had arranged for us to work with Rev. and Mrs. Krug—they were Baptist people working in the southern part of China in Kweilin. When we arrived in Hong Kong, they were there to meet us. Because we could speak the language, we quickly became involved in their evangelical meetings and Sunday School. But then ... the Communists were just a little ways from us.

Mr. and Mrs. Krug told us, "We're getting out."

We didn't want to leave after serving less than six months in China. The Communists had not taken over the interior of China yet, so Louise and I decided to go inland. We asked Baptist Mid-Missions for permission to stay, and after much prayer they said that we could. Then we faced the question of how we were going to get to the interior. We would have to fly over the Communists. So we went down to all the different airplane offices. They were all so very expensive. Finally an official at one airplane office said, "Have you checked into the St. Paul? It's a Lutheran plane."

We hadn't. So we went there and they said, "Well, we're waiting to go to Chengdu because we have half a load of bicycles that we are supposed to deliver."

Well, our luggage would fill the other half, and so God did another miracle and we were able to fly interior to Chengdu in 1949. The pilot said he often stayed at the campus of Wah Si Ba, a large Chengdu university, and maybe we could stay there too. So we all took rickshaws. It was dark as the rickshaw went through the deep water on the roads. Yet the Lord allowed us to get to Wah Si Ba. We soon found out that the mission group there was not happy that we were coming, because their missionaries were on their way out of the country. They were liberal missionaries. After we talked with them a bit, we found out that there were some conservative Baptist people who were going into Tibet. They were more our stripe than these modernists. So we went over to their house, and they agreed to rent us a room in their house because they needed the money. As long as they were there, we rented this room.

After they left, we rented an empty house on the Wah Si Ba campus that some missionaries had left. They had left the student work behind as well, so we decided to do that. We had testimony and prayer meetings in our huge living room. The room wasn't furnished much, but it had chairs in it so we could use it for this. Some of the students were truly born again. During those few months, many of them really got right with the Lord. When the time came that we had to leave that house, we took the born-again nucleus of that group with us. They were really on fire for the Lord.

While we were in Chengdu, we met up with some Baptists who worked under China Inland Mission. Once a week we would go to their house for prayer meeting, and we had good fellowship with them. We took turns giving the devotional. We were just two dumb girls, alone without others from our mission, and yet we kept going. That was a spiritual blessing to them. Most of the missionaries were leaving because they were afraid of the Communists. One day we heard that the Communists were coming to take Chengdu.

That day while riding my bicycle over to these missionaries' home, I ran into some water and fell off my bicycle. I was soaking wet, so I went to another missionary's home on the way and borrowed clothes before going on to the prayer meeting. Before I arrived, the missionaries had discussed curtailing their ministry because of the Communists. It so happened that it was my turn to lead the devotions, and I had planned to use Daniel 6:10: "Now when Daniel knew that the writing was signed, he went into his house; and his windows being open in his chamber toward Jerusalem, he kneeled upon his knees three times a day, and prayed, and gave thanks before his God, as he did aforetime." I said, "The Communists are coming, but we need to keep on praying and keep on working just as Daniel did." They started to laugh, and that was when I learned about what they had discussed before my arrival. The Lord met us that day. It was a real blessing and a challenge. All of us determined to continue on as we had been doing before, no matter what. We were convinced that God would protect us. And He did.

Well, the Communists did come. They took our passports from us, and for two weeks we didn't have a passport. When they gave them back to us, we were asked to leave, but they didn't make it easy for us. Each of us was required to have a citizen of China sign an affidavit for us that we hadn't been a troublemaker or anything and that we could leave. We really didn't want to leave. We thought that perhaps we could become Chinese citizens. To give up our American citizenship would be a difficult thing to do, and yet we were willing for the Lord, if He wanted it so. But finally we realized that we as American citizens were endangering Chinese just by being with them. There was only one choice left—to get out of China.

In February 1951 we left China. I'd served just two years and two months there. It was a great miracle of the Lord how we were able to leave and how He protected us along the way. As we came out of China, we took any kind of conveyance we could obtain. We rode on a bus, then we were on a boat on the Yangtze River. On the riverboat there were about 50 of us missionaries and embassy personnel.

The riverboat ticket salesman said that they had room in the hold of the ship where the coal and the cargo were. We could sleep there if we wanted to. Well it didn't sound too appealing, but we had to get out of China before our visas expired or we might land in jail. I was advised by some other missionaries to go into the bottom of the ship and take up as much space as I possibly could, because there would be many Chinese and foreigners also vying for that space.

So I made a big space, as long and wide as I could. One of the ladies right next to me did so too. This lady had a husband and he was taking care of my luggage as well as everybody else's. When he finally came on board ship there was no place for him. His wife pointed out to me a space around a pole and asked me to use that and to give up my big wide spot to her husband. She said that I was short enough to go around the pole, and that my spot next to hers was just the right size for her husband to roll out his bedroll.

Well, that was something. Here I had fought for this big, long spot and now I was being asked to give it up. But he had been good to me in getting my luggage safely on board ship, so I should be willing to go around the pole. While I was reading, I came across this verse, "For whatsoever is born of God overcometh the world: and this is the victory that overcometh the world, even our faith" (1 John 5:4). So I gave up my nice spot and arranged myself around the pole. Well the pole was the place where the anchor was pulled up, and when they pulled up the anchor, water would drip in there. So I had to cover myself with my oiled cloth tarp.

Of course, I had a pity party. I was thinking, "Why did I give up my nice long spot?" I managed to sleep that night. The next morning I asked the couple how they'd slept. They said that they had slept just fine. But I'd noticed a Chinese lady right next to the spot I had staked out for myself. She'd woken up very early, scratching furiously. She was pulling off lice and throwing them over to this big, long spot where I would have been. So I praise the Lord; I got a few drips but I didn't get any lice. You never know when you give up something what the Lord is protecting you from. You may think, what a pity, and yet God has something better for you.

At each port, we were thoroughly searched, but finally we arrived safely in Hong Kong. There were many, many missionaries in Hong Kong, all trying to find passage out of China. We were going here and there trying to find a way back to America. I found a French ship going to France. From France I could book passage to the United States. This was God's provision for me. He is truly Jehovah-Jireh.

The Widow's Mite
Vernon Rosenau

Vernon is the third generation of his family to have lived and served in Central African Republic (CAR). His grandparents were among Baptist Mid-Missions' first missionaries when it was founded in 1920. Vernon and his wife Jan joined BMM in 1975 and served in CAR until 1999. Vernon currently serves in BMM's Home Office as Africa and Europe Field Administrator, and Jan is a receptionist.

I was driving down the road one Sunday after a meeting in one of the villages in the bush of the Central African Republic. I saw the widow of one of our African pastors and stopped to greet her. "Good afternoon, Mama," I said, taking her hand.

"Good afternoon, child," she said, pressing 25 francs into my palm. "Take this and buy yourself a cup of coffee."

"I can't take this from you," I argued, knowing that those 25 francs were most likely all she had to live on. "I can buy my own coffee," I assured her gently.

"No," she said resolutely. "You can't deny me the privilege of giving to the Lord. You take this money and buy yourself a cup of coffee so that you will have strength to do the Lord's work."

This widow's faith in her Lord was steadfast. Her Heavenly Father had always proved Himself faithful before. She had absolute confidence that God would continue to supply her own needs if she first gave of what she had to Him.

Chastised, I gratefully accepted her 25 francs and vowed in my own heart to likewise trust the Lord with the same unshakable confidence that this widow had in her faithful Provider.

No Flour

Maribeth (Fogle) Smith

Maribeth grew up in Chad as the daughter of Martha and Lester Fogle. She and her late husband, Don Peterson, served in Central African Republic and Baptist Military Ministries from 1967 to 1992. She has been married to Andy Smith since 1998. Maribeth's brother Larry and his wife Sallie serve with BMM in the Pastoral Enrichment Program.

My husband and I were dorm parents for missionary children at Milner Memorial School located at Kaga Bandoro, Central African Republic. This was the same dormitory and school that I had attended growing up as a missionary kid, only when I was a child there, the town was called Ft. Crampel. What precious memories I have of those children—including a lesson they taught me about faith.

Feeding 20 children requires staples. We used powdered milk and ate off the land as much as we could, raising a garden and eating lots of rice. We made our own bread. The children loved homemade bread and cinnamon rolls. We also used the bread dough to make pizza crust and raised doughnuts. But bread dough requires flour, and we were running very low on flour. In primitive Africa, you never knew when the whole country might run out of a necessity like diesel fuel or flour. So we put in our order for flour with the next missionary going to the capital city. "Bring us flour—lots of flour!" we said.

When the missionary returned, he brought us the news that there was no flour to be had in Bangui. In fact, there was no flour anywhere in the country. We were told that they were waiting for a shipment of flour, but it had not arrived yet, and they didn't know when it would arrive.

Each night before bedtime, we had devotions with the children. That night we shared with them that we were out of flour and there was none to be had in the entire country. Don and I listened as the children prayed. Their prayers were all similar: "Thank You, dear Jesus that You are going to send us some flour tomorrow. We know You will, because we need it, and You have promised to give us what we need. So thank You for the flour You will send us tomorrow." The kids went to bed happy and confident.

Don and I, however, looked at each other and shook our heads. We had heavy hearts because we thought that there was no way we were going to get flour tomorrow. There simply was no flour. The children would have to go without bread for a while. We went to bed sad that night because we just knew that the answer to the kids' prayers was going to be "no flour." The next morning's breakfast was our usual rice with sugar, ground peanuts and milk, along with the last of the bread toasted in the oven of the wood stove.

We adults didn't mention to the children that the bread was gone and there was no flour to make more. The children hugged me and skipped off to school, nary a worry in their heads.

Sometime mid-morning, I heard the dinging of a bicycle bell. "What on earth?" I thought as I went out to investigate. There stood an African holding onto his bicycle.

"Madame aye ti vo farine?" he asked me. (Does Madam want to buy some flour?)

There on the back of his bicycle was a huge sack of flour—a glorious sack of flour—enough to last us until the shipment arrived in Bangui! He had ridden his bike all the way from Chad (the country to the north of us) arriving on the exact day the children were expecting flour. God's timing was perfect!

Oh, the faith and trust of children! We adults learned a lesson in faith that day. We and the children all praised the Lord together! Philippians 4:19 declares, "But my God shall supply all your need according to his riches in glory by Christ Jesus."

Forty Years Later
Herb Boyd

In 1952, Herb and his first wife Ruth were appointed as Baptist Mid-Missions' first missionaries to the Netherlands. The Boyds planted several churches in strongly Catholic areas. After Ruth passed away in 2002, Herb continued serving. He retired in 2007 after 55 years with BMM. Since 2003 he has been married to Madaline (Luce) Boyd, whose late husband pastored three churches that supported Herb and Ruth. Even in retirement, Herb and Madaline are still serving in the ongoing ministry in the Netherlands. Herb's son David and grandson Daniel and their spouses also serve with BMM in the Netherlands. Another grandson, Mark, and his wife are on the BMM Germany team.

In February of 2007 the Evangelical Baptist Church of Eindhoven in the Netherlands celebrated its 40th anniversary. As founding pastor, I was invited to be the guest speaker. It was an enjoyable day to see many friends still faithfully attending and to see the church being blessed with growth and effective ministry. After the service, a woman in her late forties named Tieneka came up to me, introduced herself, and then told me the following story.

The year the church was founded was also the first year we held a Daily Vacation Bible School, an activity previously unknown in Holland. As an eight-year-old girl, Tieneka had attended from the first day. Her mother brought her, along with a few of her friends.

"That very first day," she told me, "I wanted to accept Jesus after you told about Him, but there was no chance." (We were cautious, not wanting to scare the children from coming back!) "Finally, on the last day you said if anyone wanted to become a child of God by accepting Jesus, they should raise their hands. I was the first to raise my hand. Several others did so as well. You talked to us about what it meant and told us how to ask Him to forgive our sins and to come into our lives. I did it and was so happy that I finally could be a child of God."

She told me that when she went home, she could hardly wait to tell her mother. When she did, her mother was overjoyed. This in itself was a miracle, because most Dutch parents are very skeptical about children getting saved, not to speak of their skepticism about the whole matter of salvation.

Then her mother did something she NEVER did—she called her husband at his job to tell him Tieneka's news. On his way home from work that day, he stopped at a bakery and bought special pastry cakes. When he got home with these, he said, "There is a celebration in heaven when someone gets saved, but we are going to have our own celebration right here." Tieneka still remembers the happiness they shared as a family that day.

But … that is not the end. Years later as she grew into a young woman, the DVBS idea was catching on in Holland. Right in Eindhoven was the Christian organization that was stimulating DVBS and providing training and materials for Daily Vacation Bible Schools throughout the whole country—even into a few other European countries. Tieneka has become the person in charge of supervising and expanding this ministry. She told me that the previous year, there were over 400 Daily Vacation Bible Schools in various cities around the Netherlands. Tieneka is also the wife of the assistant pastor of the Eindhoven church, helping out with the Sunday School of the church.

This was a special blessing for me that day. Although I knew most of the facts of the story, I had never made the connection between that eight-year-old, who back in 1967 so eagerly wanted to know Jesus, and the present developments. I am glad I was still around 40 years later to hear the rest of the story.

Good News Knows No Boundaries
Karen Swedberg

Karen and her husband John have been missionaries to Brazil since their appointment in 1967. They serve in the city of São José do Rio Preto in Brazil's São Paulo State. Their son Mark and his wife Anita also serve with BMM in Brazil.

Marlene and her father had come to our city hoping to receive medical treatment for Marlene, a very sick 21-year-old. The journey by bus had taken 24 hours. When they arrived, they knew no one. There was no one to meet them when they got off the bus, no one to help them navigate the big city, no one to provide a place for them to stay.

At the hospital they were told about an evangelical home for the aged which often had extra rooms available for those who came for medical treatment. So they decided to stay there.

Medical tests revealed that Marlene had cancer in her leg. The treatment to try to eradicate the cancer would be extensive. Her father was faced with a dilemma. He was needed back in their village to care for the rest of the family. And yet someone must come and care for Marlene. The area that they were from was so undeveloped that in 1994 there were no phones in the homes. To communicate with their family they needed to phone an outstation that would then relay the message to the family. Finally, a younger sister, Marinalva, came to care for her sister, and her father returned home.

At the time, Nathan and Dawn Patefield and Penni Bresson-Burckhart worked with us in the establishment of the Good News Baptist Church. In the Lord's providence, they became aware of Marlene's problem and visited Marinalva and Marlene. They took them to church and held Bible studies with them. Marlene and Marinalva had been raised in a very backward area, and they were very insecure. But finally, both trusted Christ as their Savior.

Since Marlene was often hospitalized, Marinalva came to live with us, as we lived only six blocks from the hospital. I can remember her trying to make contact with her family over the phone. She would have to set a time so they would be at the outstation. When she would finally make contact, she would have to yell into the phone to be heard. Marlene's health continued to deteriorate, and her father came back to our town and stayed with us too.

The medical team gave no hope for Marlene's recovery, and her death was imminent. Her father wanted her buried near his home, but the cost would be prohibitive. John offered to drive the three of them home if the doctors thought Marlene could make it. One morning very early, they left on their trek to a little villa nestled in the mountains. John's fear was that Marlene would die on the way. But God, in His mercy, kept the very frail girl alive.

Since the trip was arduous, John stayed for two nights. On the second night, he had a preaching service. The family and neighbors came to hear the Word. One of their younger brothers was very interested in a Bible, and John gave him one that was in the car. A cousin wanted one too, so John mailed him one after he returned home.

Marlene lived two months before the Lord took her home. Now, 14 years later, we can see how God used her illness to reach her family in a very remote area. Marinalva is married, and her husband is the one who received the Bible through the mail. They live in our town and are active in the Good News Baptist Church, which has a national pastor. Her little brother, who was learning to read when John visited, lives with them and is faithfully serving the Lord. She told me that there are 11 in her family who are now saved.

Even though the family lived in a remote place, God was faithful to bring the gospel to them. He knows no impediment to reaching the lost.

He That Honors Me, I Will Honor
Gary Sammons

In 1993, Gary and his wife Wilma were appointed with Baptist Mid-Missions to serve with Campus Bible Fellowship International. The Lord gave them many opportunities to point college students to the Lord for salvation and discipleship. Prior to joining BMM, Gary and Wilma had served in Chile. Using this background, they have served at Editorial Bautista Independiente, BMM's Spanish publications ministry since 2008. They work with theological curriculum development, and they teach modules and hold ladies' seminars in Latin America and Spain.

In the 1981 movie *Chariots of Fire*, based on the life of Scotsman Eric Liddell, Liddell refuses to run on the Sabbath during the 1924 Olympics. Before his attempt at Olympic gold in the quarter mile, Liddell is handed a note which reads, "Him that honors Me, I will honor," referring to 1 Samuel 2:30. Liddell ends up winning the race by five meters. In our own day and age, aspiring filmmaker Drew McClean, studying at the North Carolina School of the Arts, likewise sought to honor his God with his talents and dreams.

North Carolina School of the Arts (NCSA) is one of the most distinctive schools in the country. Its mission is to train students from middle school through graduate school for professional careers in the performing, visual, film, and television arts. It consists of five professional schools: Dance, Design and Production, Drama, Filmmaking, and Music. Although NCSA is unparalleled in its class, it is permeated with humanism, vulgarity, and homosexuality.

When Drew McClean came to NCSA as a freshman to study filmmaking, he was a Christian. He realized how important Christian fellowship and nurture would be to sustain him in his new, highly secular environment. Campus Bible Fellowship International and Drew were a perfect match! He faithfully attended all our weekly Bible studies and became the president of our chapter. He delighted to go out with our gospel team once a month to share his testimony in local churches.

One of the most significant aspects of Drew's discipleship was our one-on-one Bible studies each Wednesday at 1:00 p.m. We studied every major area of doctrine in the Christian faith and life. His participation always evidenced advanced preparation, excellent insight, and dedication. It was a real thrill to be a part of this young man's development in Christ!

The thing that most impressed my wife and me about Drew was what happened when he had his interview with the filmmaking faculty between his junior and senior years. At NCSA, students are not automatically allowed to continue in their programs. They have to earn their place in their particular school each year, even if their grades are satisfactory. If they are not showing adequate advancement, other students will be allowed to take their places.

In reality, Drew's meeting with the faculty was as much his interviewing them as it was their interviewing him. Realizing how much his lifestyle and goals differed from the general tenor of the School of Filmmaking, he wanted to make sure that the faculty would want him to continue.

So, he told them that he was a Christian and that he wanted to honor the Lord in filmmaking, and that if they felt he couldn't do that studying with them, then he couldn't continue at NCSA as a student. The faculty appreciated his candor and extended him an invitation to proceed with his studies.

Our faithful and powerful Lord repeated with Drew what He accomplished in the life of Eric Liddell when he took a stand for Him. He honored Drew and made him more than a conqueror in Christ.

Eating Better for Less
Marilyn Adler

Appointed with Baptist Mid-Missions in 1958, Marilyn and her husband Allen served among Native Americans in the Southwest and in Montana. The Adlers have been retired since 2003. Their daughter Karis is a BMM missionary with her husband, Dan Mapes, in Ghana.

When we moved to Prescott, Arizona, as missionaries to the Native Americans, we had to start renting a home. It was a big adjustment to the budget. So we paid the tithe and paid the bills, and what was left over we used for groceries.

I remember one month in particular that we had only $25 for groceries for a family of seven. The Lord had been providing for us in marvelous ways—not to the point that we could forget that we were being very careful—but still He was taking care of us.

We kept our eyes open to see if we could stretch our dollars a bit further. I saw an advertisement in the newspaper for this fellow who would bring frozen food to your house and put it right in your freezer. His pitch line was "I'm going to get you eating better for less." His business was supposed to help you to really stretch your grocery money, so we invited him to come over and tell us about it.

This man came to our house one evening and started his presentation by declaring, "I'm sure I'm going to get you eating better for less!" Then he got out his questionnaire and started to ask questions about how large our family was and how much money we spent on groceries. We said that we spent approximately $75 a month on food. He started to write that down and then stopped and said, "No, I mean your total expenditure."

"That's it," I said.

He looked at me in astonishment and asked, "How do you make out?"

It was a real opening to witness to him of the Lord's provision. "Well, the Lord just takes care of us in different ways," I said. "He sends in what we need when we need it. One Christian man gave us a 100-pound sack of pinto beans one time, and that helped. A neighbor lady sent over vegetables from her garden. Some friends who are farmers brought over some melons several times."

"Well, let me figure this out," he said, "because I know I can get you eating better for ..." He stopped his pitch line right in the middle. He was not going to be able to compete with the Lord. He knew he would lose.

We never did use that fellow's business. We just continued to rely on the Lord, and He never let us down. Some of our missionary colleagues knew about our plight and apparently had mentioned it to one of the Phoenix churches. Prescott is located at an elevation of 5,250 feet in the mountains, about 80 miles north of Phoenix. One day in February, I received a call from a pastor in Phoenix.

He said, "I've got to come up to Prescott to check on a location for a camp, and my boys have never seen snow. Would you mind if my boys and my wife come along for a visit?"

"Oh no, that would be fine, just come along," I said.

Then a few days later, he called back and said, "There's another couple that really wants to come along, because their kids haven't seen snow either. So would it be all right if they came too?"

My mouth said, "Sure, come along," but my mind was screaming, "What am I going to feed 15 or so people for lunch?" I racked my brain to figure out what we could have that would satisfy all those people. Finally, I decided we would have tomato soup, cheese sandwiches, and a cake.

The day arrived, and the pastor and his friends came up to Prescott. They came in and the pastor said, "We brought some lunch with us. Do you mind if we go out to the car and bring it in here to eat?"

And I thought, "Man, I worked so hard to think of what we were going to do, and then they bring their own lunch." I felt kind of let down. They went out to the car again and brought in a sack, and then another sack, and a box, and then another box. When they were done, they had piled a corner of our house with groceries.

Our kids kept saying, "How did they know we needed those things?"

"The Lord takes care," I said.

God Is Specific

Gary Holtz

Following Gary's Air Force career, he and his wife Betty joined Baptist Mid-Missions in 1976 to serve with Campus Bible Fellowship (now called Campus Bible Fellowship International (CBFI). They have worked with several campuses in the Dayton, Ohio, area. Gary is now CBFI's Coordinator.

In Bible college, we studied systematic theology and learned the attributes of God. We learned of omniscience, omnipotence, omnipresence, holiness, and a number of other attributes. I don't recall "specificity" being among the things we had to learn, but I would humbly submit that it ought to be given consideration.

Over the years, I have never walked on water and have never fed 5,000 hungry college students with a McNuggets Happy Meal, but we have seen God provide for us in some wonderful ways. We have learned that God, in keeping His promises, can be very precise, and that His timing is impeccable. Our family has learned that God loves us immensely and is well aware of our particular situations and needs. Here are some "specific" examples:

Off to a great start

God called us into ministry with Campus Bible Fellowship International while I was on active duty with the United States Air Force at Wright Patterson Air Force Base in Fairborn, Ohio. I was released from the USAF in June of 1976, and my wife Betty and I attended Baptist Mid-Missions' candidate school at Cedarville College the following month while our three children were with their grandparents in Iowa. The Sunday morning before we were to graduate and be commissioned, Betty and I did not have a ministry team assignment in one of the area churches. So we attended our home church in Fairborn, about 12 miles from Cedarville.

As I parked our car back on the campus of Cedarville College, I glanced at one of the tires and noticed something unusual—silver wires showing through the tread. Since all four tires were of the same vintage, I looked more closely at the others. I discovered that we were desperately in need of tires all around—so much so that it would not be safe for us to begin the trip to Iowa the following Friday to get the children.

Betty and I discussed the need and prayed about it; part of the discussion was that there was no money for tires! But the need was unmistakable. During a free time on Monday afternoon, I drove to our hometown of Fairborn and had four new tires placed on the car. I arranged for a 90 days same as cash payment. The total cost was $178.08.

I returned to campus for the rest of candidate school, and we continued to pray about our need. The commissioning service was to take place that Thursday evening. Thursday at noon, as we were eating our lunch, the pastor of our church came into the dining hall looking for us. He told us that on Sunday evening our church family had taken a love offering for us. He said that although they didn't know of any specific need, they knew that we did not have regular income and that we had some traveling to do. He handed me an envelope. We opened the envelope and pulled out a check for—$178!

There was rejoicing in the dining hall, and the next morning we headed for Iowa on brand new tires—paid in full (I found eight cents in a dresser drawer at home before we left). God specifically knew our need and had provided for it before we knew the amount. It was a wonderful reminder for our entire family of His promise that He would meet our needs as we faithfully obeyed His calling—and after 32 years, He is still the same.

Unto the least of these

There are many things that could be used to describe the deputation experience, but short budgets and family separation are two that come to mind. God's provision is also a common experience during deputation, and sometimes He chooses to provide in ways that remind us of the need to have the faith of a child.

It was our second year on deputation. Our daughter Carol's 10th birthday was just a few days away when I left for a missions conference in West Virginia, leaving my wife and our three children behind so that the kids could go to school.

A few days into the conference, I called home to check on how things were going. Betty said that she had been talking with Carol the day before about what she would like for her birthday. She had said that what she would like, more than anything else, was a pink flannel nightgown. Even though Betty is an accomplished seamstress, there was no pink flannel on hand, and the "pink flannel budget jar" was empty. Betty had prayed with Carol and had tucked her into bed.

The mail on the next day brought a box from our home church in Iowa, where there was a group of ladies who met together every month to do some sewing for their missionaries. As Betty opened the box, she pulled from it several items of clothing, including some shirts for the two younger boys. Finally, there was one more item in the bottom of the box. As the children looked on, she pulled out—a pink flannel nightgown, just right for a 10-year-old girl. Our children (and Mom and Dad) once again learned a valuable lesson about God's care for us. He knows our needs, and our desires, even before we ask—even if it is a pink flannel nightgown! "Delight thyself also in the LORD: and he shall give thee the desires of thine heart" (Psalm 37:4).

You found it where?

Many of our stories of God's provision involve automobiles. After all, that's where missionaries spend a lot of their time. In 1989 we were in need of a vehicle that would meet the varying needs of a growing family and which would also be helpful in our ministry. We often had occasion to transport college students to church or to special events.

We had been shopping and had determined that, if God would provide, a Plymouth Grand Voyager minivan would be perfect for what we needed. We shopped and dreamed, picked out option packages and even chose a color—a beautiful metallic blue. And then reality set in— sticker shock!

After a time, we resigned ourselves that, apart from a miracle, we would have to lower our expectations and be content with an older vehicle. A short time later we made a trip to our local Wal-Mart, and as we parked our car, we noticed in the next parking spot a pretty blue Grand Voyager—with a sign in the window that said "FOR SALE." The sign listed the equipment options—identical to what we had picked for our dream vehicle. It had 20,000 miles on it, full transferable warranties, and was $5,000 below the list price.

A few phone calls and a few days later, we were the grateful owners of a Grand Voyager. Some 218,000 miles later, it is still a member of our family, relegated to close-to-home trips but still faithfully serving. Once again, we had a reminder that God is specific in how He answers our prayers.

Litter or God's provision?

The lessons from our Grand Voyager did not end with its purchase. God continued to remind us of His care as we have traveled many miles over the years. Betty and I were traveling on I-70 just east of Indianapolis when a loud "thump" was followed immediately by the telltale indicators of a blown rear tire. We pulled to the side of the road and quickly evaluated the situation.

We were now disabled along the side of a very busy interstate highway. Just across the road and well within vision was a state police station. Those were the days before cell phones but during the heyday of CB radios, which we carried with us. However, several distress calls yielded no response (we later learned that, at that time, the Indiana State Police did not monitor CB radios).

The vehicle was equipped with add-on running boards, which made access to the regular jacking point impossible. The only way to jack the car to change the tire was to place the scissors jack under the axle. But that was not possible because the flat tire lowered the frame so much that the jack would not fit.

After looking at our predicament and with no help in sight, I said to Betty, "What we really need is a 2"x4" so that I can back the car up on it, raise the car and get the jack in place." There were no likely sources of lumber on the horizon, but we prayed and I set out in search of something that would help us out of our dilemma. I had not walked 50 yards back down the side of the highway when I spotted it—a 2"x4" board about two feet long, lying in the ditch.

I returned to the car, beaming at my find and rejoicing in God's care. I proceeded to change the tire. After the car was jacked up and the process well under way, an Indiana state trooper pulled up behind us, turned on his lights, and watched as I completed the job! After I finished, I placed the board inside the van with the other tools. I carried it for many years as a reminder of God's care for the details of our lives.

Teeth and taxes

Medical issues also provide opportunities for God to show His power. We were traveling when I experienced excruciating pain in one of my teeth. After a couple of days of pain, a visit to an urgent care facility provided temporary relief until I could get home to visit my regular dentist. That visit revealed a cracked tooth, which would require a root canal procedure. I began to see dollar signs ($750 to be exact), because we did not have dental insurance. To make things even more interesting, before I could get to the root canal appointment, the tooth became abscessed, requiring another emergency dental visit to the tune of $150.

One more painful experience was on the horizon—it was time to prepare income tax forms. Since I was already in pain, I gathered our records and sat down to prepare the forms … and then I began to see God at work. When the state tax form was completed, we were due a refund in the exact amount of $150! Then it was on to the federal form—and the calculations yielded news of a refund—of exactly $750!

That required a call to our daughter in another state to tell her again of God's goodness. She (jokingly, I think) asked if I had started with the refund amount and worked backwards to make the figures match. But, in reality, the God of pink flannel nightgowns had shown Himself specifically powerful once again.

God's Sovereignty

God rules! The Scriptures proclaim the superiority of Yahweh. He is called Lord. King. Master. Ruler. God Most High. I AM. "Thus saith the LORD the King of Israel, and his redeemer the LORD of hosts; I am the first, and I am the last; and beside me there is no God" (Isaiah 44:6).

He has authority over all He has created—over the seas, over the land, over the wind, and over the rain. He rules over men and angels. He directs the rise and fall of governments and the unfolding of the ages. Whether people acknowledge that fact does not alter the reality of it. To be sure, there is coming a day when all humankind will acknowledge the supreme authority of God. "That at the name of Jesus every knee should bow, of things in heaven, and things in earth, and things under the earth; and that every tongue should confess that Jesus Christ is Lord, to the glory of God the Father" (Philippians 2:10-11).

God is the first and last; there is no one besides Him. The richest man in the world and the beggar in Mexico City are equally inferior to the God Most High. "And all the inhabitants of the earth are reputed as nothing: and he doeth according to his will in the army of heaven, and among the inhabitants of the earth: and none can stay his hand, or say unto him, What doest thou?" (Daniel 4:35).

Nothing in the created universe has happened or will ever happen that is not under the control of the Sovereign Lord. In the story "His Plans Are Better," God overrules the carefully laid plans of His missionaries, and the result makes a difference for eternity.

He is our Mighty King. We are His subjects. Our duty is to obey and surrender ourselves willingly to His benevolent control. God the Father is directly involved with all aspects of the lives of His individual children.

Romans 8:28-39 presents the supreme authority that God maintains over all those that are His. It starts with "And we know that all things work together for good to them that love God, to them who are the called according to his purpose."

The only way that God can promise that all things work together for good is if He maintains control of the "all things," starting from before the person comes into existence.

> Blessed be the God and Father of our Lord Jesus
> Christ, who hath blessed us with all spiritual blessings in
> heavenly places in Christ: According as he hath chosen
> us in him before the foundation of the world, that we
> should be holy and without blame before him in love:
> Having predestinated us unto the adoption of children by
> Jesus Christ to himself, according to the good pleasure of
> his will, to the praise of the glory of his grace, wherein he
> hath made us accepted in the beloved (Ephesians 1:3-6).

The word translated "predestinated" in the Greek means "to limit in advance, to predetermine." So even before our ancestors were born, God looked ahead into time and predetermined that we would believe "according to the good pleasure of His will" and not according to any foreknowledge of good works that we might do.

Then Romans 8:30 says that He "called" us. If we are believers, at some point in our lifetime we responded to that call and received Him as our Lord and Savior. We tend to think it is our idea and our choice, and yet without the "call" we would never seek Him.

"No man can come to me, except the Father which hath sent me draw him: and I will raise him up at the last day" (John 6:44). In promising to "raise him up at the last day," Jesus is promising to guard us all the days of our lives. He takes personal responsibility for His own.

> Hearken unto me, O house of Jacob, and all the
> remnant of the house of Israel, which are borne by me
> from the belly, which are carried from the womb: And
> even to your old age I am he; and even to hoar hairs will I
> carry you: I have made, and I will bear; even I will carry,
> and will deliver you (Isaiah 46:3-4).

Not only does Jesus predetermine our salvation, He also has designed specific works for us to do. He gives purpose to our lives. "For we are his workmanship, created in Christ Jesus unto good works, which God hath before ordained that we should walk in them" (Ephesians 2:10).

Stories in this section highlight what God can do with a life that is turned over to Him. In each case, God has called His child to a unique ministry—designed by God for His glory.

The Lord's great commission became their commission.

> And Jesus came and spake unto them, saying,
> All power is given unto me in heaven and in earth. Go
> ye therefore, and teach all nations, baptizing them in
> the name of the Father, and of the Son, and of the Holy
> Ghost: Teaching them to observe all things whatsoever
> I have commanded you: and, lo, I am with you always,
> even unto the end of the world. Amen (Matthew 28:18-
> 20).

The clear call of their Lord and Master could not be ignored, even though it meant relinquishing what they had once desired to keep. For the Christian to be happy and fulfilled, he or she must surrender to God the right to choose. As long as we hold on to our desire to control our own destinies, we will fall short of the best that our Master has for us. "… Eye hath not seen, nor ear heard, neither have entered into the heart of man, the things which God hath prepared for them that love him" (1 Corinthians 2:9).

Nothing in the created universe has happened or will ever happen that is not under the control of the Sovereign Lord.

> Thine, O LORD is the greatness, and the power,
> and the glory, and the victory, and the majesty: for all
> that is in the heaven and in the earth is thine; thine is
> the kingdom, O LORD, and thou art exalted as head
> above all. Both riches and honour come of thee, and thou
> reignest over all; and in thine hand is power and might;
> and in thine hand it is to make great, and to give strength
> unto all (1 Chronicles 29:11-12).

Because God is sovereign, I can trust Him in the midst of difficulties, knowing that anything that touches my life must first go through His loving and merciful hands. This is not a fatalistic approach to life that resigns itself to enduring a miserable existence. Rather it is a peaceful trust that a Heavenly Father has circumstances well under control and is doing the right thing on my behalf.

> Moreover whom he did predestinate, them he
> also called: and whom he called, them he also justified:
> and whom he justified, them he also glorified. What shall

we then say to these things? If God be for us, who can be against us? He that spared not his own Son, but delivered him up for us all, how shall he not with him also freely give us all things? Who shall lay any thing to the charge of God's elect? It is God that justifieth.

Who is he that condemneth? It is Christ that died, yea rather, that is risen again, who is even at the right hand of God, who also maketh intercession for us. Who shall separate us from the love of Christ? shall tribulation, or distress, or persecution, or famine, or nakedness, or peril, or sword?

As it is written, For thy sake we are killed all the day long; we are accounted as sheep for the slaughter. Nay, in all these things we are more than conquerors through him that loved us. For I am persuaded, that neither death, nor life, nor angels, nor principalities, nor powers, nor things present, nor things to come, nor height, nor depth, nor any other creature, shall be able to separate us from the love of God, which is in Christ Jesus our Lord (Romans 8:30-39).

Too Incredible to Be Coincidence
Mary Amesbury

Mary joined Baptist Mid-Missions in 1992 and served first in the Far East of Russia. Since 2000, she has been serving with Campus Bible Fellowship International in Cleveland, Ohio.

Of all the people and circumstances that God has used to bring me into a relationship with someone He wants to redeem, none have been more extraordinary than those that brought me to Tanya Baksheeva. Although she has yet to put her faith in the Lord Jesus Christ, I am absolutely convinced that the Father is drawing her to Himself. How can I be so sure? Because the events were far too incredible to be a coincidence.

In August of 2001, Campus Bible Fellowship International in Cleveland, Ohio, hosted for the first time "Stuff for Students," an outreach to new international students just arriving in the United States. We collected used furniture and household items and then invited international students to come and select a piece of furniture and other needed items. They also received a tract and were invited to other events where the gospel would be shared.

Since this was the first time for us to do the event, we had no idea how fast the furniture would go. We had scheduled it for 10 a.m. to 12:30 p.m., but by 10:30 a.m. all the furniture had been claimed. At about noon, one of our church members arrived and asked me if I could still use an end table that she had. She told me that she had mentioned it to me several times; however, I had absolutely no recollection of those conversations.

Nonetheless, I decided to go with her to her apartment and get the end table. As we pulled back into the church parking lot, four or five international students were coming out the back door. I called to them, "Do any of you need an end table?" The students discussed among themselves who needed the piece of furniture the most. They decided to give it to a woman with auburn hair.

"She looks Russian," I thought. My first term of service with Baptist Mid-Missions had been in Russia, and a part of my heart was still there.

"Climb in and I'll take you to where you are staying," I said. So the woman got in the back seat and we started driving to Cleveland State University. "My name is Mary, what's yours?"

"Tanya," she said.

"Where are you from?" I questioned.

"Russia," she said.

"Really? That's great. I lived there for four years. What part of Russia?" I asked.

"Siberia," she said.

In my mind I thought, "Siberia is huge. She's probably from somewhere I've never heard of." But I said, "I was in Irkutsk, teaching English at Irkutsk State University."

"That's where I'm from! And that's where I went to university!" she exclaimed.

In my surprise I nearly hit a curb. I knew this was a God moment. It was just too perfect to believe that it was a coincidence that Tanya was sitting in my car. If I had not forgotten about the end table, it would have been claimed by someone else earlier in the day. If I had pulled into the church parking lot just a few minutes later, Tanya and her companions would have been gone. If someone else in the group of students had claimed the end table, Tanya wouldn't be sitting in my car at that moment.

So I began to tell Tanya about my job with Campus Bible Fellowship International and our Bible studies. To my surprise, she didn't have even a glimmer of interest in the Bible or spiritual things. She was, however, interested in getting together to make Russian food. So that's where we started.

About a month later, Tanya came over to dinner at my house. We had a good time talking, and I showed her my Russian memorabilia and pictures. My roommate and I gave testimony of how God had furnished our house with furniture. Tanya made no comment about anything that involved God. She didn't believe or disbelieve. She just acted like I hadn't said anything. It was strange not to get some kind of reaction.

On Tanya's second or third visit, I was showing her the house and we walked into my bedroom. On the wall was a map of Russia with a picture of my former colleagues attached to it.

Tanya exclaimed, "I know of that family!"

"The Armstrongs?" I said.

"Yes, my sister was their interpreter when they bought their first apartment," she said.

That seemed just too incredible to me. We decided that I would e-mail the Armstrongs and she would e-mail her sister, and we would find out if she was right. Within a few days the answer came back. Yes, Olga had been the Armstrongs' interpreter. Wow! Unbelievable!

I shared the story of Tanya in an e-mail to my prayer supporters. One of them wrote and said that she had an exchange student from Irkutsk staying with her and her family for a year and that it would be great for the two women to meet. My friend Dawn said that if we were ever in Arizona, Tanya and I should come for a visit. At the time I was busy with ministry in Ohio, and I greatly doubted that Tanya or I would ever be anywhere near Arizona.

In December, Tanya came to Campus Bible Fellowship's International Christmas Dinner. At the dinner we had a literature table. Tanya took a copy of a booklet called *Ultimate Questions* in her native language. That was the first hint of any spiritual interest.

A few months later, Tanya e-mailed me and said that she had a conference to go to in Arizona but that hotels were too expensive. She asked me if I knew of anyone she could stay with in Arizona. The city where the conference was located was the same city where my friend Dawn lived! Tanya ended up staying with Dawn and her family and even going to church with them on Sunday. Even more amazing was that Tanya's sister Olga went to church in Russia with the Armstrongs on that very same Sunday! Coincidence? No, a powerful, purposeful God was seeking Tanya for Himself. God was piling on evidence of His sovereign control of events.

At the end of June 2002, the Armstrongs came back to the United States on furlough. They are from the West Coast, but this time they flew through New York and visited relatives before driving across the United States. On their way, they stopped in Cleveland to visit the Home Office of Baptist Mid-Missions. It worked out for me to have both the Armstrongs and Tanya over for dinner. Tanya greatly enjoyed meeting the Armstrongs and playing with their boys.

After dinner, Lisa Armstrong and I drove Tanya back to her home. Tanya was just amazed at all the connections. "What do you think is behind all these coincidences?" she asked.

"God," I said. For the next 20 minutes or so I explained to Tanya who God is and what He is like and how we can know Him personally and how I was convinced that He was seeking her. This time she was really listening! Before she got out of the car, I asked if she had a Bible. She said that she didn't have one but that she would like one in English. We planned to go to an outdoor concert in a couple of days, so I promised that I would give her a Bible then.

When I gave Tanya the Bible, I was again able to share with her how she could receive forgiveness of her sins and come into a right relationship with Jesus. I hoped she would put her faith in Christ that night, but she didn't. I didn't get to see Tanya again before she left the United States.

Tanya and I exchanged e-mail messages for a while but then gradually lost contact. At the end of April 2005 the Lord brought Tanya back to mind, and I sent an e-mail to the last address that I knew of.

Tanya wrote me back a week later. In part she wrote, "Now I'd like to tell you a story you won't believe. Yesterday I was discussing the Electronic Commerce Course with the program coordinator. Her office is situated in the public library in Irkutsk, and we accidentally started to discuss that they charge readers for books and CDs and that this is not correct for a public library. I remembered the Cleveland library and said that it is a very good one. The coordinator said, 'Oh I have a good friend in Cleveland; she works with international students at the university.' I asked her, 'What is the name of your friend?' The answer was—'Mary Amesbury.' I was VERY surprised! I said, 'You're kidding, she is my friend!' That is so unbelievable. The coordinator's name is Sonya Cheusova."

Because I was in poor health most of the time, Sonya was one of only a few Russians that I really got acquainted with during my five months in Irkutsk. That the two of them would meet the very same week that I had e-mailed Tanya and end up making the connection was, indeed, incredible.

In 2007 at the urging of one of my former students, I joined Facebook, an online social group that keeps friends connected. In an update to supporters, I mentioned that I was on Facebook. Dawn, in Arizona, was also using Facebook so we connected. Tanya found me on Facebook through Dawn. So now, after several years of lost contact, I now have regular interaction with Tanya again. Tanya has traveled to 30 cities in seven countries. She never seems settled in one place for very long. But she'll never travel further than a Sovereign God can find her. He is pursuing her in love and some day, I'm convinced, she will yield her life to Him.

Saved in Japan, Serving in Southeast Asia
Masashi Tomioka

In his story, Dr. Tomioka recounts his salvation and call to missions from his homeland of Japan. He testifies: "I have been totally changed. I have been given true peace in my heart. After my salvation, I wanted to serve for the Lord. And God called me to be a missionary in 1981." He and his wife Yoshiko joined Baptist Mid-Missions in 1988 and minister in a medical outreach in Southeast Asia.

I was born in Japan. My birthplace is not far from Tokyo. My parents were not Christians. They earnestly worshipped idols every day. When I was 10 years old, my father changed his job. He began a new job in our home. He sometimes forced me to help him with his work. So, little by little, I began to dislike my parents.

When I entered medical college, I left my home. Since I wanted to leave my parents, I was very pleased with living alone. I didn't like to obey my parents and couldn't love them.

When I was in the third year of medical college, I met Miss Evelyn Regier, a missionary with Baptist Mid-Missions. She was the instructor of an English lecture at my college. One day she invited me to her home with my five classmates. She told us about Jesus Christ. At the time I could not understand what she said. Furthermore, I did not like nonscientific thoughts. I rejected her teaching strongly.

However, when I left her home, she handed me an invitation to the local Baptist church. From that time on, I wanted to read the Bible to ascertain the existence of God. I wanted to know what the Bible was all about.

One Sunday evening in 1973, I went to church by myself. After the evening service was over, the pastor came to me and showed me Mark 7:20-23. "And he said, That which cometh out of the man, that defileth the man. For from within, out of the heart of men, proceed evil thoughts, adulteries, fornications, murders, thefts, covetousness, wickedness, deceit, lasciviousness, an evil eye, blasphemy, pride, foolishness: All these evil things come from within, and defile the man."

When I read it, I realized that I was a sinner. I understood that having hated my parents was an awful sin. So I wanted to be cleansed by Jesus Christ. I repented of all my sins before God and accepted Jesus Christ as my own personal Savior. After I got saved, God changed my mind, and my attitude toward my parents changed. He made me love them. My younger brother and sister also believed in Jesus Christ.

After I graduated from medical college, I married in 1977 and began to work as an Ear, Nose, and Throat specialist at the hospital. I began to pray that God would lead me according to His will. In the morning service of the church, in the fall of 1981, the Lord showed me one verse, Joshua 1:3: "Every place that the sole of your foot shall tread upon, that have I given unto you, as I said unto Moses." I didn't fully understand what special meaning this verse had for me. But at the time, I decided to go wherever He would lead.

Before long, the missionary who led me to Christ in 1973 wrote me a letter. She sent me a brochure concerning the medical missions of Baptist Mid-Missions. When I read it I became interested in medical missions. I wrote to the Home Office of Baptist Mid-Missions. They sent a letter in reply telling of the open door in Asia and that missionaries were needed for medical evangelism. When I read it, I felt that God was calling me to become a missionary doctor.

Then I realized why Joshua 1:3 was given to me a few months before. God had given me this verse to show me that I should go to Southeast Asia by faith, just as Joshua went into Canaan by faith. I discussed my call with Rev. Richard Rich, missionary pastor of Grace Baptist Church in Tokyo. He counseled me to enroll in the three-year missionary course at Grace Baptist Bible School in Tokyo. This I did.

My wife Yoshiko and I were accepted by Baptist Mid-Missions in July of 1988 and arrived in Southeast Asia for our first term of service in the autumn of 1990.

A Filthy Tract
Kent and Belen Albright

Kent and his wife Belén serve in Spain, Belén's homeland. Appointed with Baptist Mid-Missions in 1989, the Albrights served their early years in the Madrid area, teaching in the Bible institute and giving support to exist-

ing church plants. In 1996, the Albrights began a church in Salamanca, in western Spain. Kent is also now the director of the Spanish field's seminary program.

I am a strong believer in evangelism through literature. There are many other means, and even much more effective methods to share Christ, but a simple tract is an inexpensive way to unleash the power of the gospel. During our time here in Salamanca, Spain, we have blanketed the city and all the surrounding towns on three occasions. Since it is not illegal to stuff mailboxes, we've stuffed them a lot. This is in addition to the many other literature blitzes we've done. I estimate that our little church has distributed nearly a million tracts and brochures since our arrival.

However, our church is not filled with people who have been saved as a result. The fact is we are often surprised when someone writes in or shows up at one of our services as a result of receiving a tract. And yet it happens. The first lady to get saved in our church was a former nun who received a "Religious Survey" in her mailbox one day! Another tract success story is the testimony of Rosana.

Rosana is originally from Brazil and moved to Spain several years ago for work reasons. She's a petite, pretty woman with small features, dark complexion, thin black hair, and a captivating smile. But her life had been far from rosy. She was one of nine children, so she had to basically fend for herself. As a teen, her boyfriend left her pregnant. She loved to party at night, dressed to the hilt with very high heels. She danced the night away to counterbalance the long, weary days of survivalist jobs.

Her daughter Marcela caught her zest for the nightlife, and the two of them bar-hopped together on the weekends. One day on vacation at a nudist beach, Rosana met a Spaniard, Manolo, who later became her husband. But the party life stressed their marriage until Marcela was asked to return to Brazil for a while. It was there that she found Christ, and her life began to change dramatically. Both Rosana and Manolo could hardly believe the difference "religion" had made in her.

From Brazil, Marcela begged her mother through letters and over the phone to find a Baptist church. Rosana had hardly heard of such a church and replied that there was certainly no such thing in Salamanca. She knew the city inside out and was certain nothing like it existed … until one rainy day when she was walking to the doctor's office in Santa Marta. A brochure was lying in a puddle beneath her feet. The word "Baptist" caught her eye.

Incredulously, she picked the paper up by the corner and tried to read the mud-stained back. There it was in black and white—Iglesia Bautista de Tormes (Tormes Baptist Church). And the church was located only 200 meters from her apartment! How could she have missed it? It was Tuesday, but the brochure said they had Wednesday night meetings. Later, after she let the brochure dry, she read it cover to cover and decided to attend.

That week we'd had a church team from Ohio help us distribute thousands of brochures we'd ordered from another missionary who runs a printing press. They were disappointed that, for all their efforts, no one had shown up on Sunday. Then Rosana walked in mid-service that Wednesday evening.

That filthy tract has resulted in quite an explosion of spiritual fruit. Not only did Rosana come to Christ, but her nudist husband also bowed his head in tears to become born-again. God transformed his life, and he became a song leader and musician in our church. Manolo's daughter and father received Christ, too. Rosana's cousin in Mallorca trusted Christ; then her mother and several other sisters followed suit. Only three siblings are still unsaved. Brothers-in-law, nieces, nephews, neighbors, and other friends have found the Lord, besides the many, many others who have received testimony from this couple.

About five years ago, Rosana and Manolo moved near the town of Vitoria in southeast Brazil. A new church, headed up by missionaries, met in their home. We were saddened the day these two treasures left but God later brought them back to Spain, where they continue to attend our church, growing, learning, and serving.

God is the One who can enable filthy, sin-marred souls to find salvation, purity, and forgiveness through a soaked and soiled gospel tract.

Forgiveness
Jim Leonard

As the son of missionaries Jerry and Frances Leonard, Jim grew up sur-
rounded by ministry in Brazil. He and his wife Julie also had a heart to
serve in Brazil and joined Baptist Mid-Missions in 1986. They work with
churches and the BMM seminary in Northeast Brazil.

One Sunday night I spoke at the Peace Baptist Church in Juazeiro do Norte, a church my father had begun when I was a child. The Lord had led me to prepare a message for that night focusing on forgiveness, taken from the parable of the unmerciful servant in Matthew 18.

Just before the message, a visitor asked to share a word with the church. As this man was unknown to everybody in the congregation, this was a very unusual request, but he was permitted to speak.

Senhor Azarias, who now lives over 2,000 miles away near the Suriname border, grew up in the neighborhood of Peace Baptist Church. He confessed that as a child he and his friends would go by the church, disrupting the services by throwing rocks into the sanctuary and neighing like baby goats. They had been encouraged to do so by his parents and their priest. He recalled specifically two younger children, blond and light-skinned, whom they had chased and thrown sand at. He even remembered their names, "Jaime" and "Raquel."

Sr. Azarias had no idea both I and my sister Rachel were present on this evening more than 30 years later. With tears running down his face, this man asked the church to forgive him for what he had done as a child.

Ten years ago, after he had moved away, the Lord saved him and has greatly blessed him. Ever since then, he has wanted to come back to meet the church that had first brought the gospel into his life, though he had persecuted it.

Sr. Azarias asked us to pray for his brothers, sisters, and parents who are all unsaved and still living in the neighborhood of Peace Baptist Church. I could not have asked for a better introduction to a message on forgiveness than this one.

His Plans Are Better

Gary Hilliker

*Gary and his wife Bernice were appointed with Baptist Mid-Missions in
1966 to serve in Venezuela. Their Latin American church-planting experience served them well in 1986, when they began working at BMM's Spanish
publications ministry, Editorial Bautista Independiente, where they continue to serve.*

At the time of this episode, I was a missionary in Venezuela. The
association of Baptist churches had three men—a Venezuelan and two
men from the Warao tribe—who felt called to be missionaries to their
own people. To encourage the Warao missionaries who were trying to
start a church in a little place called Guaranoko, we decided to hold a special meeting. Fellow missionary Marilyn Pitzer and I, along with several
others, went out to Guaranoko. This village is several hours by dugout
canoe into the delta of the Orinoco River.

In the afternoon, we went out and invited people to come to the
service. We had taken along a generator and a film projector so that we
could show a film about an evangelistic work on a river. We thought that
a film would draw a crowd so that the Warao missionaries would have a
good group to preach to.

As the hour approached for the meeting, we could see the large
dugout canoe "buses" coming down the river filled with people for the
service. When the people had all arrived, we started the meeting with
several musical numbers by a Warao choir that had come from El Pajal,
where Marilyn Pitzer was working. Several people gave testimonies of
God's working in their lives.

Then it came time for the film. Everybody was really excited
about it. We got ready, turned out the light, started the projector and—
the bulb burned out. No problem, I wasn't in Boy Scouts all those years
for nothing. My motto was "Be prepared," so I had another bulb with
me. I put the bulb in, turned the switch to start the film and—pop! The
second bulb burned out!

What does a person do? Well, we started to have messages. Two
or three of the men from El Pajal gave gospel messages. Then there were

some more testimonies and an invitation. As the invitation was given, I could see some movement among the women who were sitting in front of me. They were elbowing each other and talking to one another in Warao. I asked Marilyn what they were saying, and she translated their conversation. They were saying, "I'll do it if you will. Well okay, if you go, I'll go."

Finally they started moving, and several of the women went forward to receive Christ as Savior. Then the men began to move down the aisle. Before we finished the service, some 37 Waraos went forward to accept Jesus Christ as their Savior. Sometimes God just has to take our plans and lay them aside so that He can bring glory to His name.

The Leading of the Lord of the Harvest
Heidi VanDyke

Heidi entered the BMM Family as a short-term teacher at an MK school, Fetzer Memorial Christian Academy in Lima, Peru. She was appointed for career service in Cuba in 2000. She now works alongside national leaders in the Dominican Republic.

For as long as I have worked in other countries, people have been asking me how it came about that I ended up where I am. An American residing in a poorer country is not necessarily common; a single young American lady is even more of a novelty. So people are curious about the story behind my presence.

What can I tell them, except that God is the One who leads me? During my last few months in Bible college, I asked in specific prayer if God would have me serve as a missionary and, if so, in what country. He simply impressed on my mind and heart the country of Cuba. That was so unexpected and unexplainable that I set the idea aside for two years while teaching missionaries' children in Lima, Peru.

When my commitment in Peru was coming to a close, I returned to serious prayer for direction: Stay in Peru? Return to the States? Go somewhere else? The answer again came: Cuba.

Now the answer was not so unexpected, but still unexplainable.

Cuba was a country with an oppressive government, not friendly to my own country. In fact, the Cuban government did not grant visas for missionaries to enter her territory, and the United States government rarely granted permission for her citizens to travel to the island.

My pastor and I researched the options, questioning different organizations about their past experience and current ministry in Cuba. At that time, only one had a missionary family residing in the country. It was the same organization I had worked with in Peru! I wrote the missionary family a letter through e-mail, asking whether they might be interested in my visiting and whether they thought that I could possibly work with them. Several weeks passed, and I wondered what God's answer would be. Would this idea He had planted in my heart be a direction for now, or for some time in the future?

Finally a response came from the missionaries in Cuba saying that, yes, they would welcome a visit. They apologized that they hadn't replied earlier, explaining that with the restrictions on the island they were able to review their e-mails only every couple of months. I literally jumped with excitement, looking forward to an adventure following God's leading to this "restricted access nation."

And so I began working in Cuba with the missionary family. When people in the US and Cuba asked, I told them it was a long-term commitment, dependent on God's leading. Since He had opened the way in what was to me an extraordinary manner, I expected Him to allow that work to continue for a long time. So God's next direction surprised me a little bit.

We had been praying for God to continue to arrange circumstances and protect us so that we could continue to work there. But one day we learned that a missionary with another agency working in our city had been jailed and questioned. Whether he mentioned us or not (the government claimed he had), after only a few tense days of wondering, my coworkers were also escorted out of the country. I followed after a short time, because we felt it would not be best to leave just one American in the country.

All this we accepted as God's leading, because not one part of that process was within our control. Now, of course, we did pray, wondering what was to follow: Return to Cuba? Or go somewhere else? Several months later we had the answer to the first question, since my coworkers were denied entrance on an attempted visit to Cuba.

At first, God had led me with an unexpected idea planted in my heart. Then He had led me through circumstances related mostly to other people and their actions, things I had no say in. How would He direct this time?

After leaving Cuba and seeing that the way into the country was still closed after a year, I prayed, along with my family and pastor, for direction to a new location. My heart was satisfied with the work and coworkers in Peru, so I made a visit there. But in spite of my affections, I did not sense God's direction to return. Missionaries in other countries invited me to visit and to participate in ministry, so I spent a couple weeks observing in Spain, and then a couple months teaching in Venezuela. But although I could see an extreme need in Europe, and although I felt comfortable in Venezuela, no solid decision formed, either in my mind or in my pastor's.

Meanwhile in the Dominican Republic, a group of churches was praying for renewed contact with American missionaries. Many of their ministries had been started by missionaries, but for almost 15 years none had been present to help or encourage. The pastors of this group felt a need for outside help, especially in the area of education and ministerial training. They contacted many of the veteran missionaries and representatives of the mission organization. Along with an invitation to an anniversary celebration, they made a request for renewed missionary activity in the Dominican Republic. They had yet to understand that even with the greatest desire to help, the mission organization itself did not send or lead people to any specific country. God does that.

One day I received an e-mail. This was the report of the group that had represented the mission organization in a meeting with Dominican pastors. The letter told about their visit and about the need. As I read, I was again attracted, not without logical reason, to a Caribbean island. Within a day or two I was sitting with my pastor, sharing my reaction, and was delighted to find that he, too, had seen the letter and felt God had established my direction. After two years of wondering, praying, asking, and traveling, the decision was made in just a matter of hours. God worked through the Dominican pastors to move a group of American mission representatives whose separate communications to me and my pastor caused the same result.

I've been in the Dominican Republic only a couple of years now, but I have been amazed from the very beginning by the receptive attitude of the churches, pastors, and the Dominican public. Here, God has given me abundant opportunities and freedom to serve in His Name.

FIRE at Wright State
Gary Holtz

Following Gary's Air Force career, he and his wife Betty joined Baptist Mid-Missions in 1976 to serve with Campus Bible Fellowship (now called Campus Bible Fellowship International (CBFI). They have worked with several campuses in the Dayton, Ohio, area. Gary is now CBFI's Coordinator.

No matter how many times we see the sovereignty of God on display, it is always amazing to see one more way that He shows His love and power. The following episode reminded us once again that He is in absolute control.

Campus Bible Fellowship International (CBFI) is a ministry of Baptist Mid-Missions that partners with local Baptist churches to minister to students on secular college and university campuses. The role of CBFI missionaries is to assist Christian students in forming on-campus organizations holding regular Bible studies for evangelism and discipleship. Each university has its particular requirements for approving student organizations, which may include submission of documentation, designation of a staff or faculty sponsor, a constitution, and student officers. Prospective officers may be required to complete leadership training sessions as well.

Everything was in place for the 2008-2009 academic year at Wright State University (WSU) in Fairborn, Ohio. One officer, however, failed to complete the required training, and CBFI was not recognized as a student organization and thus not approved to continue on campus. For the first time in 33 years, CBFI was not permitted to take part in club fairs to meet new students, to have information tables for recruiting new members, or to schedule meeting rooms for weekly Bible studies.

January 30 offered another opportunity to register the group for the remainder of the school year, so a different student completed the required training. Joe Hollaway, the local CBFI missionary, submitted the completed documents that day to the Student Activities office. Recognition was denied once again.

The university officials cited two reasons for denying recognition: (1) our constitution did not contain the mandatory "affirmative action" statement that we would not discriminate on the basis of religion, sexual orientation, gender identity, and gender expression; and (2) our requirement that voting members and those who would hold office "must have accepted Jesus Christ as personal Savior and must be in complete agreement with the organization's Articles of Faith." These were considered to violate the university's nondiscrimination standards, and thus CBFI was not allowed to register.

When it became apparent that the university planned to stand firm, we sought assistance from the Foundation for Individual Rights in Education (FIRE). FIRE is an organization dedicated to the preservation of basic freedoms in the academic setting and has a history of successfully assisting campus groups in similar cases. Though they do not provide legal counsel, they do provide advice based on previous legal precedents and have gained the respect of the academic world, both friend and foe. FIRE assisted us in preparing an appeal, which we presented to the university officials on February 5.

The Director of Student Activities and his assistant essentially disregarded the appeal until we directed them to recent legal decisions for similar cases—decisions that favored the student organizations. When we mentioned that we were willing to pursue litigation if necessary, the director decided that the matter would need to be referred to the university legal department for final disposition.

Three weeks passed, and our inquiries regarding a decision were not answered. In the meantime, winter quarter was drawing to a close, and CBFI was still being prevented from functioning in any way on campus. On Thursday, February 26, a representative from FIRE contacted the university to ask about their decision and to suggest that legal action would be forthcoming if there was no response. That afternoon, a phone message from the legal office at the university stated that CBFI would be reinstated for the remainder of the 2008-09 school year, but that when organizations registered in June for the 2009-10 academic year, CBFI would have to meet the same requirements which had been problematic before.

When FIRE representatives attempted to have the university legal office or Student Activities confirm this decision in writing, they refused to do so. The following day, February 27, Joe Hollaway and I went to the Student Activities office to attempt to complete registration and were refused. They had not yet received official approval to grant recognition. Again on Monday morning, March 2, Joe was turned away and FIRE decided it was time to turn up the heat. At about 2:00 that afternoon, a press release was issued, spelling out the details up to that point. The phones began to ring, both at Wright State and for CBFI staff. The story had gained the attention of Foxnews.com, a number of other web-based news sources, the local CBS TV affiliate, and several area newspapers. At 6:02 that evening, the student president for CBFI at Wright State received an e-mail stating that CBFI was reinstated, effective immediately, but that we would have to meet the same criteria as before when we applied for recognition for 2009-10. On March 3, registration was completed, and CBFI was once again a recognized student organization at WSU.

Sensing that a legal battle might still be inevitable, FIRE turned to the Alliance Defense Fund (ADF), a legal organization that provides pro bono counsel for such cases, and ADF began the process of preparing for a civil rights case in federal court, if necessary. The attorneys at ADF advised us to strengthen and further clarify the language in our constitution, to strengthen our membership numbers, and to adopt a position paper that would define the organization's expectations of conduct for voting members and for those in leadership.

As the June 19 registration deadline drew near, the university announced that it had made some changes to its registration policies; it had increased (from four to six) the number of students required to be signed up as members for the following year, and it would be making provision for an exemption from the nondiscrimination policy, providing an appeal was presented and approved. Once again, ADF assisted us in preparing our appeal, and on June 10 the registration documents, along with our appeal, were presented. On June 19 we received official word that our exemption had been granted, and that CBFI was successfully registered for the 2009-10 academic year!

Along the way, there were a couple of rather ironic developments. As a result of the increased visibility of CBFI on campus, several WSU students contacted us about becoming members of the group. While we were in dispute with the Student Activities Department of WSU, the Center for International Studies nominated Joe Hollaway for their annual International Student Advocate award, which was presented on April 18. Although another nominee actually received the award, it was an honor for Joe to be named, especially in light of the ongoing situation. Also, we were invited to participate in a panel discussion on May 14 as part of a symposium on "Legal Issues on Campus." The day was sponsored by a group of about 20 area colleges and universities and was held on the WSU campus. We were reluctant at first to participate, but decided to do so when we learned that the president of FIRE would be one of the panel members. Interestingly, another participant on the panel was a woman, now head of the Affirmative Action program at WSU, who had previously been the Director of Student Activities at Sinclair Community College in Dayton, Ohio, in 1994 and had banned CBFI from that campus for a year over these same issues.

When we arrived for the symposium, it was evident from the outset that CBFI was the guest of honor for the day—much as the turkey is the guest of honor on Thanksgiving—but overall it was a good experience, with some spirited discussion and an opportunity to present and defend our position.

During this same time period, the CBFI group at Boise State University was informed that they had two months to bring their constitution into compliance with the university's affirmative action policies, or they, along with some other religious organizations, would lose their recognized status. Once again ADF came to the aid of CBFI, and that matter was settled with an agreement that the organization must have a general membership that is open to everyone but could regulate their leadership through religious requirements.

The Scriptures remind us that the gospel message is an offense to those who do not wish to be accountable to God—thus, opposition to the truth will never end until our Lord returns. In the meantime, it is reassuring to know that He is in control, that university policy is no match for our God, and that He will use whatever means He chooses to demonstrate His power.

God Preserves His Own

Compiled from several Ghana missionaries' testimonies

Samuel Seidu was a man of prayer and a man of the Word of God. Although he had very little formal schooling before Bible school, God used him as the primary translator of the Waalii New Testament in Ghana. Samuel came from a pagan family, but many of his relatives were ardent Muslims who tried to influence him towards Islam. In his teens Samuel left his village to find work in the city. One day a friend found an Anglican songbook on the floor of a theater and brought it to Samuel. Samuel found someone who could help him read the little book. This was his first exposure to Christianity, and it whetted his appetite for more.

After some time, he lost his job and returned to his village. He told some of his acquaintances about his desire to know about God. They suggested that he go listen to the white preacher in the neighboring village of Busa. Baptist Mid-Missions missionary William Carmichael was preaching the gospel there. On Saturday, Samuel walked the 12 miles to Busa so that he could attend the service on Sunday. Samuel continued to do this for a few weeks. One week, however, he decided that he would not go to Busa that Saturday. But when Saturday came, it was like "the wind was pushing him" and so he went. That Sunday he talked with Pastor Carmichael.

Noticing his great interest in the Bible, Bill Carmichael offered Samuel a job. One day as Samuel was at work cutting firewood, the Holy Spirit convicted his heart. He knelt right there and gave his life to Jesus. When Samuel walked back to the house, Bill Carmichael could tell by his countenance that something had happened. Soon a desire to know God's Word burned within Samuel, and he aspired to study at the Baptist Bible Institute in Wa. The courses at the Baptist Bible Institute were in English, so Samuel went to one of his relatives and asked him to teach him the language. However, when the relative found out why Samuel wanted to learn English, he refused to help him anymore. Eventually Samuel was given permission to enroll at the Baptist Bible Institute even though his English was barely at the acceptable level. That first week, Samuel did not understand anything that was being taught.

He went to the Lord in anguished prayer, "Lord, I can't do this. It's too hard. I don't understand anything."

"Samuel, Who told you to go to Bible School? I have placed you here and I can keep you here," replied the Lord.

That was sufficient for Samuel. It was the Lord who had brought him to Bible school, and the Lord would enable him to learn. So each night, Samuel studied by candlelight until two in the morning to catch up with the rest of the students. He was a brilliant man with an excellent memory. After Samuel caught up with the others, he continued to study at the same intense pace as before and forged ahead of his fellow students. After graduation he became the pastor of the church in Busa.

Samuel spent at least the first two hours of every day in prayer. He allowed no other responsibility to crowd out his time with his Lord.

Oftentimes he was so focused in prayer that he was unaware that time had passed. Once, Samuel went out to Busa for a prayer meeting that began at four in the afternoon. After the meeting was over, he started home on his bicycle, but he was so overwhelmed by the needs of his congregation that he got off his bicycle and went into the bush to pray. Darkness fell while he was praying but he was oblivious to it. It was after nine p.m. before he finished praying and headed home.

He was a fearless man, preaching Christ to Muslims in the marketplace. Many times his life was threatened because he encouraged others to find the truth in Jesus Christ. One time his brother went out to prepare the family fields for planting. The rains had come and the ground was soft and ready for tilling. At the end of the day, the brother left a gourd of guinea corn for Samuel and his family to eat the next day when they came to sow.

The following day Samuel took his wife and children with him to the field. They brought along a chicken and her chicks. They could scavenge for beetles and other insects while the family worked. When they reached their destination, Samuel released the chickens from the basket. His wife went to the gourd filled with grain and prepared to grind it into flour. Their little boy—then just two years old—was filled with excitement at seeing the little chicks scurrying to and fro on the ground. He did not watch where his own little feet were going and accidentally knocked over the gourd of grain. The chicks immediately began to feed on the corn. One by one the little chicks began to flop over dead. Enemies of Samuel had come secretly in the night and mixed powdered DDT into the grain, hoping to poison the pastor and his entire family. But God preserved His own by the clumsiness of a little boy and a basketful of chicks.

Some would have said that Samuel lived an exceptionally lucky life. Those who knew him said that God had a work for him to do and was not willing that harm should come to him until it was done. That work was Bible translation. Samuel learned Greek and became the key translator for the Waalii New Testament, working alongside missionary Iola Slack. He was meticulous in searching for exact meanings without departing from the original text. The translation work had been in progress for several years when Samuel suffered several fractures to the head while standing in the back of a moving truck. He was leaning against the cab facing backwards when the truck went under a tree and a low-hanging limb caught him on the head. The doctors could do little but prescribe bed rest, which Samuel did until the fractures healed.

But several years later, a blood clot—most likely the result of the earlier head injury—loosened in his brain. God had spared Samuel's life until just a few days after Dr. Osborn, the translation consultant for Baptist Mid-Missions, had completed checking the entire New Testament with Iola and Samuel in Ghana. At age 36 Samuel went Home to be with His Savior whom he loved so much. But the Word of God in the Waalii New Testament continues to transform lives for Christ in Ghana.

¡Arriba! Seeds Bear Fruit
David Murray

David's first contact with Ecuador was through Baptist Mid-Missions' ¡Arriba! college internship program. David met his Ecuadorian wife Sonia there, and they joined Baptist Mid-Missions as full-time church-planting missionaries in 1999. They serve in Cuenca, the same city in which Sonia's brother Fernando Naranjo and his wife Laura serve with BMM. David and Sonia's passion is to reach Ecuadorians with the gospel as they start new churches for Christ.

As an ¡Arriba! student back in 1990-1991, I was burdened by God to lead as many people to Christ as possible and to make an impact for God's kingdom in Ecuador. But that task proved extremely difficult! I always wondered how much of an impact God could make through us as young "Spanglish"-speaking missionary students.

We definitely sacrificed during that year. We faced various hardships and sickness. Yet, I knew it was worth it. We saw a few people come to Christ as a result of our sharing the Good News. But somehow I felt we were dreadfully inadequate in our evangelization and edification efforts. Oh, how I longed to be used of God! But my eyes saw so few lasting results that I sometimes felt that I was almost useless that year. I felt exhausted, beaten, bruised, inadequate, and inferior. But I determined in my heart to return to this friendly, yet hard-to-reach people.

Eventually I did return as a full-time missionary with Baptist Mid-Missions. Then I began to see what I couldn't see as an ¡Arriba!

student. One foggy afternoon in 2006 I was at the police department of transportation here in the city Cuenca to register my vehicle. I noticed a man about my age who looked strangely familiar. Overwhelmed by the sense that I knew him from back in 1991 when I was an ¡Arriba! student, I determined in my heart to take the risk of being rejected. I prayed that our encounter would not end in my possible acquaintance thinking, "Who was that crazy gringo?"

I introduced myself and asked him whether his last name was Balbuena. "Affirmative," he responded with a friendly manner. Yes, the man before me was the brother of a friend of mine from a decade ago. We reminisced about how I had come to know his brother and his whole family. I told him that I still had pictures of them and how I had been praying for them all this time. I asked for his brother Rigoberto's phone number and vowed to call him soon.

Later that week I was standing before my friend Rigoberto in his office at the school he administrates. I felt it was a wonderful reunion, but I really had no idea how wonderful it was going to get in just a few minutes. For it was when I invited him to lunch and attempted to steer the conversation towards my favorite subject (the gospel) that I heard something which brought tears to my eyes and a bittersweet song of thankfulness to God in my heart!

My friend Rigoberto told me that he had received Jesus Christ as his own personal Savior several years previously. He thanked me with a smile, and with tears, for being the first person to share Christ with him. He told me that I was an instrument of God in his life, and that I was used of God to plant seeds in his heart, which softened him to future presentations of the gospel. In time he finally accepted the Lord. Praise God! How moved I was to learn that God used the seeds we planted, way back in 1990-91 to bring forth souls to His harvest! All of the effort we exerted, all of the sacrifices we made that year, seemed even more worthwhile as I learned of my good friend's salvation experience.

I continue to see fruit harvested from our efforts back in 1990-91. I can see the church we had a small part in helping to establish now flourishing with a national pastor and its own piece of land ready to be built on. I see my former Judo teacher from a decade ago, now a good friend of mine who says, "I used to teach David, but now he has become my spiritual teacher." I see a woman named Rosa, our neighbor who used to attend church faithfully back in the day. She just recently accepted the Lord into her heart for real through the ministry of the church that we helped establish. And I thank God for my Ecuadorian wife's family. All of them are saved now, and two of her brothers are in full-time ministry. One is a missionary to Ecuador with BMM!

It is a thrill to think we were actually used by God to make even a small impact for God's kingdom as students of little age and even less experience. It is God who makes things happen. We are simply His "unworthy servants." I am moved and excited to think about what God is doing and may do through us as we serve here now permanently in the gospel ministry.

A Hope and a Future
Bill and Tobi Preston

Bill and Tobi call New Zealand their ministry home, having been appointed with Baptist Mid-Missions in 1985. The Prestons serve with Calvary Baptist Church in Mt. Maunganui.

Our God is not only loving and merciful, but in His sovereignty He knows what circumstances are needed to bring us into His perfect will for our lives. Losing a job, moving to a new place away from the influence of close family, having a sick child, and needing a personal relationship with the Lord Jesus Christ, were all circumstances that came to bear in the lives of Dean and Lupe in 1990 in Tauranga, New Zealand.

We will let them share in their own words how God worked and is working now in their lives.

At the time our family arrived in Tauranga, our oldest son, John, was eight years old and our oldest daughter, Vae, was six. With our third child almost due, a new job, and a new home, it would be fair to say that things finally seemed to be looking up for us.

Then, just a week before her due date, Lupe contracted chickenpox and she gave birth with the illness, which we were told was extremely rare. In addition to this our baby, Juanita, was born breach, and only a few days out of the hospital she was readmitted with severe jaundice. The jaundice very nearly required a complete blood transfusion and almost took her life. Recovering briefly from the jaundice, she then finally succumbed to chickenpox. This tough start in life turned out to be just the beginning. Unbeknown to us, things were about to get much worse.

At six weeks, Juanita's immune system reacted badly to an immunization. The doctors and specialists were uncertain at first what the problem was. The reaction caused such extreme spasms that we feared the worst. Together, Lupe and I tried everything, but the spasms continued without interruption endlessly for months and months. When Juanita was about six months of age, the specialists resigned themselves to giving us the simple facts that either this child would outgrow the problem or she would be permanently brain damaged. We were told that there was nothing medically that could be done to help. This was a difficult time for both of us.

It is important to point out that Lupe had been born into a Christian family and had grown up to trust the Lord. While her faith in God was still strong, she felt somehow that the Lord seemed so very far away. She realized, too, that she had not been faithful since leaving her home in the Pacific many years previously. She had not attended church in years.

In contrast, I had never known the Lord Jesus and had only a remote interest in anything spiritual, despite having childhood memories of Sunday School at a very young age. While we both lived in Auckland, we had once or twice agreed to attend a church service, but for no other reason than it seemed like a good idea for our two young children to attend Sunday School. Nothing in any of those experiences caught my attention, and so after moving to Tauranga, we simply did not bother with church at all.

Despite this, Lupe always spoke to the Lord in her quiet times, and now with this latest problem, she began to talk with the Lord more earnestly. She repeatedly asked God to give her the heart to accept whatever it was the Lord had in mind for Juanita. In time, she began to accept things just the way they were.

However, the one thing that she knew for sure was that she needed to be closer to God, and she felt that the only place that this could be done was in church. So finally one Sunday morning she bundled the children into the car and said to them emphatically, "We're going to church!"

Being reasonably familiar now with the local area and where the churches were in the community, she set out with no particular church in mind. The one thing she had decided, though, was that the one place she wouldn't be visiting was Calvary Baptist Church.

She was aware of where it was and what the church starting times were as she drove past it every day. She was convinced that if she attended anything other than a church her parents approved of that they would be particularly upset with her. So, on this particular morning she drove the children the extra distance to a Presbyterian church that she had seen. This, she thought, would be a better choice and one her parents would approve of. However, the service was well underway when they arrived and she felt uncomfortable going in. She realized that she would have to quickly decide on an alternative. But where should she go? One choice was to try out a church group meeting at a local school hall, but when she arrived there the folks were already carrying in band instruments. Somehow this didn't seem right either.

By now it was 9:50 a.m. and she knew that the only other church that would start within the next 10 minutes was Calvary Baptist Church. It was within a 10-minute drive. This was a decision she knew she would have to make fast. The whole idea seemed wrong, but the critical issue at the time was the burning desire to be in God's house. So she felt that she had no other choice but to drive back to Calvary!

However, somewhere between walking in that very first Sunday and shaking hands with Pastor Preston, something changed. All the apprehension about attending this Baptist church immediately vanished. It was as if this was the place that God wanted her and the children to be on that day, and it was as if He had prepared the way.

This was the very first occasion to meet Pastor Bill and Mrs. Tobi Preston—the beginning of a very long relationship in Christ ever since. Following the morning worship service that first Sunday, Lupe asked Pastor to pray for Juanita. He agreed and then inquired if she was intending to return the next Sunday and whether her husband would come with her.

She knew that she would ... and, I guess, she was certain that I would, too. Not surprisingly, the next Sunday I did attend! We weren't to know then just what an amazing impact that first visit would have on our lives. So, the following Sunday the whole family attended and, to my surprise, the service was not at all what I had expected.

This was the first time I heard the gospel of Jesus Christ and the first time I had seen the Word of God, the Bible, treated as having relevance in our daily lives. That was a radical concept, I thought! Part of my idea of what a Christian would be was always one who believed the Book. Now I was able to see it in a different light.

We agreed to return the next week. The church began to pray for Juanita. That was a radical concept too! Then about a month after we had been attending the Sunday worship services, Juanita was miraculously healed. In fact, this miracle occurred so surprisingly and suddenly that we were unaware of when it actually took place. Juanita's very next brain scan was absolutely clear! The spasms had ended. We began to ask one another just when this had happened. It seemed that we had become so used to the crying and the pain that accompanied the spasms that we were unaware when they stopped. Immediately, Lupe acknowledged to herself God's healing. This

was a definite and real answer to prayer. But I preferred
to believe that there must have been a medical explanation to Juanita's recovery.

Looking back, it is hard to believe that we debated whether we should be attending other services during
the week and on Sunday night. We figured that attending
too many services would probably be overdoing things!
We can recall agreeing to attend the evening service provided that we stayed away from the Wednesday services.
What strange things might a group of Christians actually
be up to on a Wednesday evening?

Sometime shortly after Juanita was healed, I
discovered that I was becoming uncomfortable about my
personal convictions on life. I was convinced that each
sermon was written deliberately for me. I began to have
troublesome weeks burdened by guilt and constantly
thinking about this message of a personal Savior dying
for my sin.

All this was made worse (at least that's how it
seemed to an unsaved person), when Lupe told me after
I arrived home one day that Bill and Tobi had invited
us over to the manse for a talk. A talk with Pastor! It
seemed that Bill wanted to question my convictions
about evolution. I learned later that Lupe had mentioned
this to Pastor the week before. Following our meeting that night and a word of prayer, I knew I needed to
repent of my sins and ask the Lord Jesus to come into my
life. I tried to fight off the burden for one more week, but
before the week was over, I privately repented and acknowledged Jesus as God's Son and my personal Savior.

Now the burden of guilt was finally lifted. Lupe
was overjoyed. I was relieved. Not surprisingly, the
very next service was so incredibly different. From that
point on, our love for the Lord grew and grew. After my
salvation, Lupe rededicated her life to Jesus Christ, and
we were baptized together and became members of the
church. Calvary Baptist Church became the central focus
of our family life and it has been our church home ever
since.

Now it is fair to say that for a very long time after this we simply enjoyed being a part of God's family and were satisfied with being under the teaching of God's Word. While we were happy to serve the Lord in many ways, it took 10 long years before the conviction to serve the Lord through teaching the Word of God became prominent in our lives.

It is not that we hadn't made ourselves available to God, or so we thought. I gladly accepted the role of a trustee, and Lupe and I were always active in serving others at church. I enjoyed helping Pastor Bill with physical projects around the church and helping others in the church family. Lupe also enjoyed supporting Tobi with her role in the church. The problem we discovered was that we had convinced ourselves of an inability to be able to teach and felt an unworthiness to be useful to God in this way. Lupe was afraid of teaching and speaking in her second language. I simply made the excuse that I didn't have the time to study. But we were under conviction to be more involved, and so in 2000 I shared my first message and Lupe began to teach Sunday School. From this point on, our passion to serve the Lord grew.

Lupe now regularly teaches the Bible in schools and in Sunday School. She also enjoys the opportunity to share God's Word with the ladies group and is passionate about sharing her faith one-on-one. I now regularly speak on Sunday evenings and whenever the need arises to support the ministry. It has simply become a wonderful blessing to teach God's Word to both adults and children. We recently traveled with our family to Australia to help support a new ministry there and were able to teach and encourage others to teach while we were there. Lately we have been burdened with the need to prepare a short teaching ministry in the Pacific for the people from Lupe's homeland who have never heard or been taught the pure gospel of Jesus Christ. Our greatest desire is to be able to lead others there to the Lord.

We can only credit all of this to an awesome, loving, and compassionate God who through His leading brought us directly to the point of acknowledging His sovereignty in our lives. We also credit this to the ministry of Pastor and Mrs. Preston who have been such a blessing to us.

God has been so good to us in so many ways. Juanita is now 18 and vibrant and healthy. We have come to rejoice in the truth of Jeremiah 29:11, "For I know the thoughts that I think toward you, saith the LORD, thoughts of peace, and not of evil, to give you an expected end."

As a pastor, it is a delight to me to see how God continues to use Dean and Lupe in other ways. Dean is a vibrant testimony at his work as a foreman on our local shipping wharf. Word seems to get around, and men and women come to him for counsel, which opens the door to witness for Christ and the difference He can make in a life. Lupe has recently begun preparing some commentary information on some portions of Scripture in her native Tokelauan language to make available to her people. As a couple, they have been a constant source of encouragement and a testimony to what God can do with lives surrendered to Him.

The Long Way Around
Wilma Abbott

In 1959, Wilma Childs joined Baptist Mid-Missions as a single missionary. Here she tells the story of how God led her and her husband, Carl Abbott, together. The Abbotts served with Campus Bible Fellowship (now called Campus Bible Fellowship International) in New York, Ohio, and Australia. They have been retired since 2002.

When we surrender our lives to God to do His will, we can never imagine all that He might ask us to do—or to give up—in order to serve Him. But in His mercy He always provides the grace we need to obey whatever He requires of us. One example of this truth is illustrated by a chapter from my life.

It all started back in 1954 when God called me to serve Him in Africa and led me to Baptist Bible Seminary to prepare. I soon realized that there was no one for me to date. Only one man felt God's call to Africa, but he and I did not agree on some basic doctrinal issues. He believed in the doctrine of sinless perfection, which I didn't think was biblical. I figured it would be okay to date others as long as I wasn't distracted from God's will for my life. So I sought to enjoy the guys as brothers and the girls as sisters, as Paul had counseled Timothy in 1 Timothy 5:2.

Then in his middle year of a five-year course, Carl Abbott asked me to go to a banquet with him. I had admired Carl for his high grades and good humor, always surrounded with fun-loving guys who laughed a lot at his jokes while going through lines in the cafeteria. So I said yes. At the banquet I found myself laughing hilariously (with all who sat around us) at his jokes. He always had quick retorts to whatever was discussed. There were no lulls in the conversation … just laughs.

As time went on, we walked and talked for miles, at times stopping for ice cream at a small drugstore. In cold weather we sat and chatted in the student lounge. It was there Carl began telling me what he was looking for in a wife. I realized that the more I was with him, the more I wanted to be. So I prayed, asking the Lord what our relationship should be. The answer in my heart was, "You can either have Carl, or you can have My will for your life." I knew that no matter how much I liked Carl, I loved the Lord more and feared stepping out of His will.

At the next opportunity, I told Carl that God's will for me was Africa, and he apparently did not have the same leading. His response was, "Oh, I wouldn't want to stand in the way of God's will for you." So we stopped dating, seeing one another only as we passed in the halls. To tell the truth, there were tears of self-pity at times, but deep down I knew I had done the right thing. The peace of God reigned as He continued to prepare me for Africa and the work of the ministry there.

After I had spent 13 years evangelizing and teaching in Chad, a cultural revolution forced all nonmedical missionaries to leave the country. As I returned to the USA with 12 other missionaries, 13 Chadian pastors were in prison, and my heart ached for them in the trials they were going through. I did nothing but eat, sleep, and pray for 10 days until the Lord said, "Don't pray for them, but for their widows." So I knew their trials were over. They were with the Lord just two weeks from the time we missionaries left Chad.

Within three weeks I felt ready to begin reporting to my supporting churches, but the first question people asked was, "What are you going to do now?" Pulling my car over to the side of the road, I asked the Lord what He would have me do next. One possibility was Campus Bible Fellowship (CBF). Having attended a church conference where Leigh Adams was speaking about CBF, I didn't think I was cut out to work with students from the secular campus. I was sure they had questions I couldn't answer.

Back home I found an invitation from Betty Wallin, who was already doing campus work with Baptist Mid-Missions. The note said, "Come up and follow me around on campus for a few days. I think you'd love it." Having three days available, I went to Camillus, New York, to spend them with Betty. On campus until all hours of the night, I realized I could have answered any of the questions students asked her! That settled it. If God wanted me in CBF, I was willing.

On that trip the pastor of Betty's church invited me back to be the missionary speaker for VBS in July. This was Carl's church as well. He was on deputation seeking church support to work in—what else—CBF. When I came back during VBS, Carl and I saw each other daily for lunch, then for supper, and for long walks after VBS. Within six weeks he had proposed, and I gladly accepted with the assurance this was God's will … to work together reaching students for Christ through Campus Bible Fellowship.

Our Journey with Anorexia
Joanie Troester

Joanie and her husband Joel were appointed to serve in Brazil with Baptist Mid-Missions in 1986. In recent years, a Brazilian-led mission agency has sent missionaries to the African nation of Mozambique, where Brazil's language of Portuguese is also spoken. The Troesters have been serving alongside Brazilian missionaries in Mozambique since 2009.

Toward the end of our second term in Brazil, we had moved from São Paulo to Curitiba to partner with a Brazilian pastor. Our family of six was settling into a new work in a new city and finding new friends.

Sharon, our youngest, was losing her baby fat—not a bad thing. Soon, however, my daughters Carolyn and Kristin mentioned that Sharon's bones were sticking out. We also noticed other peculiar behavior. Yet we saw things we were pleased with: she was always the first one up in the morning, smiling from ear to ear; she was reading her Bible; and she was becoming such a servant!

At the time, our Brazilian pastor's daughter was winning her fight with leukemia. She had a terrific pediatrician, so we made an appointment. I was certain that a blood test would reveal if Sharon was anorexic and what to do about it if she was. I was totally baffled when the doctor couldn't tell us any more than we'd already figured out—she needed to eat more.

There was something else going on when all of this started. Our move from São Paulo to Curitiba meant selling our house in São Paulo so that we could buy another one in Curitiba. Missionaries had bought and sold houses for years and put them in the name of Baptist Mid-Missions of Brazil. No big deal. We put it on the market and soon had a buyer. We also found the perfect house in the perfect location in Curitiba.

As a mother, I had told God that we had to have this all settled before our oldest children, Nathan and Carolyn, went to the States for college—after all, they had to feel they had a home and had to know what their address was.

There was one thing that I hadn't planned on. All this was taking place at the time when the Brazilian government was putting their records on computer for the first time. It was discovered that our Mission accountant—a Brazilian pastor—had been embezzling money for the past seven years. Instead of paying the taxes on properties, he had been building his own house and producing false receipts.

Therefore, Baptist Mid-Missions of Brazil was in debt to the Brazilian government big time. This needed to be settled before any buying or selling of property could take place, unless the buyer could pay cash. Our buyers needed a bank loan and couldn't pay cash. This was not good news to me.

At a time when all kinds of changes and challenges were coming at Sharon, I was consumed with my "unfair" circumstances and was trying to convince God that we just had to have this house thing done so we could get on with life. Few people knew of the battle I was fighting with God. After all, I was a missionary, faithful with my devotions, active in the church and in the lives of people, and trying to do things God's way.

Yet I was evaluating my circumstances with a very wrong view of God and of His wonderful plan to use difficult situations. My wrong view of what God was doing made it easier for Sharon to also have a wrong view, and therefore, a wrong focus and wrong goals.

A few months later, we took our second furlough to put our oldest two children in college and to figure out what was wrong with Sharon. By now she was noticeably underweight, even in baggy clothes. She weighed around 80 pounds. Upon arriving in the States, we moved into a motor home to begin traveling to visit our churches. It was Joel's parents who challenged us to consider that Sharon's problem might be anorexia. We checked out books from the library and realized we needed help. But we didn't know where to turn.

During that furlough, we lived near the Hershey Medical Center in Pennsylvania. There, Sharon was put on a weight gain plan and monitored weekly. She went to a biblical counselor for a while. Since she gained weight and seemed to go from stubborn to compliant in the eating department, we thought that anorexia was history for us. In December 1999, we returned to Brazil to begin our third term.

But Sharon's heart hadn't changed and neither had mine. In fact, I didn't even know there was anything wrong with mine. Since we'd only dealt with Sharon's symptoms, by the time we'd been back for six months, she had spiraled backwards again. Many missionaries and Brazilians were involved in her life, trying to help her make wiser choices, but she continued to go downhill.

This was June of 2000. The two and a half year ordeal of selling our house was finally settled! We were starting a new work in a new area. We had found a house close to where we were holding services and near where we hoped to buy land for the church. No one wanted to leave, especially now. But a counselor in São Paulo had said that if something drastic didn't happen soon, Sharon would not be alive by Christmas.

We returned to the States with a 72-pound 17-year-old who looked like she was 12 or 13. She had spent her last week in Brazil in a children's hospital in Curitiba with a feeding tube through her nose and into her stomach. In the next three years, the feeding tube would be part of her life at least three more times.

Upon the recommendation of BMM, we plugged into the church life of Faith Baptist Church in Lafayette, Indiana, because of their track record of biblical counseling for over 30 years. The first Sunday after we arrived, Pastor Viars was beginning a series in the book of 1 Peter. He began his message with this question: "What would be better, a trial-free day, or the opportunity to display the genuineness of your faith in the midst of a trial? What would be better?" That question struck my heart. A trial-free day would definitely be my choice. How could a trial be good?

Initially, we were all in counseling. The counselors were trying to reach Sharon's heart. It took Joel and me a long time to catch on to why that was important. We were still after behavioral change in Sharon. We didn't see anything positive for a long time. I dealt with her problem by trying to force her to eat, by tricking her into eating more calories, by trying to make her feel guilty, and by arguing about her food choices and amounts. She responded by hiding food in pockets, up her sleeves, under the table and in her napkin. She secretly exercised excessively.

When Sharon's counseling ended because she wasn't cooperating, Joel and I continued counseling to help us to help her. We were slow learners. Often, after giving an account of how the week went, our counselor would ask, "So, what are we looking for here? Do we want behavior modification, or do we want to see heart change?" My response was, "Oh, that's right! Why is that so hard to remember?"

During those months and years, God showed me specific areas that needed to change in me, beginning with my overall goal in life. My goal could not be for Sharon to change or my circumstances to change. My goal needed to be to please God, whether or not Sharon or my circumstances would ever change. Second Corinthians 5:9—"Wherefore we labour, that, whether present or absent, we may be accepted of him." I can please God in spite of my circumstances.

About three and a half years after moving to Lafayette, I remember the day when a new thought struck me: "Even if Sharon never changes, this journey has been so worth it for how God has used it in my life." It was during this time that I finally realized how I had contributed to Sharon's wrong choices. The security and desire of having my own home in Brazil had become an obsessive idol in my heart. I was growing in the understanding of how biblical truth needed to be the grid through which I viewed everything. God had allowed anorexia to enter our home as a tool in His loving hands to mold me.

About that time, God brought Jen into Sharon's life. Jen had been anorexic, bulimic, and suicidal. She had gotten saved at Purdue University, and God had given her victory. Now she had a ministry with girls that wrestled with these issues. Finally, Sharon had a friend who could understand her struggles! A real turning point came when she willingly sought our help to keep her accountable in her eating.

That same week, Dr. Charles Hodges also came into the picture. He became Sharon's medical doctor. He told her, "Sharon, if you want to have victory over anorexia, you need to want to glorify God with your life more than you want to breathe. After that, the rest is easy." Again, the goal needed to be pleasing God. Sharon had heard these things for over three years and now, finally, she was beginning to make that her goal and heart's desire.

Over the next year, Sharon recorded her calorie intake for Dr. Hodges. They met weekly and he helped her identify and deal with her idols, and he gave her specific assignments that helped transform her thinking with God's truths. Growth has taken place in small steps.

Anorexia has been a family affair. Sharon's struggles have been grueling. She still needs to work at eating more than she'd like to at times. But today she is doing well. She has come such a long way. She knows that it's not really about eating or food. It's about what she's choosing to worship. I, too, have learned that every choice I make is an act of worship. And I can speak for my whole family when I say that we would not have traded this experience for anything.

Peter, the Man Sent by God
Grace Cochrane

Grace and her late husband Curtis opened the field of Ghana for Baptist Mid-Missions in 1946. The Cochranes ministered there for two decades and then transferred to North America. They retired in 1971. Grace celebrated her 100th birthday in 2009 and has long held the distinction of being BMM's oldest missionary.

God had called us to pioneer a gospel work in the Gold Coast, which was later renamed Ghana. But we didn't know the language yet and we had no other missionaries to help us. How were we to get a gospel work going? First thing, we started looking and praying for someone who spoke English and had a heart to know God. We needed someone we could teach and who would become converted and be a real helper in the work.

It was a slow, hard task. We would get some man to help us, thinking he could interpret for us, and we would try to get on with preaching the gospel. But many of these men turned out to have no understanding and little interest in the work except for the money they received as a helper. So we were constantly praying, "Lord, send us a man who will really love the work—who will love You and be a real helper to us. You know how helpless we are on our own."

One day while I was alone on the mission station, a man rode in on his bicycle, and to my surprise he could speak English quite well! He said that he had been down on the coast working for a number of years, but that he was actually a local man from one of the nearby villages. Now he had come home and wanted to put in his crops on his farm. But he felt that God wanted him to come and work with us and help us preach the gospel. He had heard us on the streets, using different interpreters to try to get the message out to the people.

We talked for a little while. He was so sure that this was what God wanted him to do. So I told him, "Come back when Mr. Cochrane is at home, and we will talk further."

So he got on his bicycle and went on to his home village to plant his fields. When Curtis came home, I told him about this man called Peter and what he wanted to do. Well, we didn't know if we would ever see him again, but true to his word Peter returned at the time he had set.

Mr. Cochrane started questioning him. Peter again explained that he had heard us preaching on the streets and wanted to help tell people about Jesus Christ and how to be saved. We came to find out that he had been exposed to a number of different kinds of religious teachings down on the coast. He had been listening to the Catholics for a while but finally decided that was not for him. He said he just couldn't believe with them. Then he got caught up in the Jehovah Witnesses and got some different ideas. So we had to get him straightened out on that.

We had Bible studies with him for some length of time. It wasn't long before Peter became convinced that he had found the right teaching from God's Word. Then he was even more determined to help us preach the gospel. He was convinced that God wanted him to interpret for us. We were praising God at how He had answered our prayer. So Peter interpreted for us and people were saved. We really enjoyed Peter. He had such a love for lost souls. Eventually he became the pastor of the local Baptist church there in the village.

An Iranian Finds Christ
Chris Vergiels

Chris and his wife Darcy came with Baptist Mid-Missions in 1993. Darcy is the daughter of Bob and the late Corrine Jones, who served for 40 years in Brazil with BMM. The Vergiels family works as church planters in the interior of Brazil's São Paulo State.

God's message of love is for the whole world—even for people whose governments would try to forbid them from hearing the good news. So sometimes God has to position people at just the right place at just the right time to hear the truth.

In June of 2003 our family was able to take a much-needed vacation to an American-style resort about two hours away from our home in the western part of the state of São Paulo, Brazil. The hotel gave us a wonderful rate for our three day, off-season getaway. After supper on our first night there, the resort activity director planned a number of games for the kids on their playground area, so Darcy and I headed back to the dining room for after-dinner coffee.

At the table next to ours were three men speaking English. They were having trouble communicating with the waiter, so we volunteered to translate their order into Portuguese. They really appreciated our help and asked us to sit with them.

In my selfish heart, I was really looking forward to some time alone with Darcy, but we accepted and were introduced to our hosts. One man was from Ireland, another from Australia, and the third was from Iran. He was there on official business for his country. He spoke English fairly well. He was very intrigued that we were Christian missionaries in an already "Christian country."

We conversed until we needed to pick up our children. However, he still had more questions, so we met afterwards and continued talking until midnight about the differences between Catholicism and biblical Christianity, church history (including the Crusades), and finally about the claims of Christ for salvation. By the end of the conversation, he was teary-eyed but not ready to trust Christ.

I asked him whether we would even be able to have this conversation if we were in Iran. He said that would not be possible and that if he ever converted to Christianity, he could be killed for his faith. I offered him my English Bible, but he said that he would have difficulty reading it. He agreed to read the Bible if I could find one for him in his native language of Farsi.

We exchanged e-mail addresses so we could keep in contact with each other. What a blessing to think of how the Lord arranged this meeting. It is also wonderful to think that we were probably the first born-again Christians this man had ever met in his life.

My linguistics professor at Bob Jones University had a contact through which I was able to purchase a Farsi Bible from the States and have it shipped to me here in Brazil. I was also able to order a discipleship booklet and some booklets in Farsi that explained salvation through Jesus Christ.

Once the Bible and booklets arrived, I needed to get them to my friend. However, that was not going to be easy. In the time since we'd met, the Iranian government had sent a Muslim "religious man" to protect him from someone like me. He did not think that I could just travel up to where he was to give him the Bible. The only way he could think of to receive the materials was for me to send it next-day air in his name to the company where he was working, addressed to him as "personal and confidential."

After much prayer, I received an e-mail from the Iranian man saying that he had received the Farsi Bible and booklets without incident. He wrote me the following e-mail. The English is a little rough, but I think the message will be a blessing:

> hi my dear friend, how are you? thank you very much for the holy bible & another books. I read something about the start of creation of the world in bible, it is about 6 days the god create every things and in 7th rest. and also I read the famous lecture of jesus on the hill near jerusaleim in the begining of his invitation. this lecture makes me very interested to continue. the words and sentenses is so beautiful and I must say that after reading that, my feeling in my heart grows and know i think like jesus much than before. thank you again. oh, i read the book dr. saeed khan kordestani also. every night i read the bible & thinking about the compationate and the mersiful of jesus. o.k of course i have many

questions, but maybe in the futher i meet you or another
pastor who can speak with me in my language or english
and answering my questions. i have a protestanian friend
here, he introduce me to the pastor of this city, we trying
to speak with a translator and at the end he invited me to
speak with the people in his church, but i can not accept
his invitation unfortunatly because the futher danger
for me in my country if thay knows. o.k thank you again
and would you excuse me please if i have some mistakes
in writing the letters in english. give my best regards to
your family.

The Farsi booklets that I sent him had a gospel presentation,
the testimony of a doctor from Iran who trusted Christ as Savior, and a
discipleship manual. I so wished it was possible for me to talk with him
personally, but the circumstances did not allow that. So we continued to
communicate for the next two months through e-mails while he traveled
through Brazil.

The last city in which he worked in Brazil was only two hours
from our home, but because of the Muslim "religious man" overseeing
the team he was working with, it was impossible for him to meet with
anyone. In his last e-mail before returning to his country, he sent me the
following message:

> ... finally i must say that after a long time think-
> ing now i wish to be one of yours and i say this to my
> lord and also to my lovely jesus christ. I pray with my
> language in my heart without any knowledge about the
> especial skill of your praying. i continue to reading the
> bible. i have a very good feeling in my heart and i pray
> for you to thanks from god to put you in my way in bra-
> zil. you are the first and only person that i tell about my
> idea, i don't tell this to my family also, then please pray
> for me...

It was so wonderful to hear of his decision to trust Christ. He is
concerned for his safety, though. I have prayed often that the Lord will
protect him and give him the freedom to tell his wife and daughter about
his decision to trust Christ.

After about a year of communicating back and forth, I did not hear from him again. Perhaps it was not possible for him to send any more messages because of the tension between the United States and Iran, or maybe there was another problem. Only the Lord knows. But I am looking forward to seeing this brother in Christ in heaven some day.

A Second Chance
Doris (Griffin) Norton

Doris and her first husband, Billy Griffin, became missionaries with Baptist Mid-Missions in 1953. They spent the majority of their service in Brazil but also served in North America. After Billy went to be with the Lord in 1996, Doris continued to serve the Lord as an active missionary for another three years. Since 2003, Doris has been married to George Norton, a missionary colleague from Brazil.

Senhor Simplicio was an old man in the village of Palhano. His daughter and granddaughter were saved in our services. They asked that we go visit him, because he wasn't able to come to the services. We went, and he told us that years ago a man went through their village selling Bibles.

He said, "I didn't accept the Lord as my Savior, but I told Him if anyone ever came here again preaching the gospel, that I would ask the Lord Jesus to come in my heart."

True to his word, Senhor Simplicio did just that. What a wonderful testimony he was to the entire village.

Mama Anna
Rene Street

Rene and her husband Howard served a decade with another agency before joining Baptist Mid-Missions in 1948. The Streets began in the Democratic Republic of the Congo but later served in Liberia. In 1966, they moved back to the US to serve with the BMM Home Office. Their final assignment was in the administration of BMM's retirement village, Missionary Acres. How-ard has been with the Lord since 2003, and Rene since 2005.

When we moved to the city of Kikwit, Democratic Republic of Congo, in 1950 we met a Congolese Christian woman by the name of Anna. After some time, she shared with me the story of her early life. Years before, soldiers from Leopoldville were dispatched to Kikwit, and among them was a young Christian soldier who attended church. He and Anna fell in love and eventually they were married. In a few years he was sent back to Leopoldville and Anna went with him. Though they loved each other dearly, Anna was not able to bear him any children. In the Congolese culture, a man must father children for posterity and to prove his manhood. Finally, out of desperation, he asked Anna if he could take a second wife who could bear him children. Anna would always be number one wife. If the first wife was barren, it was customary in the villages for a man to take a second wife for the purposes of procreation.

They discussed the matter and Anna determined that it was neither Christian nor the Lord's will for one man to have two living wives. Her husband loved her dearly, but he told Anna that if she would not consent to a second wife, she would have to return to her village. She chose to return. He took her to the riverboat, bought her ticket, and saw her off.

Her heart was broken. She was returning to her village in shame because she could not bear children. What kind of life could she look forward to? Only one of prostitution, and that was unthinkable for a Christian. She prayed and asked the Lord what He would have her to do. His answer came clearly, "As you return to your village of Kikwit, your ministry will be among the women to lead them to salvation through Christ."

Anna earned the respect of the women, and they named her "Mama Anna." One Sunday in church my husband Howard announced that if any of the women were interested in starting a ladies Bible class they should meet at our home the following Friday afternoon at two p.m. On the appointed day, three women came: Mama Anna, Mbesi Jacqueline, and Suzanne Nelson. We had our Bible study, and before the women left I asked them each to bring one lady the next week. This they did and then there were six. I asked the six ladies to each bring a lady the following week. They did and then there were 12. They could see how quickly we could enlarge our numbers by each one bringing another. This continued until there were 300 women in the class. Of course, by this time we were meeting in the church instead of our home.

Mama Anna proved to be a great leader among the women in Kikwit. She often taught the lesson in our ladies Bible class. She prayed in the language of Leopoldville as it flowed from her heart and lips. She was a blessing to me and an encouragement to many along the way.

Howard's mother visited us in the early 1950s and spent six months with us. She and Mama Anna were about the same age, but they could not converse. Mama Anna would speak in Kituba; Mother Street would respond in English. Yet each seemed to understand the heart of the other.

When it came time for Mother Street to leave us, she wanted to attend the ladies Bible class to bid them farewell. I translated for her as she told the women how happy they made her feel for having her children serving among them. She assured them that she would never forget them and would always pray for them.

Then Mama Anna asked to say a few words. She came forward, hugged Mother Street and said, "We never gave a thought that our missionaries had mothers, fathers, brothers, and sisters left in America until you came to see us. Now we know the sacrifice they have made to live among us and teach us the Word of God. Thank you, Mama Street, for giving us your son. Because he and his wife came here, many of these women have come to know the Lord as their Savior."

She paused and then continued, "Mama Street, you and I are about the same age. One of us will soon be with the Lord. If you get there first, just look for me and I will soon follow. If I get there first, I shall look for you to come. Then we can talk, and talk, and talk, and understand each other."

They hugged and each wept a little. Now they are both with the Lord, and I often think of that meeting years ago in the town of Kikwit, and then that second meeting in heaven when they were reunited and began that long talk. God is good. When we were evacuated in 1964 because of the youth rebellion, Mama Anna became the leader and teacher of that women's Bible class. Great shall be her reward!

From Farmer to Fisher of Men
Cletis Titus

Cletis and his wife Tammy are both MKs and were appointed with Baptist Mid-Missions in 2007 to serve in Jamaica. Here, Cletis tells the story of his parents, Jerry and Wyzetta, who began their BMM ministry 50 years prior—in 1957. The senior Tituses served actively with BMM for 45 years. Jerry went to be with the Lord in 2008.

During the summer after his senior year, God got hold of Jerry's heart at a Bible camp in Iowa. Jerry realized that the place for him next fall was in Bible college. The dilemma now was how to tell his dad. When you lose a boy on the farm, you not only lose a son, you also lose a farmhand, and farm workers were hard to come by in Guthrie Center, Iowa.

Jerry chose the best time he could think of to bring up the subject—when both of them were in the barn milking the cows.

"Dad, I think I need to get at least one year of college, and I was wondering if it would be alright for me to go to Omaha for a year at the Bible college?"

Jerry couldn't believe he had mustered up the courage, but now the words were out and he waited for his dad's response.

"Well, Son," his dad replied, "if that's what you think you need to do, I guess that would be okay with me. Just don't let them talk you into being one of those missionaries at that college!"

The summer ended quickly, and Jerry found himself in the big city of Omaha, Nebraska, enrolled at the Omaha Bible Institute. At six feet, three inches and weighing in at close to 300 pounds, this farm boy found himself standing out in the crowd. Nevertheless, he made many lifelong friends during his first year.

One of the highlights on the college calendar was the annual missions conference. The meetings were held in a downtown church with the old-style theater seats that folded down and then popped back into place when you stood up. These were not like the cushioned ones of today with plenty of padding and metal reinforcement; only a thin layer of veneer plywood held the occupant above the floor.

The speaker for the conference was a missionary pioneer by the name of Joe McCaba. He had served for some time in Africa and was instrumental in the founding of Evangelical Baptist Missions. Joe was a city boy from New Jersey who found himself preaching in the middle of America in an area best known for cows and corn.

Jerry was running a little late as usual and had some of his classmates save him a seat about three rows from the front on the left hand side. He listened intently as the speaker began to tell of his first experience milking a cow. "All they did was give me a bucket and point me to the cow," said Joe. "So I looked at that cow on one side and then on the other and decided that the thing hanging below was the spigot." He continued, "I put the bucket under the spigot and started looking over the cow again."

By now Jerry was ready to burst with laughter, but the next line put him over the top.

"I saw what looked like a pump handle on the back end of the cow," Joe paused for dramatic effect, "then I grabbed the tail and started pumping!"

That's all Jerry needed to hear, and he began with the rest of the students to roar with laughter. Unlike the rest of the students, though, the more Jerry thought about it, the more he laughed, and the more he laughed, the more his belly jiggled. The more he laughed, the more strain was put on that flimsy veneer seat. All of a sudden, in the middle of this packed church, the theater seat snapped, and all 300 pounds of this freshman farm boy went right to the floor.

Embarrassment would barely begin to describe his feelings as he got up off the floor and walked to the back of the long auditorium to find a metal folding chair for the duration of the service.

Yet, the speaker had his attention, and Jerry began to listen to the plea to reach the world with the gospel of Christ. It made sense that if Christ died for him, then he could live for Christ. At the end of the service, an invitation was given for the students to present their bodies as living sacrifices to the Lord.

That's exactly what he wanted to do, and for the second time in the service Jerry walked the aisle, but this time he walked not out of embarrassment but out of excitement. Not knowing what this decision would lead to, he was at least willing to follow the One who was leading.

Surrender to the will of God led Jerry Titus and his high school sweetheart, Wyzetta, first to the hills of Eastern Kentucky. It was there they were introduced to Baptist Mid-Missions and in 1957 began their ministry as church planters under the North American Field Council. Their calling led them from Kentucky to Illinois, Indiana, West Virginia, Iowa, Missouri, Arkansas, and Michigan. The Lord allowed them to be instrumental in planting three churches and bringing nine other churches to self-supporting status. The greatest joy for Jerry and Wyzetta, however, was the countless souls who have been won to Christ here in the United States, in addition to the reproducing of their ministry into the lives of at least three men who have been called to pastor under their ministry.

Their missions endeavor continues on the island of Jamaica as churches are planted and souls are won to Christ through the ministry of their son and daughter-in-law, Cletis and Tammy Titus, currently serving with Baptist Mid-Missions.

Follow Me
Steve Butler

Steve and his wife Ricka spent nearly a decade as church planters in Australia before Steve accepted his current assignment of BMM Field Administrator for North America. They have been with Baptist Mid-Missions since 1984.

This story concerns how God led my wife Ricka and me into missions. Ricka had sensed God calling her into missions as a little girl in Bible school. She came home that day and told her mother that she was going to be a missionary. Years later we met at Bob Jones University. She asked me several times during our dating years if I was sure that God didn't want me in missions. I had no burden, no sense of calling or direction to missions. I wasn't opposed to the foreign field, but I was convinced that the Lord had given direction to my life with a call to ministering here in the United States.

We married and ended up in my home state, pastoring Maranatha Baptist Church in Ripley, Tennessee. The pastor that had actually begun the church in 1948 had since retired and moved back into the community and was now a member of my first pastorate. It was a little bit of a concern to me at first, but he became a great champion of me to the people and a mentor to me privately. One of the things he challenged me to consider was starting an annual missions conference. We did that, and these conferences went on for a number of years.

The culmination of this was a missions conference where I had invited Carl Barton to come—he was then the Southern Deputation Secretary for Baptist Mid-Missions, and his job was to represent BMM in churches. Going into this conference, our church had a concerted prayer that God would allow us to send one of our own to the mission field and not just more of our money. Our missions giving had grown every year, but we had not sent anyone, and so our burden that year was that the Lord would help us in that conference to know what He would have us to do in that regard.

I had no idea what God would be doing in this conference. As we got into it, I sensed a burden for missions but I thought perhaps that this burden was simply that I needed to be more in prayer about God sending someone from our church. But by Saturday of that conference, I realized that the burden was on my own heart—that God was laying a sense of urgency for missions on me that I didn't understand at the time. The burden I felt was literally a physical feeling.

Who is the pastor's pastor? Who could I talk to about this sense of burden in the middle of this conference? If I talked to the missionary, Carl Barton, I knew what kind of answer I would get from him. I wasn't prepared for that. So Sunday morning before the service, I called John Seaton, the retired pastor, and simply told him I sensed that perhaps God was calling me to missions in this conference. I sought his counsel and asked him to pray. He said that he would pray. That seemed to be a release itself—to finally chat with someone about it and to hear that someone would be praying with me.

We had a good morning service. But by that afternoon, the sense of urgency was consuming my every thought and even my emotions. It was like a weight on my chest—there seemed to be a physical presence to this burden. That afternoon I simply shared with Ricka that I was burdened about the conference and that I was going over to the church to pray.

That Sunday afternoon I tried to pray, but I felt like nothing was being communicated. I found myself walking the central aisle of our church back and forth, contemplating the circumstances of the conference and the situation of my own heart and trying to understand this burden in my soul.

I remember coming to a point of stating, "Lord, if this is You moving me toward missions, I am willing to go, but I have to know this is You and not my emotions. Would You do something in the message tonight to confirm this from Your Word?"

We went into the evening service. Having simply prayed that prayer seemed to give a sense of release within my own heart and mind. Then Carl got up to speak, and in his very first point he used Matthew 4:19, "Follow me, and I will make you fishers of men." That verse was the only thing I heard the rest of the night. I began to argue with the Lord, "I can't do this." And that verse would ring—"Follow Me, and I will." Then I gave the Lord another reason, and that verse would smite my conscience—"Follow Me and I will." Even after praying a prayer of surrender that afternoon, I found myself arguing with the Lord. Well, I finally realized that God the Holy Spirit was wooing me with the promises of that verse.

"Steve, your part is to follow," the Holy Spirit seemed to say. "Yes, I am asking you to follow Me about this issue of missions. And I will take care of what your concerns are. I'll make you a fisher of men on the foreign field." God had brought me to a point of surrender. He had made things clear to me that night. I needed to respond to Him, and it needed to be public.

Before the service began, we had planned for Carl to bring the conference to a point, and then turn it over to me as pastor for the invitation. When I got up to endeavor to lead the congregation in an invitation, I just began to weep. I couldn't control it. It was just there. They couldn't figure out why I was weeping. I knew, and so I had to tell them.

I told them that in this conference we had been praying that God would send someone, and that I now realized that someone was me. I said that and the place was one big gasp. It became a vacuum in one second. It was an anxious moment for the church. God had knit our hearts together, and they didn't know how to take this.

Carl wasn't sure what to do, because he saw the shock on the congregation. Ricka had always felt a call to missions so she just began to cry. Ricka came forward and we knelt at the front in a moment of public commitment. Then Carl closed the service. The church was in shock and nobody said much.

Monday morning came. I got up and thought, "What in the world have I done? Where am I going? When am I going? How am I going to get there? Where is the next paycheck coming from?" There were just so many unknowns in my mind.

It's interesting how the Lord uses some things in your life. Ricka and I had a few debts that we had been working on—and right before that conference God had led me to sell a '65 Willies jeep that I had. I was going to take the money and utilize it to pay off some debts, but that Monday morning I had all those questions in my mind. I decided I'd maybe put the money from the jeep sale in a certificate of deposit. So I went to the bank of Ripley with this check from the sale of the jeep. I walked into the bank and went up to the lady that handled CDs.

"Can I help you, sir?" she asked.

"Well, I've got a check here and I'd like to open a CD and place this into savings for a time until I can make some decisions," I said, feeling more confused by the minute.

"What terms for the CD would you like?" she asked.

"I don't know," I said, lamely.

She looked at me like she was thinking, "Well you ought to have all that figured out in your mind before you walk into a bank and ask for a CD ..."

In my own expressive way I just launched into what had happened. I said, "Well, you've got to understand. Last night God called me to be a missionary and I don't know when I'm leaving and I don't know where I'm going. So I don't know how long I want this CD for."

That woman looked at me like she had seen a ghost. The blood drained from her face and she went completely white. I thought, there's a real witnessing opportunity right here. She is under some kind of conviction. So I said, "You don't know what I'm talking about, do you?"

She said, "I know exactly what you are talking about. When I was a teenager, God called me to be a missionary and I didn't go. I'm in my 50s and I have a great job and a lovely family and a nice home, but—I have never felt fulfilled in all my life because I knew God did something in my soul and I didn't follow Him. I listened to my boyfriend, who is now my husband, and my father who considered missionary work the last thing that he wanted for my life. Mr. Butler, you may not know where you are going or when you are going, but you do what God's told you to do, and you won't be sorry."

I knew from that moment on that what had happened the day before was of God. God, out of his grace, gave me a chance to hear the testimony of someone who would say what I needed to hear that Monday morning. God kept His promise, and He took care of all the questions that I had. He led us to serve Him in Australia and now in the Home Office of Baptist Mid-Missions.

The Story of Abraham Mounta
Glenn Kerr

In 1995, Glenn and his wife Becky joined Baptist Mid-Missions to serve with Bibles International (BI), BMM's translation division. Glenn's work as the Chief Translation Consultant takes him around the world. Becky works in BI's Home Office as an editor/journalist.

As a young man in Chad, Abraham Mounta wanted to marry Ruth, but because he was a Christian, her father refused and gave her to another man. Abraham also married someone else. He and Ruth went their separate ways, each having a child by their respective spouses.

Ruth's husband treated her so badly that she left and went back to her parents' home. After a time that husband died, and Abraham's first wife died also. Ruth's father decided it would have been better if he had given her to Abraham in the first place, so he consented for them to be married.

After her marriage to Abraham, Ruth went to church where she heard the gospel and also became a Christian. They both attended Bible school, and Abraham became a pastor. They had eight children together. Later, Abraham was taken prisoner along with other Chadian pastors during the time of President Tombalbaye's reign of terror. He and about 20 other pastors were kept in a Pentecostal church that had been made to serve as a prison. After a couple of days of imprisonment, they were finally told that the next day would be their execution day. The day came, and in fact it was an execution day, but someone had gotten the message wrong. It was the execution day for President Tombalbaye, who was assassinated by his own people. The reign of terror was over.

Abraham returned to Ruth to serve as a Baptist pastor for many years, being able to see the completion of the New Testament in the Sara Madjingaye language. He finally passed away peacefully at about 93 years of age, still able to read his New Testament without glasses. He died the way he lived—close to his family, his church, and his Christian friends.

A Young Man and God's Will for His Life
John Kennedy

A native of Scotland, John and his first wife Catherine served many years in Brazil with another agency. They joined the Baptist Mid-Missions Family in 1972. The Kennedys felt burdened to reach the United Kingdom for Christ, and they opened BMM's ministry there in 1973. After Catherine went to be with the Lord, John married Rillie Mae Leach, and they served throughout the United Kingdom. Even after retirement, John has continued to pursue multiple avenues of ministry. John's daughter Ruth is also a BMM missionary in Africa.

As John milked the cows, plowed the land, and planted the crops in the Highlands of Scotland, he was exposed to all the beauty of nature around him. Yet as he worked, John began to be troubled by the sin in his life. During the spring and the summer after the day's work was done, he climbed up Mount Bowie with a New Testament that he had purchased.

He read and studied. Finally he began to read in the gospel of John and found that Jesus Christ had died for him on the cross and that by believing on Him as his Savior, he could be cleansed of his sin and receive the eternal life of which the apostle John had written.

The following Saturday evening when he was in town, he began to cross the road to enjoy an evening of entertainment before he returned to the farm. There, in the middle of the street, all the verses he had read in John and the other books of the New Testament came flooding into his heart and mind. He stopped on a little traffic island in the middle of the street and prayed to the Lord asking Him to forgive his sins for which Christ had died on the cross. That night he was gloriously saved!

He sought baptism and membership in a Baptist church and also found an avenue for Christian service in a mission established after the ministry of D.L. Moody. In the open-air meetings held before the Saturday evening evangelistic services, John gave his testimony of how the Lord had saved him. This led to preaching the gospel message, knocking on doors, giving out gospel tracts, and winning souls to the Lord.

In the midst of this busy life, one day in his daily reading of the Scriptures, John read Acts 22:21, "And he said unto me, depart for I will send thee far hence unto the Gentiles."

In the days and months that followed, whenever John heard missionary speakers, and especially those from South American countries, Acts 22:21 thundered in his heart and mind. He asked the leader of his youth group to help him with this puzzle. The leader asked him, "Do you not think that God might be calling you to go as a missionary to a South American country?"

"Why me?" John argued. John discussed it with the Lord and told Him that he was quite happy serving right where he was.

One day he was plowing in a field of red land that was not supposed to have any rocks. He discovered that the Lord had placed an enormous rock in front of him. The plow wedged under the rock and the handles of the plow came up and hit him, knocking him out. When he regained consciousness, the words that rang through his mind were, "Depart for I will send you far hence unto the Gentiles." But he continued to put off the thought of going to Bible school.

Harvest time came. One day John loaded the wagons high with oat sheaves and carefully led the horse and wagon down an incline. But the Lord had placed a rabbit hole on the down side of the wagon. The bump was enough to upset the load of bouncy sheaves and over went the wagon, load, horse, and man! What a mess! The animal was not injured—but John, as he laid there semi-conscious, heard that verse ringing in his mind, "Depart; for I will send thee far hence unto the Gentiles." This stubborn Scotsman, like Jonah, kept running away from the Lord's will.

The culmination came in the fall when John was training a young horse to pull a wagon. The wagon wheels were tied, the wagon was loaded, and the horse was not supposed to be able to run. But the Lord gave that horse super strength to run, and poor John disappeared under the hooves and wheels. This time there was no damage to the wagon or the horse, but John was injured from head to toe.

All the time he was laid up in bed, Acts 22:21 shouted throughout his being, "Depart! Depart! Depart!" This time he listened and prepared to register for fall classes in a Bible college 50 miles away. Finally, he was started in the right direction. Eventually this young man served the Lord for more than 60 years in Brazil, England, Scotland, Ireland, and the United States.

Stranger in a Foreign Land
Pastor Jose Barbosa de Sena Neto

In 2007 Alice Smith received the following letter from a man in Fortaleza, Brazil, sharing the impact that Alice's late husband, Neal, had on him. Neal and Alice Smith served with Baptist Mid-Missions in Brazil from 1952 to 1992. They retired in 1993 and returned to Oregon. Neal went home to be with the Lord 10 years later in December of 2003.

Dear Missionary Alice Smith,

Grace and Peace! I suppose you think it strange that this "stranger" of Fortaleza, state of Ceara, would contact you! Let me try to explain.

Many years have gone by, nearly a whole lifetime. Though memories fade, the appearance of your beloved and unforgettable husband, Pastor Neal Smith, is still very clear in my mind.

I do not remember the year that I had the privilege to meet him, probably 1966 or 1967, however, dates are of much less importance now.

At that time I was a Franciscan seminarian doing youth seminary, studying in the so-called Seminario Serafico de Messejana in Fortaleza.

I always liked music very much, though I never studied it. I didn't have the opportunity, because when I showed an interest in it—and that interest in music was great—the friars, my superiors, thought that it was personal pride and never let me learn music, much to my frustration!

As a seminarian, we gave catechism classes to the children who live around the Church of the Sacred Heart of Jesus. One day, I stayed to eat at the house where we gave the catechism lessons. When we were about to return to the monastery, I heard the sound of an accordion being played with great enthusiasm, which grabbed my attention.

I was informed that the man was a Protestant, who was trying to bring Catholics into his church, primarily our catechism children. I became furious and decided to confront him and "get satisfaction" and ask him to play his songs and preach his messages somewhere else.

When I arrived at the other house, he was playing a hymn that has never left my head and heart! It took me many years to discover the title and the complete words of the hymn, but its melody never was erased from my memory!

I am a stranger here, within a foreign land;
My home is far away, upon a golden strand;
Ambassador to be of realms beyond the sea,
I'm here on business for my king!

This is the message that I bring,
A message angels fain would sing:
"O be ye reconciled," thus saith my Lord and King,
"O be ye reconciled to God."

When he finished playing and singing with his strong voice, he looked at me and smiled with a broad, friendly smile and invited me into that house. With a "closed face" I refused his invitation, and after a few minutes I went away. Yet in those few minutes I heard him read a text from the gospels, which speaks of the meeting of Nicodemus with the Lord Jesus.

What bothered me was that this man came to preach on the day when I taught the children catechism. Some of them wanted the lesson to end quickly, "because the American Protestant pastor was almost ready to preach." I became discouraged because of what our children were saying.

I remember that he had a Jeep, a big Jeep, and when he arrived he was very friendly with everyone in that neighborhood. His smile disquieted me greatly, because I did not know how to smile! And there he was—playing, singing, and preaching! From far away one could hear the sound of his accordion and his distinctive voice! I was curious and at the same time very angry because he was "stealing" our children.

One day I could not remain silent. I went to that house again. When I arrived he gave me a smile and came out to meet me. He gave me a bear hug. He almost "broke" me! He told me that he was glad to have me there! I wasn't accustomed to this because in the monastery, people always live very isolated from other people. We visited a little, and I forgot my intention because he had broken the barrier between us.

I asked him shyly, "Are you not going to play more?"

"What hymn would the brethren desire now?" he asked of the people present.

Very quickly, I said, "That one of the 'stranger … in a foreign land' … could you play it?"

"Oh, you like it?" he asked me.

"I heard you sing it weeks ago," I responded.

He played and sang the song! It was marvelous! He knew I was a Catholic seminarian. But he always treated me with a special kindness, which took away any desire to fight with him about our catechism children. It became my habit to listen to him a little before I returned to the monastery.

One day before beginning his work, he approached me on the sidewalk and began to talk with me. We talked and talked. He told me that he was planting a church in the Tevelandia neighborhood of Fortaleza. He asked me if I wouldn't like to go there and that he would be willing to come and take me.

"NO, I cannot!" I answered in a hurry. "I don't have freedom to leave the seminary this way, and especially with you," I informed him.

One day at the end of the year, I told him that I was being transferred to another seminary in the state of Piaui. I noticed that he became concerned and did not lose any more time. He "exploded in words" as we say around here. He spoke to me of Jesus, rapidly, and looked me in the eyes, saying, "You have the knack to be a pastor, not a priest. I have decided to help you go to our Baptist Seminary of Cariri that is in Juazeiro do Norte. But you must first accept Jesus as your only and sufficient Savior. Think about this and don't go away without first talking to me and making your decision."

I remember his words perfectly. What made the greatest impression upon me was that that man spoke to me with tears in his eyes! I didn't know how to weep anymore, I had forgotten what it was to have even one teardrop. I was being taught this—it was one of the rules of our order.

That was the last I spoke with him and he with me! I may have somewhat forgotten the appearance of his face, but his voice, the one that sang "I am a stranger here ..." has never left my mind and heart!

Oh, how the time passed! I was ordained a priest in São Paulo between 1971 and 1972. I became an iron-willed persecutor of the people of God, primarily when I returned to Ceara in the 1980s. I remained in Quixada 10 of the 22 years I was a Roman Catholic priest. I was the implacable persecutor of the believers, regardless of their denomination.

Until one day I was reached by the grace of my Lord! He is sovereign! I began my life anew at 44 years of age, when I left the so-called Roman Catholic Church. Difficult days. Many tribulations! But how good it is to be a believer in Jesus! How good it is to follow Jesus! How contagious is the joy in Him! How grand it is to praise Him and adore Him "in spirit and in truth" and have certainty of life eternal!

I went to study theology again and was consecrated to the Baptist ministry on the 8th of October of 2000. I have traveled almost all of Brazil, its capitals and principal cities, recounting my testimony of life in the Lord, fruit of the seed planted by your husband, with the sound of the accordion, and his distinctive voice singing that hymn that he always liked to sing! And how he could sing!

Today I serve my Lord, unmeritoriously, among the Bible Baptists, having assumed the responsibility with my God and Savior to always preach the "Word of truth of the gospel." I have already preached in many cities in Regular Baptist churches, having evangelistic conferences, missionary conferences, and seminars for engaged and married couples. Last year I had a missionary conference in Manaus, which commemorated the 70 years since the arrival of the first Regular Baptist missionaries here in Brazil. It was a blessing!

This last weekend, March 17 and 18, I had the privilege to preach in an evangelistic conference in the First Regular Baptist Church of Aracati, located in the middle of that city. It was planted by Bill and Dorothy Kettlewell, your friends. I was hosted and received very well by the couple and the church. The evangelistic message was simple and clear, and the results are in the hands of the Lord our all powerful God!

On one of the trips from the Kettlewell house to the church or vice versa, I told them of my vivid memory of an American Regular Baptist missionary. I told them that I had already tried to find him, describing him to other American missionaries, but I had been unsuccessful. I spoke of the accordion, of the Jeep, but no one could satisfy my curiosity.

In our conversation, Mrs. Kettlewell suggested several names. When she spoke the name, "Smith," I had no doubt. Yes, it was he, the pastor of the accordion who massaged my heart as a young man! My eyes shone and my heart began to celebrate!

I asked, "Where are they? What are they doing today? The accordion …"

Mrs. Kettlewell told me in quiet tones that Pastor Neal had died, already retired in the USA. Pastor Bill added the details of his last illness. My joy lasted but a short time! I became sad. I didn't want to believe what I was hearing!

It seemed as if I heard Pastor Neal Smith singing again, playing the accordion, with his special enthusiasm! The Lord God has His plans, which we are not capable of seeing nor understanding.

I wanted to narrate this story to you, Sister Alice, as my simple tribute to your unforgettable husband!

If only all the missionaries who work for this Brazil outside of their continental origins, which are gathered here in Fortaleza, at this time, participating in the annual reunion of Baptist Mid-Missions, would understand that it is worthwhile to be a missionary "stranger … in a foreign land."

I am overwhelmed emotionally! Forgive me!

In the Love of Jesus, our "hope of glory,"

Pastor Jose Barbosa de Sena Neto

Conclusion

What an awesome God we serve! What a privilege to be called His child. Have you glimpsed all that is ours in Christ? Think of it! There will never be a time when God is unholy towards us. There will never be a time when God doesn't love us, never a time when God ceases to be gracious or merciful. There will never be a time when God is not faithful, never a time when God is not omniscient or omnipotent. There will never be a time that God is not sovereign over all our affairs.

When trials come, we can be assured that His character has not changed and that He has not forsaken us. Although we may not be able to sense His presence, we can rest in the fact that He is there. When we take the Father at His declared Word and revealed character and are obedient to Him, fear is replaced with boldness, and worry is swallowed up in peace and rest.

It takes great faith to trust in that which is unknown and untested. But when we have God's Word and evidence of His faithfulness to that Word, it takes but the faith of a child to experience great blessings from God. Our faith is not a stretch of the will but rather the rational response to the evidence. God has not failed and can never fail. Believe God is Who He says He is. You will not be disappointed. He is such a God of love that you can safely give yourself to Him without hesitation, knowing that His will for your life will be infinitely more fulfilling than anything you could have imagined for yourself.

"Teach me thy way, O LORD; I will walk in thy truth: unite my heart to fear thy name. I will praise thee, O Lord my God, with all my heart: and I will glorify thy name for evermore" (Psalm 86:11-12).

Index

Stories

Contributors